WISDOM OF
THE GURUS

SIGS Reference Library

Donald G. Firesmith
Editor-in-Chief

Additional Volumes in Preparation

WISDOM OF THE GURUS

A Vision for Object Technology

Selected & Edited by

Charles F. Bowman

SIGS BOOKS & MULTIMEDIA

New York • London • Munich • Paris • Cologne

Library of Congress Cataloging-in-Publication Data

Wisdom of the gurus / selected and edited by Charles F. Bowman.
     p. cm. — (SIGS reference library series ; 7)
    ISBN 1-884842-55-0 (paper : alk. paper)
    1. Object-oriented programming (Computer science)
    I. Bowman, Charles F. II. Series.
    QA76.64.W57 1996
    005.1—dc20   96-41922
                                              CIP

PUBLISHED BY
SIGS Books
71 W. 23rd Street, Third Floor
New York, New York 10010
http://www.sigs.com

Composition by Fleuron.
Printed on acid-free paper.

SIGS Books ISBN 1-884842-55-0
Prentice Hall ISBN 0-13-499849-9
Printed in the United States of America
00 99 98 97 96   10 9 8 7 6 5 4 3 2 1
First Printing October 1996

For Dad

CONTENTS

PART III   PATTERNS

PART IV   LANGUAGES

C++

Smalltalk

ABOUT THE EDITOR

CHARLES F. BOWMAN IS A PRINCIPAL OF SOFTWRIGHT SOLUTIONS, INC., A consulting and training firm specializing in relational, GUI, object-oriented, and client/server technologies.

Mr. Bowman has had over 17 years' experience developing software systems and applications. As an independent consultant, Mr. Bowman has designed and developed numerous GUI applications in both the procedural and object-oriented paradigms. In addition, as part of his consulting practice, he develops courseware and training materials in a wide range of subject matter for both public and on-site delivery.

Mr. Bowman is a popular speaker, who has lectured throughout the United States and Canada, as well as the United Kingdom, France, and Germany. Popular lecture topics include Creating new widgets, Objectifying Motif, Object-oriented analysis and design, Client/server design and development, and Multiparadigm development. He was also selected as a featured speaker for Borland's nation-wide Client/Server Tour that took place throughout January of 1995.

As an Adjunct Lecturer for both St. John's University and The City University of New York, he has taught at both the undergraduate and graduate levels. Mr. Bowman has published a wide-range of articles for many prestigious journals and magazines. In addition, he is Editor-in-chief of The UNIX Developer and Series Editor for the *Managing Object Technologies* book series of SIGS Books & Multimedia. Mr. Bowman's previous books are *Algorithms and Data Structures: An Approach in C* and *Objectifying Motif*.

Mr. Bowman graduated from New York's prestigious Brooklyn Technical High School and holds a B.S. degree in Computer Science from St. John's University, and an M.S. degree in Computer Science from New York University.

PREFACE

"OVERNIGHT SENSATION." THE VERY WORDS CONJURE IMAGES OF grandeur and success. As Americans, we are enamored and obsessed with the concept. However, what we often fail to see is the years—sometimes decades—of arduous effort that precedes the overnight success. When a new musical prodigy explodes onto the scene, do we consider how many lonely hours of practice and training were required? How much research and preparation must a scientist undertake before he or she is in a position to discover a revolutionary new cure? The truth is, overnight sensations are usually years in the making.

Our industry is no exception to this phenomenon. A perfect example is the object-oriented paradigm. This "overnight sensation" took decades to emerge. It began with a small germ of an idea back in the 60s with SIMULA and Smalltalk. It has since blossomed into one of the most important trends in our industry.

However, as with any new tool, those who plan to use OO development techniques require knowledge and training. It is only by thoroughly understanding a tool's strengths and weaknesses that one can maximize its potential.

The above notwithstanding, we must respect knowledge. Moreover, it must be accurate and timely. Otherwise, we might be guilty of abusing, rather than using, the tool. An old adage states it best: a little knowledge can be dangerous. One of the ways to acquire and remain current with a body of knowledge is through professional and technical journals. Here, practitioners can follow current trends, ponder new ideas, and become versed with fast-breaking industry developments.

Unfortunately, despite the most ardent professional resolve, no one can expect to read every article in every journal. We just do not have the time. Moreover, the sheer volume of material is not our only problem. Many ideas do not pan out. Why? Some are ahead of their time, others could not withstand the test of time. Others are just plain bad. This being the case, we could spend a significant portion of our time following the seed of an idea that never bears fruit.

This brings us to yet another problem. There is often an abundance of introductory material on any given subject. However, publishers often neglect the advanced reader. It is simply a matter of economics: There are far fewer experts than novices.

All this begs the obvious question: Given all of the above, how can we even hope to remain current? How much reading, searching, and researching must we undertake to become and remain experts? How do we wade through the flotsam and jetsam of trade journals to discover the few pearls of wisdom? That is where *Wisdom of the Gurus* comes in. This text is a compendium of the most current and technically advanced body of knowledge that is focused solely on object orientation. It contains timely, accurate, and advanced material on many facets of the object-oriented paradigm. We can summarize the goals of this project as follows:

- To create a single, comprehensive source of advanced technical information. Readers will no longer need to scurry from periodical to periodical trying to locate an item of interest.
- To focus on the important and relevant trends in the industry. We have sorted through the material and eliminated the ideas that have not panned out.
- To establish a repository for advanced concepts. This is leading-edge material prepared for and by experts.

We have culled this body of knowledge from a number of important and prestigious sources:

- JOURNAL OF OBJECT-ORIENTED PROGRAMMING (JOOP)
- OBJECT MAGAZINE
- C++ REPORT
- SMALLTALK REPORT
- ROAD

These journals are well known for the timeliness and accuracy of their content. They are read—and, more important, written—by some of the most impressive names in the business. The quality and depth of the material contained in these journals cannot be overstated. Indeed, it was extremely difficult to prune the list down to the comparatively few pieces that appear in this tome. To enhance their value, we have presented the articles in a way that allows the book to read like an advanced textbook on object orientation. That is, if you read the book from cover to cover you will find a natural flow of the material.

In addition, we have divided the work into logical sections so that you can use the text as a reference. Each section opens with an overview and a description of its contents.

Some of the topics we cover include:

- design patterns,
- distributed objects,
- advanced modeling techniques,
- language influences.

We have also divided the work into logical sections so that you can use the text as a reference. Each section opens with an overview and a description of its contents.

For me, producing this work was both enriching and enlightening. As a result, I can state honestly that you will find the material as challenging as it is engrossing.

FOREWORD

I T IS WITH GREAT PLEASURE THAT I ENTHUSIASTICALLY RECOMMEND THIS COLLEC-
tion of essays, *Wisdom of the Gurus*, which was assembled by Charles
Bowman, my colleague at SIGS Books & Multimedia. Charles has done a
fantastic job in selecting and organizing work by leaders in the areas of
object modeling, development methodologies, patterns, and languages
(these are the categories that he has used in putting together this book).

I must confess to having initially some skepticism about the idea of pub-
lishing work that had been previously published in the *Journal of
Object-Oriented Programming (JOOP), ROAD, Object Magazine, C++
Report, Smalltalk Report,* or other sources. But after reading this book, I have
changed my mind. I am now convinced of the value to the reader in having
easy access to this collection of important and interesting work that Charles
has identified. Charles Bowman has put on center stage a group of essays that
were important when first published and are at least as important today.

The imprint left by Charles Bowman on this book is important to note.
He has had the challenging task of having to select from a huge collection
of meritorious material to create this new work, and, with his critical judgment, he has created tremendous "value added." There are, of course,
important "gurus" not included in this collection. No single book of this
kind can be complete. For example, in the section on languages, only C++
and Smalltalk are covered. These two languages have dominated the object-
oriented landscape for the past five years, but obviously, there have been
significant contributions by other important object-oriented language
gurus. I am sure that other similar collections of essays will be assembled in
the future that will present the ones that couldn't be included here.

Each reader of this book will find a group of favorites amongst these
high-quality pieces. My personal favorites include "Additional Aspects of
Association" by David Papurt; "Well-Structured Object-Oriented
Architectures" by Grady Booch; "From Analysis to Design Using Templates,"
by James Odell and Martin Fowler; "Formalizing Use-Case Modeling," by

Ivar Jacobson; "Defining and Developing User-Interface Intensive Applications with Use Cases," by Steven Bilow; "Use Cases: The Pros and Cons," by Donald Firesmith; "Formalizing the Output (Parts 1 & 2)," by Nancy Wilkinson; "Pattern Languages for Organization and Process," by James Coplien; "Patterns and Idioms in Circles, Complex Ellipses, and Real Bridges," also by James Coplien; and "Observations On the Role of Patterns in Object-Oriented Software Development," by Charlie Alfred and Stephen Mellor. I found these essays extremely important and most interesting when they were first published, and they are even more interesting today.

I thank Charles Bowman for assembling this important collection of work. Readers have some exciting material to peruse.

—**Richard Wiener**

Professor of Computer Science,
University of Colorado at Colorado Springs

Editor: *JOOP*
Series Editor: *Advances in Object Technology,*
SIGS Books & Multimedia

ACKNOWLEDGMENTS

I WOULD LIKE TO THANK ALL THE CONTRIBUTORS FOR GRACIOUSLY ALLOWING US to include their articles. I was extremely impressed by their collective knowledge and their ability to express it.

I would also like to thank the production staff at SIGS Books for their dedication and efforts to make this project a success: Peter Arnold, managing editor, and Beth Scalafani, graphic artist.

Finally, I would also like to thank my family: My wife, Florence, and my children, Charles, Michael, and Nicole. As usual, their patience and support was an enormous help. I love them dearly.

PART I

OBJECT MODELING

In this section we provide a number of articles that define and refine issues and techniques associated with modeling objects. This is a dynamic and changing discipline. As you will see, the following contributors are among those driving the science.

ASSOCIATION MULTIPLICITY

DAVID M. PAPURT

RELATING A PAIR OF ABSTRACT DATA TYPES, ASSOCIATION IS A RICH CONCEPT WITH many facets. My earlier columns [1,2] gave several descriptions of association: a referenced, named abstract data type; a bidirectional mapping between associated type extensions; a type with related extension and link instances; and an abstract data type with attributes, associations, and operations of its own. Each of these descriptions is from a distinct perspective and emphasizes an alternate aspect of the relationship; the latter descriptions unify seemingly different elements of the object model.

For simplicity, so far, this series of columns has restricted *association multiplicity* (or simply *multiplicity*); on the instance level, an association traversal in either direction has yielded exactly one instance. But in a more general and applicable model, a traversal can yield numbers of instances other than one. This column continues examination of association and focuses on associations wherein traversal can yield numbers of instances other than one.

First, mappings that yield multiple values are covered. Then, one-to-many and many-to-many associations are examined and described in terms of mappings that yield multiple values. Finally, association multiplicities other than one and many are examined.

MULTIPLE VALUE MAPPINGS

Mapping is a mathematical concept. My previous column[2] described two mappings that yield single values: unidirectional one-to-one mapping and bidirectional one-to-one mapping. This section extends that discussion and

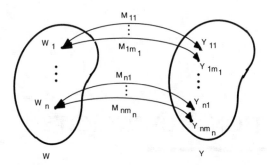 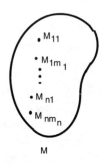

FIGURE 1A. *Bidirectional one-to-many mapping M. Sets W and Y alternate as range and domain.*

FIGURE 1B. *Mapping M viewed as a set.*

covers two additional mappings that yield multiple values: bidirectional one-to-many mapping and bidirectional many-to-many mapping.

Bidirectional One-to-Many Mapping

Figure 1 represents, with Venn diagrams, a bidirectional one-to-many mapping M two different ways. Figure 1A emphasizes that the mapping is a pair of inverse functions defined on two sets; W and Y alternate as domain and range, depending on mapping direction. Figure 1B emphasizes that the individual mapping instances form a set $\{M^{11}, \ldots, M^1m^1, \ldots, Mn^1, \ldots, Mnmn\}$.

The forward mapping function F: W→Y yields multiple values—i.e., is set valued. The reverse mapping function R: Y→W applied to any one of those multiple values yields the single value the forward function mapped originally. That is, F: W→Y and R: Y→W are constrained and must satisfy

```
R( OneOf( F(Wj) ) ) = Wj   j = 1, 2, . . ., n
where OneOf() selects any member of its set-valued argument.
```

Bidirectional Many-to-Many Mapping

Figure 2 represents, with Venn diagrams, a bidirectional many-to-many mapping N two different ways. Figure 2A emphasizes the mapping is a pair of inverse functions defined on two sets; D and V alternate as domain and range, depending on mapping direction. Figure 2B emphasizes that the individual mapping instances form a set $\{ND^1V^1, \ldots, NDdVv\}$.

Both the forward mapping function F: D→V and reverse mapping function R: V→D yield multiple values. The reverse mapping function R applied to any one value generated by the forward mapping function F yields a set

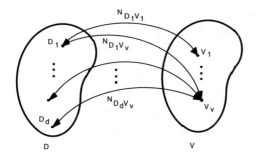

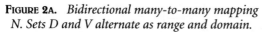

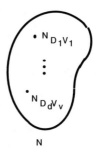

FIGURE 2A. *Bidirectional many-to-many mapping N. Sets D and V alternate as range and domain.*

FIGURE 2B. *Mapping N viewed as a set.*

that includes as a member the value the forward function mapped originally. That is, F: D→V and R: V→D are constrained and must satisfy

```
Dj ∈ R( OneOf( F(Dj) ) )
     j = 1, 2, . . ., d
```

where ∈ means *is an element of.*

ONE-TO-MANY MULTIPLICITY ASSOCIATION

Association multiplicity is the possible numbers of instances of one type participating in the association that can link to a *single* instance of the other type participating in the association. Generally, the possible numbers of instances, i.e., the multiplicity, is expressed as a set of non-negative integers. It follows from the intrinsic bidirectionality of association that there are two multiplicities for each association, one for each direction of traversal. Object type diagrams represent multiplicity with special symbols for commonly occurring multiplicities and explicit lists of numbers and intervals for less common multiplicities.[3]

> **TIP**
>
> Multiplicity is expressed as a set of non-negative integers.

The `Automobile-Person` Ownership association described in my previous column[2] had one-to-one multiplicity; the notation was a solid line between abstract data types. More precisely, in that model, every single instance of `Automobile` must link with exactly one `Person` instance, and every single instance of `Person` must link with exactly one `Automobile` instance.

Figure 3 represents the more complex `Automobile-Person` Carries (as

FIGURE 3A. *Automobile-Person Carries association. Object type diagram.*

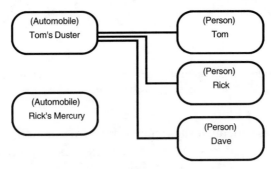

FIGURE 3B. *Sample Automobile and Person instances and Carries association links. Object instance diagram.*

passenger) association. The association is loosely described as *one-to-many,* but the solid-ball symbol in the object-type diagram of Figure 3A has more precise meaning. Reflecting that an `Automobile` can carry multiple `Persons`, the notation means that any non–negative integer (i.e., 0, 1, 2, . . .) number of `Person` instances can link to a single instance of `Automobile`. (For simplicity, this example disregards the practical maximum number of passengers that can fit into an `Automobile`.) Reflecting that a `Person` rides in only one `Automobile` at a time, the solid line going into `Automobile` means that exactly one Automobile must link to each single instance of `Person`.

The object instance diagram in Figure 3B represents a particular instance constellation—one `Automobile` carrying three `Person` instances and another empty of any `Persons`. In compliance with the association multiplicity constraints, each `Automobile` links with any number of `Persons`, and each `Person` links with exactly one `Automobile`.

One-to-Many Association as Mapping and Type

A one-to-many association is a bidirectional one-to-many mapping between type extensions. As for one-to-one association,[2] the mapping domain and range are the extensions of the types participating in the association, and they alternate depending on mapping direction.

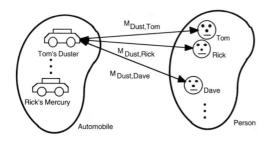 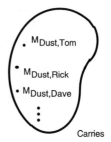

FIGURE 4A. *Automobile–Person Carries association viewed as mapping.*

FIGURE 4B. *Mapping viewed as a set, the extension of type Carries Association.*

The mapping instances—i.e., links—form a set, and the set is a type extension. Thus, a one-to-many association is a type with instances that are conceptual or actual links between associated abstract data type instances.

Figure 4 represents the `Carries` (as passenger) one-to-many association between abstract data types `Automobile` and `Person`. This Figure expresses information equivalent to Figure 3 but with different emphasis. Figure 4a emphasizes that the `Carries` association is a bidirectional one-to-many mapping, and Figure 4B emphasizes that the association mapping instances— links—form a set; that set is the extension of type `Carries Association` between `Automobile` and `Person`.

Further Observations

Unlike a one-to-one association,[2] a one-to-many association is unbalanced. The imbalance corresponds to the differing multiplicities at either end of the association. But, as in the one-to-one case, there is no preferred direction of the association, and the association can be traversed in either direction.

As in the earlier one-to-one case,[2] a link of a one-to-many association is not part of either of the two instances it connects. The link depends on both instances and contains information transcending the information in the instances.

When implementing in a programming language, often, for simplicity, a one-to-many association is implemented in a single direction only; the association can be implemented so that the link is traversed directly from the one side to the many side, or so the link is traversed directly from the many side to the one side. But never confuse such implementation issues with the conceptual model.

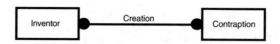

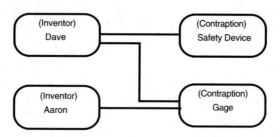

FIGURE 5A. *Inventor-Contraption Creation association. Object type diagram.*

FIGURE 5B. *Sample Inventor and Contraption instances and Creation association links. Object instance diagram.*

MANY-TO-MANY MULTIPLICITY ASSOCIATION

Figure 5a represents the *many-to-many* Creation association between abstract data types `Inventor` and `Contraption`. An `Inventor` can (and usually does) create multiple `Contraptions`, and multiple `Inventors` can work together to create one `Contraption`; the solid balls indicate that any non-negative integer number of `Contraption` instances can link to a single instance of `Inventor`, and any non-negative integer number of `Inventor` instances can link to a single instance of `Contraption`.

The object instance diagram in Figure 5B represents a particular instance constellation—two `Inventors` and two `Contraptions` connected by three links. In compliance with the association multiplicity constraints, each `Inventor` links with any number of `Contraptions`, and each `Contraption` links with any number of `Inventors`.

> **TIP**
>
> A many-to-many association describes conceptual or actual connections.

Like a one-to-one association and one-to-many association—and like associations of any multiplicity—a many-to-many association is a bidirectional mapping with domain and range that are the extensions of the types participating in the association; in this case, the mapping is many-to-many. Further—and, again, like associations of any multiplicity—a many-to-many association is a type describing conceptual or actual connections between abstract data type instances. Like any type, related instances

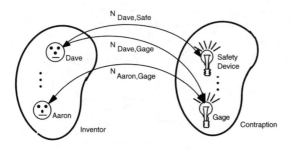

FIGURE 6A. *Inventor–Contraption Creation association viewed as mapping.*

FIGURE 6B. *Mapping viewed as a set, the extension of type Creation Association.*

and an extension of all instances exist; the instances are links, and the extension is the set of all links of the association. Figure 6 represents the many-to-many Creation association between Inventor and Contraption as a mapping and as a type.

OTHER MULTIPLICITIES

An association multiplicity constrains the number of instances of one type participating in an association that can link to a single instance of the other type participating in the association. In general, a multiplicity is a set of non-negative integers; the actual number of instances of one type linking to a single instance of the other type can be an integer only from this set. There are two multiplicities for each association, one for each direction of traversal.

Object-type diagrams denote multiplicities with special symbols for common multiplicities and explicit lists of numbers and intervals for less common multiplicities. Earlier sections presented the solid line without any terminator—indicating one—and the solid ball—designating any non-negative number (many). A hollow ball indicates optional—zero or one only—multiplicity.

> **TIP**
>
> This section describes the nomenclature.

Explicit lists of numbers and intervals written next to the association line near a type rectangle designate less common multiplicities without special symbols. For example, 1+ indicates any number greater than zero, 2–6 designates two to six inclusive, and 3, 5, 8–10 means three, five, eight, nine, or ten.

The object type diagram in Figure 7A uses an explicit list of numbers to

FIGURE 7A. *Clock-Hand association. Object type diagram.*

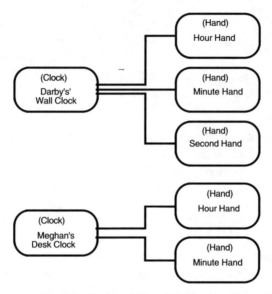

FIGURE 7B. *Sample Clock and Hand instances and association links. Object instance diagram.*

indicate that every Clock can link with either two or three Hands—any more or less violates the multiplicity constraint—and every Clock Hand links with a single Clock. The object instance diagram of Figure 7B shows a particular instance constellation.

The object type diagram in Figure 8A represents the relationship between types Street, Intersection, and Traffic Light and includes two associations; the multiplicity constraints are more complex than any seen to this point. A Street can link with as few as zero Intersections. But the 2_+ notation indicates that each Intersection must link with at least two Streets; an Intersection simply cannot exist unless at least two Streets meet or cross. An Intersection optionally links to a Traffic Light, as indicated by the hollow-ball—zero or one—multiplicity symbol, and every Traffic Light links to exactly one Intersection.

The street map of Figure 8B and object instance diagram of Figure 8C rep-

FIGURE 8A. *Street, Intersection, Traffic Light object type diagram.*

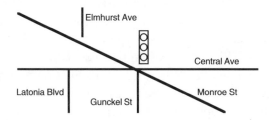

FIGURE 8B. *Sample street map.*

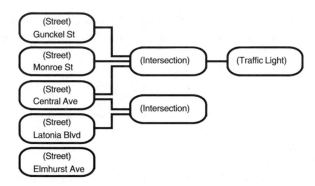

FIGURE 8C. *Object instance diagram corresponding to sample street map.*

resent the same constellation of Streets, Intersections, and Traffic Lights. Five Streets, two Intersections, and a single Traffic Light link together in one realization of the object type diagram of Figure 8A. Gunckel St., Monroe St., and Central Ave. meet at a single Intersection with a Traffic Light. Central Ave. also shares an Intersection with Latonia Blvd. The map and instance diagram show no Street Intersections with Elmhurst Ave.

SUMMARY

In a previous column,[1] type was described in terms of set theoretical concepts; the idea of type extension was central to that description. Subsequently,[2] an association was described as a bidirectional mapping between associated type extensions and as a type with related extension and link instances. These descriptions of association unified seemingly distinct elements of the object model.

But, for simplicity, in the earlier discussions, association multiplicity—the numbers of instances of one type participating in an association that can link to a single instance of the other type participating in the association—was limited to one. This column examined associations with more complex and interesting multiplicities. Where a multiplicity of one corresponds to a mapping that always yields a single value, a multiplicity other than one corresponds to a set valued mapping; even optional—zero or one—multiplicity can be viewed as a mapping that may generate the empty set. Regardless, an association is a type no matter its multiplicity.

Acknowledgment

Material for this column was adapted from INSIDE THE OBJECT MODEL: THE SENSIBLE USE OF C++.[4] The author gratefully acknowledges the permission of SIGS Books.

References

1. Papurt, D. The object model: Type and abstract data type, REPORT ON OBJECT ANALYSIS & DESIGN 1(2):11–14, 1994.

2. Papurt, D. The object model: Attribute and association, REPORT ON OBJECT ANALYSIS & DESIGN 1(4):14–17, 1994.

3. Rumbaugh, J., M. Blaha, W. Premerlani, F. Eddy, and W. Lorensen. OBJECT-ORIENTED MODELING AND DESIGN, Prentice Hall, Englewood Cliffs, NJ, 1991.

4. Papurt, D. INSIDE THE OBJECT MODEL: THE SENSIBLE USE OF C++, forthcoming from SIGS Books, New York.

ADDITIONAL ASPECTS OF ASSOCIATION

DAVID M. PAPURT

P REVIOUS COLUMNS[1-3] DISCUSSED THE BASIC FEATURES OF ASSOCIATIONS. AN association has several descriptions: An association can be viewed as a referenced, named abstract data type; as a bidirectional mapping between associated type extensions; as a type with related extension and link instances; and as an abstract data type with attributes, associations, and operations of its own. Each of the two traversal directions of an association has a multiplicity—the possible numbers of instances of one type participating in the association that can link to a single instance of the other type participating in the association.

However, association is a rich concept and has many additional facets. This column, my final one on associations, focuses on important aspects of associations not described previously: roles, order, and aggregation. Providing background for those discussions, additional topics include operations and constraints.

OPERATIONS

Introduced in an earlier column,[1] an *operation* is an abstract data type characteristic along with attribute and association. Specific to an abstract data type, an operation is behavior performed by or performed on an instance of the abstract data type. An operation is described by *what* it does, not *how* it executes.

Generally, an operation has a name, arguments with names and types, and a result type. Often, arguments or result type are left out of a description because they are implicit or unimportant in the context. A complete operation specification describes argument translation into return value and side effects.

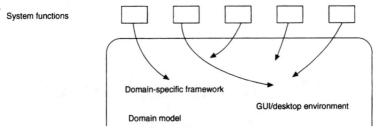

System functions

Domain-specific framework

GUI/desktop environment

Domain model

FIGURE 1. *Abstract data type Mail Carrier. The type has two operations.*

Figure 1 represents abstract data type Mail Carrier with two operations. A Mail Carrier instance can be commanded to deliver a Set of Letters. Further, the Mail Carrier instance can be queried whether rounds are complete and all Letters in the Set of Letters delivered.

This section discussed operations to enable precise description of association roles. As seen next, roles are easily understood when described in terms of operations.

ROLES

An association can be traversed in either of two directions, and association traversal yields linked instances.[2–4] Every association has two *roles*. Each role corresponds to a traversal direction and therefore fixes a source type and a target type.

A role is equivalent to an operation defined on the source type, and association traversal is equivalent to execution of that operation. The next section explains this equivalence and makes the meaning of role precise.

Operational View

In an object type diagram, role names can label each end of the line representing an association. Role names add meaning to the graphical expression of an association.

For example, Figure 2A shows two roles attached to the Carries (as passenger) association between Automobile and Person. The notation indicates each Person participating in the association plays the role of a *passenger* for the linked Automobile, and each Automobile plays the role of *transportation* for the linked Persons. Normally, role names are useful in developing a natural language description of the association.

FIGURE 2A. *Automobile–Person Carries association. Standard notation view.*

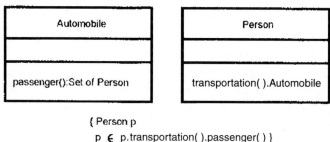

{ Person p
  p ∈ p.transportation( ).passenger( ) }

FIGURE 2B. *Automobile–Person Carries association. Operational view with explicit constraint.*

A deeper understanding of roles and association is achieved by examining an equivalent operational view of association. A standard transformation develops the equivalent operational view.

An association is transformed from the standard, line-in-an-object-type-diagram view to the operational view by defining a new operation in each of the two types participating in the association. For each type, the new operation name is the role name that appears on the opposite side of the association in the standard view; the new operation takes no arguments; and the new operation result type is the other type—or set of the other type, or list of the other type, depending upon multiplicity and order constraint (see below)—participating in the association. This operation returns all linked instances.

Thus, each role is equivalent to an operation defined on the abstract data type opposite the role in the standard view. This operational view is consistent with and refines the description, in my previous columns,[2,3] of an association as a bidirectional mapping between associated type extensions.

For example, Figure 2B represents the *Carries* association between *Automobile* and *Person* in the operational view. *Automobile* has operation *passenger()*, and *Person* has operation *transportation(); passenger()* yields a Set of *Person*, and *transportation()* yields an *Automobile*.

Role equivalent operations are constrained; the reverse operation applied to the result of the forward operation must yield the value the forward operation originally mapped. The operational view fails to capture symbolically this *inverse mapping constraint* implicit in the standard notation. So normally, an operational view of an association includes an explicit statement of the inverse mapping constraint. In the constraint appearing in the Carries association operational view (Fig. 2B), symbol Œ means the left operand *is an element of* the right operand set, and the dot operator means *apply* the right operand operation to the left operand instance.

> **TIP**
>
> Note the discussion on inverse mapping.

One of the more difficult aspects of programming an association is insuring that the inverse mapping constraint remains intact—i.e., that *referential integrity* is maintained. When one implements an association, referential integrity must be carefully maintained. The book INSIDE THE OBJECT MODEL[5] illustrates association implementation techniques.

Association role is inseparable from association operational view. But operational view is used rarely in object-oriented analysis (OOA). The standard, line-in-an-object-type-diagram notation is more concise and therefore preferable for analysis.

However, the value of the operational view is twofold. First, the operational view makes clear the meaning of association role, and so is important preparatory to analysis. Second, when one programs an association, the transformation from standard view to operational view must occur at some point during design.

Necessity

Whether or not role names appear explicitly in an object-type diagram, an association has two roles. Role names can clarify the meaning of an association but are often left out of object type diagrams without loss of meaning.

Nevertheless, certain associations always need role names, as confusion arises if they are absent. Specifically, roles are necessary for both self-associated types and multiply associated types; an example of each appears below.

Figure 3A represents the Person-type Parenting self-association in standard notation. The association expresses a relationship between parents and their children. The notation indicates each Person participating in the association plays the role of a *child* to two linked Persons playing the role of *parents*.

Figure 3B represents the Parenting association in operational view. *Person* defines operations *parent()* and *child(); parent()* yields a Pair of *Person* (a set

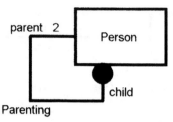

FIGURE 3A. *Person-type Parenting self-association. Standard notation view.*

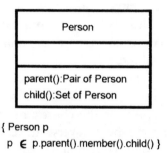

FIGURE 3B. *Person-type Parenting self-association.*
Operational view with explicit constraint.

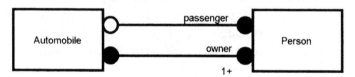

FIGURE 4. *Multiple associations between types Automobile and Person.*

of *Person* constrained to have two members), and *child()* yields a Set of *Person* (a set with an arbitrary number of members). The inverse mapping constraint appears in the figure; defined on any set (or pair), operation *member()* picks and returns a single, arbitrary member of the set.

Figure 4 contains an object-type diagram of multiply associated types *Automobile* and *Person*. The figure expresses that a *Person* can own an *Automobile* and that a *Person* can be a passenger in an *Automobile*. Appearing only at one end of each association, the role names distinguish the associations.

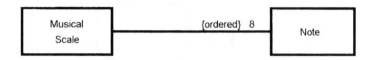

FIGURE 5. *Musical Scale–Note association. The one-to-many association is ordered.*

CONSTRAINTS

An object model might include instance, type, abstract data type, attribute, link, association, and operation components. *Constraints* are functional relationships between components in an object model; a constraint restricts the values that the components can assume.[4]

The graphical notation of an object diagram captures common constraints. For example, an association line represents the constraint that a forward traversal followed by a reverse traversal must yield the original instance.[2] A hollow ball optional multiplicity symbol represents a constraint on an association restricting the number of links.[3]

In principle, any constraint can be represented with a special graphical notation; in practice, too many graphical constructs may overwhelm the reader. So less common constraints need a general purpose notation. In object diagrams, constraints lacking specific graphical constructs are described with text delimited by braces, {}, and positioned near the constrained entity; discussed next, order is such a constraint.

ORDER

An association with many-to-many multiplicity can be constrained to be *ordered*. Ordinarily, traversal of a one-to-many association from the one side to the many side yields an unordered *set* of instances. When an order constraint applies, the traversal yields an ordered *list* of instances. In the operational view, when unordered, the role equivalent operation result type is a set; when ordered, the result type is a list.

For example, Figure 5 represents the association between a Musical Scale and Notes comprising the scale. The Notes of a Musical Scale are ordered by pitch. The constraint appears explicitly in the object-type diagram by enclosing the description—here {ordered}—in braces.

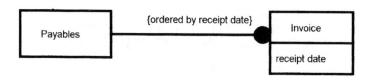

FIGURE 6. *Payables–Invoice association. The one-to-many association is ordered by the value of an attribute on the many side.*

FIGURE 7. *Year, Month, and Day aggregation.*

The basis for order can appear in the constraint description. Figure 6 represents the Payables–Invoice association. In this model, Invoices are ordered by receipt date, as opposed to, say, by company name or by invoice amount.

AGGREGATION

An *aggregation* is a part–whole relationship between a pair of types; the part is a *component* of a whole *assembly*. A line, terminated by a diamond and connecting aggregate and component types, represents an aggregation in an object diagram; the diamond appears next to the aggregate.

For example, Figure 7 represents a Year as an aggregation of many Months, and each Month as an aggregation of many Days. Figure 8 represents a Table as an aggregation of a single Table Top and three or more Legs.

Aggregation is a special case of association. (Note the similarity of their object diagram notations.) Accordingly, an aggregation can be viewed in any of the ways in which an association can be viewed. That is, an aggregation can be thought of as a bidirectional mapping between type extensions, as a type with links as instances, or as an abstract data type with characteristics.

> **TIP**
>
> Note the difference between aggregate and associated types.

However, the connection between aggregated types is stronger than the connection between associated types. An aggregation satisfies conditions not applicable to a nonaggregate association:

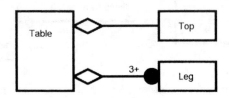

FIGURE 8. *Table, Top, and Legs aggregation.*

- An aggregation is transitive. If A is a part of B, and B is a part of C, then A must be a part of C; that is, an aggregation relationship exists between A and C.
- An aggregation is asymmetric. If A is a part of B, then B is not a part of A.

An association that fails to satisfy these conditions is not an aggregation.

A feature of aggregation is that characteristics—attributes, associations, and operations—often propagate from the assembly to components, possibly with modification. For example, in the Year, Month, and Day model of Figure 7, the day of the year attribute of a Day is computed from the month of the year attribute of Month and day of the month attribute of Day. That is, the month of the year attribute of Month propagates, with modification, and contributes to a component attribute value.

As a second example, the position and velocity attributes of an Automobile Windshield Wiper are computed, in part, from the position and velocity of the Automobile of which it is part. Likewise, operation go applied to an Automobile propagates to the Windshield Wiper—and to every other component of the Automobile as well.

Characteristic propagation is the most compelling reason to model a relationship as an aggregation instead of a nonaggregate association. Parts explosions like the Table, Top, and Legs assembly of Figure 8 are clear-cut, but ambiguous cases arise. If there is no apparent characteristic propagation, then nonaggregate association is preferable to aggregation. This approach preserves flexibility and reduces the number of constraints in the model.

CONCLUSION

This column focused on important aspects of association not covered in earlier columns: roles, order, and aggregation. Whether or not role names appear explicitly, an association always has two roles. An association role corresponds to a traversal direction or, equivalently, establishes source and destination types. A role is equivalent to an operation defined on the source type, yielding objects of the destination type, and subject to an inverse mapping constraint. Role names should be included in a model when needed to clarify the meaning of associations; in particular, role names should always appear in the descriptions of self-associated types and multiply associated types.

An association with many multiplicities can be constrained to be ordered. When an order constraint applies, traversal yields a list of instances, and not a set, and the role equivalent operation result type is a list and, again, not a set.

Aggregation—or the part–whole relationship—is a special case of association; an aggregation satisfies transitivity and asymmetry conditions. Typically, characteristics—attributes, associations, and operations—propagate from the aggregate to components, though often with modification.

Acknowledgment

Material for this column was adapted from INSIDE THE OBJECT MODEL: THE SENSIBLE USE OF C++.[5] The author gratefully acknowledges the permission of SIGS Books.

References

1. Papurt, D. The object model: Type and abstract data type, REPORT ON OBJECT ANALYSIS AND DESIGN 1(2):11–14, 1994.

2. Papurt, D. The object model: Attribute and association, REPORT ON OBJECT ANALYSIS AND DESIGN 1(4):14–17, 1994.

3. Papurt, D. The object model: Association multiplicity, REPORT ON OBJECT ANALYSIS AND DESIGN 1(5):12–15, 1995.

4. Rumbaugh, J., et al. OBJECT-ORIENTED MODELING AND DESIGN, Prentice-Hall, Englewood Cliffs, NJ, 1991.

5. Papurt, D. INSIDE THE OBJECT MODEL: THE SENSIBLE USE OF C++, SIGS Books, New York, 1995.

WELL-STRUCTURED OBJECT-ORIENTED ARCHITECTURES

GRADY BOOCH

FUNDAMENTAL TO THE BOOCH METHOD IS AN EMPHASIS ON ARCHITECTURE. A well-structured object oriented (OO) architecture consists of

- a set of classes, typically organized into multiple hierarchies
- a well-defined set of collaborations that specify how those classes cooperate to provide various system functions

Every well-structured OO architecture must consider both of these dimensions.*

The first dimension of an OO architecture—a set of classes organized into multiple hierarchies—serves to capture the static model of the abstractions that form the vocabulary of the domain. I speak of this as a vocabulary because each abstraction represents something in the language of an end-user or an implementer. For example, in the domain of credit card processing, we would find several nearly independent hierarchies relevant to domain experts, including classes representing accounts, institutions, and purchases. Each of these truly represents a hierarchy, not just a single class. For example, there exist corporate accounts, individual accounts, and joint accounts, as well as accounts whose balance may be carried over (with interest) every month and accounts that must be paid off every month. Modeling these different kinds of accounts as one class is wrong because this offers a poor distribution of responsibilities. A better approach is to define a hierarchy of accounts, starting at the most general kind of account and then

---

*There are other dimensions to every nontrivial software system, but these two are perhaps the most important. For a more complete discussion on all the views of software architecture, see P. Kruchten, *Software Architecture and Iterative Development*, Redwood City, CA: Rational Software Corporation, 1995.

TIP

Use independent hierarchies to represent semantically distant abstractions.

providing more specialized kinds of accounts through subclassing. In general, a single class hierarchy is suitable for only the most simple application; every other system should have exactly one hierarchy of classes for every fundamental abstraction in the model. Ultimately, using independent hierarchies for semantically distant abstractions provides a better distribution of responsibilities in the system.

Each independent hierarchy, together with all its close supporting classes, represents a natural grouping of abstractions in the decomposition of a system. In the Booch method, I call such groupings *class categories* because they denote architectural elements that are bigger than a class or even a hierarchy of classes. Indeed, as I mentioned before, the class is a necessary but insufficient means of decomposition: It is the class category that provides this larger

TIP

Note the discussion of class clusters.

unit of decomposition. Within each cluster there will be classes that are semantically close (such as corporate accounts and individual accounts). Between these clusters there will be classes that are semantically more distant (such as accounts vs. institutions vs. transactions). In general, class hierarchies rarely cross class category boundaries.

This first dimension is important in architecting an OO system, but it too is insufficient because it only reflects the static elements of a system. The second dimension of an OO architecture—a well-defined set of collaborations— serves to capture the dynamic model.

Each collaboration represents some behavior that arises from a set of distinct yet cooperative objects, often cutting across class category boundaries. For example, consider how information about accounts, institutions, and purchases is made persistent. Clearly, it is in our best interests to devise a consistent approach: The persistence of all of these kinds of objects should use the same mechanism, and this mechanism should be hidden from clients who want to use these objects. A reasonable solution to this problem is to define a set of classes that provide a lower-level form of persistence for atomic values and then have each persistent class use this mechanism to stream out values (for storage) or stream in values (for reconstructing the object from its persistent store). We would expect that such a mechanism would also be responsible for handling the caching of objects and resolving references or pointers, which cannot be stored directly. This mechanism fits the definition of a collaboration: there is no one class that provides this behavior, but rather, persistence in the system derives from the collaborative activity of several classes working together.

Therefore, remember that a class rarely stands alone. Especially when considering the dynamics of a system, it is important to concentrate on how certain groups of objects collaborate, so that common behavior is handled through common mechanisms. In my experience, I've found that most OO systems require less than 10 to 20 really central mechanisms. A central mechanism is one that has sweeping architectural implications, and thus represents a strategic decision. For a large class of systems, there is a set of common mechanisms that every architect must consider:

> **TIP**
>
> Classes rarely stand alone.

- persistence
- process management
- messaging
- object distribution and object migration
- networking
- transactions
- events
- exceptional conditions
- common look and feel

This list is not exhaustive, but it does represent the most common kinds of mechanisms that I find in many different systems. For each of these issues there is generally a range of possible solutions, and the task of the software development team is to explicitly decide upon and then carry out a single approach to each, suitable to all the nontechnical requirements of the system including performance, capacity, reliability, and security.

Selecting an approach to a mechanism such as object migration is indeed a strategic decision, since it has implications for the very backbone of the architecture. However, not every decision the development team makes is strategic. Some decisions are much more tactical and therefore local in nature. For example, the exact protocol every client uses to force the migration of an object is a tactical decision, made in the context of the more strategic one. However, it's often said that the devil is in the details, and so carrying out all the tactical decisions of a system in a consistent manner is just as important as making all the right strategic ones.

The key point here is that all well-structured OO systems are full of patterns, ranging from patterns such as mechanisms for object migration that shape the system as a whole to more local patterns such as idioms for handling exceptional conditions that reflect more tactical concerns. The most successful projects make the selection of these patterns an explicit part of the development process.

> **TIP**
>
> A well-structured OO architecture typically encompasses a range of patterns.

> **TIP**
>
> Idioms are at the bottom of the pyramid.

> **TIP**
>
> Note the definition of mechanism.

> **TIP**
>
> Frameworks are built atop idioms and mechanisms.

The classical definition is that a pattern is a common solution to a problem in a given context; a pattern also serves to capture its author's intent and vision. A well-structured OO architecture typically encompasses a range of patterns, from idioms to mechanisms to frameworks. For this reason, patterns are often called a system's microarchitecture.

In this spectrum of patterns, at the bottom of the food chain and closest to the code, there are idioms. An idiom is an expression peculiar to a certain programming language or application culture, representing a generally accepted convention for use of the language. Idioms represent reuse in the small. Next up are mechanisms, which build upon idioms. A mechanism is a structure whereby objects collaborate to provide some behavior that satisfies a requirement of the problem; a mechanism is thus a design decision about how certain collections of objects cooperate. As I explained earlier, mechanisms are important because they are strategic decisions that anchor the basic shape of the software system. At the top of the spectrum of patterns are frameworks, which build upon idioms and mechanisms. A framework represents a collection of classes that provide a set of services for a particular domain; a framework exports a number of individual classes and mechanisms that clients can use or adapt. Frameworks are thus a kind of pattern that provides reuse in the large.

By viewing architectures in terms of the patterns that they embody, there emerges a remarkable similarity among many well-structured OO systems. Figure 1 illustrates this canonical

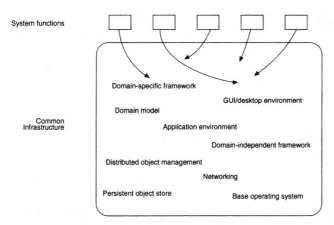

FIGURE 1. *A well-structured object-oriented architecture.*

architecture.* Each of these parts represents some framework, consisting of a set of classes and associated mechanisms.

A well-structured OO architecture typically includes the following elements:

- base operating system
- networking
- persistent object store
- distributed object management
- domain-independent framework
- application environment
- graphical user interface (GUI) desktop environment
- domain model
- domain-specific framework

At the bottom of this infrastructure, we find common platform services:

- base operating system
- networking

These two layers serve to insulate the rest of the application from the details

---

*This division of components was inspired by the work of M. Foley and A. Cortese, "OS Vendors Pick Object Standards," *PC Week*, January 17, 1994, p. 43.

TIP

This section defines the architecture of an infrastructure.

of its hardware. For some applications, the base operating system may be a large component that provides many common services (such as with Windows 95 or UNIX), but in others, it may be very small (such as in embedded controllers), providing only simple programmatic interfaces to external devices. Similarly, the networking element of this substrate furnishes all the primitive communication abstractions required by the application. This may be a major functional component in certain domains (such as an electronic funds transfer system) but nonexistent in others (such as in a stand-alone computer game).

Built on top of these facilities, we find the resources that manage object storage and distribution, which collectively define the application's plumbing:

- persistent object store
- distributed object management

In traditional terms, the persistent object store constitutes an application's database, although to some degree an object store is at a slightly higher level of abstraction than a simple relational database because an object store embodies the storage properties of a database together with some of the common behavior that characterizes these objects. Distributed object management builds upon these services and lower ones in the substrate to provide abstractions for the administration of distributed as well as mobile data in a networked environment. For example, consider a chemical engineering application that encompasses a web of computers scattered about the manufacturing floor. Some of this application's data, such as information about the inventory of various chemicals used in the process and recipes for various substances to be produced, may live on a specific node that acts as a central server for the system. Other kinds of data, such as the records about a particular production run, may be physically scattered across the network, yet appear as a logical whole to higher layers of the application.

Ultimately, the value of these two layers is that they provide the illusion to applications that objects live permanently in a large, virtual address space. In reality, an object lives on a particular processor and may or may not be truly persistent. By granting this illusion, the applications at the top of a system are ultimately much simpler, especially in geographically distributed situations. At the next highest level in the infrastructure, we find frameworks that cover domain-independent abstractions (such as various collection classes), application objects (which handle common client services such as printing and clipboard management on workstations), and the GUI facilities (which provide the primitive abstractions for building user interfaces):

- domain-independent framework
- application environment
- GUI/desktop environment

Just above this level of abstraction we find all the common abstractions that are peculiar to our given domain. Typically, these abstractions are packaged in two components:

- domain model
- domain-dependent framework

The domain model serves to capture all the classes of objects that form the vocabulary of our problem domain. For mission-critical management information systems, for example, this might include our specific abstractions of things such as customers, orders, and products, together with the business rules that apply to these things. For technical applications such as telephone switching systems, this might include things such as lines, terminals, conversations, and features, together with a specification of their behavior.

The domain-dependent framework provides all the common collaborations of these things that are specific to our domain. For example, in certain management information systems, this framework might include classes that collaborate to carry out transactions; for switching systems, this framework might provide classes that define common features such as plain old telephone service (POTS) as well as more advanced features such as call waiting, call conferencing, and caller ID.

> **TIP**
>
> The domain-dependent framework provides all the common collaborations.

In an earlier column, I explained how this canonical architecture adapts to real-time systems. Still, no matter what the application, it is essential to preserve the architectural integrity of a system. That goal is generally achieved by building architectures that are constructed in layers of abstraction, have a clear separation of concerns among these layers, and are simple.

All well-structured OO architectures have clearly defined layers, with each layer providing some coherent set of services through a well-defined and controlled interface. Each layer builds upon equally well-defined and controlled facilities at lower levels of abstraction. Such architectures are ultimately simple because they reuse patterns at various levels in the system, from idioms to mechanisms to frameworks.

FROM ANALYSIS TO DESIGN USING TEMPLATES, PART I

JAMES J. ODELL AND MARTIN FOWLER

I N RECENT YEARS A MOVEMENT HAS GROWN TOWARD DEVELOPING FORMAL PRO-cedures to increase product quality. The work has been inspired by W. Edwards Deming, who was sent to Japan after World War II to help rebuild their industry. His ideas on quality management, widely ignored in the United States, were taken up enthusiastically in Japan. Many consider this a key reason why Americans have lost so much economic and technical ground to the Japanese.

This movement toward high-quality products, often led by defense agencies, has influenced software engineering. In particular, the work of the Software Engineering Institute (SEI) has proved deeply influential.[1] Their framework proposes five levels of process maturity: initial, repeatable, defined, managed, and optimizing.

The two lowest levels are the *initial* level (often referred to cynically as the chaotic level) and the *repeatable* level. While success in level 1 depends on the heroics and competence of individuals, project developers in level 2 can rely on established management policies and implementation procedures.

These are based on the results of previous projects and the demands of the current project. Developers meet schedules and budgets. Basic project standards are defined and followed. SEI studies have shown that the vast majority of organizations are at these bottom levels of process maturity.

This column provides an approach that will support organizations wishing to take a further step-up to the *defined* level. At the defined level, an organization standardizes both its system engineering and management activities. Such an organization exploits effective software-engineering practices when standardizing its activities. Furthermore, an organization's activity standards are tailored for each project to develop their own *defined* activities.[2] One technique that supports defined-level organizations is *template-driven design.*

TEMPLATE-DRIVEN DESIGN

In this approach, design activity focuses on forming a set of design templates that can implement the analysis model (see Figure 1). These design templates are formulated using a definition of both the analysis method and the implementation environment. In theory, the design templates are applied to the analysis model, and a fully working system can be produced. This system, then, will accurately reflect the analysis model, though the system may not be the most efficient.

The analysis model should *define the interface* of the software components. When used in conjunction with the analysis model, design templates suggest the *implementation* of those components. As a result, a programmer—new to the domain, but familiar with the templates—should recognize the interface of all the components simply by looking at the analysis model. While each template is a suggested implementation, its interface is dictated by the analysis model. (In practice, achieving this goal completely may not be possible, but you should aim to get as close as possible.)

This approach enables both *consistency* and *traceability.* If a single set of design templates is used to develop code from the model, the resulting code will have a consistent style—a boon to maintenance and extension later on. This consistency comes from both naming the variables and operations and using the same mechanisms to implement bidirectional associations and subtyping. The link's directness eases tracing back from the code to the analysis model. Traceability is always useful and a key element for quality standards.[3,4]

SPECIFYING DESIGN TEMPLATES

The design templates can be specified in two ways. The first, and easiest, approach uses the design templates' document that has been adopted as a standard by a project or an organization. This document describes how to implement an analysis-level model for a particular implementation environment. Since the design templates are dependent on both the analysis approach and implementation environment, each combination of the two should have a design-template document.

The second approach encodes the design templates in a computer program.

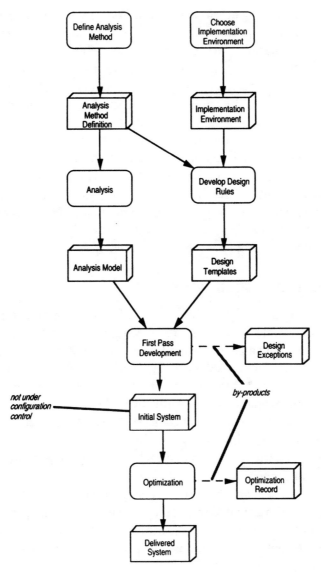

FIGURE 1. *An object-flow diagram that describes the process of template-driven design.*

(This approach is currently very limited but is becoming more important.) Of course, this encoding is exactly what compilers and code generators do. A compiler merely uses a set of design templates to transform each kind of high-level language statement into binary code. Program-language compilers are not new. However, the technology to automate design templates is still very immature—though it is being developed rapidly. Code generators do exist that can take these models and produce much of the system code using templates.

This approach naturally has practical limits. While experience in formulating templates is growing, the idea of using design templates in this way is still fairly new. Furthermore, while design templates can be provided to cover most cases, they cannot be applied to some special cases. Another practical limit is that the choice of design templates is not always well defined. Design template documents may indicate preferred implementation options, while leaving the choice to the implementor on a case-by-case basis.

This column will take a number of analysis constructs and describe possible templates for each. Here, the templates for associations are discussed in terms of both interface and suggested implementation. These general considerations and the sample template should provide readers with enough guidance to develop templates for their own environments.

TEMPLATES FOR ASSOCIATIONS

Associations—that is, relationship types and their mappings—specify how object types associate with one another. A number of OO practitioners are uncomfortable using associations in OO analysis, because they see associations as "violating" encapsulation. Encapsulation dictates that the data structure of a class is hidden behind an interface of operations. For some, the presence of associations breaks this by making the data structure public. However, associations describe the responsibilities that objects must fulfill in their relationships with other objects.

For example, Figure 2 specifies that each `Employee` object must be able to both know and change its `employer`. Conversely, each `Organization` must know its `employees` and be able to change them. In most OOPLs, this responsibility is implemented by retrieval and modification operations. Data structure may be present—and, in most cases, will be. However, data structure is a design consideration and is not specified by the analysis model.

INTERFACE FOR ASSOCIATION TEMPLATES

For each association, the OOPL interface consists of a set of operations that access and update the association. The exact terms and structure of these operations depend on the cardinalities of the relevant mappings.

In general, a single-valued mapping requires two operations: an *accessor* and a *modifier*. The accessor operation returns the object to which a given

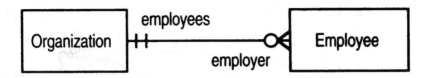

FIGURE 2. *Analysis models do not specify data structure.*

object is mapped. The modifier operation changes the mapping for a given object by reassigning the mapping pointer from one object to another. Access requests, then, require no input parameters. Modification requests, however, require an input parameter that specifies the object to which the mapping must now point. Thus, for Figure 2, the Employee class would have two operations. In C++, no standard naming convention exists. Here, many programmers use get or set somewhere in the name. For example, the names getEmployer and setEmployer (Organization org) could be used to access and modify the employer mapping. The names getEmployer and setEmployer are the most natural. However, some prefer employerSet and employerGet, because both operations will appear together in an alphabetically sorted browser. In Smalltalk, both operations are conventionally given the mapping name. Here, modifiers are distinguished from accessors by the presence of a parameter. Therefore, the Employee class would have get and set operations named employer and employer: anOrganization.

Multivalued mappings require three operations—again, with one accessor. Single-valued accessors return just one object. Multivalued accessors, however, return a set of objects. (All multivalued mappings are assumed to be sets unless otherwise indicated. The interface for nonsets will be different and is beyond the scope of this article.) Multivalued modifiers require two operations—one to add an object to a set, the other to remove an object. The accessor will usually be named in the same way that a single-valued mapping is named. However, a plural form is recommended to reinforce its multivalued nature—for example, employees or getEmployees. Modifiers would take the form of AddEmployee (Employee emp), RemoveEmployee (Employee emp), or employeeAdd: anEmployee, employeeRemove: anEmployee.

Modifiers, whether single-valued or multivalued, should also ensure that the constraints are met. For example, the SetEmployer operation should ensure that the employer mapping of Employee is not set to null. In other

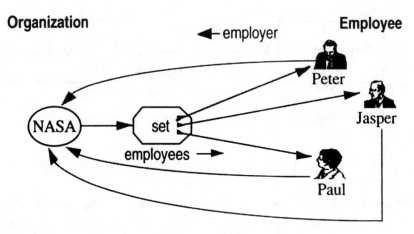

FIGURE 3. *Associations may be implemented using pointers in both directions.*

words, the modifier should ensure that both minimum and maximum cardinality constraints are met. Any other constraints, such as `invariant`, `tree`, and user-defined constraints, should also be enforced at this time.

Type checking should also be performed. For example, if a `SetEmployer: anOrganization` operation is requested, the object supplied via the `anOrganization` parameter must always be an `Organization` object. If type checking is not built into the programming language, extra code can be added to the modifier operations to ensure type integrity.

ASSOCIATION TEMPLATE OPTION 1:

Using Pointers in Both Directions

In this option, mappings are implemented by pointers from both participating classes. If a mapping is single-valued, there is a single pointer from one object to another. For example in Figure 3, each Employee has a single pointer to his employer. If a mapping is multivalued, the object will have a set of pointers to the other objects. In Figure 3, NASA points to a set of pointers which, in turn, contains pointers to Peter, Jasper, and Paul. For languages that support *containment,* an object may hold its set of mapping pointers internally rather than point to an external collection. Containment, therefore, has implications for space requirements. Since pointer sets can dramatically increase in size, an object's size can swell. Single-valued mappings can also use containment. Here, the actual object will be stored internally, instead of a pointer to that object. Typically, single-valued containment is limited to storing fundamental objects internally, such as Integer or Date objects. (Fundamental objects will be discussed later in option 6.)

In option 1, the accessor operations are relatively straightforward. For a single-valued mapping, the accessor merely returns a reference to the mapped object.* For a multivalued mapping, the accessor returns a set of references. However, it should not return *the* set of references. If it did return the set, the set's user could change the set's membership—thereby violating encapsulation. The encapsulation boundary should include all sets implementing multivalued mappings.

One solution is returning a copy of the set. Thus, if any alterations are made, they do not affect the actual mapping. However, this may incur a significant time overhead for large sets. An alternative is to use a *masking class*. A masking class is a simple class that has a single field containing the set. Only those operations that are permitted on the contained set are defined in the masking class. This way, modifications can be blocked. Another alternative, particularly for C++ implementations, uses *iterators* as described by Gamma.[5] Iterators provide a highly flexible way to access the elements of a multivalued mapping without exposing underlying representation.

Since two pointers implement each relationship, modifiers should maintain a two-way, or referential, integrity. Thus, a modifier called to change Peter's employer to IBM must not just change Peter's pointer to IBM. It must also delete the inverse pointer to Peter in NASA's employees' set and create one in IBM's employees' set.**

This template option has both benefits and drawbacks. Its accessor navigation is fast in both directions. However, ensuring referential integrity

---

*In C++, the issue about what should be returned by accessors is important. Should the object or a pointer to the object be returned? The choice should be made explicit by the design templates. A common convention is returning the value for all built-in data types such as `String` or `Integer`, the object for all fundamental classes such as `Data` and `Currency`, and a pointer for all other classes. In Smalltalk, this does not apply, since it always appears to work with objects rather than with pointers. This article refers only to returning references. For C++ and other languages that are pointer explicit, the actual templates should make clear exactly what is being returned.

**Of course, care must be taken not to enter into an endless loop. Such an example would be where `RemoveEmployee` requests `RemoveEmployer`, which requests `RemoveEmployee`, and so on. In C++, this is a typical situation that requires a friend construct. In Smalltalk a friendlike operation must be created—but marked private (which does not, of course, stop Employee from using it). In these cases, having only one modifier do the actual work is useful. The other modifier should then call just that one modifier. This will ensure that only one copy of the update code exits.

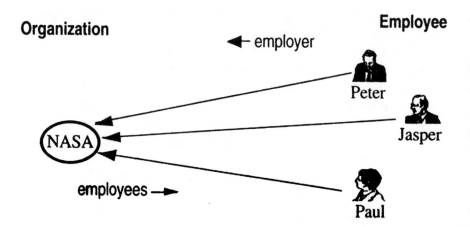

FIGURE 4. *Associations may be implemented using pointers in only one direction.*

requires extra processing time. So, while this option provides fast access, modification requires extra time. Additionally, the technique to ensure referential integrity is not trivial. However, once a solution has been chosen, replication is easy. Another disadvantage lies in the space required for this option. Not only are pointers required in both directions, but multivalued mappings can require large sets.

ASSOCIATION TEMPLATE OPTION 2:

Using Pointers in One Direction

Another option for association templates is using pointers in *one* direction only. In Figure 4, for example, the Employee objects point to their employer Organizations. However, the inverse mappings are not implemented. Therefore, if all the employees for NASA are requested, a different method than option 1, above, is required. A common technique would be to read all instances of Employee—selecting only those whose employer is NASA. The containment approach described in option 1 can also be used here.

Without implemented pointers, accessors require more logic than the preceding template option. However, modifiers require less logic, because only the class with the pointer changes the pointer. The class without the pointer just requests the modifier operation in the other class. Referential integrity will not be violated when multiple pointers get out of step. This option requires less

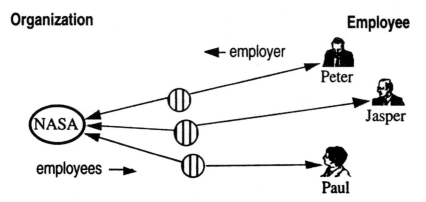

FIGURE 5. *Associations may be implemented with association objects.*

space than option 1, since it stores only one pointer per association. However, it will be slow when accessing objects to which there are no mapping pointers. So, compared to option 1, this option provides the same access time in one direction—but slower access in the other direction. Furthermore, this option requires less modification time and less pointer storage.

ASSOCIATION TEMPLATE OPTION 3:

Using Association Objects

Association objects are objects with two pointers that are simply used to link two associated objects, as illustrated in Figure 5. Typically, a table of such objects is provided for each association. Accessors work by retrieving all objects within that table, selecting those objects that point to the source, and then following each pointer to the mapped objects. Modification operations are simple. They merely create or delete the association object—thereby ensuring referential integrity without the two-way processing required in option 1. To support associations of this kind, special association classes can be built. Additionally. dictionary classes using hash-table lookups may be used to implement them.

Space is only used when associations are needed. This can be a benefit or drawback. When the objects of two classes are rarely related, few associations and less space are required. When the objects of two classes are usually related, more space is required. Furthermore, association objects provide slower access than previous options. Indexing them (by using a dictionary)

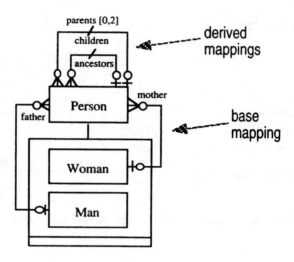

FIGURE 6. *An example of derived and base (i.e., underived) mappings.*

can improve speed. One benefit of associations, however, is that referential integrity will not be violated. In addition, no modifications are required to the data structure of the two associated classes. In this way, any number of association classes can be established or removed without having a structural impact on the associated classes.

ASSOCIATION TEMPLATE OPTION 4:

Derived Associations

Associations can be supported without any immediate data structure. For example in Figure 6, the `mother` and `father` mappings will probably be implemented with two fields that store the pointers to the `Person's` mother and father. However, the parents mapping does not require a data structure because it can be derived using the `mother` and `father` mappings. Mappings, such as parents, are usually derived in one of two ways—*eager* or *lazy.*

A lazy derivation produces its result only when a specific request is made. For instance, if the `ancestors` mapping were lazy, it would evaluate the `ancestors` only when a `getAncestors` request was issued. Implementing a data structure for a lazy association such as `ancestors` is not necessary. Lazy results are usually not stored within an object, because their results can quickly become obsolete between derivations. To ensure that a derivation is always accurate and current, eager associations are used. An eager association derives its result whenever a change in one of its component mappings occurs. For instance, if the `parents` mapping were eager, it would calculate the `parents` in the unlikely event that the `mother` or `father` of a `Person` were changed. The product of eager derivations is typically stored in the object. Otherwise, the results of the derivation could be lost. In this situation, implementing a parents data structure is useful.

In this template option, the lazy accessor method involves more than following a pointer. It involves a method that eventually derives the pointer. The eager accessor, however, follows a pointer derived earlier by a modifier. Either way, the interface remains the same. The requester does not know whether the `getAncestors` operation follows a pointer or performs a derivation. The requester only needs to know that requesting the `getAncestors` operation returns a set of `Person` objects that are the ancestors of a given `Person`.

Since the mapping is derived, modifier operations should not be available.* For instance, the ancestors mapping should not be modified directly. Any modification should be made to the mother and father mappings. If the ancestors mapping was lazy, any subsequent `getAncestors` operations would obtain the updated set of ancestors. If the `ancestors` mapping was eager, a modifier operation would have to be written to recompute and store the set of ancestors whenever `mother` and `father` mappings changed. Such a modifier should be invoked only from the `setMother` and `setFather` operations—and unavailable publicly.

ASSOCIATION TEMPLATE OPTION 5:

Hybrid Associations

Up to this point, associations have been implemented either as base or derived. Some applications may require that an association accommodate both modes. For instance, a particular ancestor of a `Person` may be known and explicitly asserted by an application. Yet, the remaining ancestors may still require derivation. In both cases, the ancestors mapping is a mapping

---

*An exception to this is hybrid mappings. Here, a mapping instance can be asserted or derived. For instance, a person's grandparents may be expressed explicitly, yet the great grandparents may be derived from the grandparents. This is particularly useful in those situations where the mother or father are unknown. Hybrid mappings, then, would require an appropriate data structure and modifier operation.

from a given `Person` to the `Person's` ancestors. However, different methods are selected to access them. Here, the template option can involve a combination of option 4 and a preceding option.

ASSOCIATION TEMPLATE OPTION 6:

Fundamental Associations

Some object types are fairly simple and prevalent throughout all parts of a model. As such, they require slightly different treatment to most object types, particularly with respect to associations. Examples of such object types are the so-called built-in data types of programming environments, such as `Integer`, `Real`, `String`, and `Date`. Additionally, good OO analysis will uncover other examples of commonly used object types, such as `Quantity`, `Money`, `Time Period`, and `Currency`. The built-in data types, together with other commonly used types, comprise the *fundamental types.*

Fundamental types, then, are commonly used types and have a certain internal simplicity. Because of their common use, they will have many associations with other types. Mappings *to* a fundamental type are not a big concern. Mappings *from* a fundamental type require a large amount of pointer space and significant effort in maintaining referential integrity. This situation would also suggest a large number of accessors to support the queries indicated for these mappings. To avoid the possibility of highly bloated interfaces, the mappings of fundamental types to nonfundamental types are typically not implemented.

Fundamental types should be declared in some way. One method marks the object type as fundamental in the glossary. For many modelers, associations with fundamental types are also referred to as *attribute types.* Declaring a mapping to be an attribute type would be a good indication to the designer that the inverse mapping should not be implemented (similar to option 2).

References

1. Humphrey, W. MANAGING THE SOFTWARE PROCESS, Addison-Wesley, Reading, MA, 1989.

2. Paulk M., B. Curtis, M.B. Chrissis, and C. Webber, Capability maturity model, Version 1.1, IEEE SOFTWARE, 10(4):18-27, 1993.

3. ISO 9001: Quality Systems—Model for Quality Assurance in Design/Development, Production, Installation and Servicing, International Organization for Standardization, REPORT ISO 9001-1987, ISO, 1987.

4. ISO 9000-3: Quality Management and Quality Assurance Standards—Part 3: Guidelines for the Application of ISO 9001 to the Development, Supply and Maintenance of Software, International Organization for Standardization, REPORT ISO 9000-3:1991, ISO, 1991.

5. Gamma, E. R. Helm, R. Johnson, and J. Vlissides, DESIGN PATTERNS: ELEMENTS OF REUSABLE OBJECT-ORIENTED SOFTWARE, Addison-Wesley, Reading, MA, 1995.

FROM ANALYSIS TO DESIGN USING TEMPLATES, PART II

JAMES J. ODELL AND MARTIN FOWLER

I N DEFINING DESIGN TEMPLATES, IT IS IMPORTANT TO KEEP IN MIND THE PURPOSES of the templates:

- to ensure that the software is structured in the same way as the analysis models, as far as is practically possible
- to provide a consistency within the software
- to provide guidelines on constructing software so that knowledge is effectively propagated around the organization

These guidelines give us an important principle. The design templates both *define the interface* of the software components and *suggest the implementation* of those components. A goal in the process should be that a programmer, new to the domain but familiar with the templates, should know what the interface of all the components is simply by looking at the analysis model. In practice it may not be possible to achieve the goal 100%, but we should aim to get as close to it as possible.

Design templates should thus provide a statement of the required interface and a number of *suggested* implementations. The interface is mandatory. However, programmers may choose the implementation from a suggested list or produce their own alternative. In other words, the class implementor may change the implementation, but may not alter the interface. The user of the class should not need to know—or care—what implementation is chosen.

Since design templates are employed using analysis information, this means that the analysis model performs two roles: as a conceptual picture of the enterprise and as a specification of the software components. As these roles are very different, the analysis model cannot satisfy them both fully. Thus, some "impurities" will appear. The alternative to this is to keep separate models. However, the overhead of keeping multiple models up to date is costly and difficult.

This column takes a number of analysis constructs and describes possible templates for each. In the previous issue, association templates were explored. In this issue, templates for generalization are discussed.

IMPLEMENTING GENERALIZATION

One of the most noticeable features about the difference between object-oriented (OO) and conventional modeling practices is the prominent use of generalization. While generalization has long been a part of many data-modeling approaches, it has been often seen as an advanced or specialized technique. The close relationship between generalization and the class inheritance of object-oriented programming languages (OOPLs) ensures a central place for it in object-oriented analysis (OOA).

Many OOA approaches use *generalization* as an equivalent to *inheritance.* However, there are several ways to implement generalization. Inheritance is just one of these. Other implementation forms are also required—particularly for those situations where objects may change their object type or be an instance of multiple object types. For instance, if a particular Employee object is changed from being a subtype of Staff to a subtype of Manager, this is known as dynamic classification. Or, if a particular object is both an instance of Property Owner and Employee, this is known as multiple classification.[1] Such require more thought because conventional OO languages only support single, static classification. The approaches to implementing multiple and dynamic classification can also be used to reorganize inheritance structures and to implement generalization in environments that do not support inheritance.

The interface for generalization will be discussed at the end of this article.

Generalization Template Option 1: Inheritance

In most OO approaches, the notions of subtype and subclass are synonymous. In other words, inheritance is the chosen method of implementing generalization. This provides the best form of implementation when such an implementation is possible. The interfaces for each object type are placed on corresponding classes and method selection is supported directly by the OOPL. Thus, this approach is usually preferred, if possible. Its disadvantages are that it does not support multiple or dynamic classification.

Generalization Template Option 2: Creating a Replacement Object

One way to handle changes in object type is to employ inheritance as described in option 1. However, when an object changes in type, remove the old object and replace it with a new one of the appropriate class. For example in Figure 1, if a Customer object becomes a Priority Customer object, the old Customer is deleted and a new Priority Customer is created. This allows the programmer to retain the advantages of inheritance and method selection while still providing dynamic classification. The full procedure for carrying this out is to (1) create the object in the new class, (2) copy over all common information from the old object to the new, (3) change all the references pointing to the old object to point to the new one, and (4) finally delete the old object.

The biggest problem, in many environments, is finding all the references to the old object and moving them to the new one. Without memory management this may be nearly impossible. Any references that are not caught will be invalid *dangling* pointers and lead to a crash that is difficult to debug. Thus, this approach is not recommended for C++. Languages with memory management can find this easier. Languages like Smalltalk make it even easier by supporting this option using the become operation.

Providing all references can be found and changed, this approach is plausible. Its remaining disadvantage is the time taken in copying common information and in finding and changing the references. This will vary considerably between environments, and the amount of time required will determine the approach's suitability.

Generalization Template Option 3: Flags

If a programmer who had never heard of inheritance was asked how she would implement Customer records to indicate whether they are priority or not she would probably answer: "with a status flag." This old-fashioned scheme is still effective for OOPLs as well because it supports both multiple and dynamic classification. Flags are easily changed at will, and one flag field can be defined for each subtype partition.

The principal difficulty with this approach is that it does not use inheri-

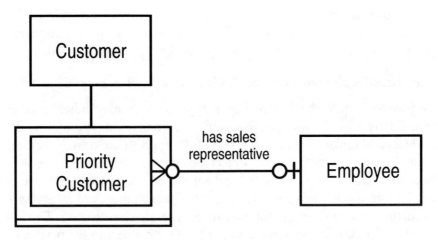

FIGURE 1. *In most OOPLs, to change a* Priority Customer *to a* Customer *requires creating a* Customer *object, moving everything from the old* Priority Customer *object to the new* Customer *object, and deleting the old* Priority Customer *object.*

tance. All operations and fields required to support subtypes, then, need to be moved to the supertype class. Thus, the Customer class in Figure 1 implements both the Customer and the Priority Customer object types—resulting in an implementation like that depicted in Figure 2. In other words, generalization is not being implemented using inheritance. Instead, it is being implemented using a flag field. In the case of Customer, the PriorityCustomerFlag is a field in the Customer class.

> **TIP**
>
> Without inheritance, the template option must guard against incorrect usage.

One of the problems that occur when inheritance is lost involves making sure that the proper operations are invoked. For example, it is clearly not appropriate to get or set the sales representative for a non-Priority Customer. If inheritance were used, such a request would cause an error (a run-time error in Smalltalk, probably caught at compile time in C++). Without inheritance, this template option must ensure that all operations originally defined on a subtype are guarded against incorrect usage. This is accomplished by checking the appropriate status flag to ensure that the correct kind of object is being accessed. For example, the getSalesRepresentative operation must make sure that the status flag indicates that the Customer object is a Priority Customer. If that check fails, the routine exits yielding some sign of the problem: usu-

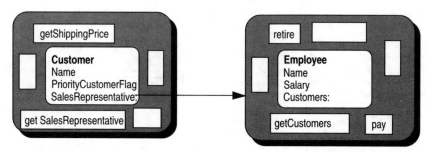

FIGURE 2. *When inheritance is not used to implement the* Priority Customer *class, one option is to add a flag field and any* Priority Customer–*related data structure to the* Customer *class.*

ally an exception. One of the drawbacks to this approach is that it is not possible to catch this kind of error until run-time.

Since inheritance is lost, its partner polymorphism is also only a memory. For instance, if a getShippingPrice operation is polymorphic for Customer and Priority Customer, selection of the appropriate method needs to be implemented by a programmer. This is typically accomplished by using a case statement inside the Customer class. A single getShippingPrice operation is provided as part of Customer's interface. In the method for that operation there must be a logical test based on the status flag of Customer—with possible calls to internal private methods. If the case statement is kept within the class and a single operation is published to the outside world, all the advantages of polymorphism remain. Thus, the soul remains even if the body is absent.

The final disadvantage of this implementation is that the class must now allocate space for all the data structures defined for its usurped subclass. In the example above, this means that the data requirements for a Priority Customer must be supported within the Customer class. Thus, all Customer objects that are not Priority Customers effectively waste this space. If the subtype has many data structures—and few instances of the subtype—this is very wasteful indeed.

Generalization Template Option 4: Combination Subclasses

Object types with multiple subtype partitions, such as those depicted in Figure 3a, usually indicate the need for multiple classification. For instance, a given object may be both a Corporate Customer and a Priority Customer. One template option to support multiple classification is by

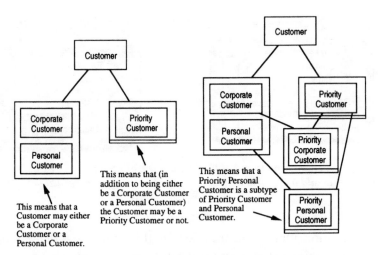

FIGURE 3. *Multiple subtype partitions (a) suggest multiple classification. One option to implement this is with combination classes (b).*

using combination subclasses. This would involve creating classes for `Priority Corporate Customer` and `Priority Personal Customer`. By using multiple inheritance, the classes can neatly capture all the required interfaces and let the programming system deal with method selection in the usual way. This approach is depicted in Figure 3b.

There are two principal disadvantages to this approach. The first is that an object type with many partitions could cause an unwieldy set of combination classes. For example, `Customer` could also be subtyped as `Large Customer`, `Medium Customer`, and `Small Customer` in one partition, and `Government-Sector Customer` and `Private-Sector Customer` in another. Including the partitions in Figure 3a, this would involve at least 24 more classes to express all the possible combinations. The other disadvantage is that this approach only supports static classification.

Some C++ authorities advocate care in using multiple inheritance. In particular, it is a common convention not to allow common root classes in a multiple inheritance lattice. The diagram in Figure 3b is one such example. Here, `Customer` is the superclass of `Priority Corporate Customer` through both `Priority Customer` and `Corporate Customer` superclasses. The alternative is to only inherit from `Customer` for one partition and use the other partition as a mixin. A mixin is designed as an abstract class that is mixed into another class to form a multiply inherited subclass.

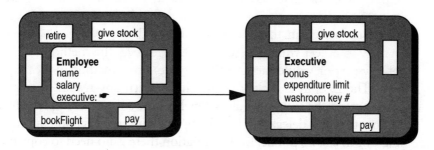

FIGURE 4. *The* Employee *class with the* Executive *subtype implementation delegated to a hidden class.*

In this example, Corporate Customer could be defined as a subclass of Customer but have Priority Customer as a mixin. Priority Customer would not be a subclass of Customer. Priority Corporate Customer would then be a subclass of Corporate Customer and Priority Customer but would no longer inherit Customer from two different directions.

> **TIP**
>
> Note the caveat on using multiple inheritance.

Note that this is an implementation technique only. In analysis, it is perfectly acceptable for the Priority Corporate Customer type to be a subtype of Customer type via two supertypes.

Generalization Template Option 5: Delegation to a Hidden Class

This template option uses *delegation* to handle the subtyping. Here, a class is defined for the subtype but is hidden from all except its superclass. A field must be provided in the superclass for a reference to the subclass (which can double as a status flag). As with flags, all the operations of the subtype must be moved to the super-

> **TIP**
>
> Delegation uses a hidden subtype.

class's interface. However, the actual methods and data structure for the subtype remain in the hidden subclass. In this way, all requests are received by the superclass. Those requests that involve a hidden subclass are then passed on to the hidden subclass for the actual processing.

For example, in Figure 4 an Executive Employee would have two objects: one Employee object and the other Executive. The Executive object, and indeed its class, would not be seen by any class other than the

Employee class. (In C++, all of its members would be *private* and Employee its *friend*.) The giveStock operation, defined only for Executive object, would be placed in the Employee class. When giveStock is sent to an Employee object with an associated Executive, the method in Employee for giveStock would merely call the giveStock method in the Executive class. The Executive class would then return any result. In this way, no other part of the system would know how the subtype is implemented.

Note that this delegation is hidden. A common delegation approach is to make both classes public. In this situation there is no need to copy the operation definitions from Executive to Employee. The user of the classes is responsible for knowing that certain operations exist on the Executive rather than the Employee. (This is often referred to as giving Employee the role of Executive.) This approach would not satisfy our requirement in this section that all the options share the same interface.

Method selection for polymorphic operations can be handled in a number of ways. One is to use an approach similar to that with flags. Employee would contain a condition to check to see if the Executive field is null. If so, it uses its usual implementation, and if not, it delegates the call to Executive. If Employee does not have the operation Employee raises an exception.

> **TIP**
>
> There are a number of ways to handle polymorphic method selection.

A different approach is to provide a separate hierarchy to handle the dynamic polymorphism. As illustrated in Figure 5, the Executive field (now renamed grading) refers to an abstract EmployeeGrading class, which is subclassed into concrete DefaultGrading and ExecutiveGrading classes. An Employee who is not an Executive would have this pointer set to a DefaultGrading, while an Executive would point to an ExecutiveGrading. The usual default implementation would be written into DefaultGrading, and Employee would always delegate the call to the class in the grading field: No condition tests are required. This structure is rather more complicated than the prior paragraph but has the advantage that new gradings can be added without changing Employee. (This approach is described in more detail as the *state* pattern in Gamma et al.[2]) The principal advantage of this option is the increase in modularity, particularly valuable if there are many hidden classes and the state pattern is used. In addition, this approach does not waste space for those objects that do not need the extended data structure.

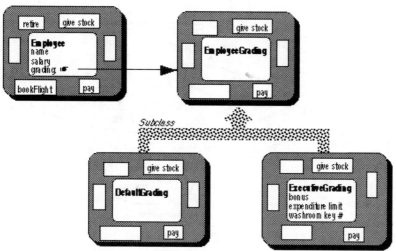

FIGURE 5. *The* Employee *class with the* Executive *subtype implementation delegated to a hidden class.*

Generalization Template Option 6: Object Slicing

This template option is a more general form of the delegation option described above. To support the dynamic and multiple classification requirements of a system, one recommended technique is called *object slicing.* In object slicing, an object with multiple classifications can be thought of as being sliced into multiple pieces. Each piece is then distributed to one of the object's various classes. For example, an object named Sigourney may be an instance of the Employed Person and Property Owner classes. To record these two facts in a single classification OOPL, one piece of the Sigourney object must become an instance of Employed Person, and the other an instance of Property Owner.

Obviously, objects cannot be "sliced" and made into instances of classes—it is a metaphor. These slices, however, can be implemented by surrogate objects. Each surrogate becomes an instance of a hidden class, as described in option 5. In addition, an unsliced version of the object must also be recorded to serve—physically and conceptually—as a unification point for its surrogates. Each original (unsliced) version of the object becomes an instance of some unhidden superclass called, for example, Conceptual Object. The instances of the other classes, such as Property Owner and Employed Person, are the object slices, where each is an instance of a dif-

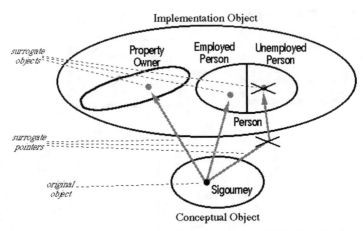

FIGURE 6. *Object slicing supports dynamic and multiple classification.*

ferent—but hidden—subclass. The instances of `Conceptual Object` are the unsliced objects, where each maintains pointers to its various slices, as described in option 5.

An example of how object slicing can be applied is illustrated in Figure 6. Here, the unsliced `Sigourney` object is represented as an instance of the `Conceptual Object` class. This one object representing `Sigourney` as a whole points to multiple `Sigourney` object slices. The instances in the `Property Owner` and `Employed Person` classes are slices of the `Sigourney` object. In other words, object slices of the whole `Sigourney` object are also `Sigourney` objects. However, the slices comply with the conventional OOPL requirement that each is an instance of only one class.

Changes in state can be accomplished by adding or removing the surrogates and the pointers to them. For instance, when `Sigourney` was classified as `UnEmployed Person`, there was a pointer from the `Conceptual Object Sigourney` to the `UnEmployed Person Sigourney` surrogate. When `Sigourney` became employed, the surrogate `UnEmployed Person` object and its pointer were removed and replaced by a surrogate `Employed Person` `Sigourney` object and its pointer.

> **TIP**
>
> Changes in state can be accomplished by adding or removing surrogates.

As each object is added or removed from the various classes, the `Construct` and `Destruct` operations would still apply. However, the object-slicing mechanism must add to these class-level operations by ensuring that objects do not have conflicting multiple states. For instance, an object can simultaneously be an instance of the `Property Owner` and `Employed Person` classes. However, it cannot simultaneously be an instance of both the `UnEmployed Person` and `Employed Person` classes: It must be an instance of one or the other. In other words, an object cannot be classified as an `Employed Person` without first removing the object from the `UnEmployed Person` class.

Object slicing is a reasonably elegant solution to a problem not yet well-supported by OOPLs. However, in addition to the programming overhead mentioned above, object slicing also requires extra logic to support polymorphism and supplement the OOPL's method-selection mechanism. This extra requirement is not used for those subtyping partitions declared as static. When a partition is static, the normal polymorphic support of the OOPL can be used. In this way, object slicing can be selectively applied. The developer must choose according to the application's requirements.

Interface for Generalization Templates

Generalization, too, has its accessors and modifiers. Accessors return an object's classification, and modifiers change the classification.

A controversial question in OOP is whether an operation *should* return an object's classification. It turns out that such an operation is often important. For example, without it, how can a process take a set of `Person` objects and filter it so as to leave only the `Women` objects? Such an operation, however, also presents a danger: that programmers will use it within a `case` statement in such a way that it subverts polymorphism. There seems little that can be done within the structure of OOP to eliminate this dilemma. An operation that returns an object's classification is often necessary and thus should be provided. Good programming style, however, dictates that such an operation should not be used *instead* of polymorphism. As a general guideline, classification information should only be requested as a part of pure information gathering within a query or for interface display.

Some conventions currently exist for finding out the classification of an object. Both Smalltalk and C++ programmers use operations named `isStateName` to determine whether an object is in a certain state. Smalltalk has a message `isKindOf: aClass` to determine class membership. C++ does not hold class information at run-time. However, sometimes opera-

TIP
This will be available with the ANSI C++ standard.

tions that effectively give this information are provided when a need is there.

Two broad naming schemes can be used. The first is to use the naming form `isTypeName`. The second is to provide a parametric operation such as `hasType (TypeName t)`. The disadvantage of the former, more conventional approach is that adding a subclass to the model forces a change in the superclass to provide the new `is TypeName` operation. The `hasType` convention is more extensible because subclasses can be added without a change to the superclass.

No naming standard exists for type changes. Names such as `makeTypeName` or `classifyAsTypeName` are reasonable. A general convention is that such operations are responsible for declassifying from any disjoint types. Thus a complete partition need only have as many modifiers as there are types in the partition. Incomplete partitions need some way to get to the incomplete state. This can be done by providing `declassifyAsTypeName` methods for each object type in the partition or by providing a single `declassifyIn-PartitionName` operation. Note that those partitions whose object types are invariant will not have these modifiers.

When these modifiers are used, associations will imply issues similar to those discussed under creation and deletion. Thus, mandatory mappings require arguments in a classification routine, and a declassification routine might lead to choices akin to single and multiple deletion.

Implementing the `hasType` Operation

Each class in the system will need a `hasType` operation. The method will check the argument against all the types implemented by the class. If flags have been used, they are checked to test for the type. Even if no flags are present, the class will almost certainly implement a particular type and that type must be checked. If any of these tests are true, a value indicating "true" is returned. If, however, none of the class' types match, the method in the superclass must be called and result of that returned. If no supertype exists, "`false`" is returned. Thus, in practice a message sent to the bottom of a hierarchy will slowly bubble up the hierarchy until it hits a match—or it runs out at the top and comes back false. This mechanism makes it easy to extend the type hierarchy because only the class that implements the type needs to check for that type.

References

1. Martin, J. and J. Odell. OBJECT-ORIENTED METHODS: A FOUNDATION, Prentice Hall, Englewood Cliffs, NJ, 1995.

2. Gamma, E., R. Helm, R. Johnson, and J. Vlissides. DESIGN PATTERNS: ELEMENTS OF REUSABLE OBJECT-ORIENTED SOFTWARE, Addison-Wesley, Reading, MA, 1995.

FROM ANALYSIS TO DESIGN USING TEMPLATES, PART III

JAMES J. ODELL AND MARTIN FOWLER

I N THE PREVIOUS TWO COLUMNS WE EXPLORED TEMPLATES. TO REVIEW, DESIGN templates both *define the interface* of the software components and *suggest the implementation* of those components. A goal in the process should be that a programmer new to the domain but familiar with the templates should know what the interface of all the components is simply by looking at the analysis model. In practice it may not be possible to achieve the goal 100%, but we should aim to get as close to it as possible.

Design templates should thus provide a statement of the required interface and a number of suggested implementations. The interface is mandatory. However, programmers may choose the implementation either from a suggested list or by producing their own alternative. In other words, the class implementer may change the implementation but may not alter the interface. The user of the class should not need to know—or care— what implementation is chosen.

> **TIP**
>
> Design templates should provide a statement of the required interface, and a number of suggested implementations.

In this column we take a number of analysis constructs and describe possible templates for each. In the previous two issues we explored association and generalization templates. In this issue, we will discuss templates for creating, deleting, and deriving objects, as well as composition.

TEMPLATES FOR COMPOSITION

Composition is just another kind of association. Therefore, the association templates described earlier can be used—with extension. Since operations may be propagated from a whole to its parts, the designer must ensure that the right operations are propagated. For instance, requesting a `rotate` operation on a `Car` object would also imply that the `rotate` operation applies to all parts of the `Car`. The `owner` field in the `Car` class could very well propagate to all of the parts as well. However, requesting a `paint` operation on a `Car` object would not imply that the `paint` operation applies to all of the parts of the `Car`—only to the exterior parts. Furthermore, an `exterior` color field in the `Car` class would not apply to all its parts.

Since propagation is not yet directly supported by object-oriented programming languages, a template is required to ensure that the proper code is in place. For those operations that are propagated, methods must be supplied for all of the appropriate parts. Furthermore, the method for the whole must ensure that the methods for the parts are also invoked. The methods for the parts, however, might not be invoked unless the method for the whole is also invoked. For example, the `move` operation on a `Car` object would also imply that the `move` operation applies to all of the parts of the `Car`. Yet, you would probably not `move` the frame if you did not also `move` the `Car`. In other words, the `move` operation is not inherited: It is propagated only.

In contrast, propagated fields do not have to be replicated to the parts. However, the part classes must have a method to access propagated fields—even if they are only contained in the whole class. In this sense, propagated fields can be thought of as being derived (as described in the previous column under Association Option 4).

TEMPLATES FOR CREATING OBJECTS

Mechanisms are required to create new objects. This applies both to those objects implemented directly by a class and to those implemented indirectly.

Interface

Each class must have a way of creating instances of the types it implements. Creation does not imply just forming a new object. The various constraints that exist for the object must also be satisfied so that it is a "legal" object. All mandatory associations must be filled during the creation operation. This implies that the creation operation must have arguments for each mandatory mapping. Similarly, any subtypes in complete partitions implemented by the class must be chosen through arguments or the naming of the creation method. Additionally, invariant associations and object types should also be chosen through arguments.

Optional and changeable features *may* also be included in the creation arguments. However, it is usually better to create the object first and then send it the necessary messages to set up these features. This reduces the size of the interface for the class. While object creation is usually carried out by the class, there are other ways to organize object creation (see the creational patterns in Gamma et al.[1]).

Template

All object-oriented languages have their own conventions for creating new objects. Typically, these provide for allocating the storage of an object and its fields. However, the initialization routine is not always an appropriate place for setting up the mandatory features passed via arguments.

In Smalltalk, the usual idiom is having each class support a creation message (often called `new`) that may take arguments. During creation, it is often arranged for the new object to be sent an `initialize` message that takes no arguments. This `initialize` is useful for setting the instance variables of multivalued mappings to a new set, but it can not support initializing associations because it takes no arguments. Such work is best done in the `new` method.

C++ provides a constructor for initialization. Much may be done here, but some compilers do make life difficult by not allowing `this` (or `self` in Smalltalk) to be used in an assignment within the constructor. Such a reference is necessary for associations implemented with references in both directions. In this case, a two-step creation is needed, using the constructor to allocate storage and a create routine to set up a legal object.

TEMPLATES FOR DELETING OBJECTS

Objects that can be created may also be destroyed.* The biggest problem in destroying objects is living with the consequences. Deleting an instance of `Order`, depicted in Figure 1, would cause a problem if there were any `Order Lines` connected to it. As specified by the mandatory association, every `Order Line` must have an `Order`. So, if the `Order` were simply deleted, the associated `Order Lines` would violate cardinality constraints.

Two approaches can be taken to this problem. The first is the *single* destruction—the kinder, gentler approach. Here, if an object's deletion

---

* Not all objects should be destroyed. Some objects, such as medical records, must live forever. Here, one alternative to destruction is archiving the object.

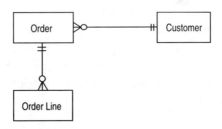

FIGURE 1. Order *objects may not be deleted when they have* Order Item *objects.* Customer *objects may not be deleted when they have* Order *objects.*

TIP

This section discusses the problems associated with deleting objects.

would cause any constraints to be violated, the destruction is not permitted to occur. The second approach is the *multiple* delete. In this approach, if an object is deleted, any objects that require it are also deleted. For instance, if an Order were deleted, its Order Lines would also be deleted—causing a ripple effect throughout the database.

In practice, delete templates will vary from mapping to mapping, not from object type to object type. So, one mandatory mapping may only permit single deletes, while another only permits multiple deletes—even though both mappings might associate the same object types. As long as the destruction is all or nothing, integrity is preserved.

Interface

Different object-oriented environments have their own approaches to destruction. All objects that may be destroyed should have a single-destruction operation. Technically, this is all a programmer needs. However, this places a burden on the user of the class to destroy things in the correct order. For example, to delete a Customer object, the programmer must also know that all Order objects for that Customer must first be destroyed. Furthermore, to delete all these Order objects, the Order Lines must first be destroyed.

Together with a single destroy, some multiple deletes may also be provided. It must be clear, however, which mappings permit multiple deletes and which do not.

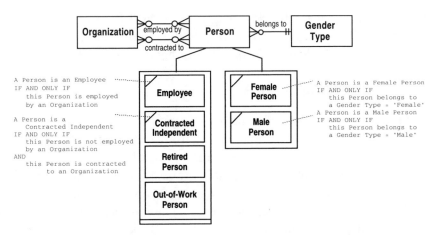

FIGURE 2. *An example of some base and derived subtypes of* Person.

Template

During destruction, memory management is a very important issue. While it makes little difference to the destruction method itself, it does affect the consequences of error. The object being destroyed must have all its links broken with associated objects—*in both directions*. Additionally, all constraints must be checked for violation. Any violations that have already occurred due to the destruction operation must be rolled back. With a non-memory-managed system the final step is to deallocate the storage. With a memory-managed system, no explicit deallocation is made. Here, once all its links are removed, the object dies of loneliness and gets "garbage collected."

TEMPLATES FOR DERIVING OBJECTS

Returning a set of objects for a particular class is reasonably straightforward. However, the instances of some classes can be derived. For example, the Person object type in Figure 2 has both derived and base (i.e., nonderived) subtypes. Employee is derived from those Person objects that are employed by an Organization. In contrast, Retired Person objects are not derived but must be explicitly classified as Retired Persons.

Derived classes are similar in nature to derived associations, discussed in Association Option 4 in our last column. They can be lazy or eager. Such classes provide only accessor operations. For lazy classes, construct and destruct operations are not permitted, since derived objects are determined by criteria external to the class. Eager classes will have constructors and destructors. However, these operations should not be available as part of the public interface—only to those operations that implement derivation rules.

TEMPLATES FOR ENTRY POINTS

At this point, a well-designed structure exists of objects that are usefully connected together. From any kind of object, using the object diagram to decide how to navigate to any other kind of object is easy. However, there is still one important question: How do you get into the object structure in the first place? This may seem odd to those who use traditional and, in particular, relational databases, since entry to these databases is via their record types. Getting hold of the data involves starting at the record type and selecting individual records. Starting from a list of all instances of a type is not always the most appropriate approach. Object-oriented systems, in particular, can provide different forms of access that can be more efficient and provide other useful abilities.

The first way in which this can be done is not to provide lists of all instances for all types of object. Consider the example in Figure 1. Since all instances of `Order Line` are connected to an instance of `Order`, there is no need to hold a reference from the type `Order Line` to all its instances. If it is considered that it would be rare for anyone to ask for all `Order Lines`, regardless of `Order` or `Product`, the reference can be neglected. In the unlikely occurrence that someone would want a list of all `Order Lines`, this could be provided by getting a list of all instances of `Order` and navigating across the mapping to `Order Line`. Thus, the storage required to hold all the references to all instances of `Order Line` can be saved at the cost of one level of indirection should all instances of Order Line ever be required. This is a purely implementation tradeoff. In a relational database, the tradeoff is irrelevant because the database uses fixed tables.

The same argument can be extended to `Order`. Here it might be considered that all instances of `Order` are required if a person wishes to select an `Order` by typing in an order number. Since the order number would typically be a `String`, references from string to `Order` would not usually be held. Certainly if an application required it, access to `Order` could be provided by way of an order number index. However, it might be argued that `Orders` were, in reality, always accessed once the `Customer` was found. In other words, references to `Order` could be obtained via the `Customer` object. Again, it is an implementation question as to whether to hold the references or not.

This argument cannot be extended to `Customer` because `Customer` lacks any mandatory relationships. Thus, a `Customer` can exist that is not related to any other object. A list of all instances of `Customer` is then necessary to ensure that such a `Customer` is found—making `Customer` a useful entry point.

Note that the decision of which object types should be entry points is purely a conceptual issue—not just an application requirements issue. Object types with no mandatory relationships must be entry points. Those with mandatory relationships may hold a list of instances, but that in itself does not make them conceptual entry points.

> **TIP**
>
> The decision of which object types should be entry points is purely conceptual.

Interface

It is useful for all objects to have an operation that returns all instances of the type. This is essential for references in one direction to work when navigating against the grain.

It can often be useful to provide some operation to find an instance according to some criteria. An example might be findCustomer (`customer Number`). While it is difficult to provide general rules, the most natural way is to use navigation. Thus, rather than asking to find all orders whose customer is ABC, it is conceptually easier to ask customer ABC for all its orders. Optimization problems may occur due to the navigational expression of the query, but these can often be resolved within `Customer`'s accessor.

When access occurs using fundamental types, this option does not apply, and a general find routine is more useful. Even then, it should be done in as general way as possible. The easiest approach is to ask for all instances of a class and then use the built-in select operation on the returned collection. This will not work very well for classes with many instances. The next move is to provide a select operation that will take any Boolean operation as argument. This allows maximum flexibility with only one operation on the class's interface. However, it is much harder to do in some languages than in others.[*] Only when these approaches are exhausted should a find with specific arguments be used. However, this should be done only when it is too expensive to do it in a more generic way. Care should always be taken not to bloat a class's

---

[*]It is easy in Smalltalk because the select operation can be invoked with an arbitrary block of code as an argument. In C++, a function has to be written that makes the whole thing a lot less elegant. One alternative is for each class to provide a general purpose find function that can be used to select instances. This can be called whenever collections of that class are needed.

interface.* Another reason for using a find operation is the presence of a relational database. Here, there may be strong optimization reasons to provide a find operation that corresponds to a structured query language select.

Note that these instance-finding operations would be as valid for nonentry points as they are for entry points. Indeed, the instance accessors should fit the same pattern.

Entry points need an additional operation to make an object fit within the structure. Merely creating an object may not place it within the structure, particularly if it is not related to any other object within the structure. Thus, entry point objects need an operation to insert them within the structure.

The above comments on interface are true for in-memory systems. Slightly different characteristics occur when using databases. Different data-management systems (either object database management systems or relational interfaces) have their own conventions. Those conventions should be used with the proviso that interfaces be as free as possible of data-management system specifics.

Implementation

The usual way of implementing an entry point is through some collection class. This collection can be a static field for the class. Asking an object for its instances means that the objects of the collection are returned. As with multivalued associations, it is important that the collection cannot be changed except through the entry point's interface. Another way is to have a manager class that looks after holding instances of entry point classes. This class is usually a singleton class.

A nonentry point will typically also have an operation to return all instances. This can be done by navigating from an entry point. Selects and finds would work in a similar way.

Reference

1. Gamma, E., R. Helm, R. Johnson, and J. Vlissides. DESIGN PATTERNS: ELEMENTS OF REUSABLE OBJECT-ORIENTED SOFTWARE, Addison-Wesley, Reading, MA, 1995.

---

*In C++, a common approach is to provide an external iterator and let the user of a class loop through the selection manually. Although this is much more awkward than using Smalltalk's internal iterators, it is often better than using C++'s internal iterators.

A Non-Procedural Process Model for Object-Oriented Software Development

Ian Graham

M OST READERS OF THESE WORDS WILL ALREADY BE CONVINCED THAT OBJECT-oriented programming is a good thing. Fewer, but only slightly fewer, I feel, will believe that prototyping and incremental development are useful. The interesting question is how to combine them.

Some three years ago, Swiss Bank Corporation successfully implemented both OOP and RADs and, in doing so, started a process that led to being rated by CSC Index as the most productive development organization in the world—or at least in their large metrics database. However, there was a problem, because the original RAD approach was a structured approach and produced results that were of little interest or direct use to the developers. About two years ago, I was charged with solving this problem. The objective was to run RADs that build shared understanding between users and developers and produce object models of use to developers using object-oriented programming languages. I started by looking at the existing RAD methods and published OOA approaches.

The remarkable thing about most published object-oriented analysis and design methods is that their life-cycle models remain thoroughly procedural. Some are really nothing more than structured methods with objects added to the entity model. I would include almost all well-known methods, such as OMT, Shlaer–Mellor, Coad–Yourdon, FUSION, and Objectory, in this category. Some methods have no life-cycle models at all, and others have very weak ones, as Booch has pointed out. (For a survey of these and many more methods, see reference 1.)

My experience has taught me that successful object-oriented rapid application development requires the complete abolition of the notion of

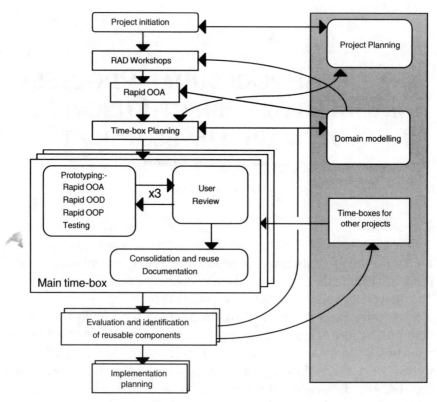

FIGURE 1. *The object-oriented SOMA life-cycle model.*

development phases. This article describes what I believe to be the first genuinely object-oriented model of the software development life cycle itself: the SOMA process model. The core idea behind this model is summed up by Figure 1. In this model, each box represents an activity object. Activities communicate by message passing, and the messages are implemented by deliverables and products.

The SOMA method[2] defines projects as networks of activities that have dependencies but no explicit sequence. An activity produces a result that must be a tested result. In particular, we test objectives by measuring them and requirements object models by walkthroughs. Task scripts are captured very early on and are used as test scripts. This helps address the debugging problem in a tool-independent fashion and places the emphasis on quality first. This tested time-box (or "right on time") philosophy means that it is quite permissible and safe to write the code before the design is done—or vice versa if that's how you like to work. Both business objects and task scripts are accumulated in a repository for reuse in subsequent workshops and projects. It is not so much that OO enhances RAD with additional benefits or vice versa. It is more that modern IT requires the benefits of both techniques applied in such a way as to be consistent with one another. Structured RADs with OO programming can be dangerous. The main benefit of the combined approach is that it makes it possible to move to specification level, rather than code level, reuse. No CASE tool known to us supported the approach adequately, which is why we produced our own tool.

To understand Figure 1 completely, the reader should be aware that rounded rectangles represent unbounded activities that have no time limit, while sharp rectangles represent bounded activities, or time-boxes. All activities are objects. All message sends are "guarded" by defined tests or preconditions. Each guard is a SOMA rule or assertion. Each rule is implemented by a test.

Project initiation, which may include throwaway prototyping, leads to workshops wherein users and developers build a business process model in the form of an object model in which the objects are task scripts. This is converted to a Business Object Model. These two object models are tested by a CRC-style walkthrough, and event traces (representing complete business processes) are produced. In the main time-box, a system is constructed, tested against these traces, and documented. The workshops also elicit objectives and measures for each objective. Objectives that cannot be measured are discarded. The task and business object models are captured using our own software tool, and report production is automated. The tool also allows us to pull down class specifications from a repository, speeding up the proceedings considerably and making the scribe's job easier.

Consolidation is the activity wherein the results of earlier or parallel time-boxes are woven into the fabric of the application. Here, developers reuse existing objects and spot opportunities for future reuse. At this point, there are several quality checks to apply to the code and documentation.

The fact that there are unbounded boxes within the main time-box, which has a definite elapsed time limit, means that the project manager has some decisions to make. Also note that the sequencing of programming and design is undetermined. This means that developers who like to code before documenting the design (like me) can do so but that more disciplined individuals, too, can be accommodated.

The pragmatic recommendation is to work the way you work best. However, the evaluation activity, which involves independent auditors, prevents this freedom from being abused. Once all tests have been passed, the implementation can be planned. Otherwise, the time-box may be rerun or the project abandoned. User review elicits evolving requirements and tests prototypes continually. Users are assigned permanently (but not full time) to time-box teams. About three or four iterations is ideal for time-boxes of three to four month's duration.

The gray area of the diagram represents activities that are outside the current project. The most interesting of these is Domain Modeling, which is where the reuse repository is created and maintained.

A three-day course is necessary to cover all the issues raised in this diagram and clearly this cannot be done in this 1,500 word column. I will elaborate on many of the surrounding issues in future columns, but the impatient reader can find the whole method explained in my book MIGRATING TO OBJECT TECHNOLOGY,[2] which also contains a software tool, SOMATiK, that supports the method. The object model represented by the diagram in Figure 1 is supplied as a SOMATiK project file. (Registered users of SOMATiK can obtain a free bug fix from the Internet.)

Experience with this life-cycle model has been positive. The users help build the object models and therefore feel that they own the system. They get a system on time and suffer no unpleasant surprises. The developers are more highly motivated, closer to the users, and less frustrated by the bureaucracy that the structured approaches usually impose. Nevertheless, the approach applies management and quality control rigorously.

References

1. Graham, I.M. (1994). OBJECT-ORIENTED METHODS, 2nd Ed., Addison-Wesley, Wokingham, UK, 1994.
2. Graham, I.M. MIGRATING TO OBJECT TECHNOLOGY, Addison-Wesley, Wokingham, UK, 1995.

BUSINESS RULES

JAMES J. ODELL

T HE REQUIREMENTS OF AN ENTERPRISE CAN BE SPECIFIED USING VARIOUS TECH-
niques: object-relationship diagrams, class hierarchies, state-transition
charts, event schemas, predicate logic, functional statements, production
rules, and so on. The object-oriented analyst/designer should choose the
specification technique that best describes the problem at hand. When specifying the various states of a telephone call, a state-transition diagram is
appropriate. A medical-diagnosis system can be specified using the production rules of an expert system. A stock analyst might use neural-network
topology diagrams for a knotty bond-analysis problem. Another rapidly
emerging technique is *rule specification* (sometimes called *business rules*).
This article focuses on answering the following:

- What are rules and why do we need them?
- How can they be expressed in the end user's natural language—while
  being, at the same time, both rigorous and formally defined?
- What is a useful way of categorizing rules?
- How can rules specify object structure as well as object behavior?
- Can certain rules be applied under some circumstances and not others?

INTRODUCTION TO RULES

Rules allow user experts to specify policies or conditions in small, stand-
alone units using explicit statements.

Rules are declarations of policy or conditions that must be satisfied.[1]

Organizational policies and conditions can be expressed in such declarations as the following:

- Pay a supplier invoice only if it has been approved.
- The product ordered from a supplier must be offered by this supplier.
- Put the orders of bad payers on a waiting list, until they pay the amounts due.
- A bad payer is a customer having more than three invoices overdue.

Rules, however, are not automatically justified, just because they provide an economical form of specification. If another technique is clearer, clarity of specification should be chosen over economy. (Coding is an entirely different story.) Therefore, if a user finds that a rule expresses a particular policy or condition more clearly, a rule should be used. The user, though, does not always have to choose between one technique or another. Rules can also be used to supplement other techniques, such as entity diagrams, data flow diagrams, and state transition diagrams.

RULES EXPRESSED IN NATURAL LANGUAGE

Rules need to be rigorous so that they form a basis for code generation. A typical rule expression in the language Prolog is:

```
sister (x,y) : - female (x), parent (x,z), parent (y,z)
```

This statement means that x is the sister of y if x is female and x and y have the same parent z. Rules presented in this manner, however, will not be understood easily by most end users. Therefore, rules should also be expressible in the end user's natural language—while being, at the same time, both rigorous and formally defined. Using this approach, the four rules above could be specified as follows:

```
Pay Supplier Invoice
ONLY IF its status is "Approved".

IT MUST ALWAYS HOLD THAT
a Product that is ordered from a Supplier
is offered by this Supplier.
```

```
WHEN requested to fill a Customer Order
IF the Customer issuing this Customer Order is a Bad Payer
THEN put this Customer Order on a Waiting List.

WHEN a Customer ceases to be a Bad Payer
THEN process backorders for this Customer.

A Customer is a Bad Payer
IF AND ONLY IF the number of Invoices
(sent to this Customer and with Due Date before today)
is greater than 3.
```

When defined in this way, rules go beyond being just explicit statements of policy. Rules can also be executable specifications for an automated system. Therefore, when a business changes its rules, its automation operates differently. Such rules do not just reflect the business, they *are* the business. Rules, then, should be:

TIP
Note the classification of rules.

- executable declarations of policies or conditions
- understandable by the user community

Until recently, this was science fiction. However, the automated support for executable and user-understandable rules is now available.

CATEGORIES OF RULES

Rules can be classified in many ways. One technique divides rules initially into two categories: constraint rules and derivation rules. Constraint rules specify policies or conditions that restrict object structure and behavior. Derivation rules specify policies or conditions for inferring or computing facts from other facts.[2] Beyond these two types of rules, further categorization can be defined (Figure 1). Again, rules can be classified in many ways. The categorization shown in Figure 1 was chosen because it reflects one way in which users think about rule specification. There is nothing holy about it. This categorization is just one useful approach to organize the presentation of rules in this book.

Stimulus/Response Rules

Stimulus/response rules constrain behavior by specifying WHEN and IF conditions that must be true for an operation to be triggered. Examples of stimulus/response rules are:

```
WHEN the stock level of a Product becomes less than the
reorder point
THEN reorder this Product.

WHEN a Library Book is requested by a Borrower
IF Copy of Library Book is available
THEN check out this Copy to this Borrower
ELSE place next available Copy of this Library Book on
             reserve.
```

TIP

Stimulus/response
rules constrain
behavior within
an event context.

Stimulus/response rules constrain behavior within an event context. In other words, the rule's IF condition only holds WHEN a particular type of event occurs. Therefore, the IF condition for an operation can differ by event stimulus. For instance, a Close Order operation can be invoked under the following conditions:

```
WHEN Order shipped or Order paid events occur
IF Order is paid and Order is shipped
THEN Close Order.

WHEN an Order cancelled event occured
IF Order is cancelled and Order is not shipped
THEN Close Order.
```

When an IF condition must be true for an operation to perform correctly (no matter what type of event occurs), a different kind of rule is required.

Operation Constraint Rules

Operation constraint rules specify those conditions that must hold before and after an operation to ensure that the operation performs correctly. Such constraints are vital to the execution of an operation and are completely independent of the event context under which the operation is invoked. Bertrand Meyer states that the presence of these rules should be viewed as a contract that binds a method and its requestors. Here, the operation says "if you call me with the precondition satisfied, I promise to deliver a final state in which the postcondition is satisfied."[3]

Operation precondition rules express those constraints under which an operation will perform correctly. The operation cannot go ahead unless these constraints are met. Examples of this kind of rule are:

```
Promote Staff employee to Manager
   ONLY IF this Employee is not a Manager.

Marry a Male and a Female
   ONLY IF this Female is not married
      and this Male is not married.
```

In contrast, *operation postcondition rules* guarantee the results. This kind of rule says that when an operation is executed, a certain state must result. Examples of this kind of rule are:

```
Promote Staff employee to Manager IS CORRECTLY COMPLETED
   ONLY IF this Employee is a Manager.

Marry a Male and a Female IS CORRECTLY COMPLETED
   ONLY IF this Female is married
   and this Male is married
   and this Female is married to this Male.
```

Structure Constraint Rules

Structure constraint rules specify policies or conditions about object types and their associations that should not be violated. A rule can constrain object structure in many ways.

> **TIP**
>
> Rules constrain object structure.

A rule can constrain the value of an attribute:

```
IT MUST ALWAYS HOLD THAT
   an Employee's salary cannot be greater than her manager's
   salary.
```

A rule can constrain the population of an object type:

```
IT MUST ALWAYS HOLD THAT
   the number of U.S. Supreme Court Justices must not be
   greater than 9.
```

A rule can constrain the cardinality of a relationship:

```
IT MUST ALWAYS HOLD THAT
   a Probationary Customer may place no more than 7 Orders.
```

Other examples of structure constraint rules are as follows:

```
IT MUST ALWAYS HOLD THAT
   the number of Employees
   (who are Managers and earning a Salary greater than 100,000)
   is less than or equal to 3.
```

```
IT MUST ALWAYS HOLD THAT
   for any given Life Insurance Policy
   the Policyholder is not the same as the Beneficiary.

IT MUST ALWAYS HOLD THAT
   every Person is a Male Person or a Female Person.

IT MUST ALWAYS HOLD THAT
   every Flight that is scheduled to depart from a City
   is not scheduled to arrive in this City.

IT MUST ALWAYS HOLD THAT
   The sum of salaries of employees working for a Department
   is less than 0.6 * budget of this Department.
```

Structure constraint rules omit references to operations, because they must hold under any operational circumstance. In other words, whenever an object's state is changed (whether this change is creation, termination, or modification), its structure constraint rules must hold. For instance, whenever an employee is added or an employee's age changes, the following rule is enforced:

```
IT MUST ALWAYS HOLD THAT
   an Employee's age cannot be greater than 75.
```

Inference Rules

Inference rules specify that if certain facts are true, a conclusion can be inferred. As such, they generally have an IF...THEN form. Such rules are generally associated with expert systems. Examples of inference rules are:

```
IF an object is an Employee
THEN that object is an Person.

IF a Polygon has a perimeter
THEN a Square has a perimeter.
```

Rules with inferences in both directions can also be specified in an IF AND ONLY IF form.

An inference rule can derive object subtypes:

```
A Person is an Employee IF AND ONLY IF
   this Person works for an Organization.

A Customer is a Bad Payer IF AND ONLY IF
   the number of Invoices
   (sent to this Customer and with a due date before today)
   is greater than 3.
```

An inference rule can derive object associations:

```
An Employee reports to a Manager IF AND ONLY IF
   this Employee works for Department
   that is headed by this Manager.
```

Computation Rules

Inference rules execute derivation merely by accessing available facts. In contrast, computation rules derive their results via processing algorithms. Computation rules can be thought of as inferences. The primary difference, however, is the manner of expressing the derivation. The inference rule is a rule conceived in an IF...THEN manner. The computation rule is a rule conceived as an equation. Some examples of computation rules are as follows:

A rule can specify value computation:

```
The net price of a Product IS COMPUTED AS FOLLOWS
   product price * (1 + tax percentage / 100).
```

A rule can specify the computation of object types:

```
The object type Woman IS COMPUTED AS FOLLOWS
   the intersection of all Female Humans and Adult Humans.
```

A rule can specify the computation of associations:

```
The parent association IS COMPUTED AS FOLLOWS
   the union of both the mother and father associations.
```

Computation rules can appear to be just another structure constraint rule, because both have an IT MUST ALWAYS HOLD quality. Structure constraints, however, are rules expressed in terms of conditional statements that must be true. Computation rules are expressed in terms of how something is derived from something else. For the OO programmer, both just become methods in a class. To a user, they describe different ways of thinking about and specifying business rules.

GLOBAL, LOCAL AND TEMPORAL APPLICATION OF RULES

The rules presented above may or may not be applied under all circumstances and at all times. For instance, the following rules would usually be in effect:

```
A Person is an Employee IF AND ONLY IF
   this Person works for an Organization.
```

```
Promote Staff employee to Manager IS CORRECTLY COMPLETED
    ONLY IF this Employee is a Manager.
```

However, some rules may have certain restrictions on the processing scope to which they apply.

```
(global unless otherwise overridden locally)
IT MUST ALWAYS HOLD THAT
    an Order must have 1 or more Line Items.

(during order acceptance)
IT MUST ALWAYS HOLD THAT
    an Order can have 0 or more Line Items.
```

Rule applicability may also depend on cultural and legal policies in force at various locations.

```
(In Omaha, Nebraska)
Marry a Male and a Female
    ONLY IF this Female is not married
        and this Male is not married.

(In Tibet)
Marry a Male and a Female
    ONLY IF this Male is not married.
```

Whether a rule is applicable may also depend upon the element of time.

```
(Before 1/1/92)
WHEN an Order is shipped and the Order is paid
THEN close Order.

(As of 1/1/92)
WHEN an Order is shipped and the Order is paid and 60 days
have elapsed
THEN close Order.
```

SUMMARY

Business policies and conditions can be expressed using several different techniques. Often such expressions can be graphical, though sometimes an explicit declarative statement is a better vehicle. Combining both techniques is also advantageous and will be presented in another article. This article has explored five categories of rules that can specify business policies and conditions using such statements. The categories presented here are just one way to think about rule taxonomy. Rules can be categorized in many other ways.

The important points are:

- Rules must express the business policies and conditions effectively.
- End users should be able to understand and express them.
- Rules need to be rigorous and formal so that they form a basis for code generation.
- Rules can be applied under all circumstances and at all times.

References and Suggested Reading

1. Object Management Group (OMG), OBJECT-ORIENTED ANALYSIS AND DESIGN, REFERENCE MODEL, Draft 7.0, unofficial position from OOA&D SIG, 1992.

2. P.M.D. Gray, K.G. Kulkarni, & N.W. Paton. OBJECT-ORIENTED DATABASES: A SEMANTIC DATA MODEL APPROACH, Prentice Hall, Englewood Cliffs, NJ, 1992.

3. B. Meyer. OBJECT-ORIENTED SOFTWARE CONSTRUCTION, Prentice Hall, Englewood Cliffs, NJ, 1988.

4. F. Van Assche. RULE-BASED IEM, James Martin and Co., internal paper, December 1991.

Systems of Interconnected Systems

Ivar Jacobson,
with Karin Palmkvist and Susanne Dyrhage

I N A PREVIOUS ARTICLE[1] WE PRESENTED AN APPROACH TO MODELING LARGE-scale systems. A recursive system construct was introduced to model a system consisting of other systems, which is a way to manage the size and complexity of a large system. This recursiveness of the system construct is here further elaborated and presented as a general construct, which we refer to as a system of interconnected systems. We will also discuss some of the many situations where this construct is useful.

Systems of Interconnected Systems

A system of interconnected systems is a set of communicating systems. There are several situations where this construct is useful, e.g., for a very large or complex system (S). Such a system is best implemented divided into several separate parts, each developed independently as a separate system. Thus, S is implemented by a set of interconnected systems, communicating with each other to fulfill the duties of S. The system S is then *super-ordinate* to the interconnected systems, and each of these is *subordinate* to S. This way, we get a separation of the superordinate system from its implementing subordinate systems, but with the relation between the different systems clear: Each subordinate system implements one subsystem of the superordinate system (see Figure 1).

> **TIP**
>
> A system of inter-connected systems is a set of communicating systems.

Separating the superordinate system from its subordinate systems has several advantages:

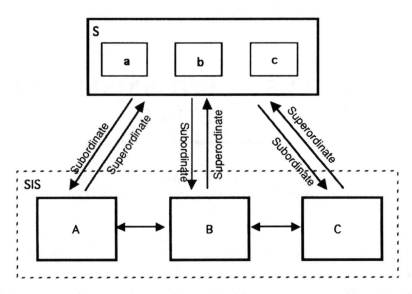

FIGURE 1. *The specification of a system S is implemented by a system of interconnected systems (SIS), where the systems A, B, and C are implementations of S's subsystems a, b, and c, respectively.*

- The subordinate systems can be managed separately during all lifecycle activities, including sales and delivery.
- It makes it easy to use a subordinate system for implementation of other superordinate systems by plugging it into other systems of interconnected systems.
- It means you can wait until late in the superordinate modeling process to decide if you need to develop entirely separate subordinate systems or if you can elaborate on the use-case and object models to implement the subsystems directly.
- It allows you to make internal changes to the subordinate systems without developing a new version of the superordinate system. New versions of superordinate systems are required only due to major functional changes.

Each subordinate system is associated with its own set of models, with strong traceability between these models and the corresponding models of the superordinate system. Thus, compared to the traditional recursion (system–subsystem–subsystem...) in most object modeling techniques today, recursion is enhanced by allowing recursion within more than one model.

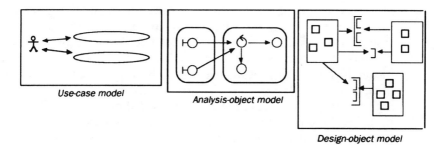

FIGURE 2. *Three models of a system, each describing the system from a specific point of view, capturing specific characteristics of the system.*

By doing so, each subordinate system can be managed as a separate system through all lifecycle activities: requirements specification, analysis, design, implementation, and testing. Naturally, the recursion may be extended to include more than one system division, even if this is seldom necessary in practice.

> **TIP**
>
> Each subordinate system is associated with its own set of models.

ACTIVITIES AND MODELS FOR SYSTEM DEVELOPMENT

A natural assumption is that the superordinate system, as well as the subordinate systems, can be modeled with the same set of models and developed by performing the same activities as for usual, noncomposite systems. Before we show how this can be done, these models and activities have to be introduced. The development activities form five different activities that are performed to get the final result, the implemented system (see Jacobson et al.[2]). These are:

- Requirements analysis, with the purpose of capturing and evaluating the requirements, placing usability in focus. This results in a use-case model, with actors representing external units communicating with the system, and use cases representing sequences of transactions, yielding measurable results of value to the actors (see Figure 2).

- Robustness analysis, with the purpose of achieving a robust system structure, in the sense that it easily accepts modification and extension. This results in a model of objects grouped into subsystems of functionally related objects. The objects are of three different kinds to achieve a robust structure: interface objects that handle all communication with the actors, control objects performing the use case–specific tasks, and entity objects corresponding to persistent objects (see Figure 2).

- Design, with the purpose of investigating the intended implementation environment and the effect it will have on the construction of the system. This results in an object model, like the previous model, but this model is extended with specifications of how the objects communicate during the flow of the use cases. This might include definitions of contracts (see Jacobson et al.[3]) for objects and subsystems, specifying their responsibilities in terms of provided operations. This object model is also adapted to the implementation environment in terms of implementation language, distribution, and so on (see Figure 2).

- Implementation, with the purpose of implementing the system in the prescribed implementation environment. This results in source code.

- Testing, with the purpose of ensuring that the system is the one intended and that there are no errors in the implementation. This results in a certified system that is ready for delivery.

There is a natural order for these activities, although they are not performed one after another but rather in cooperation with each other.

DEVELOPMENT OF A SYSTEM OF INTERCONNECTED SYSTEMS

In the previous article[1] it was shown how a use case model can be used to model the responsibilities of the superordinate system. We will extend this to show how all the models above are used and interpreted for the superordinate system. Therefore each activity will be discussed in more detail with the focus set on a system of interconnected systems. We will also discuss the relationship between the superordinate system and the interconnected systems realizing it.

> **TIP**
>
> The main goal is to define the interfaces among these subordinate systems.

What we really have to do is define how the responsibilities of a system can be distributed over several systems, each one taking care of a well-defined subset of these responsibilities. This means that the main goal is to define the interfaces among these subordinate systems. When we have accomplished this, the rest of the work is performed separately for each subordinate system, according to the "divide and conquer" principle. Therefore, this is all we have to do for the system as a whole, apart from testing it once implementation is done.

The first activity is requirements analysis. We have the same need for requirements modeling for a system of interconnected systems as for any other system. A use-case model is a very natural way to express the results.[1]

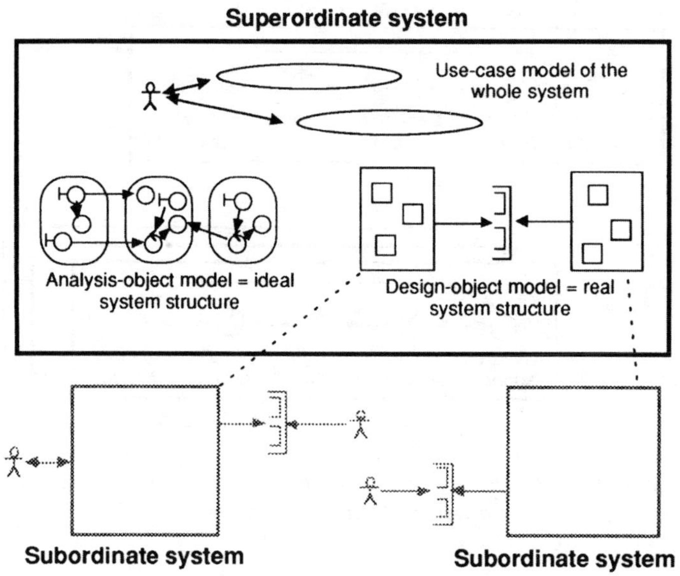

FIGURE 3. *The superordinate system is described by a set of models, where the subsystems defined in the design-object model will be implemented by subordinate systems.*

The most straightforward way to look at this superordinate use-case model is to assume that it completely captures the behavioral requirements of the system. However, this is probably seldom the case. Since we need to implement the system with other systems, the system as a whole is probably quite complex. Therefore it is not a good idea to try to be exhaustive at this level. Thus, a superordinate use-case model usually gives a complete but simplified picture of the functional requirements of the system. There is actually no need to be too detailed at this level because the detailed modeling will be performed within each of the implementing subordinate systems.

The purpose of robustness analysis is to achieve a robust structure of the system, which is of course of vital importance to a system of interconnected systems. The developers of the superordinate system must achieve a robust structure of subordinate systems, while they need not at all bother about the inner structures of these systems. We will therefore model a division of the system into smaller parts using subsystems. To get the right set of subsystems, and to get a first idea of how to distribute the responsibilities of the superordinate system over these subsystems, we develop an analysis-object

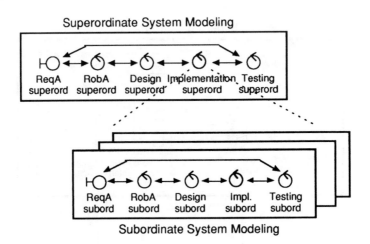

Superordinate System Modeling

ReqA
superord

RobA
superord

Design
superord

Implementation
superord

Testing
superord

ReqA
subord

RobA
subord

Design
subord

Impl.
subord

Testing
subord

Subordinate System Modeling

FIGURE 4. *A simplified picture of the activities performed to develop a system of interconnected systems.*

model. The analysis objects should represent roles played by things in the system when the use cases are performed. Therefore the analysis-object model gives a simplified picture of the complete object structure, in analogy with the use-case model.

Functionally related analysis objects are grouped together into subsystems. Thus we get a subsystem structure that is ideal in the sense that it is based upon only functional criteria, e.g., we have not taken into account any distribution requirements.

Requirements regarding how the system should be divided into several separate systems are taken into consideration when we design the superordinate system. The result of the design process may be a subsystem structure that is very different from the one we defined based upon functional criteria during robustness analysis. Thus we end up with a structure of real subsystems, which will each be implemented by a subordinate system (see Figure 3). To be able to continue the development work for each such system separately, their interfaces are defined in terms of contracts for the subsystems. In fact, the definition of contracts is the most important activity performed at the superordinate level, since contracts provide rules for development of the subordinate systems.

The next activity is implementation. As already mentioned, implementation of this kind of system is done by interconnecting other, subordinate

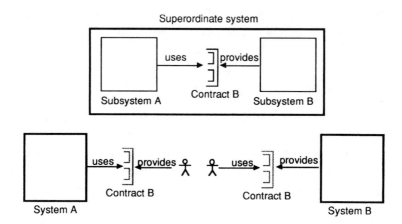

FIGURE 5. *The subsystems of the superordinate system depend on each other only through their contracts. The implementing subordinate systems therefore get the same kind of independence.*

systems that together perform all the use cases defined for the superordinate system. Each subsystem in the design-object model of the superordinate system is implemented by a system of its own (see Figure 3). In some cases there may already exist systems that can be used for this purpose, but in most cases we have to develop them. All models defined for the superordinate system serve as input to the subordinate systems development, and for each subordinate system the exact requirements are found by extracting all information that is tied to the corresponding subsystem in the superordinate system. The main requirement on a subordinate system is, naturally, that it conforms to the contracts of its subsystem.

Each subordinate system is developed in the usual way, as a black box considering other systems with which it communicates as actors (see Figure 3). We perform the usual set of activities and develop the usual set of models, as described above, for each such system. If the models at the superordinate level are exhaustive, we get complete recursiveness between the models at different levels, but as mentioned above, this is in practice seldom the case.

The final activity is testing, which in this case means integration testing when the different subordinate systems are assembled, and also testing that every superordinate use case is performed according to its specification by the interconnected systems in cooperation. Figure 4 shows the activities performed for development of the superordinate system and its subordinate systems. It is shown in terms of interacting business objects, cooperating in the development of a system of interconnected systems. This is a simplified picture, which in reality would need several business objects. The notation used is the one described in Jabobson et al.[4]

RELATIONS BETWEEN SYSTEMS

Now we have seen that the usual system development activities also can be applied to systems implemented by systems of interconnected systems. This is advantageous because it means that one does not need to handle such systems in a way different from that used with other systems. We also get a nice separation of the superordinate system from its implementation in the form of other systems.

A final note on the independence between systems involved in a system of interconnected systems:

First we take a look at the subordinate systems. Each such system implements one subsystem in the superordinate system's design-object model. The subsystems depend on each others' contracts and not explicitly on each other (see Figure 5). Thus we may exchange one subsystem for another without affecting other subsystems, as long as the new subsystem conforms to the same contract. We get exactly the same relation between the corresponding systems. Each subordinate system views its surroundings as a set of actors. This means that we can exchange a system with another, as long as the new system plays the same roles towards other systems, i.e., as long as it can be modeled with the same set of actors. Systems refer to each other's contracts as specified by the corresponding relations between subsystems and contracts in the superordinate model. A subordinate system looks upon the contracts of another system as offered by the corresponding actors, and therefore never has to refer directly to the other system (see Figure 5). Note that Contract B occurs in several places in Figure 5, indicating that it is really the same contract referred to by subsystems in the superordinate system and by the corresponding subordinate systems.

> **TIP**
>
> Each subordinate system views its surroundings as a set of actors.

How about the superordinate system, what is its relation to its subordinate systems? It is independent of its implementing systems in the following sense: Each such system is only an *implementation* of what we have specified in the models of the superordinate system, it is not *part of* this specification. For practical reasons you have to define traceability links between systems at different levels, in order to trace requirements, but the most "tidy" way to do this is to define such links only between contracts (see Figure 5). In fact, one may even say that the subordinate systems are nothing more than implementations providing the contracts defined in the superordinate models.

We can conclude that each system involved when a system is implemented by a system of interconnected systems is independent of the other *systems*, but they depend strongly upon each other's *contracts*. Thus we have a very good platform for separate development of the systems!

Application Areas

The architecture and modeling techniques for systems of interconnected systems can be used for different types of systems, such as:

- distributed systems
- very large or complex systems
- systems combining several business areas
- systems reusing other systems
- distributed development of a system

The situation may also be the opposite: From a set of already existing systems, we define a system of interconnected systems by assembling the systems.

In fact, for any system where it is possible to view different parts of the system as systems of their own, it is advisable to implement them as a system of interconnected systems. Even if it is a single system today, one may later have to split the system into several separate products, due to distributed development, reuse reasons, or customers' buying only parts of it, to mention some examples.

As a conclusion we will take a closer look at a couple of cases where the architecture for systems of interconnected systems can be used. For each of the examples we will show that the system in question has to be considered *both* as a single system *and* as a set of separate systems, indicating that it should be treated as a superordinate system implemented by a system of interconnected systems.

Large-Scale Systems

The telephone network is probably the world's largest system of interconnected systems. This is an excellent example where more than two system levels are needed to manage complexity. It is also an example of a case where the top-level superordinate system is owned by a standardization body, and different competing companies develop one or several subordinate systems that must conform to this standard. Here we will discuss the mobile telephone network GSM to show the advantages from implementing a large-scale system as a system of interconnected systems.

The functionality of a very large system usually combines several business areas. For example, the GSM standard covers the entire system, from the calling subscriber to the called subscriber. In other words, it includes both the behavior of the mobile telephones and the network nodes. Because different parts of the system are products of their own that are bought separately, even by different kinds of customers, they should be treated as systems of their own. For example, a company that develops complete GSM systems will sell the mobile telephones to subscribers and network nodes to telephone operators. This is one reason for treating different parts of a GSM system as different subordinate systems. Another reason is that it would take too long to develop such a large and complex system as GSM as one single system; the different parts must be developed in parallel by several development teams.

On the other hand, because the GSM standard covers the entire system, there is reason to also consider the system as a whole, i.e., the superordinate system. This will help developers understand the problem domain and how different parts are related to each other.

Distributed Systems

> **TIP**
>
> By definition, a distributed system always consists of at least two parts.

For systems distributed over several computer systems, the architecture for systems of interconnected systems is very suitable. By definition, a distributed system always consists of at least two parts. Because well-defined interfaces are necessary in distributed systems, these systems are very well suited also to be *developed* in a distributed fashion, i.e., by several autonomous development teams working in parallel. The subordinate systems of a distributed system can even be sold as products of their own. Thus, it is natural to regard a distributed system as a set of separate systems.

The requirements for a distributed system usually cover the functionality of the entire system, and sometimes the interfaces between the different parts are not predefined. Moreover, if the problem domain is new for the developers, they first have to consider the functionality of the entire system, regardless of how it will be distributed. These are two very important reasons to view it as a single system.

CONCLUSION

This article introduces an architecture for systems of interconnected systems. This construct allows recursion not only within one model, but also between different models. The introduced architecture is used for systems that are implemented by several communicating systems. All involved systems are described by their own models, separated from other systems' models.

The examples given illustrate that the architecture for modeling systems of interconnected systems is useful in many different application areas. In fact, you may use the suggested architecture for any system where it is possible to view the different parts as systems of their own.

References

1. Jacobson, I. Use cases in large-scale systems, ROAD 1(6):9–12, 1995.
2. Jacobson, I., M. Christersson, P. Jonsson, and G. Overgaard. OBJECT-ORIENTED SOFTWARE ENGINEERING—A USE CASE DRIVEN APPROACH, Addison-Wesley, Reading, MA, 1992.
3. Jacobson, I., S. Bylund, and P. Jonsson. Using contracts and use cases to build plugable architectures, JOURNAL OF OBJECT-ORIENTED PROGRAMMING 8(2), 1995.
4. Jacobson, I., M. Ericsson, and A. Jacobson. THE OBJECT ADVANTAGE—BUSINESS PROCESS REENGINEERING WITH OBJECT TECHNOLOGY, Addison-Wesley, Reading, MA, 1994.

PART II

DEVELOPMENT METHODOLOGIES

Object-oriented methodologies continually evolve to adapt to the ever-changing development landscape. This section presents a number of important works that have contributed to that change.

Object-Oriented Requirements Analysis, Part 1: Finding Abstractions and Their Relationships

Daniel J. Duffy

T HIS ARTICLE DESCRIBES A SIMPLE AND PRACTICAL TECHNIQUE FOR FINDING THE abstractions and domain objects from requirements documents. Furthermore, the long-term structural relationships between these abstractions are discovered and categorized. This process is called concept mapping, and its products can be used directly in well-known object-oriented methodologies, such as OMT, Ptech, and Shlaer-Mellor.

I concentrate on the static properties in this article; discussion on finding the behavior will appear elsewhere.[1]

An Introduction to Requirements Analysis

Requirements analysis is defined as the process of establishing a candidate's needs when developing a system.[2] This phase is one of the most difficult in the entire software development process and, regrettably, is one of the most neglected by the authors of the most popular object-oriented development methodologies. Most take the naive approach of mapping nouns to classes and verbs to operations on classes. Furthermore, the processes presented here demand proactive involvement between users and designers and they have deliverables that are close to the way the users view the problem.

What are Concept Maps?

A concept is defined as a regularity in objects or events designated by some label.[3] Each concept corresponds to a particular idea or understanding that we have of the world. If we possess a concept, we are then in a position to apply it to things around us. The relevance of concepts for object-oriented

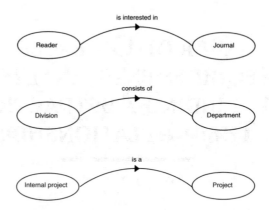

FIGURE 1. *Some simple concepts and links.*

development in general is that object-oriented analysis is a way of modeling the way people understand and process reality through the concepts that they acquire. Thus, without concepts, it is difficult to think about a given problem domain. Examples of concepts are car, wind, customer, musical instrument, and purchase.

Concepts and language are primarily tools of cognition and not of communication. Cognition precedes communication because the necessary precondition of communication is that we have something to communicate.[4] It is possible to create meaningful relationships between concepts by connecting them, thus forming propositions. A proposition consists of two or more concepts that are linked together by verbs or verb phrases to form a semantic unit. Examples of propositions are:

- A reader is interested in a journal.
- An internal project is a project.
- A division consists of departments.
- The Poisson distribution is a discrete statistical distribution.

The "glue" that connects concepts is usually verbs or verb phrases, as can be seen from the above examples. The language elements are called links. To make propositions more explicit and easier to understand than just pure text, we choose to represent propositions graphically with concepts being repre-

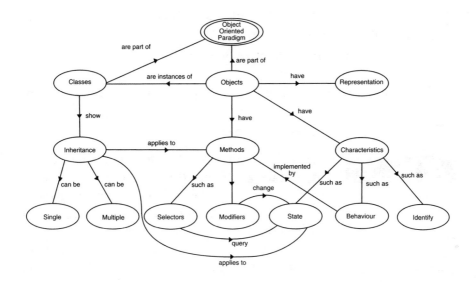

FIGURE 2. *A concept map for topics from Classes and Objects.*

sented as ellipses and links by arrows from one of the two concepts to the other one. Some examples are given in Figure 1.

Note that all propositions in this figure are called binary propositions, since they relate only two concepts with one link. It is possible to have propositions that relate three concepts (ternary propositions), four concepts (quaternary propositions), and a general number of concepts (n-ary propositions), but we try to avoid such cases as they are, first, difficult to comprehend, and second, they can be decomposed into a number of simpler binary propositions.

A concept map consists of a number of concepts and links connecting these concepts. It is a network in which the nodes are represented by concepts and the edges by links. We can form concept maps from text to see if we have understood all the concepts and relationships occurring in the text. A concept map can be seen as a window to the way someone applies his cognitive processes to knowledge acquisition. An example is given in Figure 2, which depicts a simple concept map that a novice object-oriented developer made after reading a chapter on this technology.

A more experienced OO aficionado may have some comments on this map, especially regarding its completeness or lack thereof. Typical deficiencies in concept maps are:

- They are missing some important concepts.
- Not all links have been discovered.
- Certain concepts and links are invalid or ambiguously formulated.

We shall show how to avoid and correct these problems in the next section.

THE CONCEPT MAPPING PROCESS

> **TIP**
>
> Capturing dynamic behavior belongs to a separate part of requirements analysis.

The main reason for creating concept maps is to capture parts of the requirements from a document, interviews with users or from other sources. Concept maps capture only static properties of a system, such as the main abstractions in problems and their long-term structural relationships. Capturing dynamic behavior belongs to a separate part of requirements analysis.[1] The advantages of concentrating on static properties is that it allows us to concentrate on one aspect of the system.

We note that concept maps can be used both to map requirements into their object-oriented equivalents and to determine the correct requirements by discussing them with users and domain experts.

The process consists of two stages, namely:

- Concept map preparation
- Concept map activities

We assume in this article that a requirements document in text form is available and that this is used as initial input for all discussions. The preparation stage consists in listing the nouns that appear in the requirements document. Nouns are candidates for concepts, although some of them will not attain this status. We start with an elimination process, and we should concentrate on the following:

- Attributes (properties of concepts)
- Concepts which are outside the scope of the problem
- Ambiguous and superfluous concepts

There are other ways to filter out irrelevant information.[1] Once we have completed filtering, we need to create a list of verbs and verb phrases from the requirements document that will become the linking words between the newly found concepts. These verbs and verb phrases will thus be used with concepts to form sentences.

The products of the preparation stage is a list of relevant concepts and the links between them. To summarize, the steps in this stage are:

1. Make a list of words and concepts appearing in the current problem domain.
2. Apply the filtering process already discussed.
3. Find the linking words.
4. Construct sentences using words from steps 2 and 3.

The next stage in the process is to order the concepts in some way. Some concepts are more important than others and this must be mirrored in the corresponding concept map which is to be generated. Determining that one concept is more important than another one in a particular context is highly personal and no two people will ever produce exactly the same results. Thus, there are no rules for this stage in the process except your intuition and gut feeling. Good concept maps tend to be well-structured and easily understood. Each concept map has as root an all-inclusive concept (called the key or main concept) and is placed at level 0 in the hierarchy. Links should connect the key concept with its so-called supporting concepts at level 1. A supporting concept in this context is one that is less general than its key concept at that level of abstraction. For example, the concept *classes* in the previous figure is a supporting concept for *object-oriented paradigm*. A *cross-link* is a special kind of link connecting concepts from different subtrees of the concept map hierarchy. For example, the *link affect* between a concept's *methods* and *state* is a cross-link.

The steps in constructing a concept map are:

1. List the key concept.
2. List the supporting concepts at lower levels of abstraction.
3. Create the links between the main concept and its supporting concepts.
4. Create cross-links between supporting concepts.
5. Iterate the steps in 1–4 by applying them in turn to each supporting concept.

It is important to remember that the above process is an iterative one and that it may take a number of attempts (six or seven is not unusual) before the concept map is correct. Furthermore, concept-mapping techniques lend

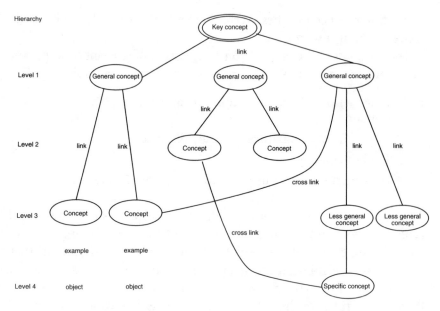

FIGURE 3. *Structuring concept maps (after [Ref. 3]).*

> **TIP**
>
> Note that this process is iterative.

themselves to either top-down or bottom-up development. Thus, you are free to choose the strategy that is most suited to you. Finally, concept maps force you to work in an object-oriented fashion, since concepts correspond to classes and links correspond to relationships between those classes.

The recommended way of producing concept maps is shown in Figure 3.

USING CONCEPT MAPS AS A FRONT-END TO OOA

The deliverables from the concept mapping phase are concepts and links. Concepts are embryonic classes, while links describe the types of relationships between concepts. There are three types of links possible: projection links, abstraction links, and partitioning links.

Projection links describe interactions between concepts and they tend to be action-based. Examples are *get, display,* and *move.* Abstraction links are related to class hierarchies, and they tend to have instances such as *is a, can be,* and *such as.* Partitioning links describe a concept in terms of its constituent parts. Examples are *consists of, has,* and is *part of.*

Discovering concepts and links give us some insight into how they are to be implemented in the analysis phase. The rules are:

- Concepts suggest objects and events.
- Projection links suggest object operations.
- Abstraction links suggest inheritance relationships.
- Partitioning links suggest aggregation relationships.

It is important to remember that a concept map is only as good as the effort that is put into making it. Choosing good names for links and concepts should be chosen as carefully as possible so that they do not mislead or convey the wrong meaning.

TEST CASE: JOURNAL REGISTRATION PROBLEM

The personnel department of a large research institute is responsible for the purchase and dissemination of journals to readers in other departments in the organization. Readers may be interested in certain specific topics relating to their research interests; it is also possible to be placed on a circulation list. Usually, readers get access to an issue of a journal for a fixed period, typically two weeks. It is possible to have access to an issue for a longer period, but permission must be granted from the personnel department.

Journals appear on a regular basis, and each journal contains information on the publisher, language, and frequency of publication.

The system should keep readers informed of the topics that are of interest to them which appear in the different journals. Furthermore, it should be possible for readers to *find* articles that deal with topics that they are interested in.

The nouns appearing in the requirements document are:

• Personnel department	• Circulation list	• Author
• Company	• Article	• Publisher
• Journal	• Keyword	• Frequency
• Reader	• Topic	• Language
• Department	• Title	

Not all nouns will be valid concepts. In particular, we need to filter entities that are attributes. These are:

- keyword
- frequency
- title
- author
- publisher
- language

Sources of noise are eliminated because they are not part of the problem. They are:

- personnel department
- department
- circulation list (this is a derivative concept)

We eliminate the concept *circulation list* because it is a derivative concept: its existence depends on Reader, Journal, and Issue.

Having carried out the filtering process, we are left with a list of candidate concepts:

- Journal
- Issue
- Reader
- Topic
- Article

The relationships between the above concepts are:

- An issue is an appearance of a journal.
- A reader is interested in a journal.
- A reader is interested in a topic.
- An issue contains articles.
- A topic may be found in an article.

TIP
Developing a concept map is an iterative process.

The next step is to arrange the different concepts in such a way that the resulting concept map is easy to understand and well structured. You will find that this is the most difficult part of the concept-mapping process, and you should discuss your results with others so that they can give their views on your work. In most cases, a concept map will undergo a number of revisions; don't be disappointed if seven or eight iterations are needed before a decent map is arrived at! It is all part of the process of understanding the essence of a given problem.

The concept map for JRP is shown in Figure 4. This is a straightforward solution. We note that the concept Circulation List does not appear in the

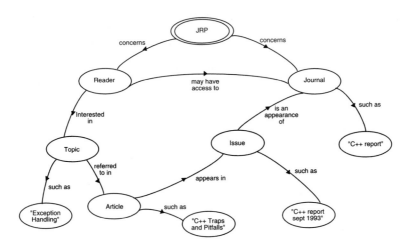

FIGURE 4. *Concept map for JRP problem.*

map. This is because we have not approached the problem from a use-case perspective. Furthermore, there is no provision for informing readers on information that is of interest to them. The two most important use cases are:

- creating circulation lists
- creating attention lists

The modified concept map for JRP is shown in Figure 5. This map implements user requirements as a central feature. Each supporting concept can then be separately analyzed, allowing us to separate the problem into different areas of concern. Furthermore, new user requirements (such as setting up special interest groups) may be implemented by creating supporting concepts at the correct level of abstraction. It might even be possible to reuse some of the concepts that have been developed in other concept maps.

THE ADVANTAGES OF USING CONCEPT MAPPING TECHNIQUES

Concept maps look easy—but try making one from a piece of text! You will be surprised how challenging it is to make one: You will be forced to think hard about the problem. It is not unusual that the first attempt is a disaster, and it can take up to six or seven iterations before you begin to get it right. The biggest advantage, however, is that the user is involved in the creation

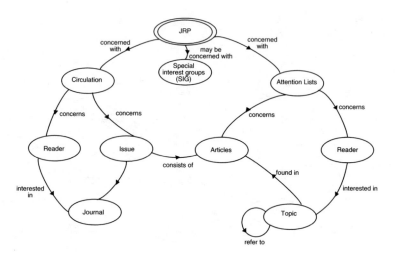

FIGURE 5. *Use-case driven concept map for JRP.*

and modification of concept maps together with the designer of the system. Finally, they can be mapped directly into OMT object diagrams.[5]

We have already said that concept maps can be approached either in a top-down or bottom-up manner. This facilitates the merging of concept maps. Concept maps are scalable if we view a given problem as a set of weakly coupled use cases.[1]

CONCEPT MAPS AND OBJECT MODELING TECHNIQUE (OMT)

Once a concept map has been created, it is not too difficult to map it into an object diagram. In fact, an object diagram is a concept map with the following extra information:

- The attributes of classes are added.
- The multiplicity of associations are registered.
- Inheritance and aggregation structures are recognized.

We have already described how the products from the concept mapping phase are mapped into object-oriented constructions. In particular, OMT object diagrams can easily be constructed. The resulting diagram is shown in Figure 6, which can be seen as an elaboration of the concept map for the registration of journals.

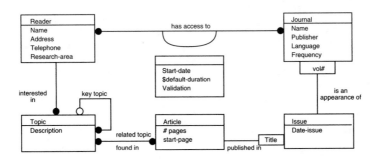

FIGURE 6. *Object diagram for JRP.*

CONCLUSION

I have given an overview of a technique that helps in determining requirements during system development. I have been employing the technique for a number of years, together with the OMT method, to help software developers with object-oriented technology. My main interest is in OMT, but concept maps can be effectively used as front-end to other well-known methodologies such at Ptech (object-relationship diagrams), Shlaer-Mellor (information structure diagrams), Objectory (domain object models), and Fusion (object model).

References

1. Duffy, D. FROM CHAOS TO CLASSES—SOFTWARE DEVELOPMENT IN C++, McGraw-Hill. New York (forthcoming in early 1995).

2. Umphress, D. and S. March. Object-oriented requirements determination, in JOURNAL OF OBJECT-ORIENTED PROGRAMMING, FOCUS ON ANALYSIS AND DESIGN, 1991.

3. Novak, J. and D. Gowin. LEARNING HOW TO LEARN, Cambridge University Press, Cambridge, England, 1984.

4. Rand, A. INTRODUCTION TO OBJECTIVIST EPISTEMOLOGY, Meridian Group, New York, 1979.

5. Rumbaugh, J., M. Blaha, W. Premerlani, F. Eddy, W. Lorensen. OBJECT-ORIENTED MODELING AND DESIGN, Prentice Hall, Englewood Cliffs, NJ, 1991.

6. Meyer, B. OBJECT-ORIENTED SOFTWARE CONSTRUCTION, Prentice Hall, Englewood Cliffs, NJ, 1988.

Object-Oriented Requirements Analysis, Part 2: Dynamic Modeling

Daniel J. Duffy

I N A PREVIOUS ARTICLE I DISCUSSED HOW A NUMBER OF TECHNIQUES THAT HAVE their roots in education and cognitive psychology can be applied to the construction of object diagrams in the object modeling technique (OMT). In particular, we used concept maps[1] to find the essential abstractions in a given problem domain and the corresponding links between these concepts. Concepts will eventually be mapped to object classes, while the links are mapped to associations, aggregation, and inheritance relationships. Concept maps have the property (as object diagrams have!) of not showing how objects are created or how objects interact with each other via message passing. This is not an objective at this stage, but we nonetheless need some tools to allow us to find the interactions between the objects and the external world. This article proposes a solution to the problem. Our objective is to find object operations that result from interactions between client and server objects in a given system. The problem is twofold: First, we have to find the events in a system, and second, we need to determine which objects receive these events. As we shall see, an event usually corresponds to an object operation, while the receiver of that event will "own" that operation. One might think that once all operations resulting from events have been discovered there are no more operations to be found, but that would be wrong, since new operations are discovered from the process (or functional) modeling phase.[2] I do not discuss this problem here. In this article I propose a simple and workable sequence of steps that, when followed, will allow us to fulfill the conditions of the following definition of what object-oriented programming is:

> Object-oriented programming is a method of implementation in which programs are organized as cooperative collections of objects, each of which represents an instance of some class, and whose classes are all members of a hierarchy of classes united via inheritance relationships.[3]

Our interest in this definition stems from the fact that objects communicate by sending messages to each other. In particular, we see a given object-oriented (OO) system as one in which messages are "relayed" from one object to another via a client/server metaphor. The "sender" of an event is called the client, while the "receiver" of the event is the called the server. In nearly all cases both senders and receivers will be objects from the concept mapping phase (or the object modeling phase in OMT). An object will be a receiver for some events and sender for other events. Another issue that has to be tackled with event-driven systems is the problem of control. By control, I mean that aspect of a system describing the sequence of operations that occurs as a response to an external stimulus.[4]

This article is "driven" by the desire to create a suitable front end to the dynamic modeling phase of OMT. In particular, the steps taken here can be executed by both the user/domain expert and the designer of the system. No knowledge of state transition diagrams is needed, and it is thus possible to create a simple prototype of a system, especially when combined with concept maps. I shall discuss how the products from this exercise can be used to produce a simple prototype in C++.

EVENTS, RESPONSES, AND CONSTRAINTS

Events describes external stimuli. In the petrol pump delivery problem (discussed later), the following external stimuli are identified:

- The attendant enables the petrol pump.
- The customer removes the gun from the holster.
- The customer replaces the gun in the holster.
- The metering device sends a pulse to the pump display.

A response describes the reaction to an event. For example, when the attendant enables the pump the following responses occur:

- start pump motor
- free clutch

Constraints describe nonfunctional characteristics of the event-response pair. Constraints describe the following:

- the maximum or minimum amount of time between an event and its response
- the range of values an entity can take on
- the probability of the occurrence of a response to an event
- the rate of occurrence of events

The main purpose of the event-response list is to enumerate as fully as possible the expectations of the user when interacting with the system. A given event-response list should only describe those events and responses which are visible to the user. It is possible to verify each event or response by observing the system. Not all event-response lists have constraints. An event may cause multiple responses, and multiple events may have to occur before a response can take place. Event-response lists are useful for verification and validation. Verification is a formal activity and it lets us define completeness aspects of the system, e.g., by formally stating in the requirements document that all output variables have been defined or that all events have been included. Verification is concerned with the question "Are we doing it right?" Validation is concerned with the question "Are we building the right system?" Validation is aimed at establishing the system's operational correctness, safety, and completeness. It is an informal process, addressed through human judgement.[5] Some rules concerning event-response lists[6]:

TIP
The event-response list enumerates the expectations of the user.

- Event-response lists are general; they do not refer to any particular scenario or use of the system.
- Event-response lists should describe visible or verifiable events and responses.
- Constraints on event-response lists should be real, validated items.
- Event-response lists should be tailored to the audience. Different types of users are interested in particular views of the system.

BENCHMARK EXAMPLE: THE PETROL PUMP STATION

To make things clearer we take a problem discussed in a number of books and articles.[7,8] We restrict attention to a subset of the problem concerned with the temporal behavior in the system. A fuller object-oriented analysis is given in Duffy.[2]

Requirements document for the petrol pump delivery problem: A computer-based system needs to be created to control the dispensing of petrol, to handle customer payment, and to monitor tank levels. Customers may use the self-service pumps, which must first be enabled by the attendant. When the pump is enabled its pump motor is started (if not already on) and the pump clutch is freed. When the trigger in the pump is depressed, a microswitch is closed, the clutch is engaged, and the petrol is pumped. When the trigger is released the clutch is freed. The gun of the pump is kept in a holster, and this holster contains a microswitch preventing petrol from being pumped until the gun is taken out. If the gun is replaced in the holster the delivery is assumed to be complete and the pump is disabled. Further depressions of the trigger have no effect as far as petrol dispensing is concerned. The delivery is considered to be finished at this stage. After a short standby period the pump motor is turned off unless the pump is reenabled. A metering device in the petrol line sends a pulse to the pump system for each 0.01 liter of petrol dispensed. Displays on the pump show the amount of petrol dispensed and the cost. Petrol is pumped up to a maximum of the required quantity in the latter case. Transactions concerning delivery are stored until the customer pays. A customer may request a receipt and will get a token for every five money units spent. Some customers leave without paying, and the attendant must annotate the transaction with suitable information, e.g., the registration number of the car. Transactions are archived at the end of each day and they may be used for ad hoc queries on sales. At present, two grades of petrol are dispensed from five pumps in the forecourt of the petrol station. Any pump may take its supply from one of two tanks, where a given tank contains a given grade of petrol. The petrol level in a tank must not drop below 4% of the tank's total capacity. If such a situation should ensue, the pump being serviced by the tank cannot be enabled to pump petrol. If a customer is pumping petrol when a tank reaches its critical level the delivery will be completed, after which the pump will be disabled, ensuring that it cannot be enabled to dispense petrol.

We show how the simple event-response techniques can be used to find object operations for this problem and that we can attain the same results as in Coleman[7] without having to resort to complicated object interaction diagrams (which would probably scare off a domain expert or future user of the system). To this end, we concentrate on the "subsystem" responsible for the actual dispensing of petrol.

With the requirements document we can create a preliminary list of events, responses, and constraints in the system:

```
E1: Enable pump              // Enables dispensing of petrol
R11: Start motor
R12: Free clutch
R13: Clear display readings
C11: Pump not already enabled
C12: Pump is not out of service

E2: Remove gun from holster   // Enables gun to pump petrol
R21: Release holster switch
R22: Enable gun

E3: Depress trigger in gun  //Start actual delivery of
petrol
R31: Close microswitch in trigger
R32: Engage clutch
C31: Pump enabled
C32: Gun enabled

E4: Release trigger in gun     // Stop delivery of petrol
R41: Free clutch
R42: Open microswitch in trigger
C31: Pump enabled
C32: Gun enabled

E5: Replace gun in holster     //No more petrol can be
dispensed
R51: Disable pump
R52: Depress holster switch
R53: Create a delivery object
R54: Send start message to timer object
C51: Pump must be enabled

E6: Disable pump               // Pump not in use
R61: Shut down pump motor
```

Once all the event-response lists have been found we can start mapping these to concepts that are used in OMT.

MOVING FROM REQUIREMENTS DELIVERABLES TO OMT

OMT uses Harel charts[4,9–11] to represent states and state transitions during the dynamic modeling phase. Object states are of particular interest. An event ensures that an object makes a transition from one state to another state. The general rules for migrating from event-response lists are:

- Events map to operations on some object.
- Responses map to events on objects, activities, or to high-level processes in the process model.[2]
- Constraints map to object states or to guard conditions in OMT.

It is important to take into account that objects send or receive events. Once we know which object receives an event we are in a position to determine the corresponding object operations. For example, the events E1 through E6 all correspond to operations on the pump object itself. These are now written in pseudo-C++:

```
enable();
disable();
remove_gun();
depress_trigger();
release_trigger();
replace_gun();
```

We still have to determine the complete signature of these operations, but this is now a minor detail. The responses in this problem all correspond to operations on the components in the pump aggregation. For example, responses R12 and R32 (for which the clutch component is the receiver) lead to the following clutch operations:

```
free();
engage();
```

Constraints map to object states. In this way we have a way of discovering states from the corresponding constraints. Some examples from the above list are:

- C11 maps to "Pump enabled state."
- C12 maps to "Pump out of service state."
- C32 maps to "Gun enabled state."

Finally, each event (and in particular each response) has a corresponding "postcondition" that corresponds to the state of the receiver once the response (which is an action in OMT) has been executed. Examples are:

- Response R12 corresponds to postcondition "Clutch in free state."
- Response R32 corresponds to "Clutch in engaged state."

We generalize this discussion to include guidelines for general OO system development:

- Draw up a list of all event-response lists (including constraints).
- Find the sender and receiver of each event.
- Determine the full signature of each event.[4]
- Map events to object operations.
- Map responses to object operations or high-level processes.
- Map constraints to object states.
- Find the postconditions corresponding to each event and response.

The product from this sequence of steps is a list of object states (object attributes), object operations, and control information. This control information can be implemented as pseudocode or even real C++ in a prototype.

SCALABILITY ISSUES

For larger problems it may not be feasible to start with a list of all events in a system. Large systems should be partitioned according to the domain approach of Shlaer-Mellor,[2,12] which I think is a practical solution to the problem of relating higher-level, more abstract views of a system to lower-level, more detailed views.[13] Splitting up the problems into manageable chunks makes life easier for the analyst because it means that each piece can be tackled independently of the others.

> **TIP**
>
> Large systems should be partitioned according to the domain approach of Shlaer-Mellor.

Object interaction diagrams break down large systems; instead, we need to view a given project as being decomposed into a number of semi-independent subsystems (in the requirements determination phase) and to analyze each subsystem separately. It is well known that the human brain can only process seven pieces of information in short-term memory. If we have no way of chunking information it means that it is almost impossible to have an overview of what the system is doing. One of the problems with the current OMT approach is that there are no guidelines for splitting the problems at an early stage in the software development process, although a number of methodologists are working on adding use cases to capture necessary requirements (see Rumbaugh[14] for more details). In the PPD problem, we could have chosen to analyze the problem in terms of its major responsibilities. Each responsibility is mapped to a subsystem or domain. Domains have static, dynamic (asynchronous), and functional relationships with each other. For example, the major subsystems in the PPD problem are:

- Dispensing
- Payment
- Monitoring

We could then analyze each chunk separately. Instead of object interaction diagrams it is possible to produce "subsystem interaction diagrams." For example, subsystem Dispensing is a client of Payment because the latter subsystem needs to know how many liters of petrol of a certain grade have been dispensed for a given customer transaction. How this is actually done is hidden in the Dispensing system. Similarly, the subsystem Monitoring is a client for Dispensing because it monitors each pulse sent to the pump from the metering device. There is a need in the OO world for more results in the early stages of development. Some state-of-the art articles are Hsia[15] and Potts.[16]

PROTOTYPING: MOVING DIRECTLY FROM REQUIREMENTS TO C++

For people in a hurry, it is possible to start writing C++ code based on event-response lists. As an example, we take the case of the pump aggregation object. From the event-response lists we can produce the following C++ class interface*:

```
// pumpass.hxx

#ifndef DS_PUMPASS_HXX
#define DS_PUMPASS_HXX

    // The enumerated type represented pump state
    enum PumpState {Enabled, Disabled, Out_of_Service};

class DS_PUMPASS
{
    // This class is an aggregate and it delegates responsibility
    // to its components via its operations

private:
    // Attributes
    int pid;        // The pump identification number
    PumpState sta;  // Current state of pump
```

---

*Copyright 1994 by Datasim BV.

```
// Components that make up the pump assembly. These have
// already been found from the concept mapping phase (or,
// alternatively, from the corresponding object diagrams)
DS_DISPLAY dis; // Display
DS_MOTOR mot;   // Pump motor
DS_CLUTCH clu;  // The clutch
DS_GHASS gha;   // Gun-holster assembly

public:
  // Constructors

  DS_PUMPASS(int pump_id);
  DS_PUMPASS(const DS_PUMPASS& pum2);
  virtual ~DS_PUMPASS();

  // Accessing functions
  PumpState state() const;    // Current state of pump

  // Modifier functions
  void enable();          // Enable dispensing of petrol
  void disable();         // Pump unable to dispense
  void remove_gun();      // Enable gun to pump petrol
  void depress_trigger();     // Start delivery of petrol
  void release_trigger();     // Stop delivery of petrol
  void replace_gun();     // Disable gun

  // Operator Overloading
  DS_PUMPASS& operator = (const DS_PUMPASS& pum2);
};

#endif
```

The events in the event-response lists have been mapped to member functions in the pump assembly class. The responses to these events are not visible in the class interface but are to be found in the bodies of the member functions. We give some examples for completeness:

```
void DS_PUMPASS::remove_gun()
{ // Enable gun to pump petrol

/*
E2: Remove gun from holster  // Enables gun to pump petrol
R21: Release holster switch
R22: Enable gun
*/

  gha.release_holster_switch();
  gha.enable_gun();
}
```

```
void DS_PUMPASS::depress_trigger()
{ // Start delivery of petrol

/*
E3: Depress trigger in gun       //Start actual delivery of
petrol
R31: Close microswitch in trigger
R32: Engage clutch
C31: Pump enabled
C32: Gun enabled
*/

  // Preconditions
  if (sta != Enabled || gha.gun_enabled() == FALSE)
    return;

  // We implement the gun-holster combination as an
    // aggregation object
  gha.close_microswitch();
  clu.engage();

}
```

CONCLUSION

I have shown in this article that it is possible to carry out a dynamic modeling exercise for a problem without resorting to computer-aided software engineering tools and we gave steps to show how the products can be used as input to OMT. I have not included scenarios or storyboards in this article; they are discussed in FROM CHAOS TO CLASSES—SOFTWARE DEVELOPMENT IN C++[2] and allow us to carry out acceptance testing on the proposed prototype.

Acknowledgments

I thank Mr. Gijs den Besten of Digital Equipment Corporation, Nieuwegein, the Netherlands, for some useful comments and suggestions.

References

1. Novak, J.D. and D.B. Gowin.. LEARNING HOW TO LEARN, Cambridge University Press, Cambridge, UK, 1984.
2. Duffy, D.J. FROM CHAOS TO CLASSES—SOFTWARE DEVELOPMENT IN C++, McGraw-Hill, London, 1995.
3. Booch, G. OBJECT-ORIENTED DESIGN WITH APPLICATIONS, Benjamin/Cummings, Redwood City, CA, 1991.

4. Rumbaugh, J., M. Blaha, W. Premerlani, F. Eddy, and W. Lorensen. OBJECT-ORIENTED MODELING AND DESIGN, Prentice Hall, Englewood Cliffs, NJ, 1991.

5. Williams, L.G. Assessment of safety-critical specifications, IEEE SOFTWARE, January 1994.

6. Umphress, D.A. and S.G. March. Object-oriented requirements determination, JOURNAL OF OBJECT-ORIENTED PROGRAMMING, 1991.

7. Coleman, D., et al. OBJECT-ORIENTED ANALYSIS AND DESIGN: THE FUSION METHOD, Prentice Hall, Englewood Cliffs, NJ, 1994.

8. Cook, S. and J. Daniels. Software isn't the real world, JOURNAL OF OBJECT-ORIENTED PROGRAMMING 7(2):22–28, 1994.

9. Harel, D., et al. On the formal semantics of statecharts,PROCEEDINGS OF THE SYMPOSIUM ON LOGIC IN COMPUTER SCIENCE, 1987.

10. Harel, D., et al. STATEMATE: A working environment for the development of complex reactive systems, 10TH INTERNATIONAL CONFERENCE ON SOFTWARE ENGINEERING, 1988.

11. Harel, D. On visual formalisms, COMMUNICATIONS OF THE ACM 31(5), 1988.

12. Shlaer, S. A comparison of OOA and OMT, Technical Report, Project Technology, 2560 Ninth Street, Suite 214, Berkeley, CA 94710, 1992.

13. Rumbaugh, J. Building boxes: Subsystems, JOURNAL OF OBJECT-ORIENTED PROGRAMMING 7(6):16–21, 1994.

14. Rumbaugh, J. Getting started: Using use cases to capture requirements, JOURNAL OF OBJECT-ORIENTED PROGRAMMING 7(5):8–12, 23, 1994.

15. Hsia, P., et al. Formal approach to scenario analysis, IEEE SOFTWARE, March 1994.

16. Potts, C., et al. Inquiry-based requirements analysis, IEEE SOFTWARE, March 1994.

OBJECT-ORIENTED REQUIREMENTS ANALYSIS: SYSTEM RESPONSIBILITIES, FUNCTIONAL MODELING, AND SCALABILITY ISSUES

DANIEL J. DUFFY

T HE OBJECT-MODELING TECHNIQUE (OMT) METHOD WAS ORIGINALLY DEVELOPED by Dr. James Rumbaugh and colleagues at General Electric.[1] The method in its current form can be described as a first-generation analysis and design technique and it has become very popular in the marketplace since its initial inception. There are plans to produce a new version of the methodology, but it is our feeling that it will take some time before it is in a form that can be used by tools. A number of shortcomings of OMT have come to light since the method was officially launched in 1991. A good overview of the main ones can be found in Fayad et al.,[2] and solutions to many of the criticisms discussed there are found in Duffy.[3] The problems that we concentrate on in this article are concerned with how functional modeling is carried out in OMT and how OMT can be configured in such a way that it can be applied to the solution of large problems. These are two major areas that need urgent attention if OMT is to be a success for large real-life problems. A number of solutions to these problems have been proposed, but they are additions to OMT in its analysis or design phases. What is needed, in our opinion, is a suite of techniques that allow us to tackle these problems in an early stage of the software development lifecycle rather than later when the structure of the system has been more or less made permanent and when changes are more difficult to bring about. To summarize, the main attention areas in this article are (1) improving functional modeling in OMT and (2) scaling OMT to large problems.

These problems are well known by now, and a number of workarounds have been proposed by several authors, including Rumbaugh himself.[4-5] It is also interesting to note that the Fusion method (as described in Coleman et al.[6]) is based on OMT and uses so-called schemas that are roughly similar to how OMT applies functional modeling and that are similar to the approach taken by us in this article. However, we take the technique a step further by showing how the products of such schemas can be directly integrated into the object diagrams that have already been found for a given problem. The advantages are that the approach remains object-oriented (OO) and that no loose ends enter the system, as is the case when we use the classical OMT approach. The results described in this article have evolved over a number of years, and we feel that we have arrived at a stage where we can analyze a problem properly before we actually embark on a classical OMT analysis. The results have been disseminated at our training courses, and we thank our students for much-valued feedback and ideas.

How Functional Modeling Is Used in OMT

OMT uses a traditional approach to functional modeling in the sense that the techniques used have their roots in structured methods and do not stem from an OO approach. The main disadvantage is that concepts are used that have no direct OO equivalent and it is not always clear how to map the deliverables from the functional modeling phase to objects, classes, or object operations. OMT uses multiple data flow diagrams to flesh out the functional model (see Rumbaugh et al.,[1] chapter 6). A data flow diagram (or DFD for short) is a graph showing the flow of data values from their sources in objects through processes that transform their destinations in other objects. The nodes in a DFD represent processes, while the edges represent data (either objects or "pieces" of objects). Processes are leveled until we get to the stage where they correspond to pure functions (no side effects). This is a stopping criterion, and when we get to this stage we know that we can map such simple processes to operations on suitable objects. The disadvantages of this approach are:

> **TIP**
>
> Note the definition of data flow diagrams.

- The coupling with the object model is very weak. OMT states that the object model is the most important of the three models (object, dynamic, and functional), but little use is made of this observation. In particular, the products of the functional modeling phase are integrated into the object model downstream during the object design phase (see Rumbaugh et al.,[1] section 10.2), and the tips for integration are obscure. It is not at all obvious which object is the owner of a given operation.

- DFDs tend to become cluttered and are difficult to modify when requirements change.
- DFDs offer no support for schema descriptions,[6] they cannot be executed, and they offer no provisions for exception handling, a topic that receives no attention in OMT (and a number of other methods for that matter). Firesmith[7] does provide support for exception handling during analysis, and similar support should find its way into OMT.
- The functional model in OMT introduces concepts that have no direct equivalent in the analysis phase; for example, a data store in OMT is defined as a passive object within a DFD that stores data for later access. This is unnecessary because all objects store data in the analysis phase and there should be no distinction between such objects and objects found in object diagrams.

On a more general note, we remark that the dynamic modeling phase of OMT uses the Harel Statechart approach, which solves some of the well-known problems of classical state transition diagrams.[8] Harel also describes activities and hence how the functional model can be integrated into his visual techniques. It would have been a great advantage if the authors of the OMT method had applied his techniques rather than using the easier option of DFDs. We note that Martin and Odell[9] apply Harel's technique to create object flow diagrams (OFDs), but the treatment is so general that it is difficult to see how it is to be applied in an OMT setting.

Our objective in the next section is to show how these problems can be solved by simple "perturbations" of the basic OMT approach. In particular, we hope to achieve our ends without introducing new diagramming techniques.

ALTERNATIVE FUNCTIONAL MODELING APPROACH

As an alternative to using DFDs we propose a method that is not new but that we can effectively apply to carry out a functional or process model. We call it "responsibility-driven process decomposition," and it is similar to classical functional decomposition, with the following exceptions:

- Flows between processes are always objects.
- Processes at the right level of granularity represent object operations.
- The object model (especially its object diagrams) is a key player in the decomposition process.

Of course, we need some way of finding all the processes in a given system.

These can sometimes correspond to responses in event-response lists (see my previous ROAD article[10] on dynamic modeling). In other words, an external event can trigger a response that is then expanded into a sequence of simpler processes. The advantages of this approach are:

- The highest-level process represents a system responsibility or goal, and hence cannot be lost in the analysis phase.
- The approach lends itself to a natural nesting mechanism.
- All processes and flows can be directly integrated into the object model.
- There are stopping criteria for the decomposition process.
- Exceptions can be introduced.

For each process we need to state what its input and output objects are as well as the preconditions under which it is supposed to operate. Violation of preconditions means in effect that the contract between client and server process is off and an exception is raised. This is a form of asynchronous communication and provision should be made for this.

The steps are:

1. Determine the top-level process, its I/O, and preconditions.
2. Decompose the top-level process into simpler processes.
3. For each process, determine its I/O and preconditions.
4. If a process can be mapped to an object operation, do so now.
5. If a process cannot be mapped to an operation, decompose it further or introduce a new data store object into a relevant object diagram.
6. Go to step 3 and continue until there are no more "stray" processes left.

TIP
It is possible to find "holes" in object diagrams.

The end result is that we have decomposed each high-level process in the system and have a direct mapping of each process to a suitable object operation. Furthermore, it is even possible to find "holes" in object diagrams, e.g., associations that could never have been found in the object or dynamic models. In this sense we see that our approach allows us to verify object diagrams.

An Example of Use

To show how the decomposition process works we take a simple example of the registration of journals that we discussed in an earlier article in ROAD.[11]

The main responsibilities lie in creating circulation lists and attention lists. We tackle the problem of creating a process decomposition for circulation lists. The input for such a process is an issue, while the output consists of a set of readers and the dates. The top-level process is described as follows:

Name: CreateCirculationList( )

Description: Creates a reader circulation list

Input: An instance of the class Issue

Output: A set of pairs, each pair consists of a Reader instance and a date

Preconditions: There must be at least one interested Reader instance

Postcondition: Set<Pair<Reader, Date> > is valid

At this stage, the process CreateCirculationList() does not correspond to any object operation and it must be decomposed. This decomposition should be carried out in such a way that it uses existing object diagrams (see Fig. 1). (Forget about the association between Issue and Reader at this stage.) The subprocesses are:

P1:   Find the Journal corresponding to the Issue.

P2:   Find the Readers and their lending period for this journal.

P3:   Calculate the expiration dates for each Reader.

Processes P1 and P2 correspond immediately to object operations, P1 with Issue and P2 with the association between Reader and Journal (remember, associations can be modeled as classes in OMT!). Process P3 is a bit more difficult because we cannot "hang" it in anywhere. It concerns Issue and Reader and hence there is an association between these whose link attribute corresponds to the expiration date before which the reader should return the issue. If classical OMT were employed, this association would probably be modeled as a data store. We now give the pseudocode that implements the about process:

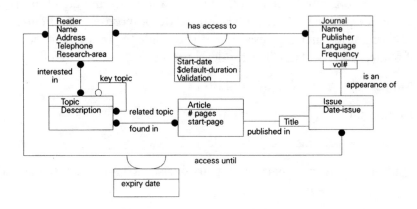

FIGURE 1. *Complete object diagram for JRP problem.*

```
Set<Pair<Reader, Date> > CreateCirculationList(Issue iss)
{
        Journal jnl = iss.journal();
        Set<Pair<Reader, Duration>> interestgroup =
findreaders(jnl);
        Set<Pair<Reader, Date>> result = calcexpiry(iss,
interest_group);
        return result;
}
```

We have found it quite easy (even for large problems) to apply this procedure for many types of problems and not just those that are administrative
in nature, such as the above problem.

RESPONSIBILITIES AND SUBSYSTEM DETERMINATION

TIP
Note the problems with partitioning.

For large problems it will be difficult to find processes initially. We need to look at the problem first and decide
how it is to be partitioned. OMT suggests doing this in
the system design phase, but this leads to many compli-
cations and we believe that a more fundamental
approach is needed. By "fundamental," we mean that
attention needs to be given to this problem in the requirements phase. OMT
tends to be a solution-oriented methodology, whereas for large systems this
approach does not work very well. Instead, what we propose is partitioning a
given problem immediately into domains (or subject areas) and then analyz-

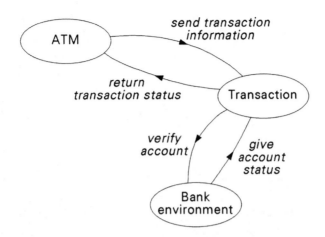

FIGURE 2. *Subsystem event-flow diagram for ATM problem.*

ing each domain separately. This is the approach taken by Shlaer and Mellor.[13] Each domain is further partitioned into subsystems in the OMT sense.

To take an example, consider the automatic teller machine (ATM) problem. In this case a customer can execute transactions on his or her bank account via an ATM machine. This is a simple problem; in this case there are three subsystems, as shown in Figure 2. The systems have been chosen in such a way that they satisfy a client/server relationship; the ATM subsystem is a client of the `Transaction` subsystem, which is in turn a client of the `Bank envi-ronment` subsystem. There is both synchronous and asynchronous communication possible. This is in keeping with the Shlaer-Mellor subsystem access model (SAM) and subsystem communication model (SCM). OMT and Fusion use event-trace and object-interaction diagrams, but these do not help well in the initial requirements phase as they are too finely grained.

LIVING WITH EXCEPTIONS

Under normal circumstances subsystems communicate by sending messages to each other. A client sends a message to a server, and under normal circumstances the server will give an answer. When the client does not obey the contract as defined by the server an exception should be raised. This represents a form of asynchronous communication from the server. We remark that our approach can handle exceptions with ease. Furthermore, we can

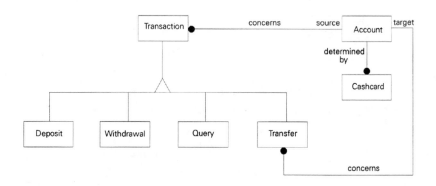

FIGURE 3. *Object diagram for transactions and accounts.*

keep pace with the new developments for interoperable objects.[14] For example, the interface for the subsystem `Bank` would contain the following functionality:

```
interface Bank
{
exception bad_account_status(string account#);
exception not_enough_funds(string account#,
    int money);
void deposit(string account#, int money)
    raises (bad_account);
void withdraw(string account#, int money)
    raises (bad_account), (not_enough_funds);
};
```

The above interface definition language (IDL) can be compiled to a number of different languages such as C, Ada, and C++. The object diagram for the combined `Transaction` and `Bank` subsystems is shown in Figure 3 without attributes or operations. These can be found by the approach taken in this article.

CONCLUSION

We have shown that by a small change in emphasis in the OMT approach some of the shortcomings of the method can be avoided without introducing new concepts, which would otherwise have to be learned by users, who already have enough to cope with. In particular, we have shown how functional modeling can be applied to OMT and how large systems can be analyzed by decomposing a problem into suitable domains or subject areas in the early stages of requirements analysis.

References

1. Rumbaugh, J., M. Blaha, W. Premerlani, F. Eddy, and W. Lorensen. OBJECT-ORIENTED MODELING AND DESIGN, Prentice Hall, Englewood Cliffs, NJ, 1991.

2. Fayad, M.E., W.T. Tsia, R.L. Anthony, and M.L. Fulghump. Object modeling technique (OMT): Experience report, JOURNAL OF OBJECT-ORIENTED PROGRAMMING 7(7):46–58, 1994.

3. Duffy, D.J. From CHAOS TO CLASSES—SOFTWARE DEVELOPMENT IN C++, McGraw-Hill, New York, 1995.

4. Gilliam, T. An approach for using OMT in the development of large systems, JOURNAL OF OBJECT-ORIENTED PROGRAMMING 5(9):56–60, 1994.

5. Rumbaugh, J. Going with the flow: Flow graphs and their various manifestations, JOURNAL OF OBJECT-ORIENTED PROGRAMMING 7(3):12–20, 1994.

6. Coleman, D., et al. OBJECT ORIENTED DEVELOPMENT—THE FUSION METHOD, Prentice Hall, Englewood Cliffs, NJ, 1994.

7. Firesmith, D.G. OBJECT-ORIENTED REQUIREMENTS ANALYSIS AND LOGICAL DESIGN, Wiley, New York, 1993.

8. Harel, M. On visual formalisms, COMMUNICATIONS OF THE ACM 31(5), 1988.

9. Martin, J. and J.J. Odell. OBJECT-ORIENTED ANALYSIS AND DESIGN, Prentice Hall, Englewood Cliffs, NJ, 1992.

10. Duffy, D.J. Object-oriented requirements analysis: Dynamic modeling, ROAD 1(6), 1995.

11. Duffy, D.J. Object-oriented requirements analysis: Finding abstractions and their relationships, ROAD 1(5), 1995.

12. Saeki, M., H. Horai, and H. Enomoto. Software development process from natural language specifications, 11th INTERNATIONAL CONFERENCE ON SOFTWARE ENGINEERING, 1989.

13. Shlaer, S. and S. Mellor. THE SHLAER-MELLOR METHOD, Project Technology Inc., Berkeley, CA.

14. Special report on interoperable objects, DR. DOBBS JOURNAL, Winter 1994/1995.

15. Potts, C., K. Takahashi, and A.I. Anton. Inquiry-based requirements analysis, IEEE SOFTWARE, March 1994.

USE CASES IN LARGE-SCALE SYSTEMS

IVAR JACOBSON

U SE-CASE MODELING IS AN ANALYSIS TECHNIQUE FOR ELICITING, UNDERSTAND-ing, and defining functional system requirements. I briefly presented use-case modeling in the first two issues of ROAD,[1,2] in which systems of moderate complexity were assumed. This article shows how the use-case approach scales up to handle the construction of large systems. To build large systems, you must solve some unique problems, including how to

- divide a large system into smaller autonomous systems
- define the interfaces among the smaller systems
- distribute the development work

In this article, by presenting an extended use-case architecture and system architecture, I show how employing use cases helps solve these problems. I also introduce the necessary method steps through an example.

USE-CASE MODEL INTRODUCTION

A use-case model consists of actors, use cases, and relationships among them.[3] Actors represent everything that must exchange information with the system, including what are usually called users. When an actor uses the system, the system performs a use case. A good use case is a sequence of transactions that yields a measurable result of values for an actor. The collection of use cases is the system's complete functionality.

Every system can be described with a use-case model. That is, any system can offer a number of use cases to a number of outside users, or actors.[4] Here, however, I consider only software and hardware systems.

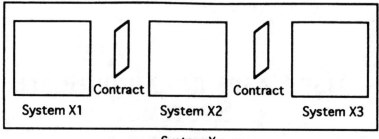

FIGURE 1. *A superordinate system X containing three subordinate systems, X1, X2, and X3. The contracts define the interfaces between the subordinate systems.*

SYSTEMS AT DIFFERENT LEVELS

In previous issues of ROAD, we have shown how to employ the use-case model to define the behavior of a complete system. This is fine for systems of moderate complexity, in which the number of use cases is small. But for very large systems, we must extend our architecture with features to manage the complexity of the system.

The use-case approach already supports a simple subsystem construct, which is a "transparent" package of objects. But this is not enough. We need a more powerful construct that can be developed separately and then connected with well-defined interfaces to form a large system. Therefore, we introduce a generalization of the system concept: Systems may contain systems recursively.

> **TIP**
>
> Systems may contain subsystems recursively.

For example, in Figure 1, the large system X contains three systems, X1, X2, and X3, which are developed by autonomous development teams.

When you must clarify what level of system you are talking about, you can refer to the overall large system (e.g., system X in Figure 1) as the superordinate system. Then, X1, X2, and X3 are referred to as subordinate systems. They are systems, not subsystems, and they should not be confused with the subsystem construct.

A large system can be divided into several levels of systems, but two levels is probably typical.

To distribute work among development teams so that each system can be developed separately, you must define the interfaces among the subordinate

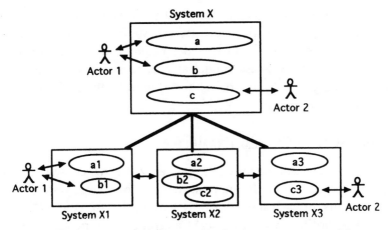

FIGURE 2: *The superordinate and subordinate use-case models.*

systems. Interfaces are one or several contracts between each pair of communicating systems. A contract is a definition of the services offered by a system. Defining contracts requires a notation. A contract is our notation to capture the interface of a system. It defines the services offered by a system. One approach, which we will present in a separate article, is to model a contract as a

number of object types, each with associated protocols. In this approach, the developers of a client system view the server system as a number of public objects that can be used as is.

USE-CASE MODELS AT DIFFERENT LEVELS

Before you can divide a system, you must understand its overall requirements and structure. That is, you must define the behavior of the complete system, at least at a high level. The use case is our technique to model system requirements. However, the developers of each subordinate system should not have to worry about overall requirements; their requirements should be assigned to them.

The need for requirements on two levels leads to two levels of use-case models: a superordinate and a subordinate level. The superordinate use-case model (use cases a, b, and c in Figure 2) defines the requirements of the entire system. The requirements of the subordinate systems are defined with a subordinate use-case model for each subordinate system. For example, the use cases a1 and b1 constitute the use-case model for system X1.

Use cases at the subordinate level that originate from the same use case in the superordinate use-case model are called subordinate use cases. For example, in Figure 2, b1 and b2 are both subordinate use cases of the superordinate use case b.

PHONE SWITCH SYSTEM EXAMPLE

A small telecommunications example, a phone switch system, illustrates how to proceed from defining requirements for a large system to defining requirements for each subordinate system. In the use-case model in Figure 3, the superordinate use case Local Call routes a phone call from the location of a calling subscriber to the location of a called subscriber. The system looks up the called subscriber in the telecommunication network, sets up the incoming call between the called and the calling subscriber, supervises the call, and, when the call is finished, releases the network.

The other superordinate use case, Subscription Changes, describes how an operator changes the stored information about the local subscriber.

The phone-switch system is divided into three systems: Trunk, Traffic Control, and Operation & Maintenance (see Figure 3). Just because these systems are part of an overall system does not mean they are small. Rather, they are of a size that is appropriate for a single development team to handle.

The system divisions are found from the use-case descriptions or directly from the requirements specification. In SOFTWARE ENGINEERING,[3] three different analysis object types—interface objects, control objects, and entity objects—are used to model a system. These same types can be used to define a system's main responsibilities. So, the criteria for finding analysis objects can be used to identify systems. In this case, Trunk and Operation & Maintenance handle the communication with the subscriber and operator actors, respectively; they are interface systems. Traffic Control controls the network and telephone lines; it is a control system.

INTERACTION DIAGRAMS AND SYSTEM INTERFACES

Before you can divide the development work among the subordinate systems, you must distribute the requirements and define the interfaces among them. I use interaction diagrams[5] to do both. An interaction diagram describes how the behavior of a superordinate use case is distributed among

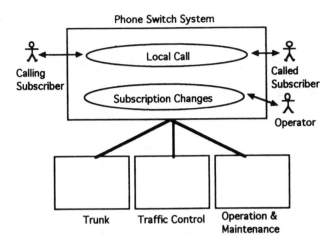

FIGURE 3: *Model of a phone-switch system.*

the systems and how the systems communicate to implement the use case. In the phone switch system, an interaction diagram for the first part of the use case Local Call would look like Figure 4. (Note that margin text describing the behavior of the use case in each system is omitted from the figure.)

You use the interaction diagrams to specify the contracts among the systems. Contracts are documented separately from the system that offers the contract. The contracts of a system should be defined and approved long before the development of this system is finished. This means, for example, that a server system can be used by developers of related client systems before the inside of the server system is implemented.

> **TIP**
>
> You use the interaction diagrams to specify the contracts among the systems.

SUBORDINATE SYSTEMS ARE SYSTEMS

Now that you have completed the modeling on the superordinate level, you can proceed to develop each individual subordinate system (in parallel of course).[6,8] We will concentrate on the Trunk. Three new actors to this subordinate system have been added, a Subscription Changer, a Coordinator, and a Digit Analyzer (see Figure 5). They represent roles played by the systems interacting with the Trunk. From the perspective of the Trunk system, these actors behave in a way equivalent to the surrounding systems. However, a one-to-one correspondence between surrounding systems and actors does not necessarily

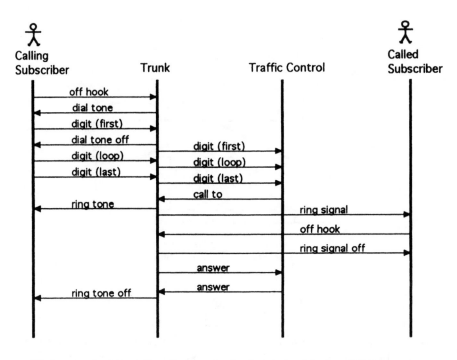

Figure 4. *An interaction diagram for the first part of the Local Call use case.*

occur. For example, the Coordinator and the Digit Analyzer together behave as Traffic Control. That is, Traffic Control is represented by two different actors, since it plays two different roles from the Trunk's perspective.

There are several reasons to view other systems as actors. First, the systems become less dependent on each other. This means that it will be easier to replace one system with another, as long as it conforms to the agreed-on interface. Second, by viewing a system as several actors that represent a separate role, respectively, you can easily let another system play one of these roles or even assign one of the roles to a system of its own. For example, the Coordinator role of the Trunk could be moved to another system's responsibilities.

To find the subordinate use cases of the Trunk, you use the interaction diagrams developed for the superordinate level. They give you enough information to divide the superordinate use cases into subordinate use cases. For example, the superordinate use case Local Call gives rise to the subordinate use case Call to/from Subscriber, and the superordinate use case Subscription Changes gives rise to the subordinate use case Changing

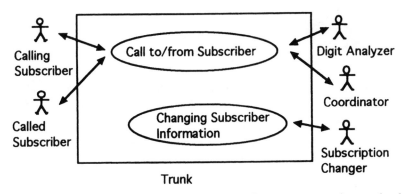

FIGURE 5: *A subordinate system is treated as an ordinary system at the next level.*

Subscriber Information in the Trunk (see Figure 5).

The requirements of the Trunk are completely defined by its subordinate use-case model and contracts. Now, Trunk can be developed in the same way as an ordinary system by a separate development team. We can identify the objects required to realize the use cases, exactly as described in one of my previous ROAD articles.[5]

MAPPING DIFFERENT LEVELS OF USE-CASE MODELS

It is important that you be able to trace use-case models developed at different system levels. Clear traceability makes it easier to assign work when going from superordinate to subordinate use cases, and later, it helps verify the subordinate use-case models against the superordinate use-case model. A formal description method for mapping was introduced in 1985.[7]

Informally, the relation between superordinate and subordinate use-case models is interpreted as if all the use cases were equivalent, as seen from the actor's perspective. This means that the use case Local Call (see Figure 3) and its subordinate use cases in Trunk and Traffic Control exhibit equivalent behavior to subscribers.

Thus, there is a type of equivalence relation between superordinate and subordinate use-case models. Each actor in the superordinate use-case model corresponds exactly to an actor in the subordinate model. Each use case in the superordinate use-case model corresponds to one or more use cases in the subordinate use-case model. Note that it is more important to identify good subordinate use cases than it is to maintain a one-to-one relationship between

> **TIP**
>
> Note the equiva-
> lence between
> superordinate and
> subordinate use-
> case models.

superordinate and subordinate use cases. In many cases, therefore, a superordinate use case will give rise to several subordinate use cases in the same subordinate system. Also, note that the name of a subordinate use case should explain the subordinate use case's behavior, which is probably not the same as the name of the superordinate use case.

Finally, each actor associated with a use case in the superordinate use-case model is usually associated with only one subordinate use case in the subordinate use-case model. (Theoretically, there is no reason why there cannot be more than one, but it is usually impractical.) This is true even in the special case in which a use case at the top level is allocated entirely, without being subdivided, to a single subordinate system.

SUMMARY

Informally, this is how you can employ use cases to define systems at different levels and relate use-case models at different levels to one another. This technique lets you continue to divide systems and use-case models in several steps. I believe, however, that even very large systems can be described with only one division, as described here.

Acknowledgments

I am greatly indebted to Staffan Ehnebom at Ericsson HP Telecommunication AB and to the process-development team at Ellemtel AB for their valuable insights in how to develop large systems.

References

1. Jacobson, I. Basic use case modeling, ROAD, 1(2):15–19, 1994.
2. Jacobson, I. Basic use case modeling, ROAD, 1(3):7–9, 1994.
3. Jacobson, I.; M. Christersson, P. Jonsson, and G. Overgaard, OBJECT-ORIENTED SOFTWARE ENGINEERING—A USE CASE DRIVEN APPROACH, Addison-Wesley Publishers Ltd., 1992.
4. Jacobson, I., M. Erikson, and A. Jacobson. THE OBJECT ADVANTAGE—BUSINESS PROCESS REENGINEERING WITH OBJECT TECHNOLOGY, Addison-Wesley Publishers Ltd., Reading, MA, 1994.
5. Jacobson, I. Use cases and objects, ROAD, 1(4):8–10, 1994.
6. Wirfs-Brock, R., B. Wilkerson, and L. Wiener. DESIGNING OBJECT-ORIENTED SOFTWARE, Prentice Hall, Englewood Cliffs, NJ, 1990.

7. Jacobson, I. CONCEPTS FOR MODELING LARGE REAL TIME SYSTEMS, Department of Computer Systems, The Royal Institute of Technology, Stockholm, September 1985.

8. Selic, B., G. Gullekson, and P. T. Ward. REAL-TIME OBJECT-ORIENTED MODELING.

FORMALIZING USE-CASE MODELING

IVAR JACOBSON

A S I WROTE IN A RECENT ARTICLE,[1] THERE IS A GROWING ACCEPTANCE OF USE cases. This is good news. It is also good news that, so far, methodologists have introduced new use-case concepts very carefully. This means there is a good chance we can achieve a standard use-case modeling technique, at least for basic use-case modeling. I have presented my contributions to this standard in several articles and the book OBJECT-ORIENTED SOFTWARE ENGINEERING—A USE CASE DRIVEN APPROACH.[2–5]

As use cases become more and more popular, interest in further developing the basic ideas will grow. Thinking on use cases will develop in both "soft" (process- or human-related) and "hard" (model- or language-related) directions, and this new thinking will come from people with different knowledge bases, such as computer scientists, software engineers, user-interface experts,[6] sociologists, and psychologists. At Objectory, we have developed use cases in both soft and hard directions: We have used use cases to model businesses,[7] and we have extended the modeling language to support recursive use-case modeling.[8,9] Recursive modeling facilitates a powerful architecture, which we call *systems of interconnected systems.*

In this column I focus on use-case modeling languages, touching only briefly on process issues. In particular, I want to describe our approach to formalizing use-case modeling. To explain what should and shouldn't be in a use-case model, I first summarize the design rationale for a basic use-case model.[3,4] Then I discuss different formalization levels and go into detail about some of them.

BASIC USE CASES: DESIGN RATIONALES FOR THE MODELING LANGUAGE

Use cases serve many roles in the various software development activities, from envisioning to requirements capture, user-interface analysis, ideal and real object modeling, testing, and so on. For a more complete list of roles see Jacobson[3] or, better, Jacobson and Christerson.[10]

> **TIP**
>
> Capture a system's functional requirements before design work starts.

The whole idea behind the use-case model is to capture a system's functional requirements before design work starts. To understand the rationale for a use-case modeling language, therefore, one must first understand who the use-case model's handlers* are.

Handlers of a Use-Case Model

A use-case model is developed during requirements analysis by people who often have a lot of experience, either in designing certain types of systems or in the business area being modeled. These analysts do not necessarily know any particular implementation technique more than superficially.

The resulting use-case model is used by many groups. It is used as a model of "What," as an outside view of the system, by

- orderers, to validate that the use-case model specifies all the needs of the supported business (i.e., all the needs of the people who will use the system

- user-interface analysts, to specify user-interface support for each use case

- function managers and project leaders (or process owners and process managers, in a process organization), to review and supervise development at different levels

- technical writers, to structure the overall work on the user manuals at an early stage

It is used as a model of "How," as an inside view of the system, by

- designers of corresponding analysis and design object models, one for each use case, to harmonize the design over all use cases and to resolve conflicts among use-case instances

- integration testers, to identify test cases at an early stage

---

*The handler concept has been described in Jacobson[11] and Jacobson, Erikson, and Jacobson.[7]

Expressability of a Use-Case Model

Requirements analysts must be able to create a use-case model that users can read. The What model, the outside view, is the model that all handlers can understand. In my experience, the best use-case models talk about a system's function (used here in its everyday meaning), not its form. It should express who the users are and what their needs are.

In a use-case model, users are actors and needs are use cases. Thus, actors and use cases are the only occurrences, phenomena, or objects in a use-case model—no more, no less. This simplicity is one reason use-case models are so easy to understand and why they have become so popular.

We have made three other important decisions about what cannot be expressed in a use-case model:

1. Internal communication among occurrences inside the system cannot be modeled. Use-case instances are the only types of objects inside the system. Therefore, they cannot communicate with one another. Otherwise, we would have to specify use-case interfaces, which would result in an internal view similar to an object model.

2. Conflicts among use-case instances cannot be modeled. Obviously there will be such conflicts in an implemented system, and these relationships are certainly very important, but they represent internal details. Such relationships should be expressed in the object models.

3. Concurrency cannot be modeled. We assume that use cases are interpreted one instance and one transaction at a time. In effect, use cases are atomic, serialized slices of a system.

Given these restrictions, one cannot use a use-case model to simulate a system at an early stage. Instead, I suggest using an early object model for this purpose. In Jacobson et al.[2] we suggested the simulation of a system using a robust-object model that has the class behavior specified. Objects are very nice simulation instruments, as the designers of Simula discovered back in the early 1960s.

> **TIP**
>
> Objects are excellent simulation instruments.

Many people have asked me why I have not developed a formal specification language for use-case modeling. In fact, I almost did. In my thesis[12] I described a formal language to specify (an early form of) use cases. The language was object-oriented, which means that I described use cases formally in terms of communicating objects. This is how I believe formal (mathematical) system specifications should be done. However, this is not use-case modeling with only use cases and actors, as described previously. This is more like using a formal object-specification language similar to Object[13,14] to specify use cases. I used an object language for the same reason I believe in object modeling in general: Objects are practical for the design of complex software. Whether you design with a programming language or a specification language is of no importance.

I believe, therefore, that simulation should be carried out by using a formal object model, not a formal use-case model. Simulation can still be done use case by use case, since an object model will have at least as many views as there are use cases. There may be more views than use cases, but there is at least one view for each use case. This means that there is a full seamlessness between use cases in a use-case model and use cases in an object model.

> **TIP**
>
> Simulation should be carried out by using a formal object model.

Formally specifying every use case can be valuable for other purposes, including test-case generation. Here too, however, I believe that each use case should be specified in terms of formally specified objects.

Having said this, I still think it is valuable to formalize use cases and actors in the use-case model. Organizations that use formal techniques to specify requirements, such as for protocols, may want to extend their use-case models with more formal techniques. The question is, how far can use cases be formalized? My answer has been consistent for many years: as far as possible without violating the three rules stated above.

LEVELS OF FORMALISMS

Use-case modeling has been formalized to different levels. Here I give an overview of these levels only, relying on your intuition to supply some of the details. I do plan to describe these levels in more detail in later articles. Remember that here I am not discussing how to map use cases to objects.[2,5] This is a very important subject, but a quite different one. After describing the basic constructs, I sketch the four principal formalisms: class associations, interaction diagrams, contracts, and state-transition diagrams.

Basic Constructs

A use-case model is a model of a system. It consists of actors and use cases (Figure 1).

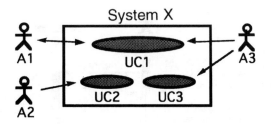

FIGURE 1. *A use-case model of system X (A1–A3 are actors
and UC1–UC3 are use cases).*

Actors and use cases have unique names within the scope of the system.
Each actor has a communication association to one or more use cases, and
vice versa.

Actors and use cases are considered to be classes that
can be instantiated. A communication association
between an actor and a use case means that an instance
of the actor will communicate with an instance of the
use case during its lifetime.

For each combination of actor and use case there
must be a description of its dynamic behavior, how the
actor instance interacts with the use-case instance. We
call these use-case descriptions, even though they also describe actor behavior. At this basic level, the behaviors of actors and use cases are described
informally, in structured English.

> **TIP**
>
> Actors and use cases
> are considered to
> be classes that can
> be instantiated.

Because actors and use cases are classes, these descriptions describe alternative, exceptional behavior. Furthermore, to each use-case description you
may want to attach a description of different use-case instances or scenarios, which will probably be used during development only to explain
different uses or different people's perception of uses (as suggested by
Rebecca Wirfs-Brock in private conversations). Finally, in some cases you
may want a static description for each actor class and each use-case class.

Class Associations

These basis modeling constructs can be enhanced with class associations.
Since one actor class can inherit another actor class, one actor instance can
use the same use cases as an actor instance in another class. A use-case class

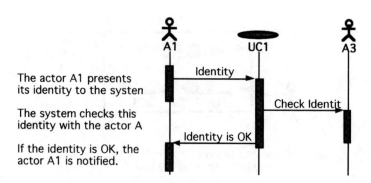

The actor A1 presents
its identity to the systen

The system checks this
identity with the actor A

If the identity is OK, the
actor A1 is notified.

FIGURE 2. *An interaction diagram describing the behavior of
the use case UC1 in system X.*

can have a "uses" association with another use-case class, which means the
classes share behavior in an abstract use-case class, or a class can have an
"extends" association, which means the behavior of one class is extended to
another class. The distinction between these two associations is tricky to
explain in a few words, so please refer to Jacobson[4] and Jacobson and
Thomas.[1]

Interaction Diagrams

Dynamic behavior, as captured in a use-case description, can be formalized
by using interaction diagrams[2,5] (Figure 2).

An interaction diagram describes the interaction among (usually) object
instances. Here the objects are actors and use cases. Each use-case description can have several interaction diagrams. Rebecca Wirfs-Brock has
suggested that an interaction diagram describes a "conversation," a term that
I think is well in line with the semantics of these diagrams. Each such conversation has a unique name within the use case.

In this case, an interaction diagram describes the sequence of interactions
among use-case and actor instances. An actor sends a stimulus to a use case,
which receives the stimulus and performs a transaction. The transaction
involves manipulating the internal attributes of the use case and then sending one or more stimuli to the originating actor or to other actors.
Structured English is used to describe a transaction. An interaction diagram
can describe different paths the conversation will follow. Thus there are constructs to describe iteration, repetition, branching, and parallelism.

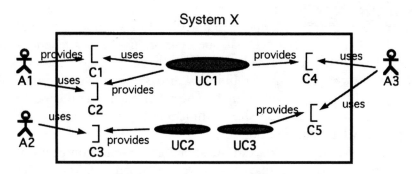

FIGURE 3. *Contracts in system X.*

Each interaction diagram that describes a conversation can be associated with pre- and postconditions. A precondition, for instance, might be "The actor A1 has logged on to the system," and a postcondition might be "The actor A1 has been notified if its identity is OK or not" (see Figure 2).

Each use case may also have pre- and postconditions. In a telecommunication system, for example, the `Local call` use case might have the precondition that the calling subscriber has acquired a subscription. A postcondition would be that the subscriber still has a subscription. In other words, the subscriber cannot lose a subscription in the middle of a call. Among other things, pre- and postconditions let you slice a system into independent use cases.

Contracts

Larger systems usually have several actors and a lot of interactions with each one. The number of different types of stimuli to and from the system may be very large—say, more than 1000. A contract (or several contracts) is a nice technique of describing a large number of stimuli between the actors and the system.[15]

A contract specifies an object's interface in detail. The "provides" relation specifies the object that is realizing a contract, and the "uses" relation specifies the object that uses the object realizing a contract, e.g., through communication (Figure 3). Thus, an actor or use case that provides a contract will realize all the stimuli defined in the contract, and an actor or use case that uses a contract will know that there is either a use case or an actor that realizes it.

We achieve a much more intelligible interface when we structure a con-

TIP

Note how to achieve more intelligible contracts.

tract in terms of objects (actually classes) and direct a stimulus to one object only. An actor provides a contract that one or more use cases use, and a use case provides a contract that one or more actors use. If they are carefully designed, several use cases can jointly provide a single contract. In such cases the use cases would also share a function, so an abstract use case should probably have been found.

Graphical user interfaces (GUIs) and communication protocols are two examples of contracts that are very well described as objects. A GUI can first be described at an abstract level as a set of contract objects. A contract object receives a stimulus and retransmits it to the associated use-case instance. One can describe objects in a contract using state-transition diagrams or preconditions and postconditions.

State-Transition Diagrams

In many cases, the static class descriptions of actors and use cases can be modeled well with state-transition diagrams.

A class can be thought of as a state machine. For example, a use-case instance traverses several machine states during its lifetime. Here a state represents the potential of the use-case instance. Which continuation the use case will follow from its current state depends on which stimulus it receives. A stimulus received from an actor instance will cause the use case to leave its current state and perform a transaction, depending on the state-stimulus combination. The transaction involves the manipulation of internal attributes of the use case and its outputs to actors. These can be the ones that created the use case or other actors that have been involved during the course of the use case. The transaction is finished when the use case has again entered a state (possibly the same one) and awaits another stimulus from an actor.

In many other cases, particularly for use cases that primarily save and retrieve information, the class can be described as a set of transactions, each one initiated by a stimulus. In these cases each transaction is associated with pre- and postconditions, to determine the state of the use case before and after the transaction.

What kind of state-transition diagram should be used? Jim Odell gives a good overview of different ways to make state-transition diagrams.[16] My own preferred notation is the CCITT/SDL[17] extended in Jacobson et al.[2] Which one you will prefer is a matter of habit and taste.

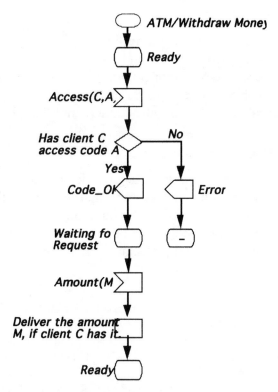

FIGURE 4. *The use case Withdraw Money of an automated teller machine (ATM) modeled with a state-transition diagram.*

In Figure 4, an instance of the use case Withdraw Money is in an initial state (Ready) when it is ready to do a cash withdrawal. It receives a stimulus, Access(C,A), from an actor, in which C is the actor identification and A is the corresponding access code. If the code is correct, the use case transitions to a new state (Waiting for Request), in which money is delivered according to the stimulus input, Amount(M). If the code is incorrect, the system generates an output stimulus and the use case returns to the initial state (Ready).

Another technique that has become popular lately is to use a modified version of Harel's hierarchical state diagrams.[18] This technique is particularly valuable when describing complex state machines, such as use cases with several transactions going on in parallel.

EXPERIENCES

In its current form, use-case modeling has been used extensively for nearly 10 years. We have become more and more convinced that use cases should be treated as a subtype of a more generic phenomena of which "normal" objects (as used in object modeling) are a subtype. Thus, use cases are classes that can be instantiated and that may have inheritance-like relations to one another.

CONCLUSION

Here I have presented the design rationale for use-case modeling and overviews of the different ways to formalize the modeling language. This, of course, is not the last word on this question. We continue to gain experience as people use our technology, and I am sure you, dear reader, have a number of proposals to further the thinking behind use cases.

References

1. Jacobson, I. and D. Thomas. Extensions: A technique for evolving large systems, REPORT ON OBJECT ANALYSIS & DESIGN 1(5):7–9, 1995.

2. Jacobson, I., M. Christerson, P. Jonsson, and G. Overgaard. OBJECT-ORIENTED SOFTWARE ENGINEERING—A USE CASE DRIVEN APPROACH, Addison-Wesley, Reading, MA, 1992.

3. Jacobson, I. Basic use case modeling, REPORT ON OBJECT ANALYSIS & DESIGN 1(2):15–19, 1994.

4. Jacobson, I. Basic use case modeling (continued), REPORT ON OBJECT ANALYSIS & DESIGN 1(3):7–9, 1994.

5. Jacobson, I. Use cases and objects, REPORT ON OBJECT ANALYSIS & DESIGN 1(4):8–10, 1994.

6. Constantine, L. and L.A.D. Lockwood. Essential use cases: Essential modeling for user interface design, OzCHI '94, November 1994, Melbourne, Australia.

7. Jacobson, I., M. Erikson, and A. Jacobson. THE OBJECT ADVANTAGE BUSINESS PROCESS REENGINEERING WITH OBJECT TECHNOLOGY, Addison-Wesley, Reading, MA, 1994.

8. Jacobson, I. Use cases in large-scale systems, REPORT ON OBJECT ANALYSIS & DESIGN 1(6):9–12, 1995.

9. Jacobson, I., K. Palmkvist, and S. Dyrhage. Systems of interconnected systems, REPORT ON OBJECT ANALYSIS & DESIGN 2(1), 1995.

10. Jacobson, I. and M. Christerson. A growing consensus on use cases, JOURNAL OF OBJECT-ORIENTED PROGRAMMING 8(1):15–19, 1995.

11. Jacobson, I. Toward mature object technology, REPORT ON OBJECT ANALYSIS & DESIGN 1(1):36–39, 1994.

12. Jacobson, I. Concepts for modeling large real time systems, Stockholm, Department of Computer Systems, The Royal Institute of Technology, September 1985.

13. Spivey, J.M. THE Z NOTATION: A REFERENCE MANUAL, Prentice Hall, Englewood Cliffs, NJ, 1989.

14. van der Linden, F.J. Object-oriented specification in COLD, Technical report no. RWR-508-re-92007, Philips Research Laboratories, The Netherlands, 1992.

15. Jacobson, I., S. Bylund, P. Jonsson, and S. Ehnebom. Using contracts and use cases to build plugable architectures, JOURNAL OF OBJECT-ORIENTED PROGRAMMING 8(2):18–24, 76, 1995.

16. Odell, J. Approaches to finite-state machine modeling, JOURNAL OF OBJECT-ORIENTED PROGRAMMING 7(8):14–20, 40, 1995.

17. CCITT specification and description language (SDL), Recommendations Z.100, March 1993.

18. Harel, D. Statecharts: A visual formalism for complex systems, SCIENCE OF COMPUTER PROGRAMMING 8:231–274, 1987.

19. Jacobson, I. and S. Jacobson. Beyond methods and CASE: The software engineering process with its integral support environment, OBJECT MAGAZINE 4(8):24–30, 1995.

DEFINING AND DEVELOPING USER-INTERFACE INTENSIVE APPLICATIONS WITH USE CASES

STEVEN CRAIG BILOW

T HIS ARTICLE DESCRIBES A SOMEWHAT NOVEL APPLICATION OF THE USE-CASE based modeling techniques originally developed by Ivar Jacobson et al.[1–5] It proposes the application of use cases and other *user-centered* design techniques to the development of products that have extensive graphical and/or multimedia user interfaces. A user-centered design technique like use-case modeling is the ideal methodology for the design of applications with complex user interfaces. This is due principally to the inherent parallels between the models required for the design technique and those required for interface specification, testing, and usability evaluation.

DESIGNING SOFTWARE SYSTEMS FOR USER INTERACTIVITY

To create a software system that provides a user with nontrivial modes of interaction, it is essential for the designer to fully and completely understand the user's needs. This is actually true of any system, but for those with complex levels of interactivity, it is even more important. To enter the process of designing a system without both analyzing and completely internalizing the user's requirements is one of the most pervasive causes of product failure.

It is indisputable that there exists a critical trade-off between the level of effort spent in the analysis phase of a development project and the product's cost. Too much time spent analyzing requirements decreases market responsiveness, increases time to market, and increases cost. In fact, at times, rapid prototyping and up-front code development may be a quite acceptable method for developing a piece of software. At the same time, the need for some level of analytical work is irrefutable. It is impossible to adequately construct an entity that is not well understood.

Where user interfaces are concerned, there are, typically, two types of analysis that must be performed: the analysis of system requirements and the analysis of usability. Traditionally, these have been accomplished by two teams using two processes. In large systems, analysis is accomplished through such engineering tools as data-flow diagrams (DFDs)[6]; user requirements are modeled with scripting and scenarios. In small projects, it is quite frequently the case that analyses are accomplished very informally and user requirements defined purely by trial and error. The latter methodology is entirely inappropriate for any project whose goals include optimum usability.

To accomplish a truly complete analysis in a reasonable time frame, an ideal process would integrate the design and analysis tasks with the usability analysis tasks into a single cohesive model. Optimally, such a technique would integrate analysis, design, and implementation techniques that focus on maintaining user requirement awareness throughout the product's life cycle. Every operation and each data structure would be directly traceable back through the development process to an entity that exists in the analysis. Each developer would consider the user regardless of the system element under construction and irrespective of the development phase. The result would be an optimally usable system that perfectly implements each intended function.

The work documented in this article strives to explore this traceable type of consistent user-centered process without sacrificing rigor, expressiveness, or the ability to quickly develop prototypes. It does not claim to have created and codified such a methodology, but it does propose that there currently exists a viable basis for one. That basis is the use case as defined by Jacobson.[1]

THE CORRELATION BETWEEN USE CASES AND USABILITY TESTING

A use case is a model of a system or subsystem that describes the way in which that system will interact with external entities. These entities are either other systems or system users. Each use case will explicitly describe an interface to the external world and, in doing so, will implicitly describe a sequence of information exchanges and contracts (transactions). Because of this, the term *use case* can best be described as *any sequence of transactions within a system that yields a measurable value to some external entity.*

On the same side of a slightly different coin is a type of model that user-interface analysts call the *script* or the *scenario*. Scripts and scenarios are written descriptions of the tasks that must be accomplished by a system and the actions that must be performed to accomplish these tasks. Note that scenarios and scripts describe transactions just like use cases; they are simply used for a different purpose. They describe information exchange sequences and, like use cases, describe those transactions with measurable value to a user.

The fundamental attribute of use cases that leads to the belief that they will serve as an excellent foundation for user-driven design is the direct relationship to scenarios. A use-case model is quite similar to a graphical depiction of the same descriptive technique used by user-interface experts. When properly developed and documented, the Use-case model will depict a complete picture of system usage. As a result, it can serve as the foundation both for system design and for user-interface analysis.

> **TIP**
>
> Use cases serve as an excellent foundation for user-driven design.

MODELING A SYSTEM WITH USE CASES

The fundamental question in object-oriented design is, How do objects interact? Objects must have well defined relationships and formal communication protocols. They require knowledge of each other, often exist as aggregates of one another, and frequently inherit other objects' behavior. An effective method of defining these relationships is essential. In complex system designs, this may be a rather daunting task.

One of the most effective methods of understanding complex object systems and their interobject transactions is to group the objects into comprehensible collections. The most rational of these groupings are those that illustrate the way an action, or requirement, is implemented.[1,4] It is necessary to examine several different views of the system and to determine the most logical structuring topology. To accomplish this, it is important to find, and consistently utilize, a simple, well-grounded modeling entity.

The use case is such an entity. A use case is a view of the system that is fundamentally rooted in the tasks that the system must perform for the user and the services it must provide to other subsystems or programs.[1,3] In designing the setup and configuration interface for an X-Window System terminal, all user requirements must be considered. In addition, it is necessary to formalize the contracts with the X server, the terminal's operating system, the nonvolatile RAM, and the boot host's file system.[7] The user, X server, O/S, and NVRAM are the external entities with which the setup client interacts. If all the relationships are correctly formalized, then the modeling methodology that describes them will be a strong foundation for a development life cycle that considers the user throughout.

EXTERNAL ENTITIES

That which is external to the system under development, whether another system or a user, is called an *actor*.[1,3,4] An actor is external to but interacts with a use case. This is the second principle concept of use-case driven design. In modeling a system, the designer should strive to define ALL the actors, ALL the use cases, and ALL the interactions. When properly modeled, it is fairly logical to conclude that the system under development meets all necessary requirements.

> **TIP**
>
> An actor is external to but interacts with a use case.

In a waterfall model of system development, this level of completeness is virtually impossible until prototypes, code, and some implementation details have been explored. But that model virtually prohibits this from taking place. An optimum development methodology is one that maintains a level of consistency where the designer is able to perform system analysis, design, and implementation in a manner free enough to return to a prior activity when discrepancies are uncovered. Use cases, actors, and their interactions provide such a method.[1–5]

A PROCESS OVERVIEW

For user interface designers, the most important set of actors in a system are the users.[7] Thus, in the course of the examples that follow, the primary emphasis is on that topic. These examples will concentrate on the definition of the use cases, actors, and objects, but, needless to say, an entire development effort is immensely more complex. One reasonable depiction of this as a sequential, linear, kinetic process would appear as:

Step 1: Find the **actors** by identifying who and what interacts with the system.

Step 2: Find the **use cases** by identifying the ACTORS needs.

Step 3: Concurrent with steps 1, 2, and 4,9 find the **domain objects** by identifying the objects that exist in the problem domain of each **use case**.

Step 4: Describe and document the **use cases**.

Step 5: Find the **design objects** by examining the way in which the use cases could be implemented effectively.

Step 6: **Distribute the behavior** among the **design objects** by looking at what each object must DO to implement the **use case**.

Step 7: Define **actions** and **services** for each **design object** by looking at how to implement the behavior for each **design object**.

Step 8: **Implement the system** by writing the code to implement each object and it's behavior.

Step 9: Test the system using the **actor** and **use case** interactions to ensure that all behavior meets the requirements.

The goals of this methodology are to allow mobility throughout the process and to ensure that all user and external requirements are met. By using use cases, it is possible to accomplish both goals while maintaining a uniform basis for system design from domain analysis through testing.

The remainder of this article will concentrate on the way in which this technique may be applied to a typical user interface. The example domain is a graphical interface, but extrapolation to multimedia interfaces is obvious.

THE EXAMPLE DOMAIN

An X Window System terminal resembles a workstation with an embedded operating system and restricted access to O/S functionality. Among the elements of such a product that most enhances it's usability is a good setup and configuration interface. Consider this interface as a subsystem of the terminal's software system. Such an interface has a number of specific uses including, but not limited to, client invocation, network configuration, server configuration, and boot configuration. External to the interface itself, are a number of entities with which interaction is required. These include the user, the O/S, and the X server. In a use-case model, the former entities may be represented as use cases; the latter are modeled as actors. An initial view of such a system is depicted in Figure 1.

This model is quite obviously incomplete. However, it is exactly the way a use-case-based design begins. An initial model is developed, expanded, repartitioned, and formalized in an iterative manner.

EXPANSION AND ITERATION OF USE CASE MODELS

The model depicted in Figure 1 can now be taken as a baseline for iterative refinement. These iterations will unquestionably uncover previously hidden details and may well modify the way the designer views the system. For example, a terminal saves its settings in non-volatile RAM, and setup must certainly communicate with that. A detail has been neglected because the

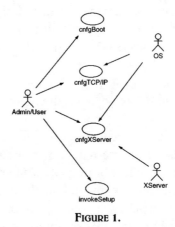

FIGURE 1.

initial model, shown in Figure 1, does not include a depiction of NVRAM.

There are also many specialized operations that the user must perform and none of these is visible in the model. The level of granularity is simply too large and must be revised. Through repetitive reanalysis and expansion, the model may be updated many times. In fact, even in design and implementation it is still possible to modify the model. A more realistic view of the system appears in Figure 2.

Among the most obvious differences between Figures 1 and 2 is the addition of many new use cases. This is quite typical, because as the designer begins to understand the system, new uses and new users are frequently discovered. In Figure 2, however, the diagram has reached a level of complexity wherein intuitive comprehensibility is no longer possible. Additional use cases can still be found, as can repartitioning and redistribution of the current use cases. The trade off manifests itself as one of granularity versus understandability.

INITIAL SUBSYSTEM DEFINITION AND THE RESTORATION OF UNDERSTANDABILITY

When a use-case model reaches a level of complexity wherein it is no longer possible to understand simply by casual observation, it is necessary to make an initial attempt at subsystem partitioning. The subsystems developed here will almost certainly not be the ones that exist when the system is complete. Obviously, with no objects yet defined, subsystem partitioning is impossible. At the same time, simple observation of the tasks being accomplished by the systems will most certainly yield certain patterns. If for no other reason, these

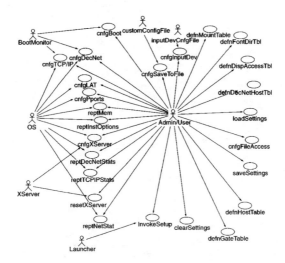

FIGURE 2.

patterns provide a way of subdividing the use-case model into smaller pieces for ease of comprehension. It to also quite probable that what the designer learns in doing this will provide tremendous insight when the "real" task of subsystem partitioning occurs.

> **TIP**
>
> Note the need to partition.

In the case of the X Window System, Figure 2, which shows the terminal configuration interface, allowing an examination of the complex use-case model, does indeed seem to illustrate a reasonably rational series of subdivisions. On initial observation, these appear to fall into the categories of configuration, table maintenance, report generation, and NVRAM control. Figures 3, 4, 5, and 6 depict the use cases and actors associated with each of these subgroupings.

AN OBSERVATION

As a side note, it seems valuable to ask one question about the diagrams in Figures 2 through 6. Of all the model's actors, which has the most associations? The answer appears to be "the user." This explains the rationale behind the premise of this article, namely, that use-case-based modeling techniques provide a profound way for the software engineer to understand the user-oriented aspects of a system. The user appears in the model more frequently than does any other external entity.

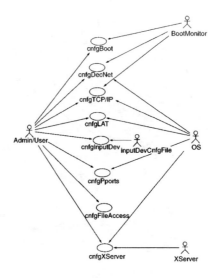

FIGURE 3.

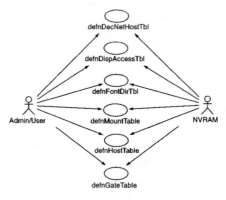

FIGURE 4.

DERIVING DOMAIN OBJECT MODELS FROM USE CASES

Once the use cases and actors that comprise a system are well understood, it is possible to define the objects that exist in the problem domain.[1,3,4] This is the subject of Figure 7, in which the use case called cnfgXServer is decomposed into one possibility of its constituent domain objects. This diagram describes two types of relationships. The dashed lines represent inheritance, while the solid lines represent acquaintance (or the need to access each other's information).

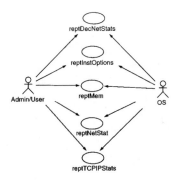

FIGURE 5.

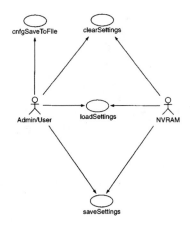

FIGURE 6.

Examples of each of these relationships include the following specifications:

1. A `multiSelection` Button is a subclass of `button`.

2. The `accessCntl` button must communicate access authorization to the display. It retrieves the information from the `hostTable` and adds it to an `xHostAddr` maintenance object.

3. `terminalCnfgFile` and `hostTable` are both subclasses of the class `file`.

4. The visual object must exchange information with both the X screen and the X window, and it receives it's visual type from the defaultVisual button.

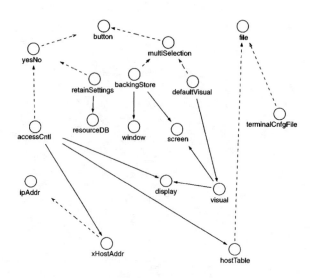

FIGURE 7.

As with any other methodology, the domain objects are not necessarily the objects that will exist in the implementation or even in the design. They simply represent the objects that exist within the domain of the problem being solved.

Like the Use Case model, the domain object model is also subject to iterative modification. As the development progresses, it is quite possible that new insights will drive design changes. For example, the entities called `hostTable` and `terminalCnfgFile` are represented in the model as classes, but in reality, they can be implemented as simple instances of the `file` class. This is also true of the `accessCtl` and `retainSettings` buttons, which are more accurately represented as instances of the `yesNo` button class, not as subclasses. These, however, are the insights to be gained from iteration, so early models will frequently be "incorrect."

In general, this should be corrected in the domain object model, but there are no strict rules. It is also possible to consider the domain accurately represented but to resolve the issues as the design object model progresses. Figure 8 illustrates this.

TRANSFORMING PROBLEMS INTO SOLUTIONS

The models shown so far have examined only the problem domain. They do not attempt to solve the problems, only to understand them. From this point

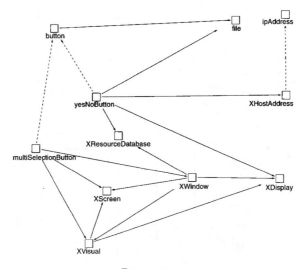

FIGURE 8.

on, it is necessary to derive design objects from the domain objects by attempting to actually solve the design problems. The goals of this process are to identify the design objects, distribute the required behavior, define the operations that objects must perform, and partition the world into subsystems.[1,3,4]

Figure 8 portrays the first of those tasks for the `cnfgXServer` use case. It is quite similar to Figure 7, but the inheritance/instantiation issues have been resolved and the objects are in the design domain rather than the problem domain. These are the objects that will actually be implemented.

BEHAVIOR: HOW THE OBJECTS INTERACT

Every class of objects will implement a set of services and will embody a number of attributes. To determine what these are, it is essential that the behavior of the objects in the system be understood. Objects interact with each other through contractual relationships that define their communication requirements. Through these, the designer comes to understand each object and

> **TIP**
>
> The designer must understand each object and its behavior.

its behavior. In use-case modeling, the technique for accomplishing this is called the interaction diagram, and it essentially builds up an object's service and attribute sets by examining all use cases in which the object participates

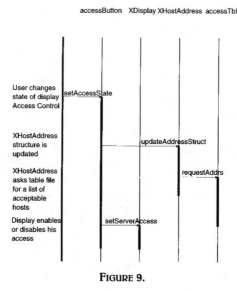

accessButton   XDisplay XHostAddress accessTbl

User changes
state of display
Access Control   setAccessState

XHostAddress
structure is
updated   updateAddressStruct

XHostAddress
asks table file
for a list of
acceptable
hosts   requestAddrs

Display enables
or disables his
access   setServerAccess

FIGURE 9.

and the actions the object must perform. On the left side of an interaction diagram is the *environment boundary*,[3] which delineates the distinction between the system being developed and the external world.[4]

To develop an interaction diagram, the use-case model and the design model are used in conjunction. For each use case, the design objects implement the required tasks. The required behavior defines the interaction and hence the necessary operations.

Figures 9 and 10 exemplify two interaction diagrams for the cnfgXServer use case. Notice that the single use case is depicted as several diagrams. In exploring the functionality to be provided for the user, it appears that the cnfgXServer use case actually consists of four discrete activities:

1. Setting Access Control.
2. Setting the ability to flush or retain resources on server reset.
3. Setting the backing store threshold.
4. Setting the terminal's visual type.

The interaction diagrams in Figures 9 and 10 are initial depictions of cases 1 and 4. Note that in the process of design, an analysis change has occurred. Having a consistent modeling technique allows the designer to simply return to the use-case model, modify it, and continue designing.

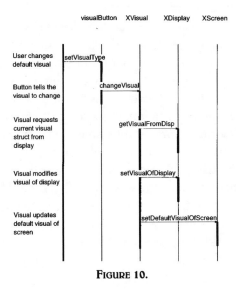

visualButton   XVisual   XDisplay   XScreen

User changes default visual — setVisualType

Button tells the visual to change — changeVisual

Visual requests current visual struct from display — getVisualFromDisp

Visual modifies visual of display — setVisualOfDisplay

Visual updates default visual of screen — setDefaultVisualOfScreen

FIGURE 10.

SERVICES AND ATTRIBUTES

Although it would be far too large a task for the scope of this article to work through an entire design example, the techniques discussed so far should clearly illustrate the process. Once the objects are defined and the developer begins to identify the interactions, all required services can be defined as a by-product of the behavioral analysis. As each use case is considered and the required objects and services are understood, the responsibilities of each object and the necessary methods will continue to become well defined. When the models are complete, all objects and the methods they must encapsulate will have been defined.

Data elements that are associated with only a single object are the object's attributes. In other words, data that is private to an object is an *attribute*, data that requires access and communication from other objects is an *object*.[3]

SUBSYSTEM PARTITIONING

When all the software system's objects have been defined and the system behavior has been distributed among the objects, it is necessary to reevaluate the subsystem partitioning. Early in the development process, an intuitive analysis of the subsystem breakdown may have been considered. In the examples in this article, that task was performed when defining use-case/actor relationships. This early partitioning is primarily for the purpose of creating use-case models with easily understandable levels of granularity. It is based on intuitive pattern analysis but has nothing whatsoever to do with object definitions. Ultimately, this partitioning may or may not be proven correct.

Correct partitioning is the result of exploring (1) which objects exist in contractual relationships, (2) which tasks are closely related, and (3) the object hierarchies and aggregation. It is also possible—and frequently necessary—to model some actors as subsystems. For example, the X Window System terminal interface is actually a subsystem of the *X Terminal* software. The terminal also has an X Server and an operating system. To correctly depict the way these interact, the server and O/S should be modeled as interacting subsystems even though they were represented in the use-case model as actors. This can easily be seen in Figure 11.

The correct partitioning of a system into subsystems is the most important activity in the definition of system architecture. The principle considerations include the following:

1. The organization of users and uses.
2. The way the system is distributed across platforms or processors.
3. The delimitation of privacy.
4. The elimination of circular dependencies.

Ideally, subsystems will represent rational groupings of objects such that actors, naming conventions, and information storage requirements are all considered. In fact, the primary methods for finding subsystems include analyzing naming patterns, grouping of information storage and retrieval activities, and grouping of activities based on actor usage.

When the subsystems have been defined, the system's objects will generally fall very directly into one subsystem or another. The distribution occurs through grouping by functional relationship. There will be a set of objects that do not fall into a single subsystem. These are generally the interface objects. Two strategies may be applied to the distribution of these objects. First, they could be grouped into a single separate subsystem. Second, they could be represented as elements of multiple subsystems. The decision making process is not formal. It simply depends on which representation appears most rational within the global system architecture.

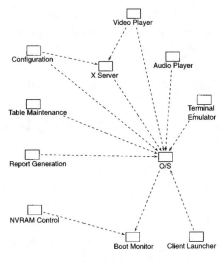

FIGURE 11.

UNDERSTANDING SYSTEM USAGE

To understand the way in which a software system will be used, it is essential that both a set of tasks and a set of design artifacts be available. Traditionally, the tasks are developed by so-called user interface experts in conjunction with domain experts who fully understand the problems being addressed by the software. The design artifacts include such items as simulations, prototypes, design documents, and the system itself.

In the X Terminal configuration client example, some of the tasks include the following: setting the IP address, setting the "Backing Store" remapping, resetting the X Server, maintaining a table of known hosts, making NFS mounts, setting access control for the X server, and saving and restoring settings from nonvolatile RAM. All these are activities that a user or system administrator will accomplish with the client. In a traditional user interface design methodology, a user interface specialist and domain expert would examine the system, a prototype, and/or the design documentation and would derive a list of applicable tasks.

When the interface has been designed with use cases, the interface evaluation will be significantly simplified. Instead of a domain expert's using the system design to derive tasks, the tasks will already exist in the form of use cases. This is not to say the use cases replace the need for user interface analysis and evaluation, but it does imply that those analyses will be extremely simple. It also implies that, unlike most other design techniques, use cases allow usability to be considered from the beginning of system development. After the very first day of development work, the basis for task analysis may be provided to the user interface analyst. This means that user interface specialists can easily work side by side with system architects from the first day of a project.

USE CASE MODELS AS A BASIS FOR USER INTERFACE DEVELOPMENT

There are many techniques in use within the user interface community, for determining the usability of an interface. Among the more interesting of these are *scenarios* and what the Tektronix Labs User Interface Laboratory calls Directed Dialog Methods.[10]

> **TIP**
>
> Scenarios are essentially a way of scripting the activities that will occur.

Scenarios are essentially a way of scripting the activities that will occur in the general use of a product. The goals being to model a product's usage and thus predict usability. Scenarios and scripts are a very mature method for accomplishing these tasks and as a result are in extremely wide use.

Directed Dialog Methods are a subclass of the class of techniques that allow the user to actually use an interface, respond to the usability verbally, and feed the response back into the design. With Directed Dialog, the user is someone who is very familiar with the problem domain is likely to use the interface in a sophisticated manner. The goal of the process involves having the user run the application through a set of typical tasks to determine the systems usability. In this particular case, *usability* is defined as the ability to use, teach, and learn the interface. It's success is based on properly defining the set of tasks to be tested.

Both of the above mentioned activities have extremely strong correlation with use-case modeling. Note that back in Figure 2, the user is the actor most often involved with the system's use cases. As has been proven in several large system developments,[2] these use cases are a profound depiction of system usage. Therefore, it follows that, to a very large extent, use cases should be able to replace scripting and scenarios. In the cases wherein there is not a one-to-one correlation, the use-case models will still enhance and simplify the development of scripts and scenarios. Of even greater interest is that they will prove to be the ideal set of tasks from which to proceed with Directed Dialog usability studies.

These conjectures imply that if one is developing a user-interface intensive system, the concept of use cases not only holds the design together homogeneously, it also provides an ideal foundation for usability testing. Therefore, a use-case-based design provides all the information necessary to ensure usability and ergonomic viability.

FORMALIZING A RIGOROUS DEVELOPMENT PROCESS

Throughout this article, the subject of iteration has been mentioned on numerous occasions. In fact, it is implicitly proposed that an iterative development process is essential to the development of a rigorous design. It has also been explicitly stated that models like the "waterfall" technique are not supportive of iteration due to their formal locking of the initial and terminal points of each phase of development. To support a model of development wherein analyses can be altered due to insights gained in design and design modification can result from programming insights, it is necessary to use a formal process that allows consistent models from activity to activity.

In use-case modeling, activity-to-activity consistency is inherent. Analysis, Design, Implementation, Test, Usability Analysis, and Maintenance are all based on a single unifying entity (the use case). Because of this, it is possible to seamlessly flow from activity to activity with little effort. As a result, it is a simple task to modify an analysis if the developer gains domain insights in the design effort. Designs can be modified in the implementation phase. Even when developing system tests, it is possible to return to analysis if one finds that a modified analysis would assist in maintenance. By utilizing use cases, it is possible to freely flow through all activities in the development effort.

Aside from the uniqueness of the process, free-flowing use-case design also requires a unique modification to the traditional project staffing requirements. In the simple example that has been explored in this article, staffing will be trivial. But, in large scale development efforts, that will not be the case. Although a large project traditionally staffs primarily analysts in the analysis phase, designers in the design phase, programmers in the implementation phase, quality engineers in the testing phase, and user-interface developers in the usability assessment, with use-case modeling, there will be staff members active in many phases simultaneously. There may not be many analysts on a project during testing, but there will be some level of analysis effort—and there will be programmers active even during analysis. The reason for this is simply that activities occur in parallel and must be staffed accordingly. This does not imply an increase in staff (it may well be a *decrease*) but it does imply a fundamental redistribution.

CONCLUSION

Although many object-oriented design techniques are becoming well known in the United States, the country of Sweden has provided the world with a profound, well proven methodology through the 25-year career of Ivar Jacobson. His work has led to a development methodology, called Objectory, which uses the concepts of use cases and actors to create a seamless iterative development process. This process allows the ways in which a system will be used to drive the design of that system.

These techniques have been proven effective is a number of large systems. But, since the American software industry is only now noticing the methodology, there are many applications of the technique that would benefit from more extensive investigation. One of those areas is the application of use-case models to the design and specification of user interfaces. It appears that use cases have the ability to form a strong foundation for this type of work. This article has attempted to prove that point by examining the application of the methodology to an X Terminal configuration client. Although incomplete, the point should certainly be clear.

Acknowledgments

This work could not have existed were it not for the work of my good friend Dr. Ivar Jacobson, who has dedicated his career to the betterment of the technology of object-oriented software. I would also like to thank Rebecca Wirfs-Brock for her support of, and interest in, my work; Sten Jacobson for providing the CASE tools; Patt Bilow for her support and editing; Patrick Jonsson, who reviewed a previous version of this article for its accuracy in representing Objectory; and The X Consortium Inc., who supported and published a previous article on this work as part of the 8th X Technical Conference. This work was informally supported by Objective Systems SF AB, KISTA, Sweden, who provided the CASE tools from which the models and supporting illustrations were derived; and Tektronix, Inc., Wilsonville, Oregon, who provided the X Terminals and the funding.

References

1. Jacobson, I., M. Christerson, P. Jonsson, and G. Overgaard, OBJECT-ORIENTED SOFTWARE ENGINEERING: A USE-CASE DRIVEN APPROACH, ACM Press/Addison-Wesley, Reading, MA, 1992.

2. Jacobson, I., Object-oriented development in an industrial environment, OOPSLA '87, Orlando, FL.

3. Objective Systems SF AB, OBJECTORY ANALYSIS AND DESIGN 3.2: PROCESS GUIDE.

4 Jacobson, I. Object-oriented software engineering—A use case driven approach, OOPSLA '93 (Tutorial Notes), Washington, DC.

5. Jacobson, I. Industrial development of software with an object-oriented technique, JOURNAL OF OBJECT-ORIENTED PROGRAMMING, Mar/Apr., 1991.

6. Yourdon, E. MODERN STRUCTURED ANALYSIS, Prentice Hall, Englewood Cliffs, NJ, 1989.

7. Bilow, S. User driven user interfaces, THE X JOURNAL, Mar/Apr. 1993.

8. Private communication from Patrik Jonsson, December 1993.

9. Private conversation with S. Bilow and Ivar Jacobson, September 1993.

10. Lynch, G. et al. TEKTRONIX LOOK AND FEEL DESIGN GUIDELINES, Standard 80009, Tektronix Inc., June 1991.

11. Objective Systems SF AB, OBJECTORY ANALYSIS AND DESIGN 3.2: TOOL GUIDE.

12. Rumbaugh, J., M. Blaha, W. Premerlani, F. Eddy, and W. Lorenson. OBJECT-ORIENTED MODELING AND DESIGN, Prentice Hall, Englewood Cliffs, NJ, 1991.

13. Objective Systems SF AB, OBJECTORY ANALYSIS AND DESIGN 3.2: TOOL GUIDE.

USE CASES: THE PROS AND CONS

Donald G. Firesmith

O VER THE LAST THREE YEARS, USE CASES HAVE BECOME WELL ESTABLISHED AS one of the fundamental techniques of object-oriented analysis (OOA). Although they were introduced by Ivar Jacobson to the object community at the 1987 OOPSLA conference,[1] it was the publication of his book OBJECT-ORIENTED SOFTWARE ENGINEERING: A USE CASE DRIVEN APPROACH[2] in 1992 that marked the true beginning of use cases' meteoric rise in popularity. Possibly in reaction to the previous structured methods, early object-oriented (OO) development methods overemphasized static architecture and partially ignored dynamic behavior issues during requirements analysis, especially above the individual class level where state modeling provides an important technique for dynamic behavior specification. Use cases provide a great many benefits in addition to correcting this overemphasis, and designers of most major OO development methods (including my own) have jumped on the bandwagon and added use cases during the last few years. In the resulting hoopla and hype, however, there has been little discussion of the limitations and potential pitfalls associated with use cases. In this column I attempt to provide a more balanced presentation and to caution against the uncritical acceptance of use cases as the latest patent medicine for all software ailments.

DEFINITIONS

The term *use case* was introduced by Ivar Jacobson et al.[1] and has been defined.[2–4] A use case is a description of a cohesive set of possible dialogues (i.e., series* of interactions) that an individual actor initiates with a system.

---

*A use case typically involves branching or looping and may depend on the state of the system and any parameters of the interactions between actors and the system.

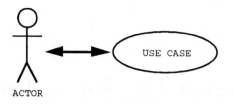

FIGURE 1. *The primary use case notations.*

An actor is a role played by a user (i.e., an external entity that interacts directly with the system) (Figure 1). A use case is thus a general way of using some part of the functionality of a system.

> **TIP**
>
> A use case is not a single scenario.

A use case is not a single scenario but rather a "class" that specifies a set of related usage scenarios, each of which captures a specific course of interactions that take place between one or more actors and the system. Therefore, the description of an individual use case typically can be divided into a *basic course* and zero or more *alternative courses*. The basic course of a use case is the most common or important sequence of transactions that satisfy the use case. The basic course is therefore always developed first. The alternative courses are variants of the basic course and are often used to identify error handling. Within reason, the more alternative courses identified and described, the more complete the description of the use case and the more robust the resulting system.

As a user-centered analysis technique, the purpose of a use case is to yield a result of measurable value to an actor in response to the initial request of that actor. A use case may involve multiple actors, but only a single actor initiates the use case. Because actors are beyond the scope of the system, use-case modeling ignores direct interactions between actors.

A use case may be an *abstract use case* or a *concrete use case*. An abstract use case will not be instantiated on its own but is only meaningful when used to describe functionality that is common between other use cases. On the other hand, a concrete use case can be instantiated to create a specific scenario.

According to Ivar Jacobson, use cases are related by two main associations: *extends* and *uses*. The extend association specifies how one use-case description inserts itself into, and thus extends, a second use-case description that is completely independent and ignorant of the first use case. Depending on some condition, the second use case may be performed either with or with-

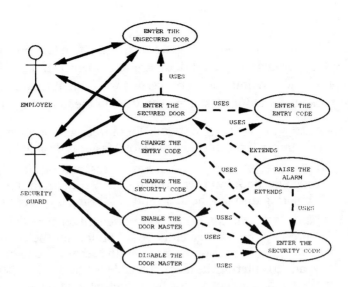

FIGURE 2. *An example use-case model.*

out the extending use case. Extends can therefore be viewed as a kind of "inheritance" between use cases in which the original use case definition is extended by the extending use case description to form a new "combined" use case. On the other hand, the uses association can be viewed as a kind of "delegation" or "aggregation"

> **TIP**
>
> Extends are a kind of "inheritance."

that captures how one or more use-case descriptions incorporate the common description of another use case. These two associations are closely related and easy to confuse. One clue as to which is which is that if A extends B, then the extended B "contains" A, whereas if A uses B, then A "calls" B. The actual distinction between these two associations is unclear, and Rumbaugh[4] has thankfully combined them into a single *adds* association from the main concrete use case to the abstract use cases that it uses.

Clearly, use cases are functional abstractions and are thus large operations, the implementations of which thread through multiple objects and classes. However, a use case need not have anything to do with objects. As pointed out by Jacobson,[5] "it should be clear that use-case modeling is a technique that is quite independent of object modeling. Use-case modeling can be applied to any methodology—structured or object-oriented. It is a discipline of its own, orthogonal to object modeling."

AN EXAMPLE

The requirements for Door Master, a security system for controlling entry of employees through a secured door, are documented in a ROAD column.[6] Except for those requirements concerned with initialization, the functional requirements for Door Master are captured in the following nine use cases:

1. ENTER_THE_DISABLED_DOOR: Employees and security guards enter freely through the door when Door Master is disabled.

2. ENTER_THE_SECURED_DOOR: Employees and security guards enter through the door by (1) entering the entry code on the numeric keypad, (2) entering through the door, and (3) closing the door behind them.

3. CHANGE_THE_ENTRY_CODE: Security guards change the entry code by (1) pressing the "change entry code" button on the control panel, (2) providing authorization by entering the security code on the numeric keypad, (3) entering the new entry code on the numeric keypad, and (4) verifying the new entry code by reentering it on the numeric keypad.

4. CHANGE_THE_SECURITY_CODE: Security guards change the security code by (1) pressing the "change security code" button on the control panel, (2) providing authorization by entering the old security code on the numeric keypad, (3) entering the new security code on the numeric keypad, and (4) verifying the new security code by reentering it on the numeric keypad.

5. ENABLE_THE_DOOR_MASTER: Security guards enable Door Master by (1) pressing the "enable" button on the control panel and (2) providing authorization by entering the security code on the numeric keypad. Door Master then (3) turns off the disabled light, (4) turns on the enabled light, and (5) locks the door.

6. DISABLE_THE_DOOR_MASTER: Security guards disable Door Master by (1) pressing the "disable" button on the control panel and (2) providing authorization by entering the security code on the numeric keypad. Door Master then (3) turns off the enabled light, (4) turns on the disabled light, and (5) unlocks the door.

The following two abstract use cases are common to, and are therefore used by, five of the concrete use cases:

7. ENTER_THE_ENTRY_CODE: Employees and security guards enter the entry code by pressing five keys on the numeric keypad followed by the "enter" key. Door Master beeps after each key and verifies the entry code.

8. ENTER_THE_SECURITY_CODE: Employees and security guards enter

the entry code by pressing seven keys on the numeric keypad followed by the "enter" key. Door Master beeps after each key and verifies the entry code.

The following abstract use case extends the ENABLE_THE_DOOR_MASTER and ENTER_THE_SECURED_DOOR use cases:

9. RAISE_THE_ALARM: The alarm is raised if the door is left open too long or if the door is not shut when Door Master is enabled. The security guards disable the alarm by entering the security code.

THE BENEFITS OF USE CASES

Use cases have become extremely popular since the publication of OBJECT-ORIENTED SOFTWARE ENGINEERING: A USE CASE DRIVEN APPROACH in 1992. They have been added to numerous OO development methods (e.g., Booch, Firesmith, Rumbaugh) because they offer many important advantages, including the following:

- As a user-centered technique, use cases help ensure that the correct system is developed by capturing the requirements from the user's point of view.

- Use cases are a powerful technique for the elicitation and documentation of *blackbox functional* requirements.

- Because they are written in natural language, use cases are easy to understand and provide an excellent way for communicating with customers and users. Although computer-aided software engineering (CASE) tools are useful for drawing the corresponding interaction diagrams, use cases themselves *require* remarkably little tool support.

- Use cases can help manage the complexity of large projects by decomposing the problem into major functions (i.e., use cases) and by specifying applications from the users' perspective.

- Because they typically involve the collaboration of multiple objects and classes, use cases help provide the rationale for the messages that glue the objects and classes together. Use cases also provide an alternative to the *overemphasis* of traditional OO development methods on such static architecture issues as inheritance and the identification of objects and classes.

- Use cases have emphasized the use of lower-level scenarios, thereby indirectly supporting Booch's important concept of a *mechanism*, a kind of pattern that captures how "objects collaborate to provide some behavior that satisfies a requirement of the problem."[7]

- Use cases provide a good basis for the verification of the higher-level models (via role-playing) and for the validation of the functional requirements (via acceptance testing).*

- Use cases provide an objective means of project-tracking in which earned value can be defined in terms of use cases implemented, tested, and delivered.

- Use cases can form the foundation on which to specify end-to-end timing requirements for real-time applications.

THE DANGERS OF MISUSING USE CASES

Because of their many important advantages and extreme popularity, use cases have become a fundamental part of object technology and have been incorporated in one form or another into most major OO development methods. In the rush to jump onto the use-case bandwagon, use cases have been perceived by some as either a panacea or as an end in and of themselves. Unfortunately, this has often led to the uncritical acceptance of use cases without any examination of their numerous limitations and ample opportunities they offer for misuse. The following provides an overview of the major risks associated with use cases:

- Use cases are *not* object oriented. Each use case captures a major functional abstraction that can cause the numerous problems with functional decomposition that object technology was to avoid. These problems include:

- The functional nature of use cases naturally leads to the functional decomposition of a system in terms of concrete and abstract use cases that are related by extends and uses associations. Each individual use case involves different features of multiple objects and classes, and each individual object or class is often involved in the implementation of multiple use cases. Therefore, any decomposition based on use cases scatters the features of the objects and classes among the individual use cases. On large projects, different use cases are often assigned to different teams of developers or to different builds and releases. Because the use cases do not map one-to-one to the objects and classes, these teams

---

*Because a use case (class) is not as specific as a usage scenario (instance), use cases may lack sufficient formality and detail to supply adequate criteria for the passing of acceptance tests.

can easily design and code multiple, redundant, partial variants of the same classes, producing a corresponding decrease in productivity, reuse, and maintainability. This scattering of objects to use cases leads to the Humpty Dumpty effect, in which all the king's designers and all the king's coders are unlikely to put the objects and classes back together again without a massive expenditure of time and effort.

TIP
Note the Humpty Dumpty effect.

- The use-case model and the object model belong to different paradigms (i.e., functional and OO) and therefore use different concepts, terminology, techniques, and notations. The simple structure of the use-case model does not clearly map to the network structure of the object model with its collaborating objects and classes. The requirements trace from the use cases to the objects and classes is also not one-to-one. These mappings are informal and somewhat arbitrary, providing little guidance to the designer as to the identification of objects, classes, and their interactions. The situation is clearly reminiscent of the large semantic gap that existed between the data flow diagrams (network) of structured analysis and the structure charts (hierarchy) of structured design. The use of the single object paradigm was supposed to avoid this problem.

TIP
The use-case model and the object model belong to different paradigms.

- Another potential problem with use case modeling is knowing when to stop. When one is building a nontrivial application, there are often a great number of use cases that can produce an essentially infinite number of usage scenarios, especially with today's graphical user interfaces and event-driven systems. How many use cases are required to adequately specify a nontrivial, real-world application? As object technology is applied to ever increasingly complex projects, the simple examples and techniques of the textbooks often have trouble scaling up. The use of concurrency and distributed architectures often means that the order of the interactions between the system and its environment is potentially infinite. Too few use cases result in an inadequate specification, while too many use cases lead to functional decomposition and the scattering of objects and classes to the four winds. Often, systems and software engineers must limit their analysis to the most obvious or important scenarios and hope that their analysis generalizes to all use cases.

- Although use cases are functional abstractions, use-case modeling typically does not yet apply all of the traditional techniques that are useful for analyzing and designing functional abstractions. Most current techniques do not easily handle the existence of branches and loops in the logic of a use case. Interaction diagrams are primarily oriented towards a simple, linear sequence of interactions between the actors and the major classes of the system. The use of abstract use cases and either extends or uses associations to solve this problem only exacerbates the functional decomposition problem. Some approach similar to that of the basis paths of structured testing would clearly help determine the adequacy of the use case model, but such an approach is not yet available to the typical developer. Most techniques do not address the issues of concurrency and the different types of messages that result. As illustrated in Rumbaugh[4] and Firesmith,[6] the concepts of preconditions, postconditions, invariants, and triggers should also be added to better analyze and specify use cases.

- Since they are created at the highest level of abstraction before objects and classes have been identified, use cases ignore the encapsulation of attributes and operations into objects. Use cases therefore typically ignore issues of state modeling that clearly impact the applicability of some use cases. Any required ordering of use cases is ignored and should be captured using some variation of Firesmith's scenario lifecycle[6] or Fusion's event lifecycle.[8] The basic ideas and techniques of use cases should also be applied to Booch mechanisms[7] and integration testing, but adequate extensions have yet to be published.

- Another major problem with use-case modeling is the lack of formality in the definitions of the terms *use case*, *actor*, *extends*, and *uses*. Similarly, the specification of individual use cases in natural languages such as English provides ample room for miscommunication and misunderstandings. Use cases provide a much less formal specification of their instances (i.e., individual usage scenarios) than do classes of objects. Whereas the inheritance relationship between classes of objects is well defined and has been automated by compilers, the inheritance and delegation relationships provided by extends and uses associations are much less well defined. While everything may seem clear at the highest level of abstraction, the translation of use cases into design and code at lower levels of abstraction is based on informal human understanding of what must be done. This also causes problems when it comes to using use cases for the specification of acceptance tests because the criteria for passing those tests may not be adequately defined.

- Another major problem is the archetypal subsystem architecture that can result from blindly using use cases. Several examples in books and papers have consisted of a single functional control object representing the logic of an individual use case and several dumb entity objects controlled by the controller object. They also may have included an interface object for each actor involved with the use case. Such an architecture typically exhibits poor encapsulation, excessive coupling, and an inadequate distribution of the intelligence of the application among the classes. Such architectures are less maintainable than more object-oriented architectures.

- Use cases are defined in terms of interactions between one or more actors and the system to be developed. However, all systems do not have actors, and systems may include signification functionality that is not a reaction to an actor's input. Embedded systems may perform major control functions without significant user input. Concurrent objects and classes need not passively wait for incoming messages to react. They may instead proactively make decisions based on results derived from polling terminators. Traditional use-case modeling seems less appropriate for such applications.

- Finally, the use of use cases as the foundation of incremental development and project tracking has its limitations. Basing increments on functional use cases threatens to cause the same problems with basing builds on major system functions. Instead of building complete classes, developers will tend to create partial variants that require more iteration from build to build than is necessary. In turn, this will unnecessarily increase the maintenance costs of inheritance hierarchies. Basing earned value on the number of use cases implemented may be misleading because all use cases may not be of equal value to the user and because of the previously mentioned problems due to functional decomposition and the scattering of partial variant objects and classes among use cases.

CONCLUSION

What, then, should developers do? Use cases clearly offer many important benefits and are powerful weapons that probably should be in the arsenal of all software analysts, designers, and testers. Unfortunately, however, they are functional rather than object-oriented and can significantly compromise the benefits of object technology if blindly added to the OO development process. Fortunately, the risks associated with use-case modeling can be mitigated through knowledge, training, and avoiding an overenthusiastic acceptance. Use cases should be only one of several ways of capturing user requirements. Models of objects, classes, and their semantic relationships should be consistent with, but not totally driven by, the use cases. Designers should beware of and minimize scattering the features of a use case's objects and classes, and they should exercise great care to avoid the creation of partial, redundant variants of classes, especially on large projects involving multiple builds and releases. The architectural guidelines of Rebecca Wirfs-Brock[9] should be followed to avoid creating excessive functional controller objects that dictate the behavior of dumb entity objects. Most importantly, use cases should not be used as an excuse to revert to the bad old days of functional decomposition and functionally decomposed requirements specifications.

References

1. Jacobson, I. Object-oriented development in an industrial environment, SIGPLAN NOTICES 22(12):183–191.

2. Jacobson, I., M. Christersson, P. Jonsson, and G. Overgaard. OBJECT-ORIENTED SOFTWARE ENGINEERING: A USE CASE DRIVEN APPROACH, Addison-Wesley, Wokingham, UK, 1992.

3. Jacobson, I., M. Ericsson, and A. Jacobson. THE OBJECT ADVANTAGE: BUSINESS PROCESS RE-ENGINEERING WITH OBJECT TECHNOLOGY, Addison-Wesley, Wokingham, UK, 1995.

4. Rumbaugh, J. Getting started: Using use cases to capture requirements, JOURNAL OF OBJECT-ORIENTED PROGRAMMING 7(5):8–12, 1994.

5. Jacobson, I. Basic use-case modeling (continued), REPORT ON OBJECT-ORIENTED ANALYSIS AND DESIGN 1(3):7–9, 1994.

6. Firesmith, D. Modeling the dynamic behavior of systems, mechanisms, and classes with scenarios, REPORT ON OBJECT-ORIENTED ANALYSIS AND DESIGN 1(2):32–36, 1994.

7. Booch, G. OBJECT-ORIENTED ANALYSIS AND DESIGN WITH APPLICATIONS, Benjamin/Cummings, Redwood City, CA, 1994.

8. Coleman, D., et al. OBJECT-ORIENTED DEVELOPMENT: THE FUSION METHOD, Prentice Hall, Englewood Cliffs, NJ, 1994.

9. Wirfs-Brock, R., B. Wilkerson, and L. Wiener. DESIGNING OBJECT-ORIENTED SOFTWARE, Prentice Hall, Englewood Cliffs, NJ, 1990.

FORMALIZING THE OUTPUT

NANCY M. WILKINSON

T HE OBJECT-ORIENTED (OO) REVOLUTION HAS ITS ROOTS IN THE PROGRAMMING community, where it remained for many years. Only in the mid-1980s did the use of formal methods for analysis and design move into the OO arena. One reason for this is that prior to that time, the OO approach was used mostly for small to medium-sized applications, where formal methods have less impact. Many projects today continue to find informal techniques preferable, and CRC cards support these projects well. When the interest in OO technology moved to organizations that had used formal structured methods in the past, such as for government or defense work, OO methods began to emerge. Methods have also become popular among groups who are new to an OO approach and who believe that formal methods will facilitate their move to the new paradigm, even if they never used formal structured methods in the past.

Many projects use informal techniques, CRC cards in particular, as a prelude to their use of formal methods and notations. Even for projects where size, sociology, or organization dictates the use of formal methods, preceding these methods with CRC cards can provide leverage along two dimensions. First, the brainstorming process that is inherent in the CRC card technique

> **TIP**
>
> Note the advantages of using informal techniques.

provides advantages to a project with a more formal bent as well. Use of the cards gets the important people together in a room, forcing joint decisions and encouraging the airing of concerns in a group setting. And using CRC card sessions to generate input allows a team to get a feel for the problem, and for objects, before having to learn and use a particular notation and tool.

Second, the information gathered in sessions and stored on the cards can be the initial basis for representing a system using a formal methodology. This use of CRC card–generated information in the formal modeling of an application is the focus of future articles.

KINDS OF METHODS

Formal methodologies and notations can generally be classified as either responsibility-driven or data-driven, depending on whether they stress behavior or data for analysis and design. Responsibility-driven approaches concentrate on class behavior to describe the what and how of a system. They view data as the support for what the classes do. Examples of responsibility-driven methods include Wirfs-Brock's responsibility-driven design (RDD),[1] Booch,[2] and Jacobson's object-oriented software engineering (OOSE).[3] Data-driven approaches concentrate primarily on the data members of classes to analyze and design the application being built. Behavior in these approaches is secondary. Examples of data-driven methods are Shlaer-Mellor[4,5] and Rumbaugh's OMT.[6] CRC card output flows more naturally into notations for responsibility-driven designs, but it can be useful as input to data-driven models as well.

The methodologies described here are just a few of the almost 30 published methods for object-oriented analysis and design (OOA/OOD). They serve as a sampling of examples of how CRC cards can provide input to different types of formal methods. The descriptions of the methodologies are cursory at best, omitting many of the details. For example, most methodologies suggest a process for OOA/OOD that we do not address, concentrating instead on the notational deliverables of the method. In particular, the emphasis is on types of deliverables that can benefit most from the input of CRC cards.

WIRFS-BROCK

The Method

Rebecca Wirfs-Brock is the inventor of RDD. The Wirfs-Brock methodology suggests two phases: a preliminary design phase and a final design phase. RDD is billed as a design methodology but incorporates analysis as a part of the preliminary design. The initial design phase is supported by the use of class cards. Each class card lists a class name, along with its responsibilities and collaborators. The cards are created and enhanced through walk-throughs of system scenarios.

The output of the preliminary design phase is then analyzed and refined to create the final design. This design is documented with a set of diagrams. Superclass and subclass relationships among classes are described in hierarchy graphs. Collaboration graphs describe the interactions of classes, compiled from the collaborations on the class cards. The responsibilities of each class are grouped into contracts, and the classes are grouped into subsystems to help simplify the collaboration graphs. A small subset of a collaboration graph for a Checkbook application is shown in Figure 1.

The semicircle numbered 1 in the graph refers to Checkbook's contract #1, perhaps called Balance and consisting of the *balance* responsibility. To fulfill this responsibility, Checkbook collaborates with Entry via Entry's contracts #3 and #4. We name contract #3 Know Contents, which is a grouping of Entry's *know entry number* and *know cleared status* responsibilities. Checkbook also needs contract #4, called Adjust Balance, as it consists simply of the *adjust balance* responsibility. To balance itself, Checkbook will also need its own contract #2, called Manage Entries, consisting of its *add entry* and *search entries* responsibilities. The boxes within the Entry box imply that Withdrawal Entry and Deposit Entry are subclasses of Entry.

RDD also includes *class descriptions*, textual supplements to the model that describe each class. They list the contracts along with the constituent operations and their signatures.

CRC Cards as Input

Responsibility-driven design is probably the most natural formal method to use as an extension to the CRC card technique. The RDD class card is virtually identical to a CRC card as we have described it. This is not a coincidence. Wirfs-Brock and Brian Wilkerson were at Tektronix when Ward Cunningham first proposed the CRC idea. They did much of the early enhancements and modifications to make the cards more usable for teaching OOD. The card I have described in these columns reflects the Wirfs-Brock evolution of the original Beck and Cunningham CRC card. Therefore, the output of CRC cards sessions is the Wirfs-Brock preliminary design model.

The cards, responsibilities, collaborations, and superclass/subclass relationships identified in the sessions provide input to the second phase of RDD design. Modifications made to the RDD model during this second

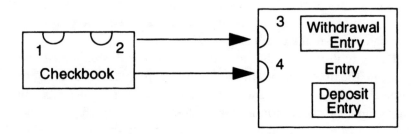

FIGURE 1. *Classes in a Wirfs-Brock collaboration graph.*

phase are done both offline and in the group and should be fed back into the CRC cards for further sessions. Hierarchies formulated in the sessions are the basis for the RDD inheritance graphs. Collaboration graphs are derived by looking at the set of collaborations written on the cards, grouping the collaborating responsibilities to identify contracts, and then representing the information graphically.

BOOCH

The Method

Grady Booch's methodology for analysis and design also concentrates on behavior, but his method includes a larger set of models and diagrams than RDD. The two main diagrams of the methodology, the *class diagram* and the *object diagram*, show relationships among classes and objects, respectively. The relationships in the class diagram are annotated to show the multiplicity of the relationship, and the form of the links denotes the type of relationship. The relationships in the object diagram are labeled with the names of messages sent between the objects and can be annotated to reflect more details of the collaboration. A small class diagram and its corresponding object diagram for the Checkbook application are shown in Figure 2.

> **TIP**
>
> Relationships in the class diagram are annotated to show the multiplicity of the relationship.

Classes in the class diagram are represented as dotted "clouds." * The

---

*Note that the clouds are not reproduced exactly here. I suspect that the difficulty of doing so inspired their choice as an icon.

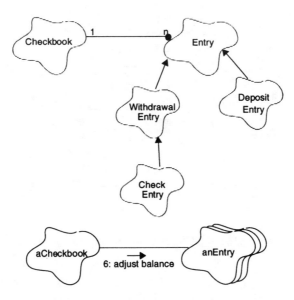

FIGURE 2. *Booch class and object diagrams.*

arrows denote inheritance, and the line shows a one-to-many *has-a* relationship between `Checkbook` and `Entry`. The corresponding object diagram solidifies the lines of the clouds as they become instantiated to reflect the objects in the model. The arrow shows the direction of the message passing and the link is labeled by the name of the message being passed, prefixed by the order of the message in the fulfillment of the scenario.

Booch's methodology also includes models such as *state transition diagrams, timing diagrams, process diagrams,* and *module diagrams.* Textual supplements include the *class template* and the *operation template.* The methodology provides a rich set of notations from which projects pick and choose as appropriate.

CRC Cards as Input

CRC cards can provide input to Booch diagrams at every phase of the lifecycle to document the emerging problem model and design. Where CRC card input will be most directly useful is in formation of the class diagram and the object diagram. The information contained in these diagrams can be derived by looking at is/the patterns of collaboration among the cards.

The set of cards on the table can provide static information for the class

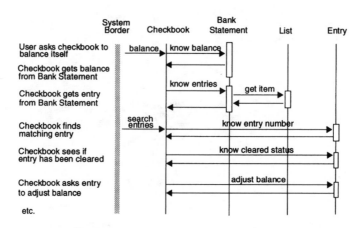

FIGURE 3. *Partial OOSE interaction diagram for balance use case.*

model. Some extra thought needs to be given to the multiplicity of the relationships, but this should not be difficult for people who have been involved in the CRC card sessions. Object model input can be derived by exercising the model with the various scenarios.

JACOBSON

The Method

Ivar Jacobson is the author of a methodology called OOSE. Developing an OO application with OOSE involves building a series of models from analysis through implementation. At the core of each of these models is the notion of a use case. Use cases are statements that begin "when . . ." and describe uses of the system. Use cases drive the analysis by providing descriptions of what the system does and the design by providing descriptions of how it does it. Use cases can be extended and arranged in hierarchies. They are documented in interaction diagrams as a series of interactions among objects. A simple use case description for the Checkbook application is shown in Figure 3 (I added a List class to hold Bank Statement's Entrys to make the interactions more interesting).

> **TIP**
>
> Use cases are statements that begin "when. . ."

Steps taken in the fulfillment of the use case are listed on the left. Classes of objects that will participate in this use case are represented in the chart as vertical lines from left to right. Arrows represent interactions of objects that must take place to complete each step. The arrows are labeled with the messages that are sent between the objects, where the message name is the responsibility of the object pointed to.

OOSE is unique among software methodologies in that it concentrates less on formal notations than most. It also stresses the need for many different models for different purposes, such as interacting with customers, designers, testers and maintainers. The accompanying software process is presented in process descriptions that focus on how the product changes throughout the lifecycle. Most important to the methodology is, of course, the notion of stressing uses of the system to build reusable and adaptable applications. Use cases have been so well received that other methodologists have begun to incorporate them in their methods and notations. For example, the latest version of Booch's method includes "scripts" and object interaction diagrams.

CRC Cards as Input

The CRC card technique maps very nicely to a formal method driven by use cases. Use cases are essentially the scenarios we use during CRC card sessions. Scenarios ask the question "what happens when . . ." How the scenarios are accomplished in the model describes the use cases. Scenario walk throughs describe object interactions in a way that can be input directly to Jacobson's documentation of use cases. As seen in Figure 3, the parts of the use case are essentially the subtasks that have been considered in the CRC card session and the labels on the interaction arrows are simply the responsibilities assigned to that object to carry out various subtasks. Since scenario descriptions are an important part of describing a CRC card model, even projects that choose not to use a formal method may decide to use the Jacobson use case diagram as part of their documentation.

References

1. Wirfs-Brock, R., B. Wilkerson, and L. Wiener. DESIGNING OBJECT-ORIENTED SOFTWARE, Prentice-Hall, Englewood Cliffs, NJ, 1990.

2. Booch, G. OBJECT-ORIENTED ANALYSIS AND DESIGN WITH APPLICATIONS, 2nd ed., Benjamin-Cummings, Redwood City, CA, 1993.

3. Jacobson, I., M. Christersson, P. Jonsson, and G. Overgaard. OBJECT-ORIENTED SOFTWARE ENGINEERING, Addison-Wesley, Reading, MA, 1992.

4. Shlaer, S. and S. Mellor. OBJECT-ORIENTED SYSTEMS ANALYSIS: MODELING THE WORLD IN OBJECTS, Yourdon Press, Englewood Cliffs, NJ, 1988.

5. Shlaer, S. and S. Mellor. OBJECT LIFECYCLES: MODELING THE WORLD IN STATES, Yourdon Press, Englewood Cliffs, NJ, 1992.

6. Rumbaugh, J., et al. OBJECT-ORIENTED MODELING AND DESIGN, Prentice-Hall, Englewood Cliffs, NJ, 1991.

FORMALIZING THE OUTPUT, PART 2

NANCY M. WILKINSON

M ETHODOLOGIES, ALONG WITH THEIR ASSOCIATED NOTATIONS AND TOOLS, provide a way for projects to formalize the process and the products of software construction. In the last column we discussed how some projects use informal techniques, CRC cards in particular, as a prelude to their use of formal methods and notations. The brainstorming process inherent in the CRC card technique brings the right people together around a table, forcing joint decisions and encouraging the airing of concerns in a group setting. More importantly, using CRC card sessions to generate input allows a team to get a feel for the problem, and for objects, before having to learn and use a particular notation and tool.

Formal methodologies can generally be classified as either responsibility-driven or data-driven, depending on whether they stress behavior or data for analysis and design. Responsibility-driven approaches concentrate on class behavior to describe the what and how of a system. They view data as the support for what the classes do. Data-driven approaches concentrate primarily on the data members of classes to analyze and design the application being built. Behavior in these approaches is secondary. Last time we described how the information gathered in CRC sessions and stored on the cards can be the initial basis for representing a system using a responsibility-driven formal methodology, e.g., Wirfs-Brock's responsibility-driven design (RDD),[1] Booch,[2] and Jacobson's OOSE.[3] Since CRC cards are a responsibility-driven technique, it is a fairly straightforward process to populate responsibility-driven models with the class, responsibility, and collaborator information derived from the cards.

The use of CRC card–generated information as a prelude to the use of data-driven formal methods, e.g., Shlaer/Mellor[4,5] and Rumbaugh's object modeling technique (OMT),[6] is less straightforward. Although the output of CRC cards does not flow as naturally into data-driven notations, information about responsibilities and collaborations can contribute greatly to the behavioral aspect of the model, which is secondary in these methods.

Caveat

Remember that the methodologies described here are just a few of the almost 30 published methods for object-oriented analysis and design (OOA/D). They serve as a sampling of examples of how CRC cards can provide input to different types of formal methods. The descriptions of the methodologies are cursory at best, omitting many of the details. In particular, the emphasis is on types of deliverables that can benefit most from the input of CRC cards.

Shlaer/Mellor

The Method

> **TIP**
>
> The information model is an extended entity-relationship diagram.

The Shlaer/Mellor analysis methodology relies mainly on three types of models to describe a problem. The *information model* is an extended entity-relationship diagram, where each object is described as a relational database table, complete with database keys. Relationships between objects are numbered, labeled with names in English text, and formalized using the keys. The objects in this model contain only data; no operations are mentioned at this stage. A subset of an information model for the Checkbook application is shown in Figure 1.

Attributes with asterisks preceding them are keys, which are used in the corresponding object to formalize relationships (note the relationship number after certain attributes). All relationships are bidirectional and labeled in both directions. The multiplicity of the relationship is indicated by the number of arrows at each end. Inheritance is indicated with the *is-a* label and is based solely on data.

Textual supplements at this stage of the analysis are object and attribute descriptions and relationship descriptions. Behavior is dealt with in the *state model* and *process model* stages, where state diagrams of each object are drawn and operations are described via data flow diagrams (DFDs).

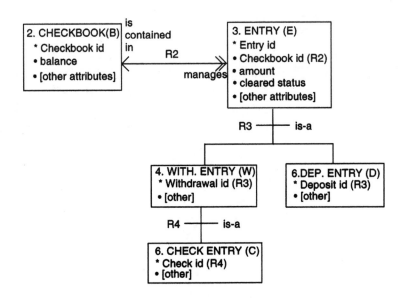

FIGURE 1. *Objects in a Shlaer/Mellor information model.*

CRC CARDS AS INPUT

The identification of the classes in a CRC card session can help build a framework for the Shlaer/Mellor information model, and the attributes from the back of the cards and *know* responsibilities can be used as starting points for determining the data for each object. The relationship names, in some cases, can be determined by looking at the overall patterns of collaborations of classes. For example, Checkbook "manages" Entries can be derived from Checkbook's responsibilities to add entry, delete entry, and search entries. In other cases, naming the relationship entails making explicit the implicit, real-world relationships that have been assumed in the sessions, e.g., Entries "are contained in" the Checkbook.

Some groups (those most comfortable with a data-driven description of a problem) like to build a Shlaer/Mellor information model first, then use CRC card sessions to add behavior to the model. Whether the CRC card sessions are done before or after the structure of the objects is determined, they provide essential information about how things get done.

CRC card responsibilities are used as input to the Shlaer/Mellor process models because they directly provide the operations to be modeled. More importantly, CRC card collaborations provide some necessary up-front information about the interactions of objects. In the Shlaer/Mellor method, the state models for each object are created, then are combined to create the object communication model (OCM). The OCM is a picture of how all objects communicate (the events sent among objects) and is similar (at a high level) to Wirfs-Brock's collaboration graph or the Booch class diagram. But a state diagram for an object is very difficult to construct without first having some idea of how that object communicates with other objects. A "preliminary" OCM must be constructed before these state models are built; and the model constructed as a result of CRC card sessions can be used as the preliminary OCM. Finally, since the Shlaer/Mellor method models superclass/subclass relationships based only on data, hierarchies based solely on behavior may be missed. CRC cards can be used to discover and create inheritance relationships based on behavior.

RUMBAUGH

The Method

James Rumbaugh's methodology, OMT, is similar to Shlaer/Mellor at a high level, but is meant for both analysis and design. The three main models of OMT capture information along the same dimensions as those in the Shlaer/Mellor method. The *object model* is similar to Shlaer/Mellor's information model but does not have the preoccupation with relational database tables and database keys. The classes in the object model also include operations as an inherent part. Various diagrams, such as the *class diagram*, where class relationships are described, and the *instance diagram*, where object relationships are documented, are parts of the object model. A subset of a Rumbaugh class diagram is shown in Figure 2.

In this class diagram, each class is modeled as a rectangle with three components: the class name, the class attributes, and the class operations. The relationship between classes, such as `Checkbook` and `Entry`, is called an association. It is described with English text above the line. The fact that it is a one-to-many relationship is indicated by the solid circle at the end of the `Entry` side of the link. Note also that the superclass/subclass relationship here is based on operations as well as data.

OMT also includes a *dynamic model*, which is a set of state diagrams for each

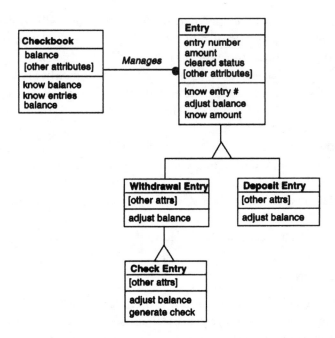

FIGURE 2. *Classes in a Rumbaugh class diagram.*

object, and a *functional model*, where DFDs describe the workings of operations. The set of relationships that can be modeled with OMT is very rich, even if you stick to the basic concepts of associations, aggregations, and generalization (inheritance). Advanced concepts include notions such as overlapping inheritance, constraints on associations, and propagation of operations. Many different flavors of diagrams can be built. They must be chosen as appropriate and consistency must be maintained between them.

> **TIP**
>
> The set of relationships that can be modeled with OMT is very rich.

CRC Cards as Input

CRC cards can provide input to the OMT method, mostly through the discovery of classes and class operations, and class interactions. Any attributes or *know* responsibilities noted during the sessions can contribute to a description of the data in the OMT class diagram as well. Names and multiplicity of relationships can be discovered in sessions and input to OMT much as they are to the Shlaer/Mellor information model. Pattern of collaborations can provide clues to good names, or a name may be the description of the real-world relationship that was assumed during the CRC card sessions. The multiplicity of relationships is evident from the number of objects which participated in the fulfillment of scenarios. The OMT instance diagram, where object interactions are documented, can be generated by recording object collaborations during the execution of scenarios. The responsibilities on the card are used to form the operations for the classes. The operations can more easily be described in the process models by people who have participated in CRC card sessions, since the execution of scenarios helps them to better understand the processing that takes place. And the construction of state models (as in Shlaer/Mellor) is aided by understanding the patterns of collaboration among classes. As CRC card sessions continue into design and the model matures, the progressive design detail can be added to the OMT models.

CONCLUSION

No matter which formal method a project team chooses, CRC cards and sessions can complement the process that uses them. Responsibility-driven methods are more natural choices as a documentation mechanism for CRC card information; however, models in data-driven methodologies can benefit from the behavioral information on the cards as well. All projects will benefit from the use of CRC cards to introduce the notion of objects, to help project members become familiar with the problem domain, and to force discussion and the brainstorming of good solutions.

References

1. Wirfs-Brock, R., B. Wilkerson, and L. Wiener. DESIGNING OBJECT-ORIENTED SOFTWARE, Prentice Hall, Englewood Cliffs, NJ, 1990.
2. Booch, G. OBJECT-ORIENTED ANALYSIS AND DESIGN WITH APPLICATIONS, 2nd ed., Benjamin/Cummings, Redwood City, CA, 1993.
3. Jacobson, I., M. Christerson, P. Jonsson, and G. Overgaard. OBJECT-ORIENTED SOFTWARE ENGINEERING, Addison-Wesley, Reading, MA, 1992.
4. Shlaer, S. and S. Mellor. OBJECT-ORIENTED SYSTEMS ANALYSIS: MODELING THE WORLD IN OBJECTS. Yourdon Press, Englewood Cliffs, NJ, 1988.
5. Shlaer, S. and S. Mellor. OBJECT LIFECYCLES: MODELING THE WORLD IN STATES. Yourdon Press, Englewood Cliffs, NJ, 1992.
6. Rumbaugh, J., M. Blaha, W. Premerlani, F. Eddy, and W. Lorensen. OBJECT-ORIENTED MODELING AND DESIGN, Prentice Hall, Englewood Cliffs, NJ, 1991.

A PRIVATE WORKSPACE: WHY A SHARED REPOSITORY IS BAD FOR LARGE PROJECTS

JAMES RUMBAUGH

THE MYTH OF THE SHARED REPOSITORY

A popular approach to parallel development by multiple developers is the *shared repository,* in which each developer sees the latest version of each model element (classes and methods) in the entire project. Several development tools support this approach. This is bad for anything but a small project. Different developers get in each other's way because their temporary changes are visible to everybody immediately. Each developer or development team needs a private workspace in which the developer can work with a stable version of the system until his or her changes are ready to be shared with everybody. This article explains the problem and the right way to handle projects.

A shared repository is a central database containing a single version of the entire system. As developers make changes to elements, the changes are visible to the entire project. This *seems* like a good approach. Everybody sees the latest changes quickly so there is less chance of inconsistency. What is wrong with this approach?

> **TIP**
>
> A shared repository is a central database containing a single version of the entire system.

A shared repository is good for a command-and-control system, such as a "war room." A war room is a command center for managing a complex, messy, real-time parallel operation, such as a battle. Nonmilitary examples include air traffic control, a city firefighting dispatch center, an overnight shipping company, and the registration desk for a conference. In all of these examples, lots of things are changing concurrently in real time. The goal of a command-and-control system is to bring together the rapidly changing information as well as possible in real time. A shared repository is useful for a command-and-control system. It allows the latest information to be absorbed and organized in a real-time system that needs fast response to a confusing collection of concurrent activity. Because there are delays and noise in gathering information, the system must not demand absolute internal consistency of information, but must expect and deal with various kinds of information errors without crashing.

We accept the inconsistencies of the war room because we have no choice if we are to react to rapidly changing real-world situations. The information is unstable because the real-world situation is unstable. This is not a good model for engineering design (unless we are trying to fix an acute problem, such as a crippled spacecraft). We would prefer to produce engineering designs in a stable environment without inherent inconsistencies caused by continual uncontrolled changes. Of course, requirements change during the development process, but we want to organize the design process so that changes are accepted at well-defined points with controlled consequences.

On anything but a tiny project, the work must be divided into parts and done in parallel by different developers. Each developer designs part of the system and uses the rest of it. But if the rest of the system is constantly changing, then the poor developer is constantly bombarded by outside changes.

The problem is that each part of a system depends on many other parts of a system. Changes to a supplier component require changes to its clients. If a developer is changing the interface to one part of the system, many other developers may have to change their work. This applies at all stages of the development lifecycle, but it is particularly acute during programming because programs are notoriously intolerant of small errors and inconsistencies that might possibly be ignored during earlier stages (but not always). It is true that all changes must be integrated into a single system before the entire system is released. But it may be inconvenient to force all developers to see all changes immediately. To force the entire system to be up to date at all times would force development to be sequential, destroying the value of parallel development. This is unacceptable on a medium or large project. Developers must be able to work with mature, stable parts of a system that are being extended by others so they can get their own work done. Eventually the work must be merged together, but if the merge process is small compared to the development time of the parallel pieces, things will get done more quickly in parallel.

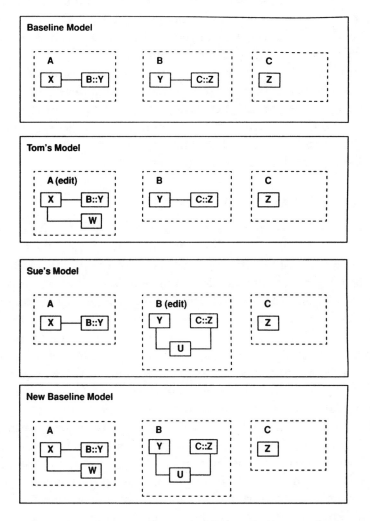

Figure 1. *Sample project showing baselines and private workspaces.*

Even if changes to a part of the system do not involve its public interface, it is an unfortunate fact of life that developers are not perfect. They make bugs. Other developers do not want to see a "work in progress" with all its bugs. They want to see other people's changes only at appropriate points of their own choosing after the changes have been validated by their developers.

For these reasons, the concept of a single shared repository is bad for engineering, such as software development. To permit parallel development with order and stability, each developer needs a private workspace whose contents are not affected by anybody else's work. Each developer needs explicit control on seeing changes by others.

Why is this different from the command-and-control system? In the real-time system, there is only one real world and it imposes its reality on us. But during a creative process, such as engineering design, different people can construct different virtual worlds. At well-defined milestones the different work must all be integrated together, but between milestones we want to have both parallel development and some stability.

PARALLEL ITERATIVE DEVELOPMENT

Iterative development is a style of work in which a system is developed in a number of *iterations,* each culminating in a new *release* of the system to customers. Each release defines a new version of the product with improved capabilities for users. Iterative development is used within a project to reduce the risk and difficulty of integrating all the changes to the release at once. Features to be added to a product are allocated to a series of internal development releases that force smaller-scale integration on a more frequent basis. Smaller integrations are easier to complete and debug, and design problems show up earlier in the development cycle. Slips to the schedule are much harder to disguise because they show up as delayed or missing releases or missing functionality. Even if a project slips behind schedule, a system with reduced functionality will be available and may be usable (which is usually not the case with a "grand implosion" model of system integration).

How do developers work in parallel? In all but the smallest one-person projects, a normal approach to system development is for two or more developers to work in parallel as part of an overall team. Each developer is assigned part of the problem. The developers cannot afford to wait for each other; they must work in parallel. This means that each developer must make modifications to the system under development but does not want to see the intermediate work of other developers, since the intermediate states of each developer's work may be inconsistent. In addition, a developer may not want to even see a consistent result from some other developer, as those changes may be inconsistent with the current state of his or her own work.

There needs to be some way to assign responsibility for parts of the system to individual developers, so that their work does not overlap and create incompatibilities that are difficult to resolve. A *category* is a user-defined subset of a model that is (by definition) a unit of access control for making changes. (I had previously used the term *subsystem*, but I have adopted Booch's term for a part of a model, reserving the term *subsystem* for a physical partition of the actual code files. There is unfortunately no consistency in terminology across different crafts and domains.) The definition of categories is a developer responsibility. They can be drawn as broadly or narrowly as desired, down to a single class or method and up to the entire system. A category should be tightly bound internally and loosely bound to the rest of the model. (In other words, there should be many internal dependencies among components of a category and fewer dependencies among categories.) Categories can be nested. The entire system model is the top-level category. The developer must draw the boundary lines correctly or unnecessary dependencies will be introduced among categories, which will complicate parallel development.

Categories are the basic units of configuration control. Each category undergoes a sequence of *versions* during its development (branching versions are also possible but I won't discuss them now). At any point during an iteration some of the categories are undergoing modification by various developers.

A *baseline* is a version of the entire system that is globally consistent and that every developer can build upon. A baseline consists of a specified version of each category in the system. The baseline is well tested and satisfies a set of objective requirements. A baseline represents a well-defined starting point for extensions to the system. Baselines corresponding to releases need to be archived so that software releases can be reconstructed if necessary in the future.

> **TIP**
>
> A baseline consists of a specified version of each category in the system.

ITERATIVE DEVELOPMENT PROCESS

On a new project, an initial project configuration is defined with a number of categories in it. This creates the initial system baseline. Each project team is assigned one or more categories. During the initial development iteration the categories must be developed individually and integrated gradually. On subsequent iterations integration of new category versions can be done by replacing previous versions within the context of an existing system baseline. Having a full system context permits testing of modifications as part of an operational system.

A project team using iterative development produces a series of baselines

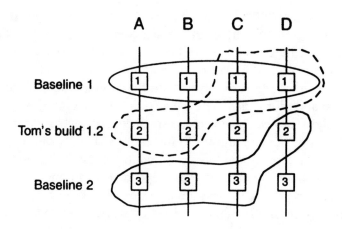

FIGURE 2. *Two baselines and a private build.*

between each release, starting from the baseline of the previous release. Each baseline represents a consistent view of the system. However, an internal development baseline may omit functionality needed in an external release. For now I assume a linear sequence of baselines, i.e., we ignore the possibility of variant branches to the development process; these deserve consideration but represent a more complicated possibility that I will not cover now.

During a system iteration each developer extends part of the system working from the previous baseline. Each developer checks out one or more categories, modifies them, and builds a private version of the system in the context of the baseline versions of all the other categories. Each developer gets a stable view of the entire system, including public and private categories, that is unaffected by changes made by other developers. Each developer sees a different version of the full system containing his or her own changes. Conceptually the developer makes a snapshot of the baseline into a private *workspace* and makes changes to the workspace without impacting other developers. Developers *check out* categories that they want to modify. Typically a configuration management system (such as Unix SCCS) prevents, or at least discourages, two developers from checking out the same category simultaneously.

Category versions, baselines, and private workspaces can be stored in a configuration management system, which can be implemented in various ways using files, databases, or third-party configuration control systems. The private workspaces can also be stored separately from the baselines. In practice, only categories that are modified by a developer must be copied into a private workspace; others could be accessed by reference from the configuration management system. The storage mechanism does not affect the semantics.

When the developer is satisfied that his or her work is correct and consistent, then a new version of each modified category is created and added to the system. However, other developers do not automatically use the latest new versions, as the new versions may be inconsistent with their own work or require additional changes that the other developers do not want to perform immediately. Developers may be notified about changes by other people, but they continue to work with their own existing view of the system. They can accept new versions from other developers whenever they want, however. Creation of new category versions does not create a new baseline, since the changes may be incomplete across the entire system. Often two developers share new versions of interdependent categories before the categories are ready for general use.

> **TIP**
>
> Developers may be notified about changes by other people.

A developer does not see changes by other developers until new versions of modified categories are created and stored in the configuration management system. (Of course a tool could permit looking at in-progress work by other developers, but nobody is forced to accept external changes until ready. Whether people can see other people's incomplete work is a political question and not part of the methodology.)

Typically a developer needs to work privately for periods ranging from part of a day to several weeks. This precludes working out of a single shared workspace in which all developers see the same version of each category. Changes during that period must go into the developer's private workspace. Both public and private versions of categories can be stored under configuration control, but they must contain enough information to keep them distinct.

Developers of interdependent categories must ensure that changes to them are compatible before a new baseline can be created. If other categories do not depend on the modified categories, new versions of the modified categories can simply be created. Otherwise other affected categories must be updated to be consistent with the modifications before the baseline is complete. In simple tools, reconciliation would be manual (the developer would have to examine the consequences of modifications and make appropriate changes to his or her categories). A more advanced tool would support some form of automatic checking and/or update. This is more difficult and requires considerable involvement with programming language semantic analysis.

Adding new categories does not create problems for other categories, but adding a new category to the system updates the configuration of the system itself. This can be handled by treating the system configuration as a module with versions of its own that is a part of the baseline. Deleting a category from the system requires moving or deleting all the information in it first.

This is a high-level statement of the process and raises many issues. In particular, it can be difficult to merge arbitrary changes to a system into a single consistent picture, since changes to different categories often interact. Modularity is an attempt to allow independent categories that can be easily reconciled without the need for manual intervention (which remains a possibility of last resort in any design process). Merging of independent changes is possible if we can separate the effects of the changes so they do not interfere.

A new baseline must specify particular versions of each of the categories (usually but not necessarily the latest version of each category). Creating a baseline is a statement that the various category versions in it are compatible and consistent. This is an assertion by the developers; there is no magic way to prove it. Syntactic and semantic checks can identify many kinds of inconsistencies, but they cannot identify all logical inconsistencies.

A SAMPLE SCENARIO

Figure 1 shows a sample project at several stages. The diagram is highly schematic and is grossly simplified compared to a real project so you can see what is going on. Categories are drawn as dotted boxes containing classes. The notation B::Y within category A means that category A contains a reference to class Y, which is defined within category B.

The initial baseline of the system is shown in the diagram. Tom checks out category A and adds a new class, W. Sue checks out category B and adds a new class, U, between classes Y and Z. Nobody modifies category C. Tom builds his system with the old version of B and tests his new code until it works. Then he puts a new version of category A back into the system configuration management. Sue continues working with the old version of category A until her code works, and then she checks a new version of B back into the system configuration management. Categories A and B are independent, so no reconciliation is needed when Sue checks her category back in. After both developers have updated their categories, the project administrator declares a new baseline using the two updated categories. The new baseline is shown at the bottom.

It is not necessary for updated versions to enter a new baseline immediately. Developers who are working together can exchange updated versions of categories without forcing everyone else to accept the changes immediately. Figure 2 shows two baselines as solid outlines. Baseline 1 includes version 1 of each category. Baseline 2 includes version 3 of categories A, B, and C and version 2 of category D. (Note that category version numbers are completely distinct from baseline version numbers.) During the second iteration, Tom accepted some of Sue's changes to category B after they had been stored as version 2 of B but before they had been incorporated into a new baseline. Sue had made some changes that Tom needs for his work. Tom made his own internal build 1.2 of the system (dotted outline) consisting of his new version 2 of A, Sue's updated version 2 of B, and the baseline versions of categories C and D. Everybody else continued to use the baseline version 1 of category A because Tom's work is incomplete. Eventually Tom updates his final changes as version 3 of category A. No one else ever uses version 2 of category A.

It is useful to keep both baseline versions and intermediate working versions of categories under configuration control. If a developer encounters a dead end and has to back off from a design approach, a set of intermediate versions can provide a clean place to restart the effort.

METAMODEL OF PROJECTS

Figure 3 shows an object modeling technique (OMT) metamodel for the structure of a project-based model. A development design tool needs to implement the concept of projects, categories, and model elements. Projects are the top-level binders of information shared across a team and across development time. A project encapsulates one or more related applications that share models and code. A category is a user-defined unit of access control during the development of a project. Categories contain model elements, such as class definitions, class imports, associations, and code bodies. Every element must be owned by one category, although it can be referenced by other categories.

Each category is owned by one project. A project can also reference categories from other projects, but cannot modify them. I call these imported categories *library categories*, since they generally come from stable libraries, but even libraries change from time to time. Each modeling element (such

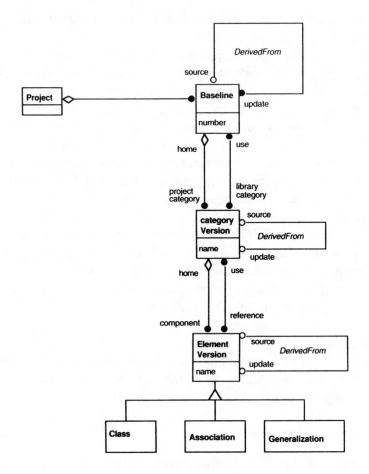

FIGURE 3. *OMT metamodel of project structure.*

as classes, associations, and generalizations) is owned by one category, but each one can be referenced by other categories as well. A developer must have checked out the "owner" category of an element to modify it. The categories in a project partition the contents of the project.

A project consists of a series of public and private baselines, each of which defines a complete build of an entire system at a moment in time. In the simple nonbranching case, a project is a linear series of baselines, each derived from the previous baseline.

Changes to categories are eventually stored as new versions. Additions of new elements pose no problems and can just be merged in. Implementation changes to classes or code bodies are invisible outside the category, so merging them is no problem. Specification changes to elements are visible elsewhere and must be propagated. Normally the developer will have to modify uses of an element (such as method calls) to make them consistent with specification changes. One special case is a name change, which should be supported by a tool. Name changes can be automatically propagated to client references if the references are clearly identified (straightforward within models, much more difficult inside code, which must be parsed within name contexts).

> **TIP**
>
> Changes to categories are eventually stored as new versions.

CHOOSING CATEGORIES

Categories have several connotations that should be observed in defining their boundaries:

A change to part of a category is likely to involve changing the rest of the category. A category represents an atomic unit of change to the model. There should be fewer dependencies across category boundaries than within a category.

A change to a category is less likely to involve changing another category. A category represents the smallest practical unit of change to the model. It is usually not necessary to place each class in a separate category, although this is possible.

It is often possible to merge changes from two or more separate categories by simply updating each category independently, if the public interfaces of the categories have not changed. Categories should be more or less independent with well-defined interfaces and dependencies.

Model elements in categories may use elements from other categories, inducing a client/supplier dependency between the categories. The dependency can be specified in terms of the public interface of the supplier. Changing the public interface of a supplier category requires the client categories to be updated to be consistent. A change to the implementation of a supplier category is encapsulated and invisible to other categories. Since most changes are to internal implementations, the amount of forced updates to a well-structured system is limited.

Two categories may be interdependent. This results from mutual client/supplier dependencies between the categories. Such cycles of dependent categories are most difficult to extend, since no single category can be modified separately.

AVOIDING CONFLICTS

Different developers can make changes that are not independent. This can arise in two ways:

- Different developers modify the same category.
- Different developers modify different categories, but the changes affect each other.

To prevent developers from accidentally making inconsistent changes to the same category, categories can be *locked*. Only one developer has permission to modify a locked category. A developer *checks out* a category by locking it and later *checks in* the modified category to return it to the mainline. Another developer can then check it out, modify it (consistent with the changes made by the first developer), and then check it back in. Locking serializes access to a category to prevent inconsistencies. Each category has a series of versions that might or might not be archived.

This process breaks down if two developers need to modify the same category simultaneously. In that case, the changes to the category have to be manually reconciled before the second developer creates an updated version of the category. There are several approaches:

- Subdivide the category so that the changes occur in different subcategories. If a category is large this should usually be the first approach.
- Forbid parallel changes to the same category. This is the normal intent of locking categories. This avoids the problem but may introduce an unacceptable delay into the development process. Applying this approach rigidly is not practical.
- Allow branching of versions of a single category. The first developer gets the mainline version of the category, and subsequent developers get branched versions that must be manually merged into the mainline version. For pragmatic reasons this possibility must usually be supported, although the goal should be to avoid it as much as possible.

Some developers have reported that rigid predefined categories may not be convenient for many kinds of development. It may be useful to allow developers to define *virtual categories* dynamically. Each dynamic category would contain a subset of model elements, but the dynamic categories could cut across the permanent logical categories. The dynamic categories would be used to control access to model elements on an ad hoc basis and would be abandoned when a given development task is complete. The same effect could be obtained by moving elements among categories, but dynamic categories would be more convenient. (It is equivalent to making temporary changes to the category organization.)

WHY HASN'T THE PROBLEM BEEN SEEN?

Many tools support the concept of a shared repository in which all users see the latest work of all other users. Why hasn't the problem with this approach been reported yet? Well, it has been reported, but awareness of the problem depends on the phase of development and the size of the model.

During high-level analysis, having everybody work out of a single shared repository that anyone can update concurrently may work acceptably for small systems. Since the model is under development and tentative in many respects, it is not critical for one developer to have a stable view of the whole system. Small inconsistencies in an analysis model do not have the same devastating consequences that small inconsistencies cause for compiled code.

This approach does not work so well for a large project. Perhaps a high-level analysis model can be created by a single small group for a small or medium project, but a large project requires work by separate teams and therefore multiple categories even during analysis. Building the design model for an entire project usually takes the effort of several developers on even a medium-sized project. Unless there is some way to divide up the system they may interfere with each other. But until the model is built there are no elements to partition! The concept of category provides a high-level partitioning before the system is populated with model elements, so that different developers can work in separate regions. However, this lack of modularity would not be apparent unless a large project were modeled to full detail. It would not show up in a quick prototype. But many early object-oriented developers have built small prototypes to get started.

During detailed design and implementation the lack of private workspaces would be more apparent. When working with code, even a small change to an imported category can prevent a program from running or even compiling, so stability of the developer's view is more critical when programming. I suspect that most users of shared-repository systems have not reached (or used the tool for) the implementation stage for a large system, so the impact of these issues will not have been seen yet.

Acknowledgments

This includes material from the forthcoming book THE OMT METHOD by James Rumbaugh. The diagrams and some of the text are taken from THE OMT METHOD TUTORIAL, copyright 1995 by James Rumbaugh. Used by permission of the author.

OBJECT-ORIENTED REGRESSION TESTING

DONALD G. FIRESMITH

R EGRESSION TESTING—THE REPETITION OF TESTING FOR THE PURPOSE OF finding new errors in previously tested software—is an absolutely critical requirement if object technology is to achieve its promised benefits. This article discusses the increased need for regression testing due to object technology and stresses the need for regression testing to be automated. It then presents three major techniques for automating regression testing, along with a discussion of their pros and cons.

THE INCREASED NEED FOR REGRESSION TESTING

Regression testing is the repetition of testing for the purpose of finding errors that may have been introduced into software after initial testing. Regression testing has many uses; its application is especially critical for object-oriented projects:

- *Reuse* will not occur without developer confidence, which regression testing can both provide and justify.
- Given an *object-oriented development cycle*, it can be used to determine whether an *iteration* has inadvertently introduced bugs into previously tested software or if a new increment invalidates software developed during a previous increment.
- Regression testing can also be used to validate the proper use of *inheritance*, which in turn can be used to support the regression testing effort.

Well-engineered object-oriented software is reusable software, and I do not restrict that statement to the ever growing number of class libraries that one

TIP
Developers will not reuse software they do not trust.

can buy from commercial vendors. As more companies embrace the object paradigm, more managers will recognize that the only way to maximize the goals promised by object technology is through the reuse of *patterns* of classes—especially domain-specific frameworks that will allow managers to achieve truly significant levels of reuse, productivity, and quality. Unless companies join with their competitors to form consortia to produce and share the necessary classes and patterns, they will find that they must develop them in-house. Developers will not reuse software they do not trust, and they often have far too many unfortunate experiences with internally produced software to trust it. The best way to gain that trust is via regression testing, but only if such testing can be made relatively quick and painless via automation.

Object-oriented development is best performed as part of an *incremental, iterative, parallel* development cycle. Because the software is developed incrementally, each new increment depends on and must be integrated with the software that was developed during the previous increments. The original software must not only continue to work, it must do so in a new environment containing classes that were either added or modified by the increment. Similarly, iteration implies making changes to existing software that must then be retested to ensure that the corrections and improvements have not inadvertently introduced bugs into the existing software. The parallel nature of the object-oriented development cycle also has testing ramifications. The developer of a class may not be the one who must later make changes to it or create new software that must collaborate with it. Thus, use of an object-oriented development cycle also increases the need for regression testing.

Perhaps the most important cause of the increased importance of regression testing is inheritance. Classes are intended to be developed incrementally by defining new derived classes in terms of one or more existing base classes. The features of these base classes must continue to function in the environment of the new derived class. Yet, combining correct new features with correct inherited features may cause subtle new bugs. For example, both new and inherited operations may interact via inherited attributes, and this use of "common local data" may cause bugs similar to those caused by common global data in traditional procedural software.* Inherited operations must

---

*Although the encapsulation of object-oriented software eliminates the all too common bugs due to the common global data of traditional procedural software, it may contain bugs due to both common local data in the form of encapsulated properties and common global objects due to a lack of language-supported building blocks larger than classes, i.e., clusters.[1]

continue to provide the correct functional abstraction, even though they may be overridden in the derived class. As in the Biblical metaphor, building on shifting sands can be dangerous. Luckily, inheritance is a double-edged sword. Not only can it cause a host of bugs,[2] inheritance can also be used for the testing of test software, thereby greatly lessening the retest effort and achieving the same benefits for test software that it has produced for deliverable software.

AUTOMATING REGRESSION TESTING OF UNITS

Because object technology makes regression testing inevitable, regression testing should be automated using a standard retest technique and test software. Standardizing on an automated regression test technique has many benefits. For example, it

TIP
Regression testing should be automated.

- decreases the test effort, which indirectly produces an increase in software quality;
- allows all developers to reuse some of the same test software, such as test drivers and error logs;
- minimizes training costs and makes it easier for different developers, test personnel, and quality assurance personnel to communicate; and
- formalizes the testing process, making it more likely that adequate testing will be performed and that test results will be captured.

The units of object-oriented software are classes, which should be incrementally developed as part of an inheritance structure. Beginning with the root class, new classes are derived from one or more base classes, and these classes should be incrementally unit tested as they are developed. Because classes are typically used only as templates for objects and are not themselves executable, they are first instantiated and then indirectly tested via one or more of their instantiated objects. Abstract classes are either instantiated for test purposes only or else used to derive concrete classes, which are then tested.

There are three main techniques that can be used to automate the regression testing of classes in an inheritance hierarchy. All three techniques use inheritance to inherit test software and test cases as well as normal software. These techniques, which are discussed in the following sections, include the following:

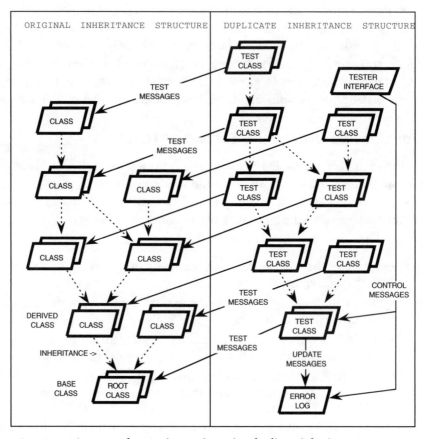

FIGURE 1. *Automated regression testing using duplicate inheritance structure.*

- developing a separate and analogous inheritance structure of test drivers;
- embedding test operations within the classes of the single inheritance structure;
- developing a separate and analogous inheritance structure of mixins that contain embeddable test operations and test cases.

Technique 1: Duplicate Inheritance Structure of Test Drivers

As illustrated in Figure 1, this technique creates a duplicate inheritance structure of test drivers that has the same topology as the inheritance structure to be tested. As each new class to be tested is derived, a corresponding test-driver class is derived. These test drivers inherit from the root test-driver class the ability to log errors and be driven by a tester interface object.

The main advantage of this approach is that derived classes of test drivers use inheritance to obtain, extend, and modify the test cases of their base classes. Numerous guidelines for the incremental testing of inheritance structures have been developed as part of the Hierarchical Incremental Testing technique.[3]

> **TIP**
>
> Derived classes of test drivers use inheritance to obtain, extend, and modify the test cases.

The main disadvantage of this technique is that it is restricted to black-box testing, and it can be very difficult to test objects from the outside due to their encapsulation and state. The behavior of an object may well depend on its state, which almost always should be hidden from its clients in the form of encapsulated attributes, links, and component subobjects. Objects often do not export operations that allow a test driver to easily place it in the appropriate pretest state and determine if it subsequently attained the appropriate posttest state. The inclusion of *get* and *set* operations in the protocol of a class merely to circumvent encapsulation for testing has several drawbacks. Such operations may be used by clients as trapdoors for other purposes, with obvious detrimental effects. Removing such test operations prior to delivery implies that different code is delivered than was tested. The use of assertions and a debugger significantly reduce these problems, but only if you are willing to give up the benefits of automated regression testing. The use of C++ offers an interesting workaround for this problem. If the classes to be tested declare their associated test classes as "friends," then these test drivers may violate the encapsulation of the objects under test and directly read and set their state.

Technique 2: Embedded Test Operations

To intentionally circumvent encapsulation and enable the easy setting and evaluation of pretest and posttest states, this technique embeds test operations directly within the classes to be tested. As illustrated in Figure 2, this technique embeds standard kinds of test operations in each class and instance. Testing a class involves the following steps:

1. Testing begins when the *tester interface* object sends the *test class* message to the class under test. The test class message will eventually

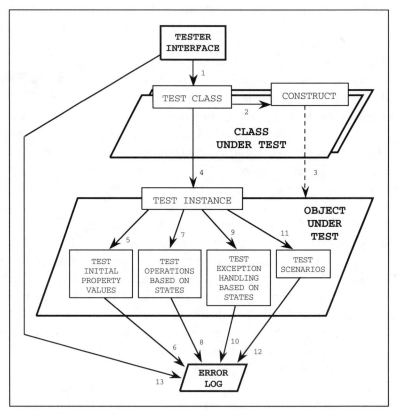

FIGURE 2. *Automated regression testing using encapsulated test operations.*

return the number of errors found to the *tester interface* object.

2. The associated *test class* operation calls the constructor.

3. The constructor constructs one or more instances (e.g., the object under test) that will be used to indirectly test the class under test.

4. The *test class* operation then sends the *test instance* message to the newly constructed object under test. After testing is complete, this message will return the total number of errors found to the *test class* operation.

5. The *test instance* operation then calls the hidden *test initial property values* operation that determines whether the object under test was properly initialized.*

---

*The hidden test operations may contain the necessary pretest and posttest states, operation parameters, and expected results as local attributes, or this test data may be stored as test attributes of the class.

6. Any errors found are then documented in the *error log* object, and the number of errors is returned to the *test instance* operation.

7. The *test instance* operation then calls the hidden *test operations based on states* operation, which tests each operation in each state by placing the object in the proper pretest state, executing the operation, and checking for the proper result including the proper posttest state.

8. Any errors found are then documented in the *error log* object and the number of errors returned to the *test instance* operation.

9. The *test instance* operation then calls the hidden *test exception handling based on states* operation, which determines if the object under test raises and handles exceptions properly.

10. Any errors found are then documented in the *error log* object, and the number of errors is returned to the *test instance* operation.

11. The *test instance* operation then calls the hidden *test scenarios* operation, which tests each usage scenario of the object. This test operation may not be necessary due to the previous test operations.

12. Any errors found are then documented in the *error log* object, and the number of errors is returned to the *test instance* operation.

13. If the number of errors returned is greater than zero, the *tester interface* object will display the number of errors on the screen and print an error report based on the *error log* object.

The primary advantage of this second technique over the first technique is that it bypasses the encapsulation of objects that make them difficult to test from the outside. The test operations have direct visibility and control over the properties of the objects, which makes the development of the test operations simpler. It also simplifies the interpretation of test results because the properties are local to the test operations. Like the first technique, this technique uses inheritance to minimize the regression test effort. Like the previous workaround using C++ `friends`, this technique allows for the automation of white-box as well as black-box unit tests. By placing the test operations within the classes to be tested, there is no need to produce a duplicate inheritance structure of test drivers. The test operations are also more likely to be used, updated, and kept consistent with the classes under test during the normal iterative incremental development process.

Unfortunately, this technique is not without its disadvantages. It bloats the size of the source code with the test operations, and *manually* removing test code prior to delivery would cause the same problems as mentioned

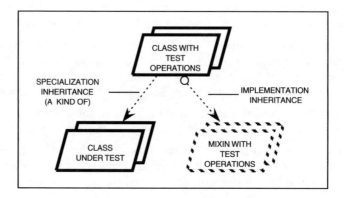

FIGURE 3. *Use of test mixins to combine both inheritance structures.*

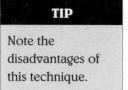

TIP

Note the disadvantages of this technique.

previously. This should not be a real problem, however, because a good optimizer should automatically delete the test operations from the deliverable object code as dead code. The proper use of assertions and exception handling supplies many of the benefits of embedded test operations and should be used where practical to minimize the development of test operations and to create more reliable and robust software. Using assertions, however, cannot replace regression testing; assertions cannot be automatically exercised in a test mode and will often find errors only during manual debugging or informally after the software has been delivered.

Technique 3: Duplicate Inheritance Structure of Test Mixins

As illustrated in Figure 3, the third technique is a combination of the first two. Like the first technique, it involves creating a duplicate inheritance structure of test classes. But this time, the test classes are mixins,* each of which contains the test software that would have been embedded in the corresponding class under test using the second technique. By multiply inheriting from both the class to be tested and its corresponding mixin class of test operations, one obtains the same classes that would have been

---

*A mixin class is defined as an abstract class that embodies a single abstraction that is used to augment the protocol and functionality of other classes by providing common resources via multiple inheritance; the abstraction of a mixin (e.g., persistence) is usually orthogonal to the abstraction of the class(es) with which it is combined.

developed using the second technique. However, the original class without the test operations can be delivered if so desired, and, although it is different from the class that was tested, the only difference is in the missing test operations. The result is the same as if a macro were used to strip out the test operations from the classes developed using the second technique.

CONCLUSION

This column has addressed the critical need for the automated regression testing of classes on projects using object technology. Three useful techniques for accomplishing this were presented. Although each involves a significant amount of effort to set up, much of this effort would have to be performed anyway during initial unit testing, and it clearly pays for itself during subsequent development and iteration. Although the use of friends in the first technique is restricted to C++ and the use of mixins in the third technique is restricted to languages (such as C++ and Eiffel) that support multiple inheritance, the ideas presented in this article can be used on any object-oriented project concerned with quality and with minimizing both the development and maintenance costs.

References

1. Firesmith, D. Clusters of classes: A bigger building block, REPORT ON OBJECT ANALYSIS & DESIGN, 1(4):18–25, 1994.
2. Firesmith, D. Testing Object-Oriented Software, in SOFTWARE ENGINEERING STRATEGIES, 1(5):15–35, 1993.
3. Harrold, M. and J. McGregor. Hierarchical incremental testing, TECHNICAL REPORT TR91-111, Dept. of Computer Science, Clemson Univ., 1991.

A VISION

SALLY SHLAER

T HIS MONTH, I WOULD LIKE TO SHARE WITH YOU A VISION FOR CHANGE—A FUN-
damental change in our profession.

Having been involved with software since the late 1950s, I have seen my share of solid successes and at least one spectacular multimillion dollar failure. As a result of the gray hairs garnered along the way, I have come to a vision of what software development might be like—can be like—if we have the understanding and dedication to make it so.

Let me quote from my company's mission statement: "to make software development a rational, controllable, reproducible engineering process."

ENGINEERING

What does it mean to be an engineer? We call ourselves software engineers, but I think you would agree that our work—at least as done today—is far different from that of electrical, mechanical, or civil engineers. We do not work with codified practices. We do not measure the products of our work in any standard way, either predictively or after the fact, as does an electrical engineer when designing a circuit or a civil engineer when designing a bridge. No, I think we call ourselves engineers because we know we aren't scientists, and we know we're doing something both technical and applied. English doesn't seem to offer us another word.

> **TIP**
>
> We call ourselves engineers because English doesn't seem to offer us another word.

For our work to become a true engineering discipline, we must base our practices on hard science. For us, that science is a combination of mathematics (for its precision in definition and reasoning) and a science of information. Today we are starting to see analysis methods that are based on these concepts. The Shlaer-Mellor method of OOA,[1] for example, is constructed as a mathematical formalism, complete with axioms and theorems. These axioms and theorems have been published as "rules"[2]; we expect that as other methods become more fully developed, they, too, will be defined at this level of precision.

REPRODUCIBILITY

When we work according to standard practices and procedures, our work becomes reproducible: reproducible in the sense that two practitioners, working independently, are able to produce essentially the same product. Today we are able to achieve this only in two areas: coding of small, well-understood classes (a List class, a Tree class), and in analysis—and the latter only when using an extremely well-defined method. We do not yet have reproducibility in the development of a class library or in system level design.

Why is reproducibility important? Reproducibility is a *sine qua non* for evaluation: until we know what the target is, how can we reasonably evaluate our products? Our current situation of "I'll recognize quality [correctness, etc.] when I see it" isn't good enough for a field that calls itself engineering.

But more significantly, when we have reproducibility, we will no longer depend on individual skills and insights, but on the maturity and knowledge of the profession as a whole. And until we can accumulate and make use of a body of recorded knowledge, we are confined to problems that can be solved with the amount of experience and know-how that can be accumulated by an individual or a small group. This isn't good enough.

CONTROLLABILITY

Today our work is still fundamentally uncontrollable. We do not have reliable, well-accepted ways to estimate our costs or to place a measure of goodness on our products. We cannot make tradeoffs in a quantitative manner: we cannot, for example, determine that it is wise to accept a lower performance design because the cost of a higher performance solution is too high.

Our lack of ability today to understand costs and benefits in a quantitative manner supports overkill in design and implementation, uncertain and unreliable schedules, and the too-true belief that software development is fundamentally unmanageable. This must change.

WORKMANSHIP

As software developers, we tend to work to make our products as good as possible—where each developer decides, for the most part, what properties are desirable or "good." In fact, we work as skilled artisans, handcrafting each design and each class with care. Our organization may be rated at SEI level 3—we have and use a defined development process—but, as individuals, we are still handcrafting. We want to make our products better, more elegant, even prettier. Remember the lovely filigree on the handles of antique pistols? This tracery served no purpose but was produced as a sign of the maker's pride in his work. We do the same thing when we name variables carefully, when we indent code so that the structure is apparent, and when we work to save a few cycles in a function that is invoked only 12 time a year. Although we can justify much (but not all) of this on the grounds of reduced maintenance, I assert that pride in workmanship is extremely important to us. We must make sure that we do not let this become an obstacle to becoming true engineers.

MANUFACTURING

Although software developers do not make 100,000 virtually identical cars, TV sets, or washing machines, our work has certain parallels with manufacturing—yet another area where engineering is applied in a serious manner. What can we learn by looking at this field?

In the history of manufacturing, one of the first breakthroughs was the concept of interchangeable parts. Our idea of interchangeable parts today includes reuse in the small (reuse of a Stack class or a small-class hierarchy) and the practice of defining an interface so as to be free to modify the internals of the process behind the interface—both good object-oriented concepts.

But we can go further. The next step is to adopt larger pre-made parts: entire components, assemblies, and frameworks the size of an architecture, an alarm service, or a process input/output domain. We already do this with user interfaces, networks, databases, and operating systems. This strategy must be continued. But we cannot truly reap the benefits of our interchangeable parts until we can interchange them, so we must develop technology that makes incorporation and interchangeability of such components a simple and straightforward endeavor. Only then will it be practical to swap out one architecture (network, operating system, etc.) for another that has more desirable features, better performance characteristics, and the like.

SOFTWARE DEVELOPMENT AS MANUFACTURING

Over the past 10 years, Steve Mellor's and my efforts—as well as those of our colleagues and clients—have been firmly directed toward turning software development into an engineering and, where appropriate, manufacturing process. We have made a great deal of progress in this undertaking, but there is more to do and many improvements yet to be made. What will life be like when this has been accomplished?

First, we will examine our materials—our information—in a considered way. We will understand where and how we get it, how to test and evaluate it for its suitability in software development, and exactly how best to use it.

We will understand the "manufacture" of our products: what the intermediate products are, how to test and evaluate them, how to identify units requiring rework.

We'll concentrate on process. The steps in the process will be defined very precisely in terms of inputs, outputs, and method. We'll identify flaws in the process through flaws in the product—less in the sense of statistical process control and more in the sense of direct causation. We will become, in part, software manufacturing engineers, refining our development process and developing automation to carry it out. And we will be willing to pay for advanced automation (much higher level compilers, translation engines, performance prediction tools); the payoff in productivity will be irresistible.

We will understand costs. Time is our largest cost by far. We'll know how much time is required at each step in the process, and we will attempt to reduce those costs by improving our process in whatever ways we can devise. Yes, we will be operating at SEI level 5 as a matter of course.

We'll consider components as a separate and serious topic. We'll develop standardized components and identify multiple sources of those components and subassemblies, and we'll use subcontractors to supply these well-defined components when they can do it less expensively by virtue of specialization.

THE FUTURE

We as practitioners must change. We must change from highly skilled artisans to being software manufacturing engineers. This is absolutely minimally required: software is a $13 billion dollar industry. We cannot afford to sit in front of our workstations and continue to build, fit, smooth, and adjust, making by hand each part of each subassembly, of each assembly, of each product.

Does this suggest that we have to give up pride in workmanship, individual innovation, creativity, etc? No, it means that we must seek these gratifications in what we do best: making our machines work for us. Computers can build software, and only skilled software developers will make this a reality.

How far away is this future? Not very far. Steve Mellor and I have codified the results of our efforts to date in the method of Recursive Design.[3] Although there are still certain spots in the process that need further exploration, we do have an end-to-end solution that is systematic, rational, reproducible, and controllable. And our New Year's resolution is to continue this effort and, working with commercial toolmakers, to put meaningful automation in your hands by year's end. I think we can do it.

References

1. Shlaer, S. and S. Mellor, OBJECT LIFECYCLES: MODELING THE WORLD IN STATES, Prentice Hall, Englewood Cliffs, NJ, 1992.
2. Lang, N. Shlaer-Mellor object-oriented analysis rules, SOFTWARE ENGINEERING NOTES, 18:1, 1993.
3. Shlaer, S. and S. Mellor, RECURSIVE DESIGN, forthcoming from Prentice Hall.

THE DEVELOPMENT TEAM

GRADY BOOCH

I T'S TIME THAT I COME CLEAN AND UNVEIL ONE OF THE DIRTY LITTLE SECRETS OF software engineering: People are more important than any process.

Remember my article a couple of issues ago, wherein I described the macro process of the Booch method in excruciating detail? Well, all of this process stuff is largely irrelevant in the presence of a jelled team of smart guys and gals. In other words, as DeMarco describes it, "Great managers don't even end up steering their projects. They don't have to. If they've succeeded in their design [of the team that builds the product], they have constructed a project that knows how to find its own way."[1]

> **TIP**
>
> Great managers do not steer.

But mark my words closely, and don't take any of them out of context with the discussion that follows. The operative word in my statement above is "jelled." This is indeed the key question of this article: For object-oriented systems, how does one best structure a development team so that it jells? Just hiring a bunch of smart guys and gals is simply not enough to ensure the success of a project. I know; I've seen projects try it time and time again. Consider the following example:

> This organization embarked on a project to build a next generation payroll system. They brought in a team of around 30 of the best and most experienced people in the company. They trained them in OO stuff. They loaded them up with the latest tools. And they utterly failed. After about a year into the project, it was painfully evident that the team was absolutely stuck in implementation. They'd devised a reasonable

architecture, but each individual contributor kept hacking away at it, adding more and more cool features that they individually thought were interesting. Ultimately, they over-engineered the poor thing, till it was so bloated with complex features that no mortal user could ever effectively use it. The company finally threw the project manager out the door, abandoned the system under development, and started all over again, this time a lot wiser but several million dollars poorer.

This example illustrates the culture of cowboy programmers, who pride themselves on individual contributions and who view every problem as a simple matter of programming.[*] Don't get me wrong, however: I'd much rather have a team of all A+ players than a multitude of B players. Furthermore, reality is that many real software innovations seem to come from A++ players organized in small teams that provide a fertile ground for their unrestrained creativity to take root.

However, this simplistic model often breaks down, because is it neither repeatable, nor does it scale up, nor does it represent a sustainable business practice. To be precise, there are three problems with merely organizing a development team around a bunch of smart guys and gals thrown together in the same room. First,

- There aren't enough smart guys and gals to go around.

I don't mean to imply that most of us in the software industry are mentally underpowered. In my experience, I've encountered perhaps only a couple of dozen or so truly world-class developers who not only were experts in their domain but who could also program circles around their peers. Consider the following:

In this particular organization, I had the honor to very briefly work with a hyperproductive developer who, for the purposes of this example, I'll call Howard.[**] Howard was an off-scale developer who could write more lines of production-quality code in a weekend than many of his peers could write in a month. We measured his work in "Howard days," wherein one Howard day was equivalent to a week or two of a mere mortal developer's time.

This suggests a rule of thumb:

---

[*] Found written on the whiteboard of one such programmer's cubicle: Methods are for wimps.

[**] I won't tell you Howard's last name, because you'd try to hire him away.

- Hyperproductive developers are, on the average, 10–20 times more productive than the average developer.

Developers like Howard are rare; if you have the good fortune to have people such as he in your organization, treat them well, because their impact on the success of your projects is beyond measure.

However, there's another rule of thumb that applies here:

- Hyperproductive developers constitute only about 1% or 2% of the entire developer population.

In other words, there aren't a lot of these kind of people to go around. You may debate whether or not such people are born or made, but either way it is clear that they are a very limited resource. Therefore, practically, most projects simply can't afford to staff themselves with all hyperproductive developers.

Continuing,

- There is a big difference between creating a simple, brilliant program that demonstrates one cool concept very well and productizing that program so that it meets the needs of industrial strength users.

Building simple, flashy things is easy. Indeed, teams of smart guys and gals often excel at rapidly crafting such software innovations. However, for most complex domains, this is simply not enough. As my earlier article on the macro process should have made clear, building production quality software is an engineering process that requires far more than just raw programming talent; rather, it demands a lot of tedious blocking and tackling to drag an inspired architecture out of the lab and into the real world. Furthermore, dealing with the multitude of details that go into productization is something that some hyperproductive developers find odious, largely because its (a) not as much fun, and (b) requires engineering compromises.

Finally,

- Some problems are so complex that they simply require a lot of hard, sustained labor, more than can be carried out by a small team of smart guys and gals.

I'm a great fan of small teams: they are easier to work with, they are more nimble, and they generally are more successful than larger teams. However, imagine trying to develop an entire national air-traffic control system with just 10 people; and imagine reengineering a multinational organization's entire billing system with only two or three really good programmers. You just can't do it. Well, actually, you can, but it would take these small teams most of their lifetimes, and by the time they delivered, the world would have changed so much that their work would be irrelevant. Object-oriented technology is great, but no technology is so great that it provides that much leverage to any single small team.

This suggests another rule of thumb:

- A small object-oriented project can be carried out with a team of only one or two people. A slightly larger project requires around five people. A modest-sized project requires a development team of a dozen or two. A team developing a moderately complex project will typically reach a peak staff of around 50. Projects of geopolitical scope may require the efforts of a few hundred developers.

The bad news is that the larger the staff, the more likely it is the project will fail. The good news is that on the average, object-oriented projects tend to require smaller staffs and less aggressive staffing profiles as compared to non-object-oriented ones. Still, it is the case that as complexity grows, so must the size of your development team. Understaffing a complex project will mean you'll never have enough raw horsepower to complete the task in a timely fashion.

For all these reasons, the dirty little secret I revealed earlier is itself not so pure. You can't just expect a project to succeed simply by staffing it with a bunch of smart guys and gals, arming them with powerful tools, showing them where to stand, and then expecting them to move the world. There just isn't enough leverage. Individuals are important, but in the world of industrial strength software development, teams are even more important. In turn, process is important in building teams because it is repeatable, it helps to address issues of scale, and it leads to a sustainable business practice.

My experience with successful object-oriented projects suggests the following practice:

- Remember that software development is ultimately a human endeavor.

Successful object-oriented projects require a skill set, a staffing profile, and an allocation of resources subtly different than for non-object-oriented projects. These topics represent the tactical issues of organizing a jelled development team, which I discuss in the following sections. However, before I do that, it's important to establish the mindset of the jelled team. Even if you organize a team with the right roles and responsibilities, your project will flounder if you fail to recognize that development is indeed a human activity.

The mindset of the successful development team has three elements, which I can best illustrate through some war stories:

> An organization staffed its projects according to the Mongolian horde principle—that is, the principle that management can overwhelm any technical problem by throwing sufficient bodies at it. Furthermore, as the organization would have it, the more developers, the more important the project would seem to be. In this one particular object-oriented project for a major new product line, management allocated 300 programmers.* My first recommendation to the project was to get rid of at least 250 developers. Management politely declined my advice; in retrospect, it was because they were more interested in building empires than they were in building software. I walked away from this project, because with this attitude, they were beyond help.

Thus:

- A project must recognize that its developers are not interchangeable parts and that the successful deployment of any complex system requires the unique and varied skills of a focused team of people.

Ignoring this principle was a large measure of the reason that the project in this example failed. In this case, management imposed some degree of structure by blindly assigning certain senior programmers as managers. Most absolutely fell flat at their task, simply because they were not skilled in leading other programmers.

Managers are not the only ones that sometimes forget that their developers are human; in a number of failed projects, I've seen senior developers share this distressing attitude:

> I was called in to a project in crisis and began my investigation by spending some time with their architect to diagnose the problem. We spent a few hours talking about certain key abstractions in the domain, and then I asked him if he would take one of these abstractions that he'd outlined and capture it in a C++ header file. He refused, with words to

---

*Honest. I'm not making this number up.

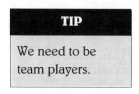

TIP

We need to be team players.

the effect "No! damn it, I'm an architect, not a coder!" It took me about three picoseconds to realize why this project was in crisis. When developers say such things, it is usually a sign of arrogance or ineptness. Unfortunately, this architect was both.

I never engaged with this project again. One of my spies on the project reported back to me later that this project eventually died a very slow and painful death.

- A project must honor the role of every one of its developers.

A coder is not a lesser person than an architect; a programmer is not a lower life form than a project manager (or, from the programmer's perspective, a manager is not a lower life form than a programmer). Indeed, the success of every project depends on the efforts of every team member, no matter how humble their contribution.

This mindset extends to individual contributors:

> At the onset of this large object-oriented project, the architect set out to jell the development team. One interview uncovered a brilliant young programmer who came highly recommended, having saved a number of projects. The interview revealed that she was smart and energetic but did not know one thing about the object-oriented programming language, nor the domain, nor any project larger than 50,000 SLOC. The architect advised her to spend at least one or two iterations in the trenches to learn about pragmatic object-oriented stuff. She was furious. She came back the following week, saying that she'd read the Booch book over the week-end and did not see why she should waste a year in the trenches, because "this OO stuff was not all that different." She very reluctantly took on the job anyway. Six months later, she joined the architecture team. At the next performance review, she admitted that this six months in the trenches had been a most formative one, allowing her to really understand what object-oriented stuff was all about. She added that despite the fact that she hated the architect's guts for a while, she thought now that this was in fact the right path to grow as a productive member of the team.*

The happy ending to this story is that the programmer in question ended

---

*Philippe Kruchten, private communication.

up being one of the best team players in the architecture group. This story suggests a third element of a project's mindset:

- Individuals on a development team must be honest about their strengths and weaknesses and not let their ego take them to places beyond their ability.

As a developer, admitting that you have certain strengths and weaknesses is the first step in growing as a professional. Every new project that a developer encounters changes that person. Successful developers recognize that fact and, in truth, welcome the challenge each new project brings, because it represents an opportunity for professional growth.

Although there may a limited pool of hyperproductive developers in the world, it is possible—and, indeed, desirable—to build a hyperproductive team using developers of average talents. The key to this approach is recognizing that different people have different skills and that every complex software project requires a balanced mixture of these skills. Furthermore, my experience suggests that the object-oriented development process requires a subtly different partitioning of skills as compared to traditional methods. In small projects, the same people may play several different roles; in larger projects, each role may be carried out by a different person or persons.

The development team includes any person who has an impact on the success or failure of a project. Every successful team encompasses three general sets of roles:

- **Core:** Responsible for actual software production
- **Supplemental:** Supports the activities of the core developers
- **Peripheral:** At the boundary of the project and its context

In traditional approaches to software development, the work of the core team would typically be divided among analysts (who gather and interpret requirements from the real world), designers (who translate those requirements into a blueprint of software artifacts), and coders (who write code against these blueprints). There are lots of problems with this monolithic model, not the least of which is that it almost forces a very strict waterfall process, wherein perfectly formed requirements are transformed into complete and unchangeable designs that are then mechanically implemented by largely unskilled coders. This utopian model of development is pure folly. Furthermore, this traditional model is absolutely the antithesis of the incremental and iterative development process found in all successful object-oriented projects, wherein the conventional activities of analysis, design, and programming are blurred. In successful object-oriented projects, a very different partitioning of skills is found. Consider the following story:

> This conservative COBOL organization found itself being dragged into the object-oriented world because of an external dictate. Management took a calm and deliberate approach to transitioning the team through a combination of mentoring, formal training, and pilot projects. Much to the surprise of the team itself, the group quickly jelled, manifest by the fact that the project soon found its own rhythm. Ultimately, the core development team organized itself around three different groups: an architect who established the system's structure; class and class category designers who managed the system's microarchitecture; and general engineers, who both implemented these classes as well as assembled them into larger parts. The health of this team was made clear when they were thrown a whole new set of requirements without schedule relief, yet did not panic.

In the successful object-oriented project, the core team is typically made up of individuals with three different roles:

- Architect
- Abstractionist
- Application engineer

This suggests a common practice:

- Organize your core development team among three groups: an architect who is responsible for the system's overall structure, abstractionists who manage the system's microarchitecture, and application engineers who implement and assemble the classes and mechanisms found in the system.

I also have a rule of thumb about the mixture of these roles in successful projects:

- Approximately 10% of the development team should be a full- or part-time member of the architecture group. About 30% of the team are abstractionists. Application engineers constitute about 50% of the whole team. The remaining 10% serve in supporting roles.

As I explained in my article on the macro process, a focus on architecture is a key principle of the Booch method. In my remaining space, let me explain the role of the architect, who is the person or persons responsible for evolving and maintaining the system's architecture. The main activities of the architect are to do the following:*

- Define the architecture of the software
- Maintain the architectural integrity of the software
- Assess technical risks relative to software design
- Propose the order and content of the successive iterations and assist in their planning
- Consult with various design, implementation, integration, and quality-assurance teams
- Assist marketing regarding future product definition

The architect is typically responsible for producing a number of deliverables, including the architecture document, parts of lower-level design documents, design and programming guidelines, elements of release plans, meeting and review minutes, and design audits of the released system.

The architect is the project's visionary. Ultimately, every project should have exactly one identifiable architect, although for larger projects, the principle architect should be backed up by an architecture team of modest size. The architect is not necessarily the most senior developer but, rather, is the one best qualified to make strategic decisions, usually as a result of his or her extensive experience in building similar kinds of systems. Because of this experience, such developers intuitively know the common architectural patterns that are relevant to a given domain and what performance issues and other forces apply to certain architectural variants. Architects are not necessarily the best programmers either, although they should have adequate programming skills. Just as a building architect should be skilled in aspects of construction, it is generally unwise to employ a software architect who is not also a reasonably decent programmer. Project architects should also be well versed in the notation and process of object-oriented development, because they must ultimately express their architectural vision in terms of clusters of classes and collaborations of objects.

---

*Kruchten, P. April 1994. SOFTWARE ARCHITECTURE AND ITERATIVE DEVELOPMENT, Santa Clara, California: Rational Software Corporation, p.53.

The architect must have real project experience, have good communication skills, exhibit strong leadership skills, and be proactive and goal oriented. An architect should also be a person who sometimes likes to color outside of the lines. Every good architecture requires some element of risk, and therefore, architects should not be afraid to take bold or novel action that might lead to a breakthrough that generalizes or simplifies the architecture.

This suggests the following practice:

- Choose an architect who possesses a vision large enough to inspire the project to great things, the wisdom born from experience that knows what to worry about and what to ignore, the pragmatism necessary to make hard engineering decisions, and the tenacity to see this vision through to closure.

References

1. DeMarco, T. Standing naked in the snow, AMERICAN PROGRAMMER 7(12):30, 1994.

PART III

PATTERNS

The identification and reuse of patterns is among the most important emerging. The articles that follow both summarize and extend that body of knowledge.

Pattern Languages for Organization & Process

James O. Coplien

Limits to Perfection in Objects

The object paradigm's promise for new and powerful abstraction techniques has heightened software engineering expectations for the past decade. Software designers who use these techniques to build new systems often find that their products can be understood and modified more easily than ever before. Objects also bring new development methods and processes to software engineering, with a focus on iteration and concurrent engineering, that make it possible to validate customer expectations frequently and directly. With architectural clarity comes ease of maintenance, and a promise of at least some relief for developers of all large software systems, right?

Yet nature abhors panaceas. We are now finding that objects alone aren't enough. Some systems just don't bend to abstract data types or inheritance hierarchies. While object-oriented design techniques may outshine "traditional" techniques in many domains, databases still shine in others. Procedural programming, and even the traditional methods that support it, still seem to have their place. Even in a system that is built purely of objects, important design relationships between objects are neither objects themselves, nor have any stature in most design methods. We find that interesting systems use multiple paradigms—often a tasteful mix of procedures, objects, and databases—to suit customer needs. While programming languages like C++ have risen to the challenge of multiparadigm design, we still lack design techniques that derive their power from multiple design perspectives. How can we manage the complex, yet important, patterns of relationships in object-oriented systems?

The Generative Patterns movement has risen to this challenge. Patterns are a way of describing, documenting, and creating system architectures for software, just as patterns have always permeated the architectures of great buildings. The patterns in a building contribute to its aesthetics and elegance, its durability, and even its utility. What elegance lies in the layout of windows of different sizes in the front elevation of a building? What patterns make a building look strong or, indeed, make it strong? These patterns can't be understood or explained in terms of the bricks or beams of the building alone, yet each reflects an important intent of the architect. So it should be with software: we should be concerned with the patterns of relationship in the system as a whole. Yes, classes and objects are still important—they are the bricks and girders that are all the rage in today's software toolkits—but the timelessness of a program lives in the patterns that tie its parts together. Some of these patterns, like the balance of commonality and variability along lines of inheritance, are truly object oriented. But many others are not. Even within an object-oriented system, designers think beyond objects to use intricate patterns as they frame and craft the system as a whole. Many designers do so unwittingly, while others introspect more deeply and consciously use patterns to their advantage.

Many contemporary object-oriented designers—including Grady Booch,[1] Kent Beck,[2] Ward Cunningham, Ralph Johnson,[3] and Peter Coad[4]—have turned to the work of Christopher Alexander (not a software architect, but a real architect) as a model for building software architectures from patterns. Alexander's TIMELESS WAY OF BUILDING[5] is a masterpiece of systems thinking. Both in buildings and in software, patterns capture specific practices that master designers use at the system level. Captured in written form, these patterns help guide inexpert designers. Software patterns are now a recurring theme at software conferences, and are making their way into corporate research and development programs worldwide.

LIMITS TO PERFECTION IN PROCESS

We noted already the role that an iterative development process plays in object-oriented development. While we have concrete languages, and lots of methods and courses on object-oriented software and its structure, process hasn't attained nearly the same level of maturity. There seems to be some kind of object-oriented cosmic consciousness that iteration is good, and that old step-by-step processes are bad. Yet organizations, and even insightful individuals, have difficulty understanding how to shift from their old ways of doing things to the new, seemingly radical, iterative way of doing development. Introducing any new development process into an organization has always been a risky business, and attaching the word "iteration" to a process makes it even riskier in the eyes of today's software managers. We are being told that the old paradigm of dividing our processes into analysis, requirements, design, and coding no longer works. We are told that sales and marketing should not stand in the way of direct dialogue between the customer and the software engineer. This points to a shift in organizational principles and business practices at least as large as the software engineering shift from structured design to object-oriented design.

And, once again, we turn to patterns for answers. We have long understood that organizations and business practices are full of patterns: patterns of organization structure, patterns of information flow, patterns of control. Much of organization is culture; the study of culture is anthropology, and one common textbook

> **TIP**
>
> Business practices are full of patterns.

definition of anthropology is the study of patterns of relationships in a culture. By understanding the patterns in our software development organizations, we can better understand ourselves as software engineers and our domain of software development. And if we understand these patterns in enough depth, we can turn them around as the tools we use to lay the architectural foundations for new organizations and processes that support our business goals.

Work in both generative software patterns and in generative organizational patterns is in its formative stages. Most pattern work to date has been empirical, recovering recurring patterns from outstanding software[6]; this is a necessary first step to cataloging good patterns. As useful patterns emerge, and as we see how patterns interact, we can assemble and publish them as tools that support construction of new systems.

Patterns are one component of the process research being carried out at AT&T. While most pattern research in the industry is concerned with software architecture, we believe that organizational architecture also can benefit from a pattern-based approach. In fact, patterns may frequently cross over between these domains. Just as the process community has borrowed abstraction techniques such as Petri Nets from software engineering, so it might take patterns under its wing. And as patterns have long been important to people who study organizations and processes, so software might take a cue from research in organizational patterns.

WHAT IS A PATTERN?

What exactly do we mean by this new sense of the word "pattern," now becoming a buzzword in the software community? Like a dressmaker's pattern, it tells us how to make something, like part of a software system or part of an organization. But it is not just a set of obscure instructions that, if followed, produce the intended product as kind of a surprise at the end. We can tell what a pattern will achieve by studying it. A pattern is both a thing and a description of how to make that thing. Patterns are not a formal specification of a system, but appeal to our sense of aesthetics and intuition about the system's purpose. The same is true for a dressmaker's pattern. Christopher Alexander claims that the same is true for the great architectures of history, for works like the Chartres Cathedral—its splendor was the product of more than blueprints. For example, his pattern "Light on Two Sides" suggests that the best rooms have light sources on at least two of the walls. We want organizational patterns to be similarly descriptive and clear without prescribing details. They should let us shape the solution to the context in which it is being applied, just as we do with a dress pattern or one of Alexander's patterns.

> **TIP**
>
> A pattern tells us how to make something.

Patterns solve problems. A pattern captures, structures, and presents a morsel of key knowledge about some domain. Experts in a given domain know the tricks of their trade, why they work, and when to apply them. Novices often miss important tricks of the trade, or blindly apply the ones they do know with mixed success. Patterns capture these key knowledge morsels by describing the problem they solve, the trade-offs they resolve in whole or in part, the context in which they apply, and the particulars of the implementation. Capturing the knowledge in this form raises the chances for success for an inexpert practitioner.

Let's consider the simple problem of how to create group boundaries in a new department we are building to develop a new line of products. This problem won't give you any great insights into organizational theory, but will show how patterns apply to the domain of organization and process.

Pattern Name:
Organization Follows Geography

Problem:
How should you assign tasks to geographically distributed organizations?

Context:
A product must be developed in several different hallways, on different floors of a building, in different buildings or at different locations.

Forces:
Communication patterns between project members follows geographic distribution.

Coupling between pieces of software must be sustained by concomitant coupling between the people maintaining that software.

People avoid communicating with people who work in other buildings, other towns, or overseas.

People in an organization usually work on related tasks, which suggests that they communicate frequently with each other.

Solution:
The architectural partitioning should reflect the geographic partitioning, and vice versa.

Design Rationale:
Research has found that social distance goes up rapidly with physical separation. Our empirical experience with co-development overseas reveals that failure to follow this pattern can lead to complete project failure.

FIGURE 1. *A simple organizational pattern.*

PROCESS PATTERNS BY EXAMPLE

Each product has its own market segment. One of the markets is in the country of Napaj, and part of the code will be written by people in our corporate facility there. A small architecture team has made a first cut at the architecture. What are the patterns we follow to partition the group?

A good solution principle is that organizations should be maximally decoupled. If organizations can work independently, they will need fewer meetings, have more decision autonomy, feel in control of their destiny, and be able to work undisturbed. But what kind of coupling should we focus on? We could group the organizations by their geographical collocation, with one group in Napaj and another in our home country. Another alternative would be to group them by market segment; yet another would be to divide people along the lines of the straw software architecture. Each of these perspectives presents a different facet of the same problem. Each perspective is a separate context. A pattern is a solution to a problem in a context.

Let us quickly look at patterns for each of the partitioning problems. In successful projects, geographic boundaries don't cut across the organization structure: that is a pattern. We can describe tendencies, called forces, that contribute to this pattern (Figure 1). The forces for this pattern are obvious, as described in the figure. There is a tension between these forces that is dangerous to leave unresolved. A good pattern resolves one or more of the forces present in the problem. The pattern we apply here is called "Organization Follows Geography." By aligning organizational boundaries with geographic boundaries, we resolve all these forces. And we feel good about the resolution: A good pattern is like a small play that builds toward a climax, and we should feel a sense of catharsis at the end.

How about grouping by market segment? Again, the problem is the communication coupling between organizations, coupling we can avoid by partitioning the organization the right way. The forces are:

- Development organizations should track and meet customer needs.
- Customer needs are similar, and much of what they all need can be done in common.
- Different customers expect results on different schedules.

The solution is to reflect the market structure in the development organization. One frequently overlooked and powerful pattern is a "core" organization that supports only what is common across all market segments. It is important to put this organization in place up front. We call this pattern "Organization Follows Market." This is a remarkably obvious pattern, and what's more remarkable is how many large development organizations ignore it. Patterns are a way of capturing the experience of experts for new generations of practitioners. With this pattern in hand, the organization designer can avoid a multitude of problems that plague organizations supporting multiple markets.

MORE PATTERNS TO FINE-TUNE THE PROCESS

Now let's shift the context a bit. The organizations are formed and jobs are staffed. Each organization starts selecting its local development process. Many choose a standard waterfall model: requirements, design, implementation, and test. They create roles to flesh out the process model: Designer,

Coder, Project Manager, Inspector, Test Writer, and others. They start development, but bog down as delivery dates approach. They uncover analysis and design errors during coding and unit testing. Early friendly user testing with the customer does not go well. What is wrong with the process?

The organization had presumed that the analysis, design, and coding phases were separable and independent. In a postmortem they found that, in fact, analysis, design, and most implementation activities were tightly coupled to each other. They found that back-end activities, such as testing, product packaging, delivery, and customer support, were also tightly coupled to each other. Most back-end activities were nonetheless decoupled from design and coding. They also found that they were using the same general review process for both documents and code, whereas their process design hadn't foreseen that commonality.

These, too, are patterns. As described here, it is often the case that organizations discover them only in retrospect. Such patterns can be discovered empirically by analyzing the day-to-day workings of a particular organization and process. Role playing is one process and organizational analysis tool used at AT&T, drawing on Beck and Cunningham's CRC design techniques.[7] Role playing takes place in sessions where software developers build a model of their own organization. We analyze this data with a tool called Pasteur, searching for patterns in organization and process. One thing Pasteur can do is to draw adjacency diagrams like that of Figure 2, which shows an empirical model of communication structures in the project. The individual clusters are locales of mutual interest; the picture provides hints about organization structure.

Using a pattern language for process and organization, we choose a pattern that reforms the organizational structure around communities of interest. We call this pattern "Form Follows Function" (a term coined, curiously enough, by the building architect Louis Sullivan); the architect Alexander had an analogous pattern called "Circulation Paths." If you can discover major communication centers early enough, you can build an organization around the paths of communication.

Patterns can be used to continually evolve processes as new insights surface and as the landscape changes. Look at the adjacency diagram again. Although there appear to be separate processes for review (at the top left), front-end activities (top right), and back-end activities (at the bottom), the Coder role is tightly coupled to all of them. The apparent autonomy of these processes is maintained at the expense of the individuals at the bottom of the

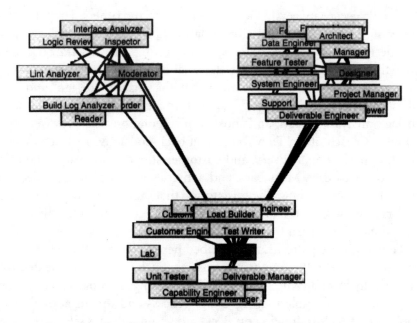

FIGURE 2. *Coupling in this partitioned design/coding process can be reduced by rearranging coder's responsibilities.*

food chain: the poor implementors of all those lines of C++ code. Why are they so tightly coupled to the front-end and review processes? Well, because that's how real work gets done. To unburden coders, the insightful process architect can shift their responsibilities to other roles, or add roles to support the coders in their work (perhaps by implementing chief programmer teams, for example). Such rearranging should not be done arbitrarily, of course. The adjacency diagram is only a hint, and an organization should change its structure and process only in light of the organization's goals, its roles' cohesiveness, and its employees' special talents.

PATTERNS: BEYOND THE SCIENCE OF MODELING TO THE ART OF BUILDING

We can organize patterns into an ordered structure called a generative pattern language. Alexander describes a pattern language for building architecture in his book; software engineers are developing pattern languages for software system architectures (such as Johnson's framework patterns); and research at

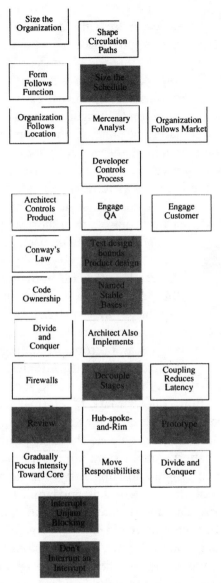

Figure 3. *Key patterns of a generative pattern language for organizations and processes.*

AT&T is evaluating pattern languages to create organizations and development processes (Figure 3). Pattern languages can generate all possible organizations and processes for a given context, just as the English language can generate all possible OBJECT MAGAZINE articles. A good pattern language captures the transformations—or patterns—that consistently succeed in building architecture, software architecture, or organizational architecture. Architects who subconsciously apply these patterns build distinguished works, which are as much the product of art and intuition as of rigorous science. Patterns give stature and voice to the artistic nature of practical endeavors such as building a house, writing a program, or guiding the work of a community of people. A pattern language helps the novice understand the key workings of a virtuoso. While a pattern language can't make a virtuoso out of everybody, it can guide inexpert practitioners away from novice errors—an important consideration in leading-edge fields where true virtuosos are in short supply.

A good pattern language guides the inexpert practitioner away from typically inexpert mistakes. In a pattern language for human interfaces, it might guide the developer away from dialogue boxes or moded interfaces. In a pattern language for organizations (such as in Figure 3), it would guide the organizational analyst away from presuming that managers actually control their subordinates. For our organization decomposition patterns, the language would specify the order in which we apply "Organization Follows Market," "Form Follows Function," and the other decomposition patterns. It may even suggest how to combine them, or might stipulate that they all yield the same partitioning.

While these patterns might seem almost mechanical, they still must be guided by human insight and familiarity with the context at hand. Users of any language must draw on their skills and familiarity with the problem being solved as they articulate and elaborate a solution. Anyone who builds an organization must be keenly aware of whom the organization is to serve, what the expected products and profits are, and what similar organizations look like. Good patterns support their solution with a design rationale. Novices shouldn't follow patterns blindly, but should understand the rationale for each one, and exercise judgment in applying patterns as their knowledge grows.

PATTERNS: COMING SOON TO A DOMAIN NEAR YOU

We believe that organization-building should be nurtured as an art and a skill, not just as "management science." Just as great builders can build magnificent edifices, we believe the great managers of the future will be able to craft great organizations as artisans rather than as scientists. In fact, that's probably what makes great managers great today. If we can capture the insight that great managers use to build organizations, then we can do for organizational science what Alexander aspired to do for architecture: To give the workaday individuals the tools they need to work with aesthetic sensitivity, functional utility, and organizational architecture. Patterns can be the blueprints from which many future systems might be built, be they software, buildings, or the communities of people who grace their chambers.

We hope that by assembling enough of these patterns, we can detect recurring themes that portend for high productivity or high quality, and assemble such patterns as a basis for new organizations.

References

1. G. Booch. Patterns, OBJECT MAGAZINE 3(2):24–27, 1993.

2. K. Beck. Patterns and software development, DR. DOBB'S JOURNAL 19(2):18–23.

3. R. E. Johnson. Documenting frameworks using patterns, ACM SIGPLAN NOTICES 27(10), 1992.

4. P. Coad. Addendum to the Proceedings of OOPSLA '92, OOPS MESSENGER 4(2), 1993.

5. C. Alexander, THE TIMELESS WAY OF BUILDING, Oxford University Press, New York, 1979.

6. E. Gamma. Design Patterns: Abstraction and reuse of object-oriented designs, PROCEEDINGS OF THE EUROPEAN CONFERENCE ON OBJECT-ORIENTED PROGRAMMING, Oscar Nierstrasz, Ed, Springer Verlag, Berlin, 1993.

7. K. Beck. Think like an object, UNIX REVIEW, September, 1991.

PATTERNS AND IDIOMS IN CIRCLES, COMPLEX ELLIPSES, AND REAL BRIDGES

JAMES O. COPLIEN

P ATTERNS ARE A GENERALIZATION OF PROGRAMMING LANGUAGE IDIOMS—OR are they? Patterns have a problem-oriented focus, while many idioms are more solution-oriented. A designer who has mastered idioms and their use can draw on their knowledge to solve a host of programming problems. Are patterns just the bridge—er, gate—that takes an inexpert designer from ignorance to proficiency with idioms that makes them master architects? By mastering a few simple solution idioms, can a designer develop much the same proficiency as with a larger number of patterns? Discussions between design experts show that the mapping from patterns to idioms is many-to-many and complex, even for problems that are intuitive and well-known in the literature. It appears that there are roles for both patterns and idioms in software design.

Late last year and early this year, I participated in a CompuServe study group forum (DBADVISOR Section 20) that focused on the book ADVANCED C++ PROGRAMMING STYLES AND IDIOMS. A recurring design problem surfaced in the discussion: what is the design relationship between a `Circle` and an `Ellipse`? Does `Circle` have a `resize` member function that changes it into an `Ellipse`? If so, then:

- Maybe `Circle` shouldn't be a distinct class; only `Ellipses` should appear in the implementation;
- Or maybe `resize` should be a `const` member function that yields an `Ellipse` result, leaving the original alone;
- Or maybe resize should change the type of a Circle object to be an `Ellipse` object, as appropriate.

The first solution ignores the presence of `Circles` in the domain vocabulary, and may miss important opportunities for optimization (e.g., the formula for the area of a circle is simpler than that for an ellipse). The second object produces a new object instead of resizing the object being operated on; those aren't the semantics we'd expect from a drawing package. The third option is difficult to express in a statically typed language like C++.

The envelope/letter idiom in ADVANCED C++ (Section 5.5)[1] provides one way out of this dilemma. That idiom separates the interface into one class, and the (possibly numerous) implementations into separate classes. The interface can be sufficiently robust to support multiple implementations. A programmer can instantiate an "envelope" object representing the `Ellipse` interface. That object can bind itself to a "letter" object for either a concrete `Ellipse` or a `Circle`. If we stretch an object representing a `Circle`, it can rebind its implementation to an `Ellipse` representation. A single instance built with the general Ellipse interface can bind itself to the appropriate implementation. The implementation classes are derived from the interface class, which guarantees that the implementations comply with the interface.

The same idiom also addresses a seemingly unrelated inheritance dilemma. Consider the inheritance relationship between two numeric classes, `Complex` and `Real`. Our intuition tells us to derive `Real` from `Complex`, because a `Real` IS-A `Complex`. A publicly derived class should be a subtype of its base class, yet it can have no less internal state than its base. The more abstract a type is, the wider its range of values. That means derived class state should be more constrained than for the corresponding base class; in good object-oriented design, base and publicly derived class member functions obey semantics. We intuitively expect the implementation to reflect these semantics: there should be fewer bits in a base class than in its derived classes. If class `Complex` has eight bytes, we probably expect class `Real` to be four bytes. However, inheritance can only add state information to a base class; a derived class object always carries at least as many bits as its base class object. Envelope/letter pairs solve this by breaking the class apart: state and type can be fully separated.

Envelope/letter class pairs are a single solution that addresses both these problems; we find a similar solution structure at the heart of many design patterns. Perhaps they seem fundamental because of DeBruler's maxim: "Most interesting problems in computer science reduce to what's in a name, and can be solved by one more level of indirection." Does that mean that the problems are fundamentally related to each other? Furthermore, the

`State` and `Bridge` patterns of the DESIGN PATTERNS (DP) book, solve related problems. What is the relationship between `State`, `Bridge`, the envelope/letter idiom, and the problems they solve? This month's column summarizes highlights from recent electronic mail discussions about these two problems and the patterns and idioms that address them. The dialogue pushes the envelope about the relationship between patterns, idioms, problems, solutions, and what kinds of designers should use them.

I organized my thoughts into two patterns based on the `Circle/Ellipse` example and the `Complex/Real` example, and posted them to the electronic pattern discussion list (patterns@cs.uiuc.edu) to elicit opinions from the pattern community. The first pattern describes the `Circle/Ellipse` problem and its solution:

Problem: Even though a derived class seems to be a proper subtype of its base class, some base class operations are overconstrained for the derived class context. Stated another way, some operations that are closed under the base class are not closed under the derived class.

Context: A statically typed language that expresses subtyping as inheritance. The base class has an operation whose parameters correspond to degrees of freedom in its state space. We want to inherit that operation in the derived class (which takes away at least one degree of freedom present in the base class; see the example).

Forces:

- We usually use (public) inheritance (in the languages defined in the context) to express subtyping.

- A base class member function may take one parameter for each of the degrees of freedom in its state space.

- Because the derived class is a subtype of the base class, it has fewer degrees of freedom than the base class.

- To inherit a base class operation whose parameters map onto degrees of freedom in the state space, the derived class must elide one argument (or otherwise constrain the arguments).

- Any base class operation inherited by the derived class should exhibit the same signature in both classes.

Example:

```
class Ellipse {
public:
    Ellipse(Pdouble majorAxis, Pdouble minorAxis, Point center);
```

```
    virtual void resize(Pdouble majorAxis, Pdouble minorAxis);
    . . . .
};
class Circle: public Ellipse { // because a Circle IS-A Ellipse
public:
    Circle(Pdouble radius, Point center):  Ellipse(radius,
        radius, center) { }
    void resize( ? );
};
```

Solution: Capture the subtyping relationship using inheritance. Use the envelope/letter idiom to separate the representation of the base and derived classes as two classes derived from a common abstract base. The base can be an arbitrary new class (as in the DP Bridge pattern) or can be the more abstract of the two classes (as in the envelope/letter idiom).

The code is actually pretty involved.

Resulting context: Consider the example. An Ellipse may result if the resize operation is applied to either a Circle or an Ellipse. Because a Circle IS-A Ellipse, resize may yield a Circle (as an optimization) to satisfy the expected post-condition that the object be of type Ellipse.

The new context leaves some efficiency issues to be addressed.

Rationale: At first glance, resize(Pdouble, Pdouble) seems to apply to Ellipses but not to Circles. It is easy to conclude this, because resize is closed under Ellipse, but not under Circle. However, resize applies equally to Circles as to Ellipses, and is closed under Ellipses in general. This means that any attempt to resize a Circle changes it into an Ellipse. Such dynamic retyping is difficult to support in the given context of statically typed languages. To overcome this restriction, use idioms (like the envelope/letter idiom) or design patterns (like the DP Bridge) that allow dynamic retyping of an object at run-time. Here, the type is a function of the number of degrees of freedom in the state. This is a subtle difference from the DP State pattern alone, where type depends on value.

Here is the second pattern I proposed. It solves a bit different problem, one of the obvious conflicts between inheritance and subtyping.

Problem: Mixing inheritance and subtyping leads to unused data members.

Context: A language that does not separate subtyping and inheritance.

Forces:

- Subtyping is inheritance in this context.

- If class B is a subtype of class A, then class B is more restrictive in the sense that its state space is a proper subset of the state space of its base class. This is often enforced using method pre- and post-conditions.

- A class should carry only the data necessary for its semantics; irrelevant base class states should be "canceled."
- You can't remove base class members from a derived class; base class data members become part of derived class objects.

Example:

```
class Complex {
public:
  Complex(double, double);
  Complex operator+=(const Complex&);
friend Complex operator+(const Complex&, const Complex&);
  . . . .
protected:
  double r, theta;
};

class Real: public Complex {
  . . . .
// sizeof(Real) == 8
};
```

Solution: Factor the class state spaces from the type hierarchy into a separate inheritance hierarchy (`State` pattern or envelope/letter idiom). The application classes contain only a single data member, which is a pointer to the implementation classes. The implementation classes contain the "real" state. `Application` classes follow normal design subtyping relationships. The inheritance hierarchy of the implementation class, or lack thereof, is immaterial.

Example:

```
class Number {
public:
Number(double d1, double d2 = 0) { u.rep = d2? new
Complex(d1,d2) ? new Real(d1);
}
 Number() { }
   virtual Number &operator+=(const Number &n) { return
     u.rep->operator+=(n); }
   virtual ~Number() { delete u.rep; }
friend Number operator+(const Number&, const Number&);
  . . . .
protected:
  union { Number *rep; double aDouble; } u;
};

class Complex: public Number {
```

```
friend Number;
protected:
  Complex(double d1 = 0, double d2 = 0): Number(),
    rpart(u.aDouble), ipart(d2) {

 u.aDouble = d1;
 }
 ~Complex() { u.rep = 0; }
 Number &operator+=(const Number&);
 . . . .
private:
  const double &rpart; double ipart;
};

class Real: public Number {
friend Number;
private:
  Real(double d = 0): Number(), rpart(u.aDouble)
    { u.aDouble= d; }
 ~Real() { u.rep = 0; }
  Number &operator+=(const Number&);
  const double &rpart;
  . . . .
};
```

Resulting context: A compact representation can be used, independent of the interface presented to the application programmer. Though this saves the memory of the extra datum inherited from the base class, it adds space for a pointer.

These two patterns generated a deluge of responses in the mailing group. Bruce Cohen of Servio was the first to note that both these patterns had something to do with the tension between "the needs of the type relationship and the needs of the inheritance relationship," which he felt explained the forces. Robert Martin (Object Mentor Association) cast the problem as "subtypes that are more constrained than their supertypes." He claims:

> In the first case, it is the interface of the subtype: `Circle` that is more constrained than the supertype `Ellipse`. In the second case it is the state information that is more constrained (the subtype `Real` has fewer state variables than the supertype `Complex`).

Robert and I had some dialogue about the relationship of constraints like this to subtyping. Our dialogue taught me that the number of internal state bits shouldn't be used to measure subtyping relationships, but that the interface semantics are the final arbiter. However, it's likely (as in `Real` and

`Complex`) that inheritance causes the derived class to end up with extra state. The extra state doesn't cause a subtyping problem, but, as Robert pointed out, it can be confusing to a user attempting to manipulate a derived class object through a base class interface. It's also just dead weight.

Karl Puder presented yet another solution, at least for the case of `Complex` and `Real`: derive both from a more abstract class like `Number`. This is the solution taken by ADVANCED C++, and is in fact the example used to motivate the envelope/letter idiom in Section 5.5. This gives the compiler a slightly weaker static type model to work with, which may mean more work at run time.

Dirk Riehle wasn't sure that the problem had been well-enough specified that it merited a pattern, but said he'd give it a shot, anyhow. He claims such objects have non-deterministic semantics. This is an expansion of Puder's solution. Here's Dirk's offering:

Motivation: Use the notion of non-deterministic semantics to reconcile differences between types related to each other through an is-like-a relationship.

Problem: Two types/classes are very similar but slightly differ in some of their operation's semantics. How shall the supertype abstracting out the commonalities of both types treat these differences?

Context: Finding the right abstraction is one of the most fundamental problems of building good type hierarchies. [He noted he should add something about subtyping and the Liskov substitutability principle.]

As an example, consider the `Circle/Ellipse` problem. Both types have an operation Resize that has (vaguely) the same meaning but is so distinct that it even has different parameters:

```
void Circle::Resize( int diff );
void Ellipse::Resize( int xdiff,  int ydiff );
```

Operations that will be closed in subtypes of types that are neighbors in the subtype lattice need to have an open semantics in their supertype that entails at least those possibilities, the subtypes will require to have.

Therefore:

Solution: Evaluate the domain, i.e., the range of possible semantics for the critical operations and specify them as the semantics of those operations. They shall not determine which possibility will be chosen for a subtype; i.e., they are nondeterministic.

With respect to the `Circle/Ellipse` problem, neither circle nor ellipse are subclasses of each other, but both are subclasses of `Shape`. We have to introduce not only a common supertype but also a new abstraction encapsulating the resize parameters to keep things going on the technical level:

```
void Shape::Resize( ResizeAction* ra );
void Circle::Resize( ResizeAction* );
void Ellipse::Resize( ResizeAction* );
```

The additional abstraction `ResizeAction` is nondeterministic from `Shape`'s perspective and will be specialized to fit the needs of specific subtypes (`1dResizeAction` and `2dResizeAction`), `1dResizeAction` for circles and squares and `2dResizeAction` for ellipses and rectangles closing the semantics. It might have the operation:

```
ResizeAction::JustDoIt( Resizable* );
ResizeAction::BuildFromMouseMove( int xdiff, int ydiff );
```

with `1dResizeAction` and `2dResizeAction` casting the parameter to `1dResizable` or `2dResizable` (where `Circle` is derived from `1dResizable` and `Ellipse` from `2dResizable`).

Types with non-deterministic semantics should always be made abstract classes. Actually, it seems to me to be close to the characteristic description, i.e., the definition of abstract type.

> **TIP**
>
> Types with non-deterministic semantics should always be made abstract classes.

This solution ensures that the base class interface accommodates all the derived class cases. Bill Hopkins suggested a variant of this pattern using argument defaulting. The `Resize` operation might have two parameters; it would do one-dimensional resizing if the caller supplied one parameter, and two-dimensional resizing if both parameters were supplied.

Giuliano Carlini recast the original patterns into a new pattern called "Mutation Contract." The pattern is too long to reproduce here, but it solved the problem of a constant type interface to a representation with dynamic structure. His solution is to choose the most efficient representation possible for the result of a given computation. The solution is reminiscent of the implementation of arithmetic operations in many Smalltalk implementations.

BERCZUK'S SYNOPSES

Steve Berczuk (MIT Center for Space Research) distilled the discussion into three patterns. All of them solve the same problem. The specific problem is: How do you express the relationship between `Circle` and `Ellipse`? The more general problem is: How do inheritance and subtyping interact with each other? The first pattern suggests we do away with class `Circle` entirely:

Name: Instance as Classification

Context: A system where round shapes are manipulated, and `Circles` are an implementation convenience but not as an interface. For example, we want to create round objects with semi-major axis == semi-minor axis by specifying only one number, but we will never inquire about the specific properties of a circle such as diameter.

Solution: Treat circles as instances of the `Ellipse` class. Provide a constructor with one argument rather than two.

This is a lot like the `State` pattern in the DP. His second pattern solves the same problem, but in a different context. It re-introduces the `Circle` when the context dictates that significantly different behaviors align with the design abstractions:

Name: Subclassing

Context: A system where the `Circle/Ellipse` distinction is important for different behavior. `Circle` responds to all `Ellipse` messages, and also has behavior specific to circles. (You can then have a `List<Circle>` and process it appropriately.) The fact that `Ellipse` requires more state than a `Circle` is not important to your application.

Solution: Use inheritance. Derive `Circle` from `Ellipse`, and use `Circles` when appropriate. Many operations can be handled by the base class.

This pattern provides yet another solution, in the context where the user doesn't really care whether the abstraction is a circle or an ellipse (i.e., it is just an optimization):

Name: Use state for changing type.

Context: A System where a "fat" interface is permissible (One can make `Circle`-specific requests to an `Ellipse`, but they will be ignored, or an error value will be returned) and we don't necessarily want to distinguish between `Circles` and `Ellipses` other than in behaviors. We want to allow for an `Ellipse` that gets created, and later resized so that semi-major axis == semiminor axis to become a circle. We don't want extra state information and we also want to take advantage of the of any simplifications that can be had by assuming `Circles`.

Solution: Use something akin to the `State` pattern in DP, with the `Context` class being `Ellipse`, with `State` classes `Circular` and `GeneralEllipse`.

This isn't a complete set, of course. Consider a situation where one cared about superfluous state information, but the context was otherwise the same as for the Subclassing pattern. This will give us a different pattern with slightly different Solution (perhaps using a union in the base class which can either be a double or a pointer to a struct). This emphasizes the point that patterns are the combination of context and problem with the resulting solution. A given solution may not work for a problem unless the contexts match quite closely. Combining problems and contexts with solutions can yield a number of interesting patterns.

Berczuk talks more about the relationship between pattern problems and solutions in his article, "Finding solutions through pattern languages."[3]

LESSONS LEARNED TO DATE

The discussion groups covered considerable ground in the thread that explored the two initial patterns. It explored the envelope/letter idiom, the State and Bridge patterns, some type theory, and many new patterns to deal with the original perceived problem. The envelope/letter idiom provides a solution for both of the original problems:

- It makes it possible for an object to change its behavior (type) at run time so that state changes caused by operations like resize make equal sense for both Circles and Ellipses;
- It makes it possible to separate the structure of a concrete type from the interface, making it possible to get rid of superfluous state information that inheritance would force on the derived class.

I have usually thought of the envelope/letter idiom as a "restatement of the State pattern for C++," but this exercise suggests that we should view them differently. Why? A pattern is a solution to a problem in a context. The envelope/ letter idiom solves two different problems (and several more) equally well. In summary:

- The State pattern is a solution to the problem of how to make behavior depend on state;
- The Bridge pattern is a way to separate implementation from interface;
- The envelope/letter idiom is a solution to the problem of how to make class–both implementation structure and behavior–depend on state.

We can model (or implement) the State pattern using a state machine, where "[f]or each state, a table maps every possible input to a succeeding state."* Envelope/letter handles "indeterminacies" that are more complex than state machines alone can handle (though state machines fall out of envelope/letter as a special case). Envelope/letter is curiously reflective, since the state embedded in one structure is used to select a new structure—whose state is derived from the state of the original structure. For example: If we resize a `Circle` to make it an `Ellipse`, it takes on more state (what used to be the radius becomes a major and minor axis), though the new state comes from the original center and radius of the `Circle`, and from the parameters supplied to resize.

The structure of `State` and `Bridge` are identical (except that `Bridge` admits a hierarchy of envelope classes, whereas `State` allows only one). The two patterns use that same structure to solve different problems: `State` allows an object's behavior to change along with its state, while `Bridge`'s intent is "[to d]ecouple an abstraction from its implementation so that the two can vary independently." Many other patterns use this same envelope/letter-like structure to solve additional design problems: for example, `Strategy` uses this structure to organize alternative algorithms in letter classes that support a single generic envelope class.

Does this mean that envelope/letter is a more general solution than `State`? Or is it a broad implementation technique that supports the `State` pattern, as well as other patterns like `Proxy`, or `Adapter`, or `Bridge`? The answer admits a bit of both. Idioms are solutions in search of problems: a well-equipped architect can use them as multipurpose tools that address a wide variety of problems. Idioms might even solve problems that were unforeseen at the time they were written, whereas patterns tend to focus on specific problems with well-known solutions. The DP patterns `Bridge`, `Strategy`, and `State` (and to some degree, `Adapter`) have similar solution structures. Figure 1 presents one perspective on the relationship between these patterns and the idioms that embody the underlying solution structures. According to Gamma et al., `Bridge` is a synonym for the handle/body idiom-including the specialized use to support representation sharing in the `Counted Body` idiom. They suggest that envelope/letter is a generalization of `State`. Though `State`, `Strategy`, and `Bridge` all share elements of the handle/body idiom, they differ in intent—that is, they solve different problems.

We can make a gross generalization that patterns are problem-focused, and idioms are solution-focused. We can approach design from either end,

---

*See page 308 of Gamma et al.[2]

and each has its own benefits and liabilities. Let's look at the `Bridge` pattern again for another example. `Bridges` support implementation sharing, a fact made explicit in the Applicability section for the `Bridge` pattern.[2] A parenthetic note suggests that the shared implementation might be reference-counted. As Figure 1 shows, that means the `Bridge` pattern subsumes the `Counted Body` idiom. Reference counting is widely applied as a form of garbage collection—yet there is nothing in the `Bridge` pattern that would lead a novice to use it for memory management. The `Counted Body` idiom focuses on the memory management problem. This focus on memory management suggests than the `Counted Body` idiom shouldn't be lumped into the `Bridge` pattern along with the handle/body idiom, but that it should stand as a pattern in its own right.

The challenge of a problem-focused approach is formalizing the problem you're solving: different people interpret problems in different ways. Gamma et al. formalized the `Counted Body` problem as the `Bridge` pattern: decoupling an abstraction from its implementation. Consider the `Complex/Real` pattern: what problem does it solve? The designer might perceive this as being any of the following problems:

- Mixing inheritance and subtyping leads to unused data members
- Behavior and representation are tied too closely together
- Inheritance structures and type structures are orthogonal
- Static typing misses opportunities to convert an object to a more compact representation

There is (at least) one solution-the envelope/letter idiom-that solves all these problems. We could build a pattern language containing a pattern for each alternative view: several problem-solution pairs, all of which share the same solution. But imagine trying to generate a list of all the problems solved by this idiom! That would make an unreasonably large search space for the novice developer seeking a solution.

What if we taught the envelope/letter idiom to novice developers so it became a tool in their tool box? Knowing the tools at their disposal, they could pick the right tool for the right job as problems arose. However, that means that every novice would have to re-discover the problems on their own. Some problems are so common that they should be part of a novice's

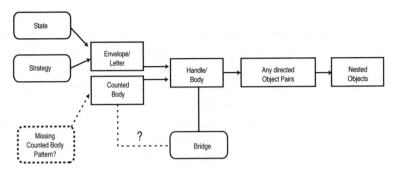

FIGURE 1. *Some structural relationships between idioms (rectangles)and patterns (ellipses).*

training. The counted body idiom is a good example of a problem/solution pair that every C++ programmer should learn.

Which is better: The problem-focused approach found in the patterns community, or a solution-based approach? To replay a familiar theme, each approach is suitable to its own context. The same is true in architectural design as it is in software. Consider the origin of the arch during the expansion of the Roman Empire. As the empire grew, transplanted officials expected many of the commodities of Roman home life, including good water, good communications, and the ability to dispatch military force rapidly if necessary. The solutions were aqueducts and (curiously enough) bridges. The arch made both of these possible, and the Romans were first to use it on a grand scale. The Romans later went on to use arches in more decadent contexts, as we find in the Coliseum and in decorative arches throughout the Roman empire.

Here, arches solve two problems: how to build fairly level roads over hilly terrain, and how to make water flow to a city from a distance. An experienced architect who understood both these needs, and who understood arches as well, would have foreseen arches as a component of both solutions without consciously analyzing the problems and their forces. Experienced architects understand the intent of arches in general. We would have to point out the arch solution to an inexpert architect (or an architect who predated the Roman era).

Maybe software patterns are the same way. One of the "Aha's" that people experience when they read a pattern is, "Gee, I never thought of doing that!" Maybe one overlooked value of patterns is as an advertisement for useful solutions. Most of the design patterns being discussed in contemporary literature have more value in their solutions than in their mapping from problem to solution. The patterns discussed here for subtyping and inheritance fall into this category. I believe that patterns also exist for specific application domains where novices can't understand the solution unless they understand the problem it addresses. For example, round-robin scheduling may not appear to be a particularly modern regimen, but it has substantial advantages over priority-driven schemes in real time systems. To appreciate that round-robin scheduling is a solution at all, one must understand both the problem and the context. I believe patterns will shine in these highly specialized domains, where expertise will always be scarce.

Both problem-oriented approaches like patterns and solution-based design techniques like idioms have their place. Both help us learn-that is, they make lasting changes in our design practice. Patterns are important for novices, since they point out the common pitfalls that experienced practitioners have already discovered. Solution-based approaches are the raw material that we can assemble in new ways to address unforeseen problems. The psychologist Piaget notes that our early stages of intellectual development are guided by externally imposed rules. As we gain respect for these rules over time and as we see those solutions work, we're able to abstract better and deal with more complexity. Though Piaget's model relates primarily to childhood intellectual development, it's a good analogy for how we learn new paradigms as well. Richard Helm notes (in mail of January 9, 1995):

> Descriptions of patterns/idioms start out as solution-directed. After all, they are discovered in the context of creating a solution. Initially you understand only the specific solution for the problem at hand... Only when you have used the pattern to solve multiple problems does your understanding of it become more abstract and solution-directed. You see the range of problems that the pattern can solve. It becomes solution-directed.

I empathize with this view, but would say that "only when you have used the solution part of a pattern to solve multiple problems does your understanding of it become more abstract and solution-directed." You then see the range of problems that the solution addresses: each of these becomes a pattern with its own problem statement. Extracting a `Counted Body` pattern from `Bridge` is a good example.

In a recent discussion with Larry Constantine at WOOD/95, he (and several others) went even further to suggest that we should separate problem patterns (e.g., for analysts) from solution patterns (for designers).

Alexander says that expert architects don't need patterns, as the patterns have already become part of them. Patterns are just the gate through which architects pass until they develop the sensitivity to know which solutions work well together. Such architects still know the stock solutions they learned in college and during their

> **TIP**
>
> Expert architects don't need patterns.

apprenticeships; those never go away, just as the need for programming language idioms is ever-present. Patterns prevent novice architects from shooting themselves in the foot. Experience with patterns, and in particular with the workings of their solutions, nurtures the quality without a name.

Acknowledgements

I'm grateful to Steve Berczuk, Giuliano Carlini, Richard Helm, Bill Hopkins, Robert C. Martin, Karl Puder, and Dirk Riehle for their patterns, comments, and criticisms of this paper.

References

1. Coplein, J. ADVANCED C++ PROGRAMMING STYLES AND IDIOMS, Addison-Wesley, Reading, MA, 1992.

2. Gamma, E., et al. DESIGN PATTERNS, Addison-Wesley, Reading, MA, 1995.

3. Berczuk, S. "Finding solutions through pattern languages," IEEE COMPUTER, 27(12):75–76, Dec. 1994.

PATTERN MINING

James O. Coplien

P ATTERNS DON'T JUST COME OUT OF THIN AIR—THEY CAPTURE PROVEN DEVEL-
opment experience. Gems of knowledge come from projects with
proven track records, and it takes work to extract them. Pattern-mining
activities at AT&T have produced a wide variety of patterns now being used
by new development projects. We use knowledge extraction techniques
analogous to those used by knowledge engineers to feed expert system
knowledge bases.

New projects are using these patterns as an architectural basis; existing
projects are using them as architectural documentation. Patterns have
found some surprising applications as well, including requirements generation and validation.

Our early experience with patterns has uncovered challenges that we will
face in the near future: how to review patterns and admit them to project
repositories, and how to index and organize them.

In the previous Column Without a Name, I talked about how difficult it
will be to bring the tenets of the pattern culture to an organization of computer scientists. In spite of the obstacles, we're starting to see some success.
This month, I'll focus on a pattern "technology transfer" effort in a large
project at AT&T, describing how the organization is starting to embrace patterns. There are many early indications of success. However, because
architectural benefits usually pay off over many years, this is necessarily a
preliminary assessment.

The following components must be present to make patterns work in an
organization:

- *Recognized need for design expertise support.* Unless someone understands they need to create or improve a design infrastructure, patterns don't have a place in a development organization
- *A source of design expertise.* It does no good to have willing customers if there is no source of useful patterns, and a process to mine and refine them.
- *A groundswell of pattern advocacy.* An individual or small group must carry the pattern vision into a receptive organization and nurture it until it takes root.

I touch on all of these in this column, but focus on the second item. I call this item *pattern mining.* I've heard others call it "pattern harvesting." The pattern-mining approach has been successful so far, and it builds on a major tenet of the pattern discipline: that patterns should capture broad practices that have been proven good. It takes work to find those, organize them, and publish them. Pattern mining is certainly not the only path to effective use of patterns. I encourage others to write to me at cope@research.att.com. to relate their own experiences, and I'll try to summarize and relate them here.

RECOGNIZING THE NEED FOR DESIGN EXPERTISE

This pattern story starts with a successful legacy system seeking to move into next-generation markets by building on new technologies and disciplines. The original system was large, rich in functionality, and based on custom technology that isn't (and never has been) taught in academic software curricula. Many of the project's deep design principles live in the heads of senior engineers with 20, 30, or 40 years of professional experience in the industry.

The new project was staffed with engineers whose expertise was in markets different than those for the original system. Confidence nonetheless ran high, fueled by faith in distributed processing, object-oriented programming, reuse, and other technologies and disciplines. No one took the architectural task lightly, but the project hadn't yet come to grips with its architectural blind spots.

In December 1994, I gave a presentation to some managers and engineers from this organization to point out the importance of building on historic architectural strengths instead of building each new system from first principles. Though much of the new system software would be written from scratch to take advantage of technological advances, many of the underlying principles of the existing system still applied to the new one.

To make my point, I drew an architectural analogy that was familiar to the audience. It was a building whose original architecture embodied a major symbol of the tenant's business, a symbol that was visible only to those who could see the big picture of the plot layout. As the building aged and staff turned over, fewer and fewer people even knew about the symbol. The plot was reshaped to add parking lots and extend the building, to the point that the occupants unwittingly evolved the symbolism out of the architecture. Could the new software project be headed down the same road if it ignored the architectural principles of the legacy architecture that was its heritage? I offered patterns as one way to sustain corporate memory. Whether it was the analogy or something else, the talk was a turning point: a few weeks later, we started to plan how to capture the patterns of the original project for use by the new project.

> **TIP**
>
> Pattern mining draws on the architectural principles of legacy systems.

PATTERN MINING

How do you mine the patterns of an existing system? There is a widely-held claim for object-oriented design (which I do not believe) that "objects are just there for the picking." I am even more sure that patterns aren't there for the picking: they must be sought out, verified, and carefully codified.

Pattern mining reminds me of what knowledge engineers do when they search for the rules that drive their expert systems. Patterns are rules, too, but they are rules that will be executed by human inference engines with the intelligence to accept, reject, or reshape those rules. As knowledge engineers must work with diligence to understand and codify the rules buried in the experts' heads, the pattern miner must work with double diligence. Not only must we capture the rules, but the thought processes behind them. It isn't a matter of creating new thought, but of bringing long-standing good practice out of its shell (leaving the rest of the hatching analogy to a columnist better versed in such matters).

Reflecting on our pattern mining efforts from that perspective, it is amazing that we were able to collect patterns at all. We did some things right, and we were lucky. We also learned from our mistakes. Some of the key insights follow.

Key People

We approached management of the legacy project, and asked them for the names of experts who could provide us deep architectural insights. The request sometimes needed clarification, and we would explain that we wanted people who understood the system at as many levels as possible. We found that these people show up in a variety of roles. Curiously—or perhaps not so—they have unusually frequent contact with field support, particularly for problems that are escalated to high levels. In our case, the management recommendations worked out great, though the pattern miner should in general be wary of being sent to politically accomplished experts instead of experienced and authoritative engineers.

Speaking in Patterns

TIP
Pattern miner's role.

Our goal as pattern miners is, of course, to produce patterns. But perhaps we should view ourselves as pattern-smiths instead of miners, just as goldsmiths and silversmiths take the raw material of the mine as an intermediate form to process it into a final product. We shouldn't expect patterns to come forth from the mine! One role of the pattern miner was to take the raw domain expertise and reshape it as patterns.

We felt that we should give the domain experts some insight on who we were and what we were doing, to increase their level of buy-in and to engage them as peers. We bought copies of A PATTERN LANGUAGE[1] for some of our domain experts; some of them procured it on their own. I set up no expectation that the domain experts describe their knowledge in pattern form: I made it clear that I would sort that out later.

The domain experts quickly picked up on what we were after, and their presentation often made our job easy. I found that at least two of the folks we interviewed "spoke in patterns," and always had. One of them kept a list of key architectural principles on his PC, accumulated over years of experience. It was a list of patterns, though of course he didn't know that: a fact which we didn't let bother either of us. Another domain expert, who had read Alexander and found it intriguing, just seemed to speak in patterns: problem, context, forces, solution, and rationale. I found I could transcribe much of his material directly into the form.

Classic Knowledge Engineering Challenges

There were, of course, those who didn't speak in patterns. One of our domain experts knew so much, that I don't think he knew what he knew. More to the point, he probably didn't know what I didn't know, and what he presumed was common knowledge to the whole world was either profound or unintelligible to me. These are the kind of people that the knowledge engineers warned us about, and we expected to run into more of them than we did.

Enlisting one domain expert as an interpreter for another worked well for us. I also found it worked well to bring in a domain expert who had read Alexander and who was comfortable with patterns. He could either draw the patterns out of the other domain expert, by asking the right questions, or he could extract them from our notes later. This worked particularly well when trying to extract knowledge from a senior expert (with 40 years of experience) using a junior expert as the interpreter (someone who has merely 20 years of experience). The junior expert made these sessions a priority because *he* learned so much at them. In fact, he was playfully jealous of *me* because I was able to get time with key experts, on a level that most project members would find impossible.

TIP

Enlist domain experts as interpreters.

Pacing the Interviews

I found these interviews to be intense, and limited them to 1.5 hours each. I found I could handle about two of these a week without getting behind in my work to shape them into patterns, and to convert them into HTML. We produced about 100 published patterns from two interviewees over a total of six sessions, which is more productive than we expected. Some of this productivity owes to my familiarity with the domain (though I was unfamiliar with most of the patterns); much of it owes to our luck in finding great interviewees.

CAPTURING THE PATTERNS

We have followed Doug Lea's lead at SUNY Oswego by capturing the patterns online in HTML. We use a variety of forms, but strive for brevity and simplicity. Examples and protracted rationales can be hidden behind hyperlinks.

I can't say enough for the value of HTML to link together related patterns. The nonlinear nature of pattern literature seems to grow as the pattern language grows; our current set of patterns is rich in structure.

Scrubbing the Patterns

TIP
Not all patterns are worth recording.

Not every design principle earns its wings as a pattern, and not every pattern should be published. In this project, we were careful about what practices were cast as patterns, but we probably could have been more careful about which patterns we published to the organization. We identified patterns by culling interview notes, searching for practices that met the following criteria:

- The practices must have a good track record. The pattern must have been broadly applied (I like to cite Ted Biggerstaff's "Rules of 3"[2] and look for at least three applications of the principle).

- A pattern must pass the test of time. The time factor is subjective, but for the project in question, the patterns typically date back 15 to 25 years.

- The source must be authoritative. Patterns for any given topic area must come from someone widely recognized as an authority in the area covered by the pattern. This not only helps the credibility of the pattern, but it enhances our chances of meeting the other criteria.

- Good patterns don't solve pat problems; they generate emergent behaviors that solve problems indirectly. Alexander used the term "generative" to describe this nature of good patterns; hence the term, "generative pattern language."

TIP
"Being OO" is not a requirement for a good pattern.

In some sense, it's not worth the trouble to write a good pattern if the solution and rational are immediate, intuitive, and obvious; one might as well use a table of rules. Of course, what is "obvious" and not is a subjective question, open to interpretation and discussion in a writer's workshop. The forces and rationale in a good pattern bear on problems where the solution is obscure or counterintuitive. A good pattern helps the designer understand why the "obvious" solutions don't work, and helps them understand why the suggested solution does, and under what conditions. Good patterns like this are hard to write, but worth the effort.

- Being object-oriented is not a quality we look for in good patterns. While most of our patterns (like *Riding Over Transients*, below) work perfectly well in an object environment, there isn't anything particularly object-oriented about them. Most of the good patterns seem to be in a different dimension: they are less about objects than about the mechanisms and arrangements that hold them together.

- Good patterns improve human quality of life. It's one thing to tell how to solve a technical problem, and quite another to explore the sociological, psychological, and humanistic side of a solution. Consider `Riding Over Transients`*:

Name: `Riding Over Transients`.

Problem. How do you know whether a problem will work itself out or not?

Context. A fault-tolerant application where some errors, overload conditions, etc., may be transient. The system can escalate through recovery strategies, taking more drastic action at each step. A typical example is a fault tolerant telecommunication system using static traffic engineering, where you want to check for overload or transient faults.

Forces. You want to catch faults and problems. There is no sense in wasting time solving a problem that goes away by itself. Many problems work themselves out, given time.

Solution. Don't react immediately to detected conditions. Make sure the condition really exists by checking several times, or use `Leaky Bucket Counters` to detect a critical number of occurrences in a specific time interval. For example: by averaging over time or just by waiting a while, give transient faults a chance to pass.

Resulting Context. Errors can be resolved with truly minimal effort. The human operator need not intervene for transient errors (as in the pattern `Minimize Human Interaction`).

Rationale. This pattern detects "temporally dense" events. Think of the events as spikes on a time line. If a small number of spikes (specified by a threshold) occur together (where "together" is specified by the interval), then the error is a transient. If the episode transcends the interval, it's not transient: the leak rate is faster than the refill rate, and the pattern indicates an error condition. If the burst is more intense than expected (it exceeds the error threshold) then it's unusual behavior not associated with a transient burst, and the pattern indicates an error condition. Used by `Leaky Bucket Counters`, `Five Minutes of No Escalation Messages`, and others.

This pattern works; it has been proven in many telecommunication systems over time. Multiple authoritative sources vouched for the pattern. The pattern is a powerful, generative solution that attacks a problem (transient errors) indirectly. The human tie is there, too: it tells us how systems avoid unnecessarily alerting the operator.

We also found that good patterns group together. Riding Over Transients is a widely applicable principle; though it tells us *what* to do, it doesn't tell us *how*. Here is a specific "instance" of Riding Over Transients, called Leaky Bucket Counter:

Name. Leaky Bucket Counter

Problem. How do you deal with transient faults?

Context. Fault-tolerant system software that must deal with failure events. Failures are tied to episode counts and frequencies.

One example from 1A processor systems in AT&T telecommunication products: As memory words (dynamic RAM, called "cells" in 1A processor terminology) got weak, the memory module would generate a parity error trap (a trap refresh failure). Examples include both 1A processor dynamic RAM and 1B processor static RAM.

Forces. You want a hardware module to exhibit hard failures before taking drastic action. Some failures come from the environment, and should not be blamed on the device.

Solution. A failure group has a counter that is initialized to a predetermined value when the group is initialized. The counter is decremented for each fault or event (usually faults) and incremented on a periodic basis; however, the count is never incremented beyond its initial value. There are different initial values and different leak rates for different subsystems: for example, it is a half-hour for the 1A memory (store) subsystem. The strategy for 1A dynamic RAM specifies that the first fault in a store (within the timing window) causes the store to be taken out of service, diagnosed, and then automatically restored to service. On the second, third, and fourth failure (within the timing window) you just leave it in service. For the fifth episode within the timing window, take the unit out of service, diagnose it and leave it out.

Resulting Context. A system where errors are isolated and handled (by taking devices out of service), but where transient errors (e.g., room humidity) don't cause unnecessary out of service action.

Rationale. Periodically increasing the count on the resource creates a sliding time window. The resource is considered sane when the counter (re-)attains its initialized value. Humidity, heat, and other environmental problems could cause transient errors which should be treated differently (i.e., pulling the card does no good).

See, for example, Fool Me Once.

Uses Pattern Riding Over Transients

These criteria helped us identify candidate patterns. These candidates now must be screened for broader publication to the project. While our present screening criteria are weak, we know some techniques that work, and can imagine others:

- The pattern starts with an authoritative source, is shaped into pattern form by someone skilled in the pattern form and organization, and is reviewed by the original expert. This is how most of our patterns made their way into the published pattern catalogue.

- A more formal review process would ask that the project convene writers' workshops to refine patterns and screen them for suitability to the project. Some patterns will remain "doggerel": they are kept around for reference, but aren't broadly published or endorsed by the project.

> **TIP**
>
> Formal reviews help maintain pattern viability.

An ideal writers' workshop would be a standing body with allegiance to the organization that is to use the patterns. Such organizations exist as architecture review forums, but patterns haven't matured far enough in the culture to be accepted by these institutional bodies. The composition of such a standing body leads to difficult technical questions (how to balance the depth of expertise and breadth of coverage) and it is often a difficult political question as well. So far, these factors have prevented the formation of a standing writers' workshop.

All told, this project is currently using about 200 patterns in two or three domains.

PREPARING THE ORGANIZATION

It's one thing to extract patterns from the established practices of a legacy organization: we have knowledge engineering as one model of the strategies that work and the challenges one expects to encounter. It's quite another thing to introduce those patterns into a client organization. How do you teach an organization to use patterns?

I believe that one must write patterns before using others' patterns effectively, which means that pattern-writing should be at the core of any pattern training program. I designed a two-day pattern workshop that builds on the reflective learning techniques that I've learned from my friend Bruce Anderson.[3] I served as a facilitator for the workshop, usually in collaboration with one to three colleagues from research and development organizations.

For the first course offering, I asked that the organization limit attendance to those with a key architectural stake in the project. My (not so) hidden agenda was to use the group as a source of new patterns; the overt agenda was to seed architectural leaders with the skills necessary to bring patterns into the foundation architecture of the new system. The audience was broader than I expected (in the sense that there was a wide variation in years of professional experience), and I didn't harvest many patterns from that workshop. However, at a later offering of the same course for a different organization, the students produced remarkably high-quality patterns. That organization used those patterns to seed its own pattern library.

Last, but certainly not least, it's important to enlist folks from the client organizations as pattern advocates to teach, gather, and organize patterns. Once started, such an effort can be self-sustaining. One domain expert has taken up that banner in the legacy project; he and I often work together as a team. The pattern program in that organization will soon be self-sustaining, and I'm eager to use it as a model for new pattern mining efforts. There are pockets of strong pattern advocacy in the organization for the new product, because they've seen how patterns can help them.

How They're Being Used

If this were a simple story, I'd note that the patterns are helping to shape the architecture of the emerging project, pronounce victory, and move on. Patterns have addressed some unforeseen project needs, so we have some serendipitous results to report as well.

- *Architecture documentation for the legacy organization.* The existing project originally budgeted limited time and staff to patterns as one mechanism to help the next-generation product developers understand the existing architecture. The organization that maintains the existing system found that patterns captured their own architecture so well that they have invested further resources into pattern work. The legacy organization now employs one experienced architect half-time to collect, capture, and organize patterns. These patterns amplify and complement existing project architecture documentation.

- *Training.* Both organizations use these patterns as training material for new hires.

- *Requirements generation.* This is a wholly unanticipated result; it sounds a little backward at first, so follow closely. The next-generation product tried to map each legacy system patterns to one or more domains in the new system. Some didn't fit at all, but some did. The original point of this exercise was design reuse: How much of the old system could carry over to the new?

Customers and engineers had already provided requirements for the new system. These requirements had also been mapped into the domains. If one of the legacy patterns seemed to apply in a next-generation system domain, but couldn't be traced back to a requirement for that domain, it indicated a missing requirement. Many of these are "design-level" requirements: constraints that point to technologies or approaches that wouldn't be clear from end-user requirements alone. In short, these patterns helped the next-generation project refine its requirement documents. That supported architectural and business planning.

TIP
Pattern mining can identify missing requirements.

I should emphasize here that these projects do not view themselves as pattern-driven projects, in the same sense that a project that has learned an OO programming language and method might view itself as an OO project. I would have been concerned had patterns taken the project by storm. Patterns are one tool in a designer's tool kit, and the projects are expecting no more from a pattern discipline than I believe the discipline can deliver.

Earlier in this article, I touched on the importance of generative patterns: patterns that work indirectly to solve a problem. I believe in a grass-roots approach; changes from the troops filter up and into the organization. People start using patterns because they believe they will help them, not because there's a policy statement that says they're good. A bottom-up approach keeps expectations in line, but doesn't prevent broad application of pattern techniques.

YET TO BE DONE

We still have much to learn about organizing patterns. We already support multiple topical indices, and we link patterns with their specialized instances.

As described above, we find that the patterns' *Intents* serve a useful indexing purpose. We plan to engage AT&T knowledge engineers to help us better organize the patterns and to refine our pattern organization principles.

Writers' workshops afford the author useful feedback, but they are not a forum for technical dialogue with the author. Many believe that such a forum would be useful. We still need to introduce both this forum and the writer's workshop into our review culture. One organization is taking steps to institute informal reviews; that may be sufficient in itself, or it may point the direction to more formal review procedures. Time will tell.

SIGNPOSTS

Many thanks to my colleague Bob Hanmer at AT&T, who has been one of the principal development-side advocates of patterns in the company.

Oisin McGuinness at Sumitomo Bank in New York pointed out that, in my previous column,[4] I inaccurately related an anecdote regarding Heaviside and Laplace. Laplace (1749–1827) indeed predated Heaviside (1850–1925), so it's impossible that "a prior derivation by Oliver Heaviside was dismissed" in favor of Laplace's work. However, the Heaviside transform was in wide use by the engineering community at the beginning of this century before Laplace's techniques had made practical inroads. At the turn of the century, the Heaviside operational calculus was a "technique," and the Laplace transform was "research." Even contemporary mathematical literature notes that "The modern Laplace transform ... [i]n the 1920s and 1930s ... was seen as a topic of front-line research; the applications that call upon it today were then treated by an older technique—the Heaviside operational calculus."[5] The engineering community had not yet derived a formal basis for the Heaviside techniques, which caused the scientific (mathematical) community to cast aspersions on it. The relationship between the practical community and the mathematical research community is typified by the experience of Carson, who demonstrated an isomorphism between the Heaviside transform and an interesting class of Laplace transforms in 1926. The work of Carson, who worked in the area of electrical circuits, was unfairly criticized in a 1937 publication of Doetsch, a mathematician. Many thanks to Dr. McGuinness for pointing out the HISTORY OF EXACT SCIENCE reference.[5]

References

1. Alexander, C., *et al.* A Pattern Language. New York: Oxford University Press, 1977.

2. Biggerstaff, T., and C. Richter. Reusability framework, assessment, and directions. Hawaii International Conference System Sciences, Jan. 7–10, 1987: 502–512.

3. Anderson, B. Task and Reflection in Learning to Learn, in Empowerment through Experiential Learning: Explorations of Good Practice, by J. Mulligan and C. Griffin, Eds., London: Kogan Page, 1992: 239–246.

4. Coplien, J. Software development as science, art and engineering, C++ Report 7(6), 1995: 14–19.

5. Deakin, M. A. B. The ascendancy of the Laplace transform and how it came about, Arch. Hist. Exact Science 44(3) 1992: 265–286.

Observations on the Role of Patterns in Object-Oriented Software Development

CHARLIE ALFRED AND STEPHEN J. MELLOR

T HE 21ST CENTURY IS A MERE FOUR YEARS AWAY. IF YOU'RE A SOFTWARE DEVELoper today, what kind of job will you have five years from now? If you've been too busy to give much thought to this question, perhaps now is the time to slow down a bit, take a break, and do some serious contemplation. In the year 2000, you may find that the job title "Software Developer" has vanished, and the vast majority of those who hold that job today will find themselves holding one of the following types of jobs:

1. *Analyst:* An expert in some problem domain who is able to develop a complete, detailed, executable, and testable implementation-independent model of a system.

2. *Designer:* An expert in a technology area or abstract problem domain who is able to work with a catalog of patterns, recognize the occurrence of these patterns in a domain analysis, and use the constraints of the problem to select an appropriate implementation for each pattern.

3. *Integrator:* An expert in combining subassemblies of implementation-specific patterns and manufacturing, testing, and deploying a complete system.

4. *Other:* Someone who was too busy to become an expert in one of the above three areas, and finds him- or herself asking the question: "Would you like fries or a soft drink with your order today?"

If you're skeptical, then we invite you to read on. We think that there's a pretty compelling case for why the computer software industry of today is about to experience its own industrial revolution.

279

THE SOFTWARE INDUSTRIAL REVOLUTION

In 1986, Brad Cox wrote about the upcoming "Software Industrial Revolution."[1] He drew the analogy between the computer software industry of today, and the gun manufacturing industry of the 1790s. Brad observed that prior to Eli Whitney, most gun manufacturers were craftsman who, with lots of painstaking effort, carefully crafted and assembled each component into the finished product. Assembly-line style manufacturing came on the scene in 1798 and changed the face of this industry forever. Very soon, the craftsman were virtually extinct, replaced by the industrialists. An isolated pattern? We think not. It happened again in the automobile industry in 1910 when Henry Ford introduced the Model T, and more recently in the computer hardware industry in the 1970s with the emergence of *large-scale integration* (LSI) chip technology.

The advent of the object paradigm was supposed to do the same thing for the software industry: transform it from a craftsman-style cottage industry into a post-modern industrial manufacturing process. Object orientation offered the promise of wide-scale reuse. Cox spoke of developers ordering software modules from catalogs like electronic parts, and entire industries devoted to the very specialized manufacturing and distribution of these components. Object-oriented programming, as we know it today, first emerged around 1980 with the commercial availability of the Smalltalk-80 language. Several other object-oriented programming languages, the most widespread of which today is C++, arrived on the scene over the subsequent decade.

Here we are in the late '90s, and what has really changed? On the whole, not much. Sure, some things are different. A commercial class library industry has sprung up, with products available for user-interface, database, math, and general-purpose (strings, containers, etc) applications. A few organizations have discovered how to build libraries that model their specific business and reuse them as a common foundation for several different production applications. However, the wide-scale reuse that object orientation seemed to promise has not yet occurred in practice. Why not? A major reason is that code reuse is difficult. In many cases, implementation is too low a level of abstraction to discover truly reusable components. There are likely to be too many application-specific details that pollute the interface and/or implementation of a component that is a candidate for reuse. Retroactive factoring of class hierarchies is time-consuming, error prone, and just plain expensive. It is faster and cheaper to use the old implementation as a model, and build a similar set of components for the application at hand. A second, and somewhat related problem, is that individual classes are of too fine a granularity to be reusable. Coupling between classes often forces the prospective reuser to include many different components just to get the one or two reusable ones.

THE CONTRIBUTION OF PATTERNS

In their recently published book, DESIGN PATTERNS,[2] Erich Gamma et al. applied the ideas of building architect Christopher Alexander, and suggested that reuse on a much wider scale is possible at a higher level of abstraction. In this article, we'd like to extend these ideas a bit, and show how reusable patterns can provide the glue that links together the various stages of the software development lifecycle.

WHAT IS A PATTERN?

A pattern is a common mechanism that solves a set of similar problems. Patterns may be structural (patterns of things and how they interconnect) or behavioral (patterns of events and how they interconnect), or both. The best patterns occur when the structure naturally supports the desired pattern of events. An example of a structural pattern would be a joint. In the human body, knees, elbows, wrists, hips, and ankles all are examples of joints. Joints aren't limited to human anatomy; all vertebrates have them. Joints aren't even limited to the biology domain. Machines and other kinds of manmade structures also use joints. Basically, joints are an abstract mechanism that connect a pair of things, while allowing freedom of movement. An example of a behavioral pattern is the check-in version, check-out version, create branch, and merge branch operations in a configuration management subsystem. Another way of looking at it is that a pattern is what's left when you abstract all the problem domain-specific details out of the objects. In that respect, a pattern is a collection of objects that belong to an abstract domain.

> **TIP**
>
> A pattern is a common mechanism that solves a set of similar problems.

A PATTERN-INFLUENCED SOFTWARE DEVELOPMENT PROCESS

The *waterfall model* of the software development lifecycle decomposes the development process into requirements gathering, analysis, design, implementation, unit testing, integration, and system testing phases. The *spiral model*, suggested by Boehm in 1981,[3] describes a process composed of several iterations, each one following the waterfall phases. In either lifecycle model, the only complete, executable representation of the system is the source code.

We'd like to describe a variant of the spiral model that we see as achievable by most organizations during the next five years. Let's take a closer look at the design phase, and identify three distinct concepts:

- *Design knowledge base*—A design knowledge base is a database of patterns for abstract domains, one or more implementations for each pattern, and the rules for how to select a specific implementation. The important thing to note is that the pattern implementations in this knowledge base will be captured in a higher-level form than a specific programming language. Also, the patterns are as general as possible. Each one identifies a specific problem that occurs across many domains, and describes an abstract mechanism to address the problem

- *Design process*—The design process (or phase) begins with a detailed analysis model of a domain. This model describes the objects, their attributes and relationships, and the collaborations between objects in terms of states, events, actions, and transitions. In short, it is complete and executable. We combine this model with a set of domain and implementation-specific constraints, including expected usage patterns, scale, response time requirements, hardware capabilities, etc. The design process is one of assessing trade-offs and choosing appropriate structural representations to transform the analysis model into a good design model.

- *Design*—A design is a detailed view of a domain-specific structural model of a system (or subsystem). A higher-level view of the same model is called a software architecture.[4] In principle, a design is programming language independent. In practice, the degree to which this is achieved depends largely on how well the system was partitioned into domains. In other words, a design is more likely to be programming language independent if the programming language and operating system issues were factored into their own domains.

Our view of how these three aspects of design influence the software development process is as follows. It is the job of the analyst to be aware of the patterns available in the design knowledge base and match them to problems that occur in each domain being analyzed. The analyst uses the abstract pattern and "colors" it in with domain-specific attributes and behaviors. For each pattern in the analysis model, the designer applies the rules in the knowledge database to this set of domain- and implementation-specific constraints. The designer assesses the trade-offs inherent in the set of pattern implementations and chooses an appropriate one for this problem. Once a particular implementation is selected, producing a "colored pattern implementation" is a mechanical transformation. The additional attributes and behaviors added to the pattern during analysis must be merged with the implementation-specific structure, attributes, and behaviors of the selected pattern implementation.

Our view of implementation is highly mechanical, and, in fact, automatable. We produce the implementation by a process of translation,[5] instead of elaboration used by today's approaches in which the designer elaborates the analysis models by reorganizing, adorning, and adding detail.

Patterns in the Requirements Phase

Usage patterns are one of the most important aspects to discover in the requirements view of a system model. Many of the high-level architecture and low-level design decisions made later on will depend heavily on the expected usage patterns. Different kinds of systems give rise to different forms of usage patterns. For example, let's consider two basic kinds of systems: purposeful and reactive. A purposeful system is one where the external actors interact with a predictable, well-behaved system to accomplish some predefined goal. An ATM network or a Frequent Flier Awards system are both examples of purposeful systems. A reactive system, on the other hand, is one where the streams of external events are arbitrary, and the behavior of the system is highly dependent on its internal state. Most real-time control systems fall into this category.

Use case scenarios, as described by Jacobson, are an excellent way to describe the usage patterns for a purposeful system. For each use case, we need to estimate the number of actors who will invoke the use case and how frequently they do so. For reactive systems, use case scenarios unfortunately aren't much help. In this case, the best we can do is estimate the time distribution between successive occurrences of the same event.

> **TIP**
>
> For reactive systems, use case scenarios aren't much help.

For example, in a system that models the response of a city to natural disasters, we might estimate the time between primary earthquake shocks on a particular fault line. Sometimes in a reactive system, the occurrence of one external event will increase the likelihood of some others. In an earthquake, a primary shock often is followed by several nearby after-shocks of lesser magnitude.

Patterns in the Analysis Phase

Analysis patterns can be described as abstract mechanisms that occur across a wide variety of domains. An analysis pattern may have several different structural representations, but all of these can be encapsulated by a common external interface to the pattern. For example, Ordered Container and Iterator patterns occur in the analysis of virtually every domain. We can describe the external interface of an Ordered Container and its Iterator regardless of whether we implement the container as a doubly-linked list or an adjustable length array.

Patterns in the Design Phase

Design patterns are very closely related to analysis patterns. A particular analysis pattern will give rise to one or more design patterns. The exact number depends on how many useful ways there are to represent the internal details of the components. Each design pattern describes the organization and behavior of the underlying components of the mechanism (i.e., what roles does each component play and how do they interact). Different design patterns have different space, time, and flexibility trade-offs. The choice of a particular design pattern will depend on the usage patterns discovered during the analysis phase of the project and the performance and scalability goals of the system. For example, an adjustable length array is a more compact way to represent an ordered container than a doubly-linked list, and is somewhat faster to iterate over. On the other hand, if the usage patterns suggest that the container will be subject to frequent insert and delete actions and the number of members in the collection will vary widely over the lifetime of the collection, a doubly-linked list might be a better choice.

AN ILLUSTRATIVE EXAMPLE

Consider the case of an airline operation. During the normal course of business, it experiences occasional flight delays. Each delay may cause several passengers to miss connecting flights (which are running on schedule). If several delays occur at the same time, then each connecting flight might be missed by passengers from more than one delayed flight. It is the airline's responsibility to make alternate flight arrangements for the passengers inconvenienced by a delay.

A system that seeks to address this application must address the problem of how to best allocate scarce resources. In this case, there may be more passengers who need to travel from city X to city Y than there is space on the available alternate flights. In addition, certain alternate flights are more attractive than others and some passengers are a higher priority to the airline than others.

A simple pattern that solves this problem might be called "Dispatcher." A Dispatcher is responsible for multiple Clients and multiple Servers. Each Client has a certain level of demand; each Server has a certain level of available supply. In an airline, passenger groups are clients and their demand is equal to the number of seats in a particular cabin. Flights are servers and their supply is equal to the number of unreserved seats in each cabin.

Each potential assignment of a Client to a Server would be an Option. The Dispatcher might use a ConstraintPolicy to eliminate impossible or inefficient Options. In the airline example, the ConstraintPolicy might specify that multipassenger groups must travel together, or passengers needing wheelchairs cannot take a flight making more than one connection. Also, the Dispatcher might use a PriorityPolicy to determine the relative value of two Options. As a result, each Client and Server hold ordered lists of Options. For the Clients, the list represents a ranking of preferred Servers; for the Servers, the list represents a ranking of preferred Clients.

The algorithm used by the Dispatcher to assign Clients to Servers would assign Options that were the first choice for both Client and Server. When the Client's demand (or Server's supply) is satisfied, the remainder of its Options are deleted. The pattern might include a re-prioritization step after each assignment. This would be useful to let the PriorityPolicy increase the value of remaining Options as the Client runs out.

This pattern shows up in a lot of different application domains. In local-area pickup and delivery dispatching (i.e., Federal Express, etc) Clients are Stops and Servers are Drivers. Also, these problem domains wouldn't be limited to transportation and logistics. In software hotline support, Clients are support calls, Servers are support engineers, and the ConstraintPolicy might deal with feature or platform expertise. In distributed object systems, Clients might be messages, Servers might be objects, and the PriorityPolicy might deal with load-balancing issues.

In any case, the essential relationships and collaborations between the `Dispatcher`, `Client`, `Server`, `Option`, `ConstraintPolicy`, and `PriorityPolicy` classes are part of the abstract domain, and as a result are part of the pattern. The details about how `Client` demand and `Server` supply are represented (or computed) and how `ConstraintPolicy` or `PriorityPolicy` instances are specified are not part of the pattern, but instead are part of the application domain.

Also, the particular implementation of the `Dispatcher` pattern might make certain space/time trade-offs. For example, if the number of `Clients` and `Servers` is small, then the full suite of `Options` might be generated and ranked at once. For larger numbers, it might be useful to generate a subset of the possible options at the start, and then generate additional ones as they are needed.

CONCLUSION

We're convinced that the emerging concept of patterns will have a significant and lasting impact on the process of how we analyze, design, and implement software systems. In particular, we believe that several specific things are likely to occur:

1. Robust application generators (i.e., capable of producing the source code for an entire application) based on (one or more) design model logical notations (i.e., the concepts that underlie the visual notation) will be commercially available very soon. It wouldn't surprise us to see these application generators rated in terms of "programmer power" much like today's automobile engines are rated in terms of horsepower.

2. Design (and architectural) pattern and policy databases will become commercially available. There is still a lot of work to be done to identify, catalog, and represent analysis, design, and architectural patterns in a formal language. Also, we still need a formal way to classify application constraints and specify a formal policy notation. The presence of these items will allow design generators to automate the production of a design model from a detailed analysis model and set of application constraints.

3. CASE tools able to produce complete, detailed, testable analysis models will enjoy widespread use. For the first time in the history of the software industry, there will be an economic incentive to produce such an analysis model that is so large few development teams will be motivated to rush from an incomplete analysis into design and implementation.

Once the cost of producing design and implementation models from a complete, detailed, testable analysis model is sufficiently low, system analysis will take the place of what we know today as software development. Industries that support this automated, low cost manufacturing process (such as suppliers of design and implementation generators, and design and architectural pattern/policy databases) will flourish and the software development process we know today will vanish to the pages of a history book.

References

1. B. Cox and A. Novobilski, OBJECT-ORIENTED PROGRAMMING: AN EVOLUTIONARY APPROACH, Addison-Wesley, Reading, MA, 1986.

2. E. Gamma et al. DESIGN PATTERNS, Addison-Wesley, Reading, MA, 1995.

3. B. Boehm, SOFTWARE ENGINEERING ECONOMICS, Prentice Hall, Englewood Cliffs, NJ, 1981.

4. S. Shlaer and S. J. Mellor, OBJECT LIFECYCLES: MODELING THE WORLD IN STATES, Prentice Hall, Englewood Cliffs, NJ, 1991.

5. S. Shlaer and S. J. Mellor, RECURSIVE DESIGN: IMPLEMENTATION THROUGH TRANSLATION, Prentice Hall, Englewood Cliffs, NJ (forthcoming).

Using Design Patterns to Evolve System Software from UNIX to Windows NT

Douglas C. Schmidt and Paul Stephenson

D EVELOPING SYSTEM SOFTWARE THAT IS REUSABLE ACROSS OS PLATFORMS IS challenging. Due to constraints imposed by the underlying OS platforms, it is often impractical to directly reuse existing algorithms, detailed designs, interfaces, or implementations. This article describes our experiences using a large-scale reuse strategy for system software based on design patterns. Design patterns capture the static and dynamic structures of solutions that occur repeatedly when producing applications in a particular context.[1,2] Design patterns are an important technique for improving system software quality since they address a fundamental challenge in large-scale software development: communication of architectural knowledge among developers.[3]

> **TIP**
>
> Design patterns capture the static and dynamic structures of solutions.

Our experiences with a large-scale reuse strategy based upon design patterns are described here. This strategy has been used to facilitate the development of efficient OO telecommunication system software at Ericsson. In this article, we present a case study that describes the cross-platform evolution of portions of an OO framework called the ADAPTIVE Service eXecutive (ASX).[4] The ASX framework is an integrated collection of components that collaborate to produce a reusable infrastructure for developing distributed applications.

The ASX framework supports event-driven distributed applications. One of the key components in the ASX framework is the `Reactor` class category.[5] The `Reactor` integrates the demultiplexing of events and the dispatching of the corresponding event handlers. Event handlers are trig-

TIP

The ASX framework supports event-driven distributed applications.

TIP

It was possible to reuse the underlying design patterns.

gered by various types of events such as timers, synchronization objects, signals, or I/O operations.

We recently ported the ASX framework from several UNIX platforms to the Windows NT platform. These OS platforms possess significantly different mechanisms for event demultiplexing and I/O. To meet our performance requirements, it was not possible to directly reuse many of the components in the ASX framework across the OS platforms. However, it was possible to reuse the underlying design patterns that were embodied in the ASX framework, thereby reducing project risk.

The remainder of the article is organized as follows: the first section outlines the background of our work using OO frameworks for telecommunications system software; the second section presents an overview of the design patterns that are the focus of this article; the third section examines the issues that arose as we ported the components in the `Reactor` framework from several UNIX platforms to the Windows NT platform; the fourth section summarizes the experience we gained, both pro and con, while deploying a design pattern-based system development methodology in a production software environment; and concluding remarks are given in the fifth section.

BACKGROUND

The design patterns and framework described in this article are currently being applied at Ericsson on a family of client/server applications.[6] These applications use ASX framework as the basis for a highly flexible and extensible telecommunication system management framework. The ASX framework enhances the flexibility and reuse of system software that monitors and manages telecommunication switch performance across multiple hardware and software platforms.

The system software we are developing provides essential services and mechanisms used by higher-level application software. Our system software frameworks are comprised of components that access and manipulate hardware devices (such as telecommunication switches) and software mechanisms residing within an OS kernel (such as alarms, interval timers, synchronization objects, communication ports, and signal handlers).

In general, developing system software that is capable of being directly reused on different OS platforms is challenging. Several factors complicating cross-platform reuse of system software are outlined as follows:

Efficiency

Since applications and other reusable components will be layered upon system software, the techniques used to develop system software must not degrade performance significantly. Otherwise, developers will reinvent special-purpose code rather than reuse existing components, thereby defeating a major benefit of reuse.

> **TIP**
>
> The techniques used to develop system software must not degrade performance significantly.

Portability

To meet performance and functionality requirements, system software often must access nonportable mechanisms and interfaces (such as device registers within a network link-layer controller or event demultiplexing mechanisms) provided by the underlying OS and hardware platform.

Lack of functionality

Many OS platforms do not provide adequate functionality to develop portable, reusable system components. For example, the lack of kernel-level multithreading, explicit dynamic linking, and asynchronous exception handling (as well as robust compilers that interact correctly with these features) greatly increases the complexity of developing and porting reusable system software.

Need to master complex concepts

Successfully developing robust, efficient, and portable system software requires intimate knowledge of complex mechanisms (such as concurrency control, interrupt handling, and interprocess communication) offered by multiple OS platforms. It is also essential to understand the performance costs associated with using alternative mechanisms (such as shared memory versus message passing) on different OS platforms.

There are trade-offs among the factors described above that further complicate the reuse of system software across OS platforms. Often, it may be difficult to develop portable system software that does not significantly degrade efficiency or subtly alter the semantics and robustness of com-

TIP

Many traditional
OS kernels do not
support preemptive
multithreading.

monly used operations. For instance, many traditional OS kernels do not support pre-emptive multithreading. Therefore, writing a portable user-level threads mechanism may be less efficient than programming with thread mechanisms supported by the kernel.[7] Likewise, user-level threads may reduce robustness by restricting the use of OS features such as signals or synchronous I/O operations.

Design Pattern Overview

A design pattern is a recurring architectural theme that provides a solution to a set of requirements within a particular context.[1] Design patterns facilitate architectural level reuse by providing "blueprints" or guidelines for defining, composing, and reasoning about the key components in a software system. In general, a large amount of reuse is possible at the architectural level. However, reusing design patterns does not necessarily result in direct reuse of algorithms, detailed designs, interfaces, or implementations.

OO frameworks typically embody a wide range of design patterns. For example, the ET++ graphical user-interface (GUI) framework[8] incorporates design patterns (such as Abstract Factory[1]) that hide the details of creating user-interface objects. This enables an application to be portable across different window systems (such as X windows and Microsoft Windows). Likewise, the InterViews[9] GUI framework contains design patterns (such as Strategy and Iterator[1]) that allow algorithms and/or application behavior to be decoupled from mechanisms provided by the reusable GUI components.

In the context of distributed applications, OO toolkits such as the Orbix CORBA object request broker[11] and the ADAPTIVE Service eXecutive framework[4] embody many common design patterns. These design patterns express recurring architectural themes (such as event demultiplexing, connection establishment, message routing, publish/subscribe communication, remote object proxies, and flexible composition of hierarchically related services) found in most distributed applications.

This article focuses on two specific design patterns (the Reactor[5] and Accepter patterns) that are implemented by the ASX framework. Components in the ASX framework have been ported to a number of UNIX platforms, as well as Windows NT. The ASX components, and the Reactor and

`Accepter` design patterns embodied by these components, are currently used in a number of production systems. These systems include the Bellcore Q.port ATM signaling software product, the system control segment for the Motorola Iridium global personal communications system, and a family of system/network management applications for Ericsson telecommunication switches.[6]

The design patterns described in the following section provided a concise set of architectural blueprints that guided our porting effort from UNIX to Windows NT. In particular, by employing the patterns, we did not have to rediscover the key collaborations between architectural components. Instead, our development task focused on determining a suitable mapping of the components in the pattern onto the mechanisms provided by the different OS platforms. Finding an appropriate mapping was nontrivial, as we describe later. Nevertheless, our knowledge of the design patterns significantly reduced redevelopment effort and minimized the level of risk in our projects.

> **TIP**
>
> By employing the patterns, we did not have to rediscover the key collaborations.

The Reactor Pattern

The `Reactor` pattern is an object behavioral pattern.[1] This pattern simplifies the development of event-driven applications (such as a CORBA ORB,[10] an X-windows host resource manager, or a distributed logging service[5]). The `Reactor` pattern provides a common infrastructure that integrates event demultiplexing and the dispatching of event handlers. Event handlers perform application-specific processing operations in response to various types of events. An event handler may be triggered by different sources of events (such as timers, communication ports, synchronization objects, and signal handlers) that are monitored by an application. The callback-driven programming style provided by a Motif or Windows application is a prime example of the `Reactor` pattern.

The `Reactor` pattern provides several major benefits for event-driven distributed applications:

- *Improve performance:* it enables an application to wait for activity to occur on multiple sources of events simultaneously *without* blocking or continuously polling for events on any single source.

- *Minimize synchronization complexity:* it provides applications with a low-overhead, coarse-grained form of concurrency control. The

Reactor pattern serializes the invocation of event handlers at the level of "event demultiplexing and dispatching" within a single process or thread. For many applications, this eliminates the need for more complicated synchronization or locking.

- *Enchance reuse:* it decouples application-specific functionality from application-independent mechanisms. Application-specific functionality is performed by user-defined methods that override virtual functions inherited from an event handler base class. Application-independent mechanisms are reusable components that demultiplex events and dispatch pre-registered event handlers.

Figure 1 illustrates the structure of participants in the Reactor pattern.* The Reactor class defines an interface for registering, removing, and dispatching Event_Handler objects. An implementation of the Reactor pattern provides application-independent mechanisms that perform event demultiplexing and dispatch application-specific concrete event handlers. The Reactor class contains references to objects of Concrete_Event_Handler subclasses. These subclasses are derived from the Event_Handler abstract base class, which defines virtual methods for handling events. A Concrete_Event_Handler subclass may override these virtual methods to perform application-specific functionality when the corresponding events occur.

> **TIP**
>
> The Reactor triggers Event_Handler methods in response to events.

The Reactor triggers Event_Handler methods in response to events. These events may be associated with handles that are bound to sources of events (such as I/O ports, synchronization objects, or signals). To bind the Reactor together with these handles, a subclass of Event_Handler must override the get_handle method. When the Reactor registers an Event_Handler subclass object, the object's handle is obtained by invoking its Event_Handler::get_handle method. The Reactor then combines this handle with other registered Event_Handlers and waits for events to occur on the handle(s).

When events occur, the Reactor uses the handles activated by the events

---

*Relationships between components are illustrated throughout this article via Booch notation.[11] Dashed clouds indicate classes; nondashed directed edges indicate inheritance relationships between classes; dashed directed edges indicate a template instantiation relationship; and an undirected edge with a solid bullet at one end indicates a composition relation. Solid clouds indicate objects; nesting indicates composition relationships between objects; and undirected edges indicate some type of link exists between objects.

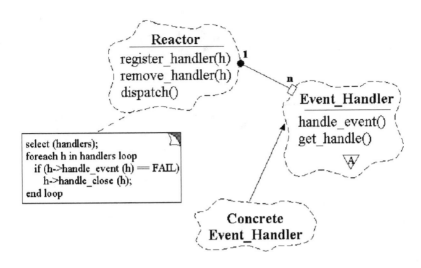

FIGURE 1. *The structure of participants in the reactor pattern.*

as keys to locate and dispatch the appropriate `Event_Handler` methods. The code annotation in Figure 1 outlines the behavior of the `dispatch` method. The `handle_event` method is then invoked by the `Reactor` as a "callback." This method performs application-specific functionality in response to an event. If a call to `handle_event` fails, the `Reactor` invokes the `handle_close` method. This method performs any application-specific cleanup operations. When the `handle_close` method returns, the `Reactor` removes the `Event_Handler` subclass object from its internal tables.

An alternative way to implement event demultiplexing and dispatching is to use multitasking. In this approach, an application spawns a separate thread or process that monitors an event source. Every thread or process blocks until it receives an event notification. At this point, the appropriate event handler code is executed. Certain types of applications (such as file transfer, remote login, or teleconferencing) benefit from multitasking. For these applications, multithreading or multiprocessing helps to reduce development effort, improves application robustness, and transparently leverages off of available multiprocessor capabilities.

Using multithreading to implement event demultiplexing has several drawbacks, however. It may require the use of complex concurrency control schemes; it may lead to poor performance on uniprocessors[4]; and it may not

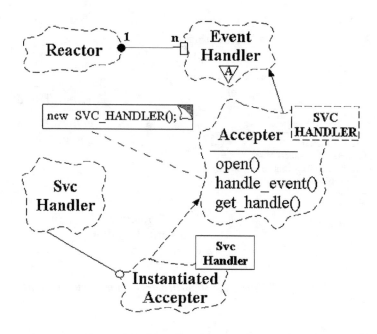

FIGURE 2. *The structure of participants in the acceptor pattern.*

be available on widely available OS platforms (such as many variants of UNIX). In these cases, the Reactor pattern may be used in lieu of, or in conjunction with, OS multithreading or multiprocessing mechanisms, as described in the next section.

The Accepter Pattern

The Accepter pattern is an object creational pattern[1] that decouples the act of establishing a connection from the service(s) provided after a connection is established. Connection-oriented services (such as file transfer, remote login, distributed logging, and video-on-demand) are particularly amenable to this pattern. The Accepter pattern simplifies the development of these services by allowing the application-specific portion of a service to be modified independently of the mechanism used to establish the connection. The UNIX "superserver" inetd is a prime example of an application that uses the Accepter pattern.

To build upon the interfaces and mechanisms already provided by the Reactor pattern, the Accepter class inherits the Event_Handler's demultiplexing and dispatching interface (shown in Figure 1). Figure 2 illustrates the structure of participants in the `Accepter` pattern. The `open` method in template class `Accepter` initializes a communication endpoint and listens for incoming connection requests from clients. The `get_handle` method returns the I/O handle corresponding to the communication endpoint.

When a connection request arrives from a client the `Reactor` triggers a callback on the `Accepter`'s `handle_event` method. This method is a *factory* that dynamically produces a new `SVC_HANDLER` object. In the example in Figure 2, `SVC_HANDLER` is a formal parameterized type argument in the `Accepter` template class. The `Instantiated_Accepter` class supplies an actual `Svc_Handler` class parameter. The `Svc_Handler` parameter implements a particular application-specific service (i.e., transferring a file, permitting remote login, receiving logging records, sending a video sequence, etc.).

Note that the `Accepter` pattern does not dictate the behavior or concurrency dynamics of the `Svc_Handler` service it creates. In particular, a dynamically created `Svc_Handler` service may be executed in any of the following ways:

- *Run in the same thread of control:* This approach may be implemented by inheriting the `Svc_Handler` from `Event_Handler` and registering each newly created `Svc_Handler` object with the `Reactor`. Thus, each `Svc_Handler` object is dispatched in the same thread of control as an `Accepter` object. The implementation described in the third section uses this single-threaded behavior.

- *Run in a separate thread of control:* In this approach, the `Reactor` serves as the master connection dispatcher within an application. When a client connects, the `Accepter`'s `handle_event` method spawns a separate thread of control. The `Svc_Handler` object then processes messages exchanged over the connection within the new slave thread. Threads are useful for cooperating services that frequently reference common memory-resident data structures shared by the threads within a process address space.[7]

> **TIP**
>
> Threads are useful for cooperating services that frequently reference common memory-resident data structures.

- *Run in a separate OS process:* This approach is similar in form to the previous bullet. However, a separate process is created rather than a separate thread. Network services that base their security and protection mechanisms on process ownership are typically executed in separate processes to prevent accidental or intentional access to unauthorized resources. For example, the standard UNIX super-server, `inetd`, uses the `Accepter` pattern in this manner to execute the standard Internet `ftp` and `telnet` services in separate processes.[12]

The ASX framework[4] provides mechanisms that support all three of these types of concurrency dynamics. Moreover, the selection of concurrency mechanism may be deferred until late in the design, or even until run-time. This flexibility increases the range of design alternatives available to developers.

In addition, the `Accepter` pattern may be used to develop highly extensible event handlers that may be configured into an application at installation-time or at runtime. This enables applications to be updated and extended without modifying, recompiling, relinking, or restarting the applications at runtime. Achieving this degree of flexibility and extensibility requires the use of OO language features (such as templates, inheritance, and dynamic binding), OO design techniques (such as the `Factory Method` or `Abstract Factory` design patterns[1]), and advanced operating system mechanisms (such as explicit dynamic linking and multithreading [4]).

EVOLVING DESIGN PATTERNS ACROSS OS PLATFORMS

Motivation

Based on our experience at Ericsson, explicitly modeling design patterns is a very beneficial activity. In particular, design patterns focus attention on relatively stable aspects of a system's software architecture. They also emphasize the strategic collaborations between key participants in the architecture without overwhelming developers with excessive detail. Abstracting away from low-level implementation details is particularly important for system software since platform constraints often preclude direct reuse of system components.

> **TIP**
>
> Explicitly modeling design patterns is a very beneficial activity.

In our experience it is essential to illustrate how design patterns are realized in actual systems. One observation we discuss in the fourth section is that existing design pattern catalogs[1,2] do not present "wide spectrum" coverage of patterns. Often, this makes it difficult for novices to recognize how to apply patterns in practice on their projects. We believe the development sequence that unfolds in this section will provide a technically rich, motivating, and detailed (yet comprehensible) roadmap to help shepherd other developers into the realm of patterns.

With these goals in mind, this section outlines how the `Reactor` and `Accepter` design patterns were implemented and evolved on BSD and System V UNIX, as well as on Windows NT. The discussion emphasizes the relevant functional differences between the various OS platforms and describes how these differences affected the implementation of the design patterns. To focus the discussion later, C++ is used as the implementation language. However, the principles and concepts underlying the `Reactor` and `Accepter` patterns are independent of the programming language, the OS platform, and any particular implementation. Readers who are not interested in the lower-level details of implementing design patterns may wish to skip ahead to the fourth section, where we summarize the lessons we learned from using design patterns on several projects at Ericsson.

> **TIP**
>
> Patterns are independent of the programming language and any particular implementation.

The Impact of Platform Demultiplexing and I/O Semantics

The implementation of the `Reactor` pattern was affected significantly by the semantics of the event demultiplexing and I/O mechanisms in the underlying OS. In general, there are two types of demultiplexing and I/O semantics: *reactive* and *proactive*. Reactive semantics allow an application to inform the OS which I/O handles to notify it about when an I/O-related operation (such as a read, write, and connection request/accept) may be performed without blocking. Subsequently, when the OS detects that the desired operation may be performed without blocking on any of the indicated handles, it informs the application that the handle(s) are ready. The application then "reacts" by processing the handle(s) accordingly (such as reading or writing data, accepting connections, etc.). Reactive demultiplexing and I/O semantics are provided on standard BSD and System V UNIX systems.[12]

In contrast, proactive semantics allow an application to proactively initiate I/O-related operations (such as a read, write, or connection request/accept) or general-purpose event-signaling operations (such as a semaphore lock being acquired or a thread terminating). The invoked operation proceeds asynchronously and does not block the caller. When an operation completes, it signals the application. At this point, the application runs a completion routine that determines the exit status of the operation and potentially starts up another asynchronous operation. Proactive demultiplexing and I/O semantics are provided on Windows NT[13] and VMS.

For performance reasons, we were not able to completely encapsulate the variation in behavior between the UNIX and Windows NT demultiplexing and I/O semantics. Thus, we could not directly reuse existing C++ code, algorithms, or detailed designs. However, it was possible to capture and reuse the concepts that underlay the `Reactor` and `Accepter` design patterns.

UNIX EVOLUTION OF THE PATTERNS

Implementing the ReactorPattern on UNIX

The standard demultiplexing mechanisms on UNIX operating systems provide reactive I/O semantics. For instance, the UNIX `select` and `poll` event demultiplexing system calls inform an application which subset of handles within a set of I/O handles may send/receive messages or request/accept connections without blocking. Implementing the `Reactor` pattern using UNIX reactive I/O is straightforward. After `select` or `poll` indicate which I/O handles have become ready, the `Reactor` object reacts by invoking the appropriate `Event_Handler` callback methods (i.e., `handle_event` or `handle_close`).

One advantage of the UNIX reactive I/O scheme is that it decouples 1) event detection and notification from 2) the operation performed in response to the triggered event. This allows an application to optimize its response to an event by using context information available when the event occurs. For example, when `select` indicates a "read" event is pending, a network server might check to see how many bytes are in a socket receive queue. It might use this information to optimize the buffer size it allocates before making a `recv` system call. A disadvantage of UNIX reactive I/O is that operations may not be invoked asynchronously with other operations. Therefore, computation and communication may not occur in parallel unless separate threads or processes are used.

The original implementation of the `Reactor` pattern provided by the ASX framework was derived from the `Dispatcher` class category available in the InterViews OO GUI framework.[9] The `Dispatcher` is an OO interface to the UNIX `select` system call. InterViews uses the `Dispatcher` to define an application's main event loop and to manage connections to one or more physical window displays. The `Reactor` framework's first modification to the `Dispatcher` framework added support for signal-based event dispatching. The `Reactor`'s signal-based dispatching mechanism was modeled closely on the `Dispatcher`'s existing timer-based and I/O handle-based event demultiplexing and event handler dispatching mechanisms.*

The next modification to the Reactor occurred when porting it from SunOS 4.x (which is based primarily on BSD 4.3 UNIX) to SunOS 5.x (which is based primarily on System V release 4 (SVR4) UNIX). SVR4 provides another event demultiplexing system call named poll. Poll is similar to select, though it uses a different interface and provides a broader, more flexible model for event demultiplexing that supports SVR4 features such as STREAM pipe band-data.[12]

The SunOS 5.x port of the Reactor was enhanced to support either select or poll as the underlying event demultiplexer. Although portions of the Reactor's internal implementation changed, its external interface remained the same for both the select-based and the poll-based versions. This common interface improves networking application portability across BSD and SVR4 UNIX platforms.

A portion of the public interface for the BSD and SVR4 UNIX implementation of the Reactor pattern is shown as follows:

```
// Bit-wise "or" these values to check
// for multiple activities per-handle.
enum Reactor_Mask { READ_MASK = 01,
    WRITE_MASK = 02, EXCEPT_MASK = 04 };
class Reactor
{

public:
    // Register an Event_Handler object according
    // to the Reactor_Mask(s) (i.e., "reading,"
    // "writing," and/or "exceptions").
    virtual int register_handler (Event_Handler *,
                Reactor_Mask);
    // Remove the handler associated with
    // the appropriate Reactor_Mask(s).
    virtual int remove_handler (Event_Handler *,
                Reactor_Mask);
    // Block process until I/O events occur or
    // a timer expires, then dispatch Event_Handler(s).
    virtual int dispatch (void);
// ...
};
```

Likewise, the Event_Handler interface for UNIX is defined as follows:

---

*The Reactor's interfaces for signals and timer-based event handling are not shown in this article due to space limitations.

```
typedef int HANDLE; // I/O handle.
class Event_Handler
{
protected:
    // Returns the I/O handle associated with the
    // derived object (must be supplied by a subclass).
    virtual HANDLE get_handle (void) const;
    // Called when an event occurs on the HANDLE.
    virtual int handle_event (HANDLE, Reactor_Mask);
    // Called when object is removed from the Reactor.
    virtual int handle_close (HANDLE, Reactor_Mask);
// ...
};
```

The next major modification to the `Reactor` extended it for use with multithreaded applications on SunOS 5.x using Solaris threads.[7] Adding multithreading support required changes to the internals of both the `select`-based and `poll`-based versions of the `Reactor`. These changes involved a SunOS 5.x mutual exclusion mechanism known as a "mutex." A mutex serializes the execution of multiple threads by defining a critical section where only one thread executes the code at a time.[7] Critical sections of the `Reactor`'s code that concurrently access shared resources (such as the `Reactor`'s internal dispatch table containing `Event_Handler` objects) are protected by a mutex.

The standard SunOS 5.x synchronization type (`mutex_t`) provides support for *nonrecursive* mutexes. The SunOS 5.x nonrecursive mutex provides a simple and efficient form of mutual exclusion based on adaptive spinlocks. However, nonrecursive mutexes possess the restriction that the thread currently owning a mutex may not reacquire the mutex without releasing it first. Otherwise, deadlock will occur immediately.

While developing the multithreaded `Reactor`, it quickly became obvious that SunOS 5.x mutex variables were inadequate to support the synchronization semantics required by the `Reactor`. In particular, the `Reactor`'s `dispatch` interface performs callbacks to methods of pre-registered, application-specific event handler objects as follows:

```
void Reactor::dispatch (void)
{
    for (;;) {
    // Block until events occur.
    this->wait_for_events (this->handler_set);
    // Obtain the mutex.
    this->lock->acquire ();

    // Dispatch all the callback methods
```

```
// on handlers who contain active events.
for each handler in this->handler_set {
if (handler->handle_event
   (handler, mask) == FAIL)
// Cleanup on failure.
   handler->handle_close (handler);
}
// Release the mutex.
this->lock->release ();
}
}
```

Callback methods (such as `handle_event` and `handle_close`) defined by `Event_Handler` subclass objects may subsequently re-enter the `Reactor` object by calling its `register_handler` and `remove_handler` methods as follows:

```
// Global per-process instance of the Reactor.
extern Reactor reactor;

// Application-specific method called
// back by the Reactor.

int Accepter::handle_event (HANDLE handle,
                            Reactor_Mask)
{
    Concrete_Event_Handler *new_handler =
       new Concrete_Event_Handler;

    *new_handler = this->accept (handle);

    // Re-enter the Reactor object.
    reactor.register_handler (new_handler,
                              READ_MASK);
    // ...
}
```

In this code fragment, nonrecursive mutexes will result in deadlock since 1) the mutex within the `Reactor`'s `dispatch` method is locked throughout the callback and 2) the `Reactor`'s `register_handler` method tries to acquire the same mutex.

> **TIP**
>
> Note that nonrecursive mutexes result in deadlock.

One solution to this problem involved recoding the `Reactor` to release its mutex lock before invoking callbacks to application-specific `Event_Handler` methods. However, this solution was tedious and error-prone. It also increased synchronization overhead by repeatedly releasing and reacquiring mutex locks. A more elegant and efficient solution used *recursive* mutexes to prevent deadlock and to avoid modifying the `Reactor`'s concurrency control scheme. A recursive mutex allows calls to its `acquire` method to be nested as long as the thread that owns the lock is the one attempting to reacquire it.

> **TIP**
>
> The current implementation of the UNIX-based `Reactor` pattern is about 2400 lines of C++ code.

The current implementation of the UNIX-based `Reactor` pattern is about 2,400 lines of C++ code (not including comments or extraneous whitespace). This implementation is portable between both BSD and System V UNIX variants.

Implementing the Accepter Pattern on UNIX

To illustrate the `Reactor` and `Accepter` patterns, consider the event-driven server for a distributed logging service shown in Figure 3. Client applications use this service to log information (such as error notifications, debugging traces, and status updates) in a distributed environment. In this service, logging records are sent to a central logging server. The logging server outputs the logging records to a console, a printer, a file, or a network management database, etc.

In the architecture of the distributed logging service, the logging server shown in Figure 3 handles logging records and connection requests sent by clients. These records and requests may arrive concurrently on multiple I/O handles. An I/O handle identifies a resource control block managed by the operating system.*

> **TIP**
>
> A single-threaded server must not block indefinitely reading from any individual I/O handle.

The logging server listens on one I/O handle for connection requests to arrive from new clients. In addition, a separate I/O handle is associated with each connected client. Input from multiple clients may arrive concurrently. Therefore, a single-threaded server must not block indefinitely reading from any individual I/O handle. A blocking `read` on one handle may significantly delay the response time for clients associated on other handles.

A highly modular and extensible way to design the

---

*Different operating systems use different terms for I/O handles. For example, UNIX programmers typically refer to these as file descriptors, whereas Windows programmers typically refer to them as I/O HANDLEs. In both cases, the underlying concepts are the same.

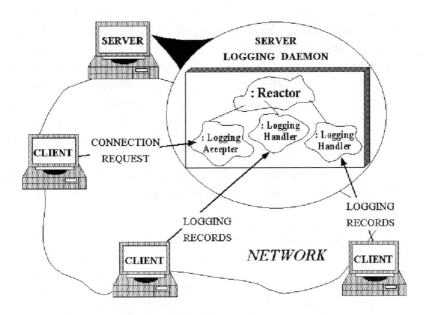

FIGURE 3.

server logging daemon is to combine the Reactor and Accepter patterns. Together, these patterns decouple 1) the application-independent mechanisms that demultiplex and dispatch preregistered Event_Handler objects from 2) the application-specific connection establishment and logging record transfer functionality performed by methods in these objects.

Within the server logging daemon, two subclasses of the Event_Handler base class (Logging_Handler and Logging_ Accepter) perform the actions required to process the different types of events arriving on different I/O handles. The Logging_Handler event handler is responsible for receiving and processing logging records transmitted from a client. Likewise, the Logging_Accepter event handler is a factory that is responsible for accepting a new connection request from a client, dynamically allocating a new Logging_Handler event handler to handle logging records from this client, and registering the new handler with an instance of a Reactor object.

The following code illustrates an implementation the server logging daemon based upon the Reactor and Accepter patterns. An instance of the Logging_Handler template class performs I/O between the server logging daemon and a particular instance of a client logging daemon. As shown in the following code, the `Logging_Handler` class inherits from `Event_Handler`. Inheriting from `Event_Handler` enables a `Logging_Handler` object to be registered with the `Reactor`. This inheritance also allows a `Logging_Handler` object's `handle_event` method to be dispatched automatically by a `Reactor` object to process logging records when they arrive from clients. The `Logging_Handler` class contains an instance of the template parameter `PEER_IO`. The `PEER_IO` class provides reliable TCP capabilities used to transfer logging records between an application and the server. The use of templates removes the reliance on a particular IPC interface (such as BSD sockets or System V TLI).

```
template <class PEER_IO>
class Logging_Handler
    : public Event_Handler
{

public:
    // Callback method that handles the reception
    // of logging transmissions from remote clients.
    // Two recv()'s are used to maintain framing
    // across a TCP bytestream.

    virtual int handle_event (HANDLE, Reactor_Mask) {
        long len;
    // Determine logging record length.
    long n = this->peer_io_.recv (&len, sizeof len);

    if (n <= 0) return n;
    else {
        Log_Record log_record;

        // Convert from network to host byte-order.
        len = ntohl (len);
        // Read remaining data in record.
        this->peer_io_.recv (&log_record, len);

        // Format and print the logging record.
        log_record.decode_and_print ();
        return 0;
    }
}

// Retrieve the I/O handle (called by Reactor
// when Logging_Handler object is registered).

virtual HANDLE get_handle (void) const {
    return this->peer_io_.get_handle ();
}

// Close down the I/O handle and delete the
```

```
// object when a client closes the connection.

virtual int handle_close (HANDLE,
                          Reactor_Mask) {
    delete this;
    return 0;
}

private:
    // Private ensures dynamic allocation.
    ~Logging_Handler (void) {
    this->peer_io_.close ();
    }

    // C++ wrapper for data transfer.
    PEER_IO peer_io_;
}
```

The Logging_Accepter template class is shown in the C++ code below. It is a generic factory that performs the steps necessary to 1) accept connection requests from client logging daemons and 2) create SVC_HANDLER objects that are used to perform an actual application-specific service on behalf of clients. Note that the Logging_Accepter object and the SVC_HANDLER objects it creates run within the same thread of control. Logging record processing is driven reactively by method callbacks triggered by the Reactor.

The Logging_Accepter subclass inherits from the Event_ Handler class. Inheriting from the Event_Handler class enables an Logging_Accepter object to be registered with the Reactor. The Reactor subsequently dispatches the Logging_Accepter object's handle_event method. This method then invokes SOCK_ Accepter::accept, which accepts a new client connection. The Logging_Accepter class also contains an instance of the template parameter PEER_ACCEPTER. The PEER_ACCEPTER class is a factory that listens for connection requests on a well-known communication port and accepts connections when they arrive on that port from clients.

```
// Global per-process instance of the Reactor.
extern Reactor reactor;

// Handles connection requests
// from a remote client.

template <class SVC_HANDLER,
       class PEER_ACCEPTER,
       class PEER_ADDR>
class Logging_Accepter
    : public Event_Handler
{
```

```
public:

    // Initialize the accepter endpoint.

    Logging_Accepter (PEER_ADDR &addr)
        : peer_accepter_ (addr) {}

    // Callback method that accepts a new
    // connection, creates a new SVC_HANDLER object
    // to perform I/O with the client connection,
    // and registers the new object with the Reactor.

    virtual int handle_event (HANDLE, Reactor_Mask) {
        SVC_HANDLER *handler = new SVC_HANDLER;

        this->peer_accepter_.accept (*handler);
        reactor.register_handler (handler, READ_MASK);
        return 0;
    }

    // Retrieve the I/O handle (called by Reactor
    // when an Logging_Accepter object is registered).

    virtual HANDLE get_handle (void) const {
        return this->peer_accepter_.get_handle ();
    }

    // Close down the I/O handle when the
    // Logging_Accepter is shut down.

    virtual int handle_close (HANDLE,
                              Reactor_Mask) {
        return this->peer_accepter_.close ();
    }

private:
    // Factory that accepts client connections.
    PEER_ACCEPTER peer_accepter_;
};
```

The following C++ code shows the main entry point into the server logging daemon. This code creates a `Reactor` object and an `Logging_Accepter` object and registers the `Logging_Accepter` with the `Reactor`. Note that the `Logging_Accepter` template is instantiated with the `Logging_Handler` class, which performs the distributed logging service on behalf of clients. Next, the main program calls `dispatch` and enters the `Reactor`'s event-loop. The `dispatch` method continuously handles connection requests and logging records that arrive from clients.

The interaction diagram shown in Figure 4 illustrates the collaboration between the various objects in the server logging daemon at runtime. Note that once the `Reactor` object is initialized, it becomes the primary focus of the control flow within the server logging daemon. All subsequent activity is triggered by callback methods on the event handlers controlled by the `Reactor`.

```
// Global per-process instance of the Reactor.
Reactor reactor;

// Server port number.
const unsigned int PORT = 10000;

// Instantiate the Logging_Handler template.
typedef Logging_Handler <SOCK_Stream>
    LOGGING_HANDLER;

// Instantiate the Logging_Accepter template.
typedef Logging_Accepter<LOGGING_HANDLER,
                         SOCK_Accepter,
                         INET_Addr>
                         LOGGING_ACCEPTER;

int
main (void)
{
    // Logging server address and port number.
    INET_Addr addr (PORT);
    // Initialize logging server endpoint.
    LOGGING_ACCEPTER accepter (addr);

    reactor.register_handler (&accepter, READ_MASK);

    // Main event loop that handles client
    // logging records and connection requests.
    reactor.dispatch ();
    /* NOTREACHED */
    return 0;
}
```

This C++ code example uses templates to decouple the reliance on the particular type of IPC interface used for connection establishment and communication. The SOCK_Stream, SOCK_Accepter and INET_Addr classes used in the template instantiations are part of the SOCK_SAP C++ wrapper library[14] SOCK_SAP encapsulates the SOCK_STREAM semantics of the socket transport layer interface within a type-secure, OO interface. SOCK_Stream sockets support the reliable transfer of bytestream data between two processes, which may run on the same or on different host machines in a network.[12]

By using templates, it is relatively straightforward to instantiate a different IPC interface (such as the TLI_SAP C++ wrappers that encapsulate the System V UNIX TLI interface). Templates trade additional compile-time and linktime overhead for improved runtime efficiency. Note that a similar degree of decoupling also could be achieved via inheritance and dynamic binding by using the `Abstract Factory` or `Factory Method` patterns.[1]

Evolving the Design Patterns to Windows NT

This section describes the Windows NT implementation of the `Reactor` and `Accepter` design patterns performed at the Ericsson facility in Cypress, CA. Initially, we attempted to evolve the existing `Reactor` implementation from UNIX to Windows NT using the `select` function from the Windows Sockets (WinSock) library.* This approach failed because the WinSock version of `select` does not interoperate with standard Win32**

I/O HANDLEs. Our applications required the use of Win32 I/O HANDLEs to support network protocols (such as Microsoft's NetBIOS Extended User Interface (NetBEUI)) that are not supported by WinSock version 1.1. Next, we tried to reimplement the `Reactor` interface using the Win32 API system call `WaitForMultipleObjects`. The goal was to maintain the original UNIX interface, but transparently supply a different implementation.

Transparent reimplementation failed to work due to fundamental differences in the proactive-versus-reactive I/O semantics on Windows NT and UNIX outlined in the fourth section. We initially considered circumventing these differences by asynchronously initiating a 0-sized `ReadFile` request on an overlapped `I/O HANDLE`. Overlapped I/O is a Win32 mechanism that supports asynchronous input and output. An overlapped event signals an application when data arrives, allowing `ReadFile` to receive the data synchronously. Unfortunately, this solution doubles the number of system calls for every input operation, creating unacceptable performance overhead. In addition, this approach does not adequately emulate the reactive output semantics provided by the UNIX event demultiplexing and I/O mechanisms.

It soon became clear that directly reusing class method interfaces, attributes, detailed designs, or algorithms was not feasible under the circumstances. Instead, we needed to elevate the level of abstraction for reuse to the level of design patterns. Regardless of the underlying OS event demultiplexing I/O semantics, the `Reactor` and `Accepter` patterns are applicable

---

*WinSock is a Windows-oriented transport layer programming interface based on the BSD socket paradigm.

**Win32 is the 32-bit Windows subsystem of the Windows NT operating system.

for event-driven applications that must provide different types services that are triggered simultaneously by different types of events. Therefore, although OS platform differences precluded direct reuse of implementations or interfaces, the design knowledge we had invested in learning and documenting the Reactor and Accepter patterns *was* reusable.

The remainder of this section describes the modifications we made to the implementations of the Reactor and Accepter design patterns in order to port them to Windows NT.

Implementing the Reactor Pattern on Windows NT

Windows NT provides proactive I/O semantics that are typically used in the following manner. First, an application creates a HANDLE that corresponds to an I/O channel for the type of networking mechanism being used (such as named pipes or sockets). The overlapped I/O attribute is specified to the HANDLE creation system call (WinSock sockets are created for overlapped I/O by default). Next, an application creates a HANDLE to a Win32 event object and uses this event object HANDLE to initialize an overlapped I/O structure. The HANDLE to the I/O channel and the overlapped I/O structure are then passed to the WriteFile or ReadFile system calls to initiate a send or receive operation, respectively. The initiated operation proceeds asynchronously and does not block the caller. When the operation completes, the event object specified inside the overlapped I/O structure is set to the "signaled" state. Subsequently, Win32 demultiplexing system calls (such as WaitForSingleObject or WaitForMultipleObjects) may be used to detect the signaled state of the Win32 event object. These calls indicate when an outstanding asynchronous operation has completed.

The Win32 WaitForMultipleObjects system call is functionally similar to the UNIX select and poll system calls. It blocks on an array of HANDLEs waiting for one or more of them to signal. Unlike the two UNIX system calls (which wait only for I/O handles), WaitForMultipleObjects is a general purpose routine that may be used to wait for any type of Win32 object (such as a thread, process, synchronization object, I/O handle, named pipe, socket, or timer). It may be programmed to return to its caller either when any one of the HANDLEs becomes signaled or when all of the HANDLEs become signaled. WaitForMultipleObjects returns the index location in the HANDLE array of the lowest signaled HANDLE.

Windows NT proactive I/O has both advantages and disadvantages. One advantage over UNIX is that Windows NT WaitForMultipleObjects provides the flexibility to synchronize on a wide range Win32 objects. Another advantage is that overlapped I/O may improve performance by allowing I/O operations to execute asynchronously with respect to other computation performed by applications or the OS. In contrast, the reactive I/O semantics offered by UNIX do not support asynchronous I/O directly (threads may be used instead).

On the other hand, designing and implementing the `Reactor` pattern using proactive I/O on Windows NT turned out to be more difficult than using reactive I/O on UNIX. Several characteristics of `WaitForMultiple Objects` significantly complicated the implementation of the Windows NT version of the `Reactor` pattern.

> **TIP**
>
> Overlapped I/O may improve performance by allowing I/O operations to execute asynchronously.

First, applications that must synchronize simultaneous send and receive operations on the same I/O channel are more complicated to program on Windows NT. For example, to distinguish the completion of a `WriteFile` operation from a `ReadFile` operation, separate overlapped I/O structures and Win32 event objects must be allocated for input and output. Furthermore, two elements in the `WaitForMultipleObjects` HANDLE array (which is currently limited to a rather small maximum of 64 HANDLEs) are consumed by the separate event object HANDLEs dedicated to the sender and the receiver.

Second, each Win32 `WaitForMultipleObjects` call only returns notification on a single HANDLE. Therefore, to achieve the same behavior as the UNIX `select` and `poll` system calls (which return a set of activated I/O handles), multiple `WaitForMultipleObjects` must be performed. In addition, the semantics of `WaitForMultipleObjects` do not result in a fair distribution of notifications. In particular, the lowest signaled HANDLE in the array is always returned, regardless of how long other HANDLEs further back in the array may have been pending.

The implementation techniques required to deal with these characteristics of Windows NT were rather complicated. Therefore, we modified the NT `Reactor` by creating a `Handler_Repository` class that shields the `Reactor` from this complexity. This class stores `Event_Handler` objects that registered with a `Reactor`. This container class implements standard operations for inserting, deleting, suspending, and resuming `Event_Handlers`. Each `Reactor` object contains a `Handler_Repository` object in its private data portion. A `Handler_Repository` maintains the array of HANDLEs passed to `WaitForMultipleObjects` and it also provides methods for inserting, retrieving, and "reprioritizing" the HANDLE array. Reprioritization alleviates the inherent unfairness in the way that the Windows NT `WaitForMultiple Objects` system call notifies applications when HANDLEs become signaled.

The `Handler_Repository`'s re-prioritization method is invoked by specifying the index of the HANDLE that has signaled and been dispatched by the `Reactor`. The method's algorithm moves the signaled HANDLE toward the end of the HANDLE array. This allows signaled HANDLEs that are further back in the array to be returned by subsequent calls to `WaitForMultiple Objects`. Over time, HANDLEs that signal frequently migrate to the end of the HANDLE array. Likewise, HANDLES that signal infrequently migrate to the front of the HANDLE array. This algorithm ensures a reasonably fair distribution of HANDLE dispatching.

The implementation techniques described in the previous paragraph did not affect the external interface of the `Reactor`. Unfortunately, certain aspects of Windows NT proactive I/O semantics, coupled with the desire to fully utilize the flexibility of `WaitForMultiple Objects`, forced visible changes to the `Reactor`'s external interface. In particular, Windows NT overlapped I/O operations must be initiated *immediately*. Therefore, it was necessary for the Windows NT `Event_Handler` interface to distinguish between I/O HANDLEs and synchronization object HANDLEs, as well as to supply additional information (such as message buffers

> **TIP**
>
> Windows NT overlapped I/O operations must be initiated immediately.

and event HANDLEs) to the `Reactor`. In contrast, the UNIX version of the `Reactor` does not require this information immediately. Therefore, it may wait until it is *possible* to perform an operation, at which point additional information may be available to help optimize program behavior.

The following modifications to the `Reactor` were required to support Windows NT I/O semantics. The `Reactor_Mask` enumeration was modified to include a new `SYNC_MASK` value to allow the registration of an `Event_Handler` that is dispatched when a general Win32 synchronization object signals. The `send` method was added to the `Reactor` class to proactively initiate output operations on behalf of an `Event_Handler`.

```
// Bit-wise "or" these values to
// check for multiple activities per-handle.
enum Reactor_Mask { READ_MASK = 01,
```

```
    WRITE_MASK = 02, SYNC_MASK = 04
};

class Reactor
{
public:
    // Same as UNIX Reactor...

    // Initiate an asynchronous send operation.
    virtual int send (Event_Handler *,
                      const Message_Block *);

// ...
};
```

Likewise, the Event_Handler interface for Windows NT was also modified as follows:

```
class Event_Handler
{
protected:
    // Returns the Win32 I/O HANDLE
    // associated with the derived object
    // (must be supplied by a subclass).
    virtual HANDLE get_handle (void) const;

    // Allocates a message for the Reactor.
    virtual Message_Block *get_message (void);

    // Called when event occurs.
    virtual int handle_event (Message_Block *,
                              Reactor_Mask);

    // Called when object is removed from Reactor.
    virtual int handle_close (Message_Block *,
                              Reactor_Mask);

// Same as UNIX Event_Handler...
};
```

When a derived Event_Handler is registered for input with the Reactor an overlapped input operation is immediately initiated on its behalf. This requires the Reactor to request the derived Event_Handler for an I/O mechanism HANDLE, destination buffer, and a Win32 event object HANDLE for synchronization. A derived Event_Handler returns the I/O mechanism HANDLE via its get_handle method and returns the destination buffer location and length information via the Message_Block abstraction.[4]

The current implementation of the Windows NT-based Reactor pattern is about 2,600 lines C++ code (not including comments or extraneous whitespace). This code is approximately 200 lines longer than the UNIX version.

The additional code primarily ensures the fairness of WaitForMultiple Objects event demultiplexing, as discussed above. Although Windows NT event demultiplexing is more complex than UNIX, the behavior of Win32 mutex objects eliminated the need for the separate Mutex interface with recursive-mutex semantics discussed in the unix reactor section. Under Win32, a thread will not be blocked if it attempts to acquire a mutex specifying the HANDLE to a mutex that it already owns. However, to release its ownership, the thread must release a Win32 mutex once for each time that the mutex was acquired.

Implementing the Accepter Pattern on Windows NT

The following example C++ code illustrates an implementation of the Accepter pattern based on the Windows NT version of the Reactor pattern:

```cpp
template <class PEER_IO>
class Logging_Handler : public Event_Handler
{
public:
    // Callback method that handles the
    // reception of logging transmissions from
    // remote clients.  The Message_Block object
    // stores a message received from a client.

    virtual int handle_event (Message_Block *msg,
                              Reactor_Mask) {
        Log_Record *log_record =
            (Log_Record *) msg->get_rd_ptr ();

        // Format and print logging record.
        log_record.format_and_print ();
        delete msg;
        return 0;
    }

    // Retrieve the I/O HANDLE (called by Reactor
    // when a Logging_Handler object is registered).

    virtual HANDLE get_handle (void) const {
        return this->peer_io_.get_handle ();
    }

    // Return a dynamically allocated buffer
    // to store an incoming logging message.

    virtual Message_Block *get_message (void) {
        return new Message_Block (sizeof (Log_Record));
    }
```

```
            // Close down I/O handle and delete
            // object when a client closes connection.
            virtual int handle_close (Message_Block *msg,
                                        Reactor_Mask) {
                delete msg;
                delete this;
                return 0;
            }

    private:
            // Private ensures dynamic allocation.
            ~Logging_Handler (void) {
                this->peer_io_.close ();
            }

            // C++ wrapper for data transfer.
            PEER_IO peer_io_;
    };
```

The Logging_Accepter class is essentially the same as the one illustrated in the UNIX listen section. Likewise, the interaction diagram that describes the collaboration between objects in the server logging daemon is also very similar to the one shown in Figure 4.

The application is the same server logging daemon presented in the UNIX listen subsection. The primary difference is that Win32 Named_Pipe C++ wrappers are used instead of the SOCK_SAP socket C++ wrappers in the main program as shown here:

```
// Global per-process instance of the Reactor.
Reactor reactor;

// Server endpoint.
const char ENDPOINT[] = "logger";

// Instantiate the Logging_Handler template
typedef Logging_Handler <NPipe_IO>
    LOGGING_HANDLER;

// Instantiate the Logging_Accepter template
typedef Logging_Accepter<LOGGING_HANDLER, NPipe_Accepter,
                        Local_Pipe_Name>
    LOGGING_ACCEPTER;

int
main (void)
{
    // Logging server address.
    Local_Pipe_Name addr (ENDPOINT);
    // Initialize logging server endpoint.
    LOGGING_ACCEPTER accepter (addr);

    reactor.register_handler (&accepter,
                            SYNC_MASK);
```

```
    // Arm the proactive I/O handler.
    accepter.initiate ();

    // Main event loop that handles client
    // logging records and connection requests.
    reactor.dispatch ();
    /* NOTREACHED */
    return 0;
}
```

The `Named Pipe Accepter` object (`accepter`) is registered with the `Reactor` to handle asynchronous connection establishment. Due to the semantics of Windows NT proactive I/O, the `accepter` object must explicitly initiate the acceptance of a `Named Pipe` connection via an `initiate` method. Each time a connection acceptance is completed, the `Reactor` dispatches the `handle_event` method of the `Named Pipe` version of the `Accepter` pattern to create a new `Svc_Handler` that will receive logging records from the client. The `Reactor` will also initiate the next connection acceptance sequence asynchronously.

Lessons Learned

Our group at Ericsson has been developing OO frameworks based on design patterns for the past two years.[6] During this time, we have identified a number of pros and cons related to using design patterns as the basis for our system design, implementation, and documentation. We have also formulated a number of "workarounds" for the problems we observed using design patterns in a production environment. This section discusses the lessons we have learned thus far.

Pros and Cons of Design Patterns

Ironically, many pros and cons of using design patterns are "duals" of each other, representing "two sides of the same coin:"

Patterns are underspecified.

They generally do not overconstrain an implementation. This is beneficial since it permits flexible solutions that may be customized according to application requirements and the constraints imposed by the OS platform and network environment.

> **TIP**
>
> Many pros and cons of using design patterns are "duals" of each other.

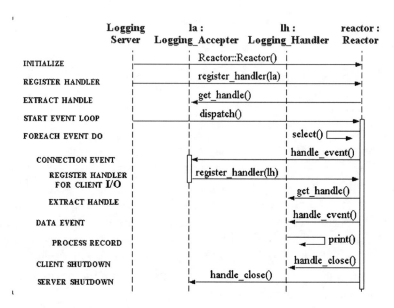

FIGURE 4. *Server logging daemon interaction diagram.*

On the other hand, it is important for developers and managers to recognize that understanding a collection of design patterns is no substitute for design and implementation skills. For example, recognizing the structure and participants in a pattern (such as the Reactor or Accepter patterns) is only the first step. As we describe in the fourth section, a major development effort is often required to fully realize the pattern correctly and efficiently.

Patterns enable large-scale architectural reuse.

> **TIP**
>
> Our task became much simpler when we recognized how to leverage off our prior development effort.

Even if reuse of algorithms, implementations, interfaces, or detailed designs is not feasible. Understanding these benefits was crucial in the design evolution we presented in the fourth section. Our task became much simpler when we recognized how to leverage off our prior development effort and reduce risk by reusing the Reactor and Accepter patterns across UNIX and Windows NT.

It is important, however, to manage the expectations of developers and managers, who may have misconceptions about the fundamental contribution of design patterns to a project. In particular, patterns do not lead to automated code reuse. Neither do they guarantee flexible and efficient design and implementation. As always, there is no substitute for creativity and diligence on the part of developers.

Patterns capture implicit knowledge that is implicitly understood.

Our experience has been that once developers are exposed to, and properly motivated by, the concepts of design patterns, they are generally very eager to adopt the nomenclature and methodology. Patterns tend to codify knowledge that is already understood intuitively. Therefore, once basic concepts, notations, and pattern template formats are mastered, it is straightforward to document and reason about many portions of a system's architecture and design using patterns.

The downside of the intuitive nature of patterns is a phenomenon we termed "pattern explosion." In this situation, all aspects of a project become expressed as patterns, which often leads to relabeling existing development practices without significantly improving them. We also noticed a tendency for developers to spend considerable time formalizing relatively mundane concepts (such as binary search, a linked list, or opening a file) as patterns. Although this may be intellectually satisfying, it does not necessarily improve productivity or software quality.

TIP
Watch for pattern explosions.

Patterns help improve communication
within and across software development teams.

Developers share a common vocabulary and a common conceptual "gestalt." By learning the key recurring patterns in their application domain, developers at Ericsson elevated the level of abstraction by which they communicated with their colleagues. For example, once our team understood the `Reactor` and `Accepter` patterns, they began to use them in many other projects that benefited from these architectures.

As usual, however, restraint and a good sense of aesthetics is required to resist the temptation of elevating complex concepts and principles to the level of "buzz words" and hype. We noticed a tendency for many developers to get locked into "pattern-think," where they would try to apply patterns that were inappropriate simply because they were familiar with the patterns. For example, the `Reactor` pattern is often an inefficient event demultiplexing model for a multiprocessor platform since it serializes application concurrency at a very coarse-grained level.

Patterns promote a structured means of documenting software architectures.

This documentation may be written at a high-level of abstraction, which captures the essential architectural interactions while suppressing unnecessary details.

One drawback we observed with much of the existing pattern literature[1,2] however, is that it is often *too* abstract. Abstraction is a benefit in many cases since it avoids inundating a casual reader with excessive details. However, we found that in many cases that overly abstract pattern descriptions made it difficult for developers to understand and apply a particular pattern to systems they were building.

Solutions and Workarounds

Based on our experiences, we recommend the following solutions and workarounds to the various traps and pitfalls with patterns mentioned previously.

- *Expectation management:* Many of the problems with patterns we discussed previously are related to managing the expectations of development team members. As usual, patterns are no silver bullet that will magically absolve managers and developers from having to wrestle with tough design and implementation issues. At Ericsson, we have worked hard to motivate the genuine benefits from patterns, without hyping them beyond their actual contribution.

- *Wide-Spectrum pattern exemplars:* Based on our experience using design patterns as a documentation tool, we believe that pattern catalogues should include more than just object model diagrams and structured prose. Although these notations are suitable for a high-level overview, we found in practice that they are insufficient to guide developers through difficult design and implementation tradeoffs. Therefore, it is very useful to have concrete source code examples to supplement the more abstract diagrams and text.

Hypertext browsers, such as Mosaic and Windows Help Files, are particularly useful for creating compound documents that possess multiple levels of abstraction. Moreover, in our experience, it was particularly important to illustrate multiple implementations of a pattern.

This helps to avoid "tunnel vision" and overconstrained solutions based upon a limited pattern vocabulary. The extended discussion in the third section is one example of a wide-spectrum exemplar using this approach. This example contains in-depth coverage of tradeoffs encountered in actual use.

- *Integrate patterns with OO frameworks:* Ideally, examples in pattern catalogs[1,2] should reference (or better yet, contain hypertext links to) source code that comprises an actual OO framework. We have begun building such an environment at Ericsson, in order to disseminate our patterns and frameworks to a wider audience. In addition to linking online documentation and source code, we have had good success with periodic design reviews where developers throughout the organization present interesting patterns they have been working on. This is another technique for avoiding "tunnel vision" and enhancing the pattern vocabulary within and across development teams.

CONCLUSION

Design patterns facilitate the reuse of abstract architectures that are decoupled from concrete realizations of these architectures. This decoupling is useful when developing system software components and frameworks that are reusable across OS platforms. This article describes two design patterns, `Reactor` and `Accepter`, that are commonly used in distributed system software. These design patterns characterize the collaboration between objects that are used to automate common activities (such as event demultiplexing, event handler dispatching, and connection establishment) performed by distributed applications. Using the design pattern techniques described in this article, we successfully reused major portions of our telecommunication system software development effort across several diverse OS platforms.

This case study describes how an OO framework based on the `Reactor` and `Accepter` design patterns evolved from several UNIX platforms to the Windows NT Win32 platform. Due to fundamental differences between the platforms, it was not possible to directly reuse the algorithms, detailed designs, interfaces, or implementations of the framework across the different OS platforms. In particular, performance constraints and fundamental differences in the I/O mechanisms available on Windows NT and UNIX platforms prevented us from encapsulating event demultiplexing functionality within a directly reusable framework. However, we were able to reuse the underlying design patterns, which reduced project risk significantly and simplifed our redevelopment effort.

Our experiences with patterns reinforce the observation that the transition from OO analysis to OO design and implementation is challenging.[11] Often, the constraints of the underlying OS and hardware platform influence design and implementation details significantly. This is particularly problematic for system software, which is frequently targeted for particular platforms with particular nonportable characteristics. In such circumstances, reuse of design patterns may be the only viable means to leverage previous development expertise.

The UNIX version of the ASX framework components we described here are freely available via anonymous ftp from the Internet host ics.uci.edu (128.195.1.1) in the file gnu/C++_wrappers.tar.Z. This distribution contains complete source code, documentation, and example test drivers for the C++ components developed as part of the ADAPTIVE project[4] at the University of California, Irvine and Washington University.

References

1. Gamma, E., R. Helm, R. Johnson, and J. Vlissides. DESIGN PATTERNS: ELEMENTS OF REUSABLE OBJECT-ORIENTED SOFTWARE, Reading, MA, Addison-Wesley, 1994.
2. Buschmann, F., R. Meunier, H. Rohnert, and M. Stal. PATTERN-ORIENTED SOFTWARE ARCHITECTURE—A PATTERN SYSTEM, Wiley, New York, 1995.
3. Coplien, J. O. A development process generative pattern language, in PATTERN LANGUAGES OF PROGRAMS, J. O. Coplien and D. C. Schmidt, Eds., Addison-Wesley, Reading, MA, June 1995.
4. Schmidt, D. C. ASX: An object-oriented framework for developing distributed applications, PROCEEDINGS OF THE 6TH USENIX C++ TECHNICAL CONFERENCE, Cambridge, MA, USENIX Assoc., Apr. 1994.
5. Schmidt, D. C. Reactor: An object behavioral pattern for concurrent event demultiplexing and event handler dispatching, in PATTERN LANGUAGES OF PROGRAMS, J. O. Coplien and D. C. Schmidt, Eds., Addison-Wesley, Reading, MA, June 1995.
6. D. C. Schmidt and P. Stephenson. An object-oriented framework for developing network server daemons, PROCEEDINGS OF THE 2ND C++ WORLD CONFERENCE, Dallas, TX, SIGS, Oct. 1993.
7. Eykholt, J., S. Kleiman, S. Barton, R. Faulkner, A. Shivalingiah, M. Smith, D. Stein, J. Voll, M. Weeks, and D. Williams. Beyond multiprocessing... Multithreading the SunOS kernel, PROCEEDINGS OF THE SUMMER USENIX CONFERENCE, San Antonio, TX, June 1992.
8. Weinand, A., E. Gamma, and R. Marty. ET++—An object-oriented application framework in C++, PROCEEDINGS OF THE OBJECT-ORIENTED PROGRAMMING SYSTEMS, LANGUAGES AND APPLICATIONS CONFERENCE, ACM, Sept. 1988, pp. 46–57.

9. Linton, M. A., J. Vlissides, and P. Calder, Composing User Interfaces with InterViews, IEEE COMPUTER, vol. 22, pp. 8–22, Feb. 1989.

10. S. Vinoski, Distributed object computing with CORBA, C++ REPORT, 5(6), July/August 1993.

11. Booch, G. OBJECT-ORIENTED ANALYSIS AND DESIGN WITH APPLICATIONS, 2nd ed., Benjamin/Cummings, Redwood City, CA, 1993.

12. Stevens, W. R. UNIX NETWORK PROGRAMMING, Prentice Hall, Englewood Cliffs, NJ, 1990.

13. Custer, H. INSIDE WINDOWS NT, Microsoft Press, Redmond, WA, 1993.

14. Schmidt, D. C. IPC_SAP: An object-oriented interface to interprocess communication services, C++ REPORT, 4(6), Nov./Dec. 1992.

PART IV

LANGUAGES

Every programming paradigm requires an implementation language. As I am sure you are aware, there are several that have shaped the object-oriented landscape. This section discusses the important trends and features of these languages.

C++

THE BEAUTY AND POWER OF C++

I F YOU BELIEVE THAT IT'S POSSIBLE FOR A PERSON TO BE TRANSPORTED AS A BEAM of brilliant energy, as in Star Trek, then you should know that it is likely to be choreographed by highly polymorphic software systems. Polymorphism literally means "more than one form"; it denotes a single thing having multiple forms. In the object-oriented software area, polymorphism means that a single thing is able to behave in many different, but related ways. Or that a single thing can elicit many different, but related behaviors. Or finally, that a single thing is able to accept many different, but related forms of data for processing. Only through the workings of software which is extremely adaptable, and flexible can things like energy beam transfer occur and these workings are the kind of characteristics which highly polymorphic systems offer. Of course, there's no question that any software system de-materializing, and re-materializing people had better be extremely successful, robust, and reliable. Extremely high flexibility, and reliability are qualities that can be realized together in object-oriented software systems developed using C++.

One of the major ways many well designed C++ systems achieve these qualities is by making extensive and significant use of inheritance based polymorphism, along with strong type checking. Inheritance based polymorphism has been shown to be the most powerful of the many forms of polymorphism. Inheritance based polymorphism allows us to develop systems which are extremely adaptable, and flexible.

C++ inheritance based polymorphism allows us to develop systems which behave efficiently and effectively in a wide variety of circumstances, contexts, and conditions. Polymorphic systems are the most capable for effectively addressing a wide variety of application needs, and demands.

C++ inheritance based polymorphic systems perform well in the face of a wide variety of input conditions, and output necessities.

Dynamic substitution is the mechanism which underlies much of the polymorphism found in many C++ systems. Dynamic substitution takes place within (horizontally), as well as across (vertically) the various levels of C++ systems having a layered architecture.[1] Dynamic substitution allows these systems to attain a high degree of flexibility. Flexible systems are adaptable to many different circumstances.

Visually, the structures and architectures of well designed C++ programs which are highly polymorphic are beautiful, and conceptually these programs are elegant. When you use the proper levels of abstraction, and make judicious use of inheritance based polymorphism in C++, it is an experience echoing Dijkstra's comment that well abstracted code is self-documenting. And that as you write the code, it is apparent that it is correct.[2]

With these things in mind we will explore the best ways to implement, and exercise inheritance based polymorphism using C++. C++ easily supports constructing amazing, mind bending, and highly polymorphic systems.

WORKING ON VEHICLES

Let's take a look at the two major classes we will use to illustrate a system with a high degree of polymorphism. They are the classes Vehicle and BodyDivision; a Vehicle is worked on by the BodyDivision:

```
class Vehicle
{
  private:
        int exportStatus
  public:
        int isExport()
        {
                return exportStatus;
        };
  };
  class BodyDivision
  {
      public:
        void doStripes(Vehicle aVehicle)
        {
                //stripe aVehicle
        };

        void testForStripe(Vehicle aVehicle)
        {
```

```
            if(aVehicle.isExport())
            {
                    doStripes(aVehicle);
            }
        };
    };
```

The two might be used like this:

```
main()
{
    Vehicle ourVehicle;          // create a Vehicle object.
    BodyDivision ourBodyDivision;
                        // create a BodyDivision
    BodyDivision.testForStripe(ourVehicle);
                        // send ourVehicle to
                        // ourBodyDivision to test
                        // for stripes.
};
```

In the BodyDivision class, if a Vehicle is for export, the BodyDivision class has the function Stripe() to give the Vehicle stripes.

DYNAMICALLY SUBSTITUTING IMPLEMENTATION

Using inheritance based polymorphism in C++, it is easy to change the specifics of *how* something is implemented* on the fly; it is possible to change how something is done dynamically during program execution. This is *dynamic substitution* of implementation.

In real life there isn't just one kind of vehicle, there are various kinds such as sports, off-road, and van vehicles. More than likely the striping process is somewhat different for each kind of vehicle. As things stand now BodyDivision would have to use an "if" or "switch" statement to deal with each kind of vehicle. Something like this fragment:

```
switch (kinds_of_vehicles) {
{
    case sportsVehicle:
        // do sports Vehicle stripes
    break;
    case off-roadVehicle:
        // do off-road Vehicle stripes
    break;
```

---

*Although implementation is sometimes referred to as *details*, it's better to think of it as *not policy*. This gets us away from thinking that *details* necessarily equals *low level*.

```
    // etc.
};
```

It would be inconvenient to have to specify the striping process for every kind of new vehicle introduced into a program. It also error prone because we might forget to add the appropriate striping operation in the switch construct when a new kind of vehicle is introduced.

To get around this we can implement (define) the striping procedure, `Stripe()`, specific to each kind of vehicle inside the class code for each kind of vehicle; we will take `Stripe()` out of the `BodyDivision` class. When the `BodyDivision` works on each kind of vehicle it can ask the vehicle to stripe itself.

To make this work efficiently in C++, the various kinds of vehicles can be publicly inherited[5] (publicly derived) from a common vehicle class. The classes would be arranged in a hierarchy, much like an organizational chart with the common vehicle class where the president would be placed and the various derived classes where the vice-presidents would be located. The common class may be thought of as a *parent* class and the various kinds of vehicles which inherit from it may be thought of as *child* classes.

In this case let's call the common, parent class, `Vehicle` (ignoring the fact that we used the name for an earlier class). We will call the child subclasses derived from the `Vehicle` class: `OffRoadVehicle`, `Sports-Vehicle`, and `VanVehicle`.

As we proposed, the `Stripe()` function will be implemented inside each of the children vehicle types. Given such a scenario in C++, the common base class, in this case `Vehicle`, simply declares (announces) the operations, such as `Stripe()`, common to all of the classes which inherit from it. It declares the common function, but leaves the implementation up to each child vehicle subclass.

When we simply declare a common function, such as `Stripe()` in the `Vehicle` class, we prepend the declaration with the word "`virtual`" and append it with the pure virtual specifier "`= 0`". "Pure" means that we are only declaring, not defining, the function in the `Vehicle` class declaration. This forces the child subclasses of `Vehicle` to define (implement) the function declaration themselves. Here is the new `Vehicle` class serving as the base class of our vehicle hierarchy of classes:

```
class Vehicle {
{
    public:
```

```
    virtual int isExport() = 0;
    virtual void doStripes() = 0;
};
```

When a C++ class has at least one "`virtual`" function appended with the pure virtual specifier "`= 0`" it is an abstract class. So we see that class `Vehicle` is an abstract class.

Here is one of the child types, a `SportsVehicle` subclass, inheriting from our new `Vehicle` class. Notice in the code how the `SportsVehicle` subclass inherits from `Vehicle` by placing a colon after its name followed by the `Vehicle` class name:

```
class SportsVehicle : public Vehicle
{
private:
    virtual int isExprt() { return TRUE; }
    virtual void doStripes()
    {
        // specific striping code for SportsVehicles
    };
};
```

Next is an example of the `BodyDivision` class which is able to process the various subclasses of `Vehicle`. As we proposed earlier, the function `Stripe()` is no longer a member of the `BodyDivision` class. Because a subclass of the abstract `Vehicle` base class is now being passed into the `BodyDivision` class, not a `Vehicle` class itself, as before, an asterisks follows the name `Vehicle` when it is used in the `BodyDivision` class:

```
class BodyDivision
{
  public:
      void testForStripe(Vehicle* VehiclePointer)
      {
          if (VehiclePointer->isExport() == TRUE)
          {
              VehiclePointer->doStripes();
          }
          else
          {
              sendToShipping(VehiclePointer);
          }
      };
};
```

The arrow means that the variable "`vehiclePointer`" activates the functions is `Export()`, and `Stripe()`.

With this new `BodyDivision` class, during run-time (dynamically) the implementation of striping can change, depending on which `Vehicle` child class is being processed by `BodyDivision`. In other words we can "dynamically substitute" one kind of implementation process, or procedure for another. There is no need to make changes to `BodyDivision` whenever it receives a new kind of `Vehicle` subclass for export.

Our program, or system is less subject to changes which might break it in various places. `BodyDivision` does not have to be modified to work on any new subclass of `Vehicle`; it is open to any new subclasses of `Vehicle` which may be introduced into the program any time in the future.[6] This is a significant way to use abstract base classes, and their subclasses to achieve polymorphism, and dynamic substitution in C++.

OBJECTS AND POINTERS

Before going on, it should be explained that while the abstract `Vehicle` base class has various concrete subclasses—`OffRoadVehicle`, `SportsVehicle`, and `VanVehicle`—these concrete subclasses, in all but rare cases, must be instantiated into unique objects to be useful. Instantiation means that a copy of a class, or subclass is given the ability to operate its functions, or store its data by the operating system.

> **TIP**
>
> A class or subclass may have zero, one, or any number of unique object instances.

A class, or subclass may have zero, one, or any number of unique object instances, each having a different state from the others. For instance, the set of actual `SportsVehicle` objects in a program at any one time may be a set of different colored Mazda RX-7s, or a set combining various makes such as RX-7s, Triumph GTBs, Nissan 340Zs, etc.

While the children subclasses of the `Vehicle` classes may be instantiated into objects, it is not possible to instantiate the `Vehicle` class into an object. That is because when we modified the `Vehicle` class, we made it a C++ abstract base class (ABC). It is not possible to create (instantiate) objects of a C++ ABC. However, the good thing about C++ ABC's is that we may use them as gateways, or interfaces to elicit the behavior of their children subclasses.

This is done by using a pointer variable,[7] which has the type of the ABC, to call (invoke) the specific behavior of each child subclass. The "vehiclePointer" argument, in our new Vehicle class, is a pointer variable which has the type of the Vehicle ABC. It may contain the address of instantiated objects which are copies of any of the subclasses inherited from Vehicle: OffRoadVehicle, SportsVehicle, and VanVehicle.

Every C++ variable has a compile time (static) type and for "vehiclePointer" its static type is the Vehicle class. If we were going to use "vehiclePointer" for more than just passing data to functions, we could declare it like any other variable:

```
Vehicle* vehiclePointer; // declare a Vehicle type pointer
```

Since the various Vehicle subclasses all inherit from Vehicle, a pointer variable having a Vehicle class static type may contain the address of any object instantiated from any of these subclasses. Again, this is why Vehicle in the stripeOrShip() function, of the new BodyDivison class, has an asterisks after it.[8]

DYNAMICALLY SUBSTITUTING POLICY

Now let's gain more flexibility by dynamically changing, or substituting policy as necessary. With policy we are more concerned with what will be done not how it is done.

The following code fragment from the function stripeOrShip() in the new BodyDivision class, is an example of dynamically changing, or substituting, policy as necessary. The pointer interface to the Vehicle hierarchy, "vehiclePointer," and the BodyDivision functions, Ship(), and Stripe() are entities within the same horizontal layer of our program[9]:

```
if (vehiclePointer->isExport() == true) {
vehiclePointer->Stripe(); } else {
Ship(vehiclePointer); }
```

Here the policy switch is made using the "if" construct. We have dynamically chosen our policy by testing whether, or not an actual Vehicle subclass object (for example a given actual Mazda RX-7 object of the SportsVehicle subclass represented by vehiclePointer) is for export. In this code we are determining "what" should be done. If the subclass object will be exported, it is given stripes, else it is sent to Shipping.

Earlier we dynamically invoked a specific striping implementation (how something is done) for each `Vehicle` subclass class—`OffRoadVehicle`, `SportsVehicle`, or `VanVehicle`—using the pointer to the `Vehicle` base class "vehiclePointer." In the "if" statement example, we have used the same pointer to determine policy, or "what" will be done, not implementation (how) it will be done.

While the abstract pointer, "vehiclePointer," exists within the same horizontal layer as the functions of `BodyDivision`, the concrete functions the pointer calls generally exist in layers below (vertical to) to that of `BodyDivision`. The "vehiclePointer" variable, may be used as an abstract, horizontal, interface to vertical, concrete objects.

HORIZONTAL AND VERTICAL SYSTEM POINTERS

Let us call abstract base class pointers to functions of policy, *horizontal pointers*. Abstract base class pointers to functions of implementation, let us call *vertical pointers*. Policy pointers are called horizontal pointers because, for systems with a layered architecture, policy generally changes within a horizontal layer. Implementation pointers are called vertical pointers because for systems with a layered architecture, implementation generally takes place in layers below the policy abstraction layer.

While, horizontal, and vertical pointers are two very useful ways of thinking about (conceiving) C++ pointers, in layered architecture systems, the C++ language standard does not define entities called horizontal pointers, or vertical pointers.[10]

Figure 1 is an example diagram of a C++ layered architecture system conceived with horizontal, and vertical system pointers.

Because all of the individual horizontal, and vertical pointers of a C++ program may vary the both the specific subclass, and specific object address within a subclass they point to, the topology, and operation of a running C++ program is highly variable, and dynamic. This allows the system to flex, and adapt well to a wide range of circumstances. Included in this adaptability is the ability of highly polymorphic systems to offer a wide variety of inputs, outputs and services.

The ability of an ABC pointer variable, like "vehiclePointer," to vary the address of the subclass objects it points to during program execution is called dynamic substitution. Dynamic substitution allows the capabilities of a highly polymorphic system to change as needed. It also allows the system

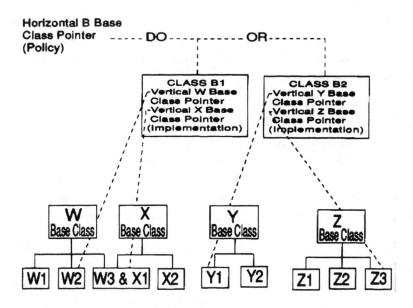

Figure 1.

to be highly extensible. At any one instance the configuration of a highly polymorphic system is different from the next, sometimes radically so. It is almost as if some extremely polymorphic systems were intelligent, and alive with self will.

Highly polymorphic systems make extensive use of both horizontal, and vertical base class pointers. It is through wise system design, and use of both horizontal, and vertical pointers that highly flexible and adaptable software systems may be created. The topology, and structure of a highly polymorphic system varies instant by instant according to the ever changing configuration of its horizontal and vertical pointers.[11] These are the same kind of pointers as, "`vehiclePointer`," used by the `BodyDivision` class example in Figure 1.

> **TIP**
>
> Highly polymorphic systems make extensive use of both horizontal and vertical base class pointers.

Of course, what is horizontal in one context is vertical in another, and vice versa. And it is no different for horizontal, and vertical pointers. The determination of what is a horizontal pointer versus what is a vertical pointer is relative to the level of the system being examined. In other words, it depends on the context. Also, it should be noted that, the same pointer may have opposite designations, as to whether, or not it is horizontal, or vertical, depending on the level of the system under consideration, even within a single application, or system.

Clients and Servers

In our example the BodyDivision class is a client which uses, a Vehicle class as a server (using is a client role).[12] The decision as to how horizontal pointers are configured at any particular time occurs within clients. Clients use conditional statements to select between hierarchies of vertical, or what is the same thing, implementation servers. Vertical pointers are determined by servers. What vertical path is taken is determined by which server is being used.

Servers, like SportsVehicle, are implemented in a hierarchy of classes. They are subclasses in an inheritance hierarchy of classes, as SportsVehicle is in the Vehicle hierarchy of classes. Such a hierarchy of classes need not have many levels of inheritance. Often a simple one level hierarchy of siblings inherited from a parent is sufficient. The Vehicle class hierarchy has been constructed to allow clients such as BodyDivision to use any of its server subclasses.

Taking an overall system view, servers may be clients and clients may be servers. The basis for classifying an object as a server, or client depends on the level of the system, and context under consideration.

A major way to view client, and server classes should be as agents of dynamic substitution, and change within a system. Both clients, and servers may dynamically alter the structure, and configuration of a software system. Highly polymorphic systems, through clients, and servers, can flexibly, alter and adapt their structure, and nature to deal with a wide variety of changes in the application environment. It is this which gives highly polymorphic systems, their general, advantage over systems with little or no polymorphic substitution.

The Root of the Power of Inheritance

Through the use of C++ class, and object inheritance we can easily construct systems which allow both dynamic substitution of one horizontal, or policy class for another, and substitution of one vertical, or implementation class for another. So how exactly is inheritance being taken advantage of to allow this?

Inheritance based dynamic substitution, and polymorphism rest on taking advantage of the commonality[13] found in classes, and subclasses arranged in an inheritance hierarchy, as in our `Vehicle` example. The commonalities among classes in a hierarchy we want to take advantage of are common responsibility, common interface, and common type.

Polymorphism is generally viewed to be a focus on taking advantage of type commonality. The parent class is seen as a specific type (kind of thing) and its children are seen as specializations, or extensions of the parent's type, as with our vehicle hierarchy of classes. This is the typical is-a relationship found in many object-oriented programs.

Dynamic substitution, on the other hand, should be viewed as being more focused on responsibility, and interface commonality present across a hierarchy, as opposed to polymorphism which additionally emphasizes type commonality. Dynamic substitution casts a wider net than polymorphism. Polymorphism is simply one aspect of dynamic substitution.

Taking advantage of commonality, along with templates, and function name overloading are the major sources of polymorphism for most C++ applications. It should be noted that, taking advantage of a class hierarchy's commonality is the only way to dynamically substitute the horizontal, and vertical components of a C++ application.

The commonality of the class hierarchy is represented by an abstract base class (ABC) in C++. An abstract class has functions which represent the commonality of the class hierarchy. It declares the operations, or functions that subclasses of the hierarchy must define to be a part of the hierarchy. these undefined operations are called abstract, or, pure virtual functions. (While abstract classes must have at least one abstract function declaration, they may have one, or more, non-abstract functions declared as members also.)

A pointer having the compile-time (static) type of the abstract class at the base of the hierarchy, such as the `Vehicle` base class, is used by clients, such as `BodyDivision`, to gain services from subclasses in the hierarchy. The client uses the base class pointer to call the abstract functions that each hierarchy subclass defines on its own. Just as in our example, "vehiclePointer," which is of static type `Vehicle`, was used by `BodyDivision` to call abstract functions like `Stripe()` to acquire services, or information from the various subclasses of the Vehicle ABC.[14]

All of the classes in a hierarchy, from top to bottom, must require no more, nor provide any less than what the others do. The ABC provides a contract to clients, or users of the hierarchy. This contract specifies, on the one had, what the hierarchy requires to function properly, and on the other, what services, or responsibilities all classes in the hierarchy will provide, or carry out.

Because of the abstract functions an abstract class is said to be an abstract interface. Because the class commonality an abstract base class embodies is the source of a class hierarchy's polymorphism, the writer formulated the term abstract polymorphic interface, or polymorphic interface (PI), to refer to a pointer having the static type of an abstract base classes. This captures the nature of the idiomatic usage of such a pointer in C++.

It would be a mistake to fail to make as much use of the power available through this topological, commonality arrangement of classes as we can. The class hierarchy's topological arrangement should, in most cases, reflect the structure of relations between real abstractions in the application domain. It would be a mistake to fail to use as much inheritance based dynamic substitution as necessary through the use of PI's.

A final word on the root power of inheritance. Considering time and space, inheritance has been found to the most efficient of the various mechanisms used to achieve polymorphism. To quote Budd, "Tomlinson provides a good analysis of the time and space requirements of delegation and inheritance,[15] concluding that inheritance is generally faster and, surprisingly, requires less space."[16] Booch, Rumbaugh et al., and others, concur with this analysis.[17] They understand that inheritance based polymorphism is superior, overall, to polymorphism based on other means. So that, dynamic substitution of policy, and implementation via the inheritance mechanism is the most effective and efficient means of doing so.

ONE BODY TWO ARMS

A nice feature of C++ is that inheritance based polymorphism may underlie both *function name* and *argument polymorphism*.[18] And you can get both features very easily by using pointers of the static type of abstract base classes.

Function name polymorphism in C++ uses an abstract class pointer to dynamically substitute the behavior of one subclass' function for the same name function of another subclass, or object. Here is an illustration of the syntax of function name polymorphism from our previous examples:

```
vehiclePointer->Stripe();
```

Of all of the `Stripe()` functions defined in each of the subclasses of the `Vehicle` hierarchy, the specific one executed depends on the class type—`OffRoadVehicle`, `SportsVehicle`, or `VanVehicle`—of the specific object "`vehiclePointer`" points to when the statement is executed during run-time.

Argument polymorphism uses pointers to a base class, such as `Vehicle`, as arguments to functions. Again from our example:

```
stripeOrShip(Vehicle* vehiclePointer);
```

The argument to the function `stripeOrShip()`, "vehiclePointer," may refer to an object belonging to any one of the `Vehicle` hierarchy subclasses: `OffRoadVehicle`, `SportsVehicle`, or `VanVehicle`. We are not restricted to passing only variables of one type, or class, as the function's argument.

It is obvious that being able to dynamically substitute any subclass object of the `Vehicle` class hierarchy into the argument variable, allows us to have a high degree of flexibility in our programs. We can pass into the `stripeOrShip()` function a range of different kinds of objects.

A last word on function name, and argument polymorphism is that they may be combined in a process known as double dispatching. Let's say that we now have derived subclasses of the `BodyDivision` class in addition to the subclasses we have previously derived from Vehicle. The various `BodyDivision` subclasses are referred to through the pointer, "bodyDivisionPointer." We may now execute a statement such as:

```
bodyDivisionPointer->Stripe(Vehicle* vehiclePointer);
```

We have double dispatching because we have, in a single statement during a running program, the ability to execute any `Stripe()` function from amongst all of the objects instantiated from all of the classes derived from `BodyDivision`, and because during a running program, we can pass as an argument to "`Stripe()`" any object instantiated from any class derived from the `Vehicle` class.

So with C++ double dispatching we can combine the two forms of polymorphism to create even greater polymorphism in a software system. Double dispatching allows us to specify two dynamic substitutions in a single statement.[19]

A Sparkling Diamond is Born

Creating a class hierarchy should mainly be based upon the analysis phase (logical) "splitting and merging" of application classes. Bjarne Stroustrup, the creator of C++ recommends taking this approach.[20] Doing so helps to make C++ systems more flexible, and extensible.

TIP
Code implementation within server classes can be changed without having to recompile client users.

A key side benefit of creating an analysis phase abstract PI, with its corresponding concrete hierarchy of classes is the breaking of compilation dependency between clients using the PI, and the hierarchy of server classes. Code implementation within server classes can be changed without having to re-compile client, users of the server classes. This reduces the compilation time of a C++ program, and minimizing compilation time is a very important goal of good, C++, physical design.

There is a dialectic (interaction) between dynamic substitution based on the analysis phase splitting, and merging of classes on the one hand, and breaking physical client/server compilation dependency on the other. The result of the dialectic gives birth to an intensely high degree of adaptability, and robustness for many C++ software systems.

COMPLEX SYSTEMS AND DYNAMIC SUBSTITUTION

Dynamic substitution of a software system's policy, and implementation reflects a part of the behavior of many complex systems in the real world.

An example of dynamic substitution of implementation in real world systems is how the human immune system substitutes various antibodies in its fight against foreign organisms. An example of dynamic substitution of policy in real world systems is how the human immune system decides whether, or not to even send antibodies into a fight. Before fighting, the system must determine whether, or not an organism it encounters should be resisted; it must determine whether, or not the organisms it encounters are a part of the body, or foreign. This points out the efficacy of the dynamic substitution of policy, and implementation in complex systems.

One of the major thrusts of object orientation in software development is the conscious incorporation of significant characteristics of real world complex systems into software systems. Understanding the operation of dynamic substitution in complex systems, and keeping them in mind during software development seems to offer significant benefits.[21]

POLYMORPHISM AND TYPE CONSTRAINT

Of course, in most cases, systems do, and should have limits. Constraints can be applied to a system via its type system. The nature of the configuration of both horizontal, and vertical pointers, at any one time, in a system are partially constrained by the C++ type system.[22] The nature, and extent of what a path of horizontal, and vertical pointers can, or should do is set by the static class (or subclass) types of the pointers in the path.

Of course, a subclass function in the path can be overriden in an irresponsible way by a programmer. However, good object-oriented programmers will not attempt to override a `draw()` subclass function by throwing away the drawing functionality and putting in its place telephone answering capability, for instance.[23]

The type system is not only capable of suppressing inappropriate behavior, but can provide other kinds of integrity even within highly flexible polymorphic systems. Specific object types or other entities can be blocked from flowing along certain paths, while others are allowed. Using the type system, certain operations can be allowed and others prohibited, for a variety of circumstances.

We see from the preceding discussion that the combination of C++ inheritance based polymorphism, and the C++ type system provides adaptability, extensibility and system integrity all at once.

SCALABILITY, COMPONENTS AND DYNAMIC SUBSTITUTABILITY

The use of C++ inheritance based dynamic substitutability is scalable. Just as the `BodyDivision` client class dynamically invoked the functions of various `Vehicle` hierarchy subclass objects for implementation, subclasses of components, or what are the same thing, categories, and groups of class, may be dynamically selected for substitution, and activation in a system. And just as the `BodyDivision` client dynamically selected between horizontal policies, components may be dynamically selected for horizontal policy.

So that in a single system, there may exist micro substitution at the class level, and macro substitution at the component level. Component dynamic substitution adds a totally new dimension to the matter of instant by instant system configuration.

Components may be used as a subsystem on their own, or as elements of a larger subsystem of many components. There are four primary ways to group classes into components in C++ and they may intermixed: the "`#include`" mechanism, the use of file module visibility rules, the new feature of namespaces, and the grouping together of mixin classes into a single aggregate class.[24] It is by using the latter, aggregate class mechanism that we can dynamically substitute one component for another.

Mixin classes get their name from the fact that they are generally not instantiated on their own. They are usually inherited, as a group, into a component interface class, which is then instantiated. The class that mixins are inherited into is called an aggregate class. So here we have a single class which represents a component.

The single aggregate class representing a component may be inherited from to form subclass components in a hierarchy below the first component, aggregate class. These subclasses may include other component, aggregate classes (or even one or more independent, single classes, though that would not be common).

Just as we made use of the hierarchy of subclasses in our `Vehicle` example, by using a pointer of the type of the base `Vehicle` class, we can make use of an inheritance hierarchy of components by using pointers to the base component, aggregate class. Deft use of this base pointer allows us to dynamically substitute both horizontal policy components, and vertical implementation components. With pointers to base aggregate components we can access, and exercise class functions, and data in derived aggregate components.

Use of base component pointers allows extremely adaptable use of components on their own, as subsystems, or as elements of subsystems. Employing base component pointers we can dynamically substitute, or swap out, entire subsystems of our program systems. We can replace one subsystem for another during run-time. We can dynamically add, replace, or delete a system's subsystems.[25]

This offers untold flexibility for our programs and systems. In fact, for most C++ systems it is through dynamic substitution of components of policy and components of implementation that decidedly observable differences in system behavior will occur. Nevertheless, dynamic substitution does occur at the class, or object level. And thus we have two major aspects of dynamic substitution in C++ software systems—class, or micro, based on the one hand, and component, or macro, based on the other.

The ability to dynamically swap both components, and individual classes demonstrates that the mechanism of dynamic substitution may be "shared" throughout all layers of a system's hierarchy of layers.[26] The shared mechanism of dynamic substitution may also be present in each of the vertical processes slicing across two, or more horizontal layers of a software system.

Also, just as with classes, components can have a client/server relationship to each other. In a system with a layered architecture, component clients within a horizontal layer make policy decisions for that layer by dynamically substituting component aggregate subclasses. Implementation components in vertical layers provide services for clients through the same process of dynamic substitution.

References

1. Like the 7 layer ISO Open Systems Interconnect (OSI) Reference Model for communications.

2. Donald Knuth, Literate Programming (California: Center for the Study of Language and Information, 1992) 73.

3. Every class has a constructor which creates runnable copies of the class (objects). Objects will be explained in more detail shortly. In this constructor we are simply initializing the two class variables, "exportStatus," and "vehicleType." C++ class variable initialization should generally be done using a mechanism called an initializer list, but for simplicity we will use ordinary assignment.

4. Although implementation is sometimes referred to as "details", it's better to think of it as "not policy". This gets us away from thinking of "details" as operations necessarily at an assembly language like level of abstraction.

5. Versus private inheritance used mainly for implementation, and not generally for dynamic substitution.

6. Read Barbara Liskov's Data abstraction and hierarchy, SIGPLAN NOTICES 23(5):25, 1988, for more on this.

7. A pointer is a way of indirectly referring to something.

8. See listing 1 for a complete example using the latest Vehicle and BodyDivision classes.

9. The various functions of a class, such as BodyDivison, should generally operate within the same horizontal layer, not vertically across layers.

10. The concept of horizontal, and vertical pointers is a logical construct.

11. The value of calculus integration , for a highly polymorphic system at any instant, varies according to the specific configuration of its horizontal, and vertical pointers at that instant.

12. This is a paradigm of good C++ design we should adopt in most cases. In general we should consciously construct classes and objects as either clients, or servers. We see from our examples that the "using" relationship of the BodyDivision class with respect to a Vehicle may be extended and made dynamic by taking advantage of the commonality, or is-a relationships amongst Vehicle server classes. We will explore more about hierarchy commonality, and is-a relationships in the next section.

13. isomorphism

14. The Stripe() function belonging to an object of a Vehicle subclass currently assigned to "vehiclePointer" is found, in most C++ compiler implementations, by using a virtual table (vtbl) mechanism. The vtbl holds pointers to the various Vehicle subclass implementations of Stripe().

15. Chris Tomlinson, Mark Scheevel and Won Kim, "Sharing and Organizing Protocols in Object-Oriented Systems" Journal of Object-Oriented Programming, 2(4): 25-36, 1989.

16. Timothy Budd, An Introduction to Object-Oriented Programming (Massachusetts: Addison, 1988) 276.

17. Grady Booch, Object-Oriented Analysis and Design (California: Benjamin, 1994), Budd, IOOP, James Rumbaugh, Michael Blaha, William Premerlani, Frederick Eddy, and William Lorenson, Object-Oriented Modeling and Design (New Jersey: Prentice, 1991).

18. ad hoc and pure polymorphism, respectively

19. We could add any number of pointer arguments to the function. Then it would more like multiple dispatching.

20. Bjarne Stroustrup, C++ Programming Language (Massachusetts: Addison, 1991).

21. Grady Booch is a leader in promoting the view that we should consciously incorporate the mechanisms of real world complex systems into software systems, and his book OOA&D clearly reflects this.

22. The configuration of a system's pointers are also constrained by the choices made at various conditional locations in both clients, and servers.

23. Though of course in some exceptional cases, doing so may be desirable for whatever reason.

24. Booch, OOA&D. Booch discusses the mixin/aggregate mechanism in some detail throughout OOA&D. But especially see 63, 127-8, 373, and 515.

25. How about if we add "self modifying" code to the mix?

26. Booch, OOA&D 10-11.

A Perspective on ISO C++

BJARNE STROUSTRUP

As C++ Programmers, we already feel the impact of the work of the ANSI/ISO C++ standards committee. Yet the ink is hardly dry on the first official draft of the standard. Already, we can use language features only hinted at in the ARM and THE C++ PROGRAMMING LANGUAGE (second edition), compilers are beginning to show improved compatibility, implementations of the new standard library are appearing, and the recent relative stability of the language definition is allowing extra effort to be spent on implementation quality and tools. This is only the beginning.

We can now with some confidence imagine the poststandard C++ world. To me, it looks good and exciting. I am confident that it will give me something I have been working towards for about 16 years: a language in which I can express my ideas directly; a language suitable for building large, demanding, efficient, real-world systems; a language supported by a great standard library and effective tools. I am confident because most of the parts of the puzzle are already commercially available and tested in real use. The standard will help us to make all of those parts available to hundreds of thousands or maybe even millions of programmers. Conversely, those programmers provide the community necessary to support further advances in quality, programming and design techniques, tools, libraries, and environments. What has been achieved using C++ so far has exceeded my wildest dreams and we must realistically expect that the best is yet to come.

The Language C++ supports a variety of styles—it is a multiparadigm programming language. The standards process strengthened that aspect of C++ by

> **TIP**
>
> C++ is a multiparadigm language.

providing extensions that didn't just support one narrow view of programming, but made several styles easier and safer to use in C++. Importantly, these advances have not been bought at the expense of runtime efficiency.

At the beginning of the standards process, templates were considered experimental; now they are an integral part of the language, more flexible than originally specified, and an essential foundation for standard library. Generic programming based on templates is now a major tool for C++ programmers.

The support for object-oriented programming (programming using class hierarchies) was strengthened by the provision for runtime type identification, the relaxation of the overriding rules, and the ability to forward declare nested classes.

Large-scale programming—in any style—received major new support from the exception and namespace mechanisms. Like templates, exceptions were considered experimental at the beginning of the standards process. Namespaces evolved from the efforts of many people to find a solution to the problems with name clashes and from efforts to find a way to express logical groupings to complement or replace the facilities for physical grouping provided by the extra linguistic notion of source and header files.

Several minor features were added to make general programming safer and more convenient by allowing the programmer to state more precisely the purpose of some code. The most visible of those are the `bool` type, the explicit type conversion operators, the ability to declare variables in conditions, and the ability to restrict user-defined conversions to explicit construction.

A description of the new features and some of the reasoning that led to their adoption can be found in D&E. So can discussions of older features and of features that were considered but didn't make it into C++.

The new features are the most visible changes to the language. However, the cumulative effect of minute changes to more obscure corners of the language and thousands of clarifications of its specification is greater than the effect of any extension. These improvements are essentially invisible to the programmer writing ordinary production code, but their importance to libraries, portability, and compatibility of implementations cannot be overestimated. The minute changes and clarifications also consumed a large majority of the committee's efforts. That is, I believe, also the way things ought to be.

For good and bad, the principle of C++ being "as close to C as possible—and no closer"[3] was repeatedly reaffirmed. C compatibility has been slightly strengthened, and the remaining incompatibilities documented in detail. Basically, if you are a practical programmer rather than a conformance tester, and if you use function prototypes consistently, C appears to be a subset of

C++. The fact that every example in K&R[2] is (also) a C++ program is no fluke.

COHERENCE

ISO C++ is not just a more powerful language than the C++ presented in The C++ PROGRAMMING LANGUAGE (second edition)[5]; it is also more coherent and a better approximation of my original view of what C++ should be.

The fundamental concept of a statically typed language relying on classes and virtual functions to support object-oriented programming, templates to support generic programming, and providing low-level facilities to support detailed systems programming is sound. I don't think this statement can be proven in any strict sense, but I have seen enough great C++ code and enough successful large-scale projects using C++ for it to satisfy me of its validity.

You can also write ghastly code in C++, but so what? We can do that in any language. In the hands of people who have bothered learning its fairly simple key concepts, C++ is helpful in guiding program organization and in detecting errors.

C++ is not a "kitchen sink language" as evil tongues are fond of claiming. Its features are mutually reinforcing and all have a place in supporting C++'s intended range of design and programming styles. Everyone agrees that C++ could be improved by removing features. However, there is absolutely no agreement which features could be removed. In this, C++ resembles C.

During standardization, only one feature that I don't like was added. We can now initialize a static constant of integral type with a constant expression within a class definition. For example:

```
class X {            // in .h file
    static const int c = 42;
    char v[c];
    // ...
};

int X::c = 42;      // in .c file
```

I consider this half-baked and prefer:

```
class X {
    enum { c = 42 };
    char v[c];
    // ...
};
```

I also oppose a generalization of in-class initialization as an undesirable complication for both implementors and users. However, this is an example where reasonable people can agree to disagree. Standardization is a democratic process, and I certainly don't get my way all the time—nor should any person or group.

AN EXAMPLE

Enough talk! Here is an example that illustrates many of the new language features. It is one answer to the common question "how can I read objects from a stream, determine that they are of acceptable types, and then use them?" For example:

```
void user(istream& ss)
{
   io_obj* p = get_obj(ss);      // read object from stream

   if (Shape* sp = dynamic_cast<Shape*>(p)) { // is it a
Shape?
      sp->draw();            // use the Shape
                             // ...
   }
   else // oops: non-shape in Shape file
         throw unexpected_shape();
}
```

The function `user()` deals with shapes exclusively through the abstract class `Shape` and can therefore use every kind of shape. The construct

```
dynamic_cast<Shape*>(p)
```

performs a runtime check to see whether p really points to an object of class Shape or a class derived from Shape If so, it returns a pointer to the Shape part of that object. If not, it returns the null pointer. Unsurprisingly, this is called a dynamic cast. It is the primary facility provided to allow users to take advantage of runtime type information (RTTI). The `dynamic_cast` allows convenient use of RTTI where necessary without encouraging switching on type fields.

The use of `dynamic_cast` here is essential because the object I/O system can deal with many other kinds of objects and the user may accidentally have opened a file containing perfectly good objects of classes that this user has never heard of.

Note the declaration in the condition of the `if statement`:

```
if (Shape* sp = dynamic_cast<Shape*>(p)) { ... }
```

The variable `sp` is declared within the condition, initialized, and its value checked to determine which branch of the `if` statement is executed. A variable declared in a condition must be initialized and is in scope in the statements controlled by the condition (only). This is both more concise and less error-prone than separating the declaration, the initialization, or the test from each other and leaving the variable around after the end of its intended use the way it is traditionally done:

```
Shape* sp = dynamic_cast<Shape*>(p);
if (sp) { ... }
// sp in scope here
```

This "miniature object I/O system" assumes that every object read or written is of a class derived from `io_obj`. Class `io_obj`. must be a polymorphic type to allow us to use `dynamic_cast`. For example:

```
class io_obj {    // polymorphic
public:
  virtual io_obj* clone();
  virtual ~io_obj() { }
};
```

The critical function in the object I/O system is `get_obj()` that reads data from an `istream` and creates class objects based on that data. Let me assume that the data representing an object on an input stream is prefixed by a string identifying the object's class. The job of `get_obj()` is to read that string prefix and call a function capable of creating and initializing an object of the right class. For example:

```
typedef io_obj* (*PF)(istream&);

map<string,PF> io_map;    // maps strings to creation functions

io_obj* get_obj(istream& s)
{
  string str;
  if (get_word(s,str) == false)    // read initial word into str
    throw no_class();

  PF f = io_map[str];    // lookup "str' to get function
  if (f == 0) throw unknown_class();    // no match for "str'
  return f(s);    // construct object from stream
}
```

The map called `io_map` is an associative array that holds pairs of name strings and functions that can construct objects of the class with that name.

The associate array is one of the most useful and efficient data structures in any language. This particular map type is taken from the C++ standard library. So is the `string` class.

The `get_obj()` function throws exceptions to signal errors. An exception thrown by `get_obj()` can be caught be a direct or indirect caller like this:

```
try {
    // ...
    io_obj* p = get_obj(cin);
    // ...
}
catch (no_class) {
    cerr << "format error on input";
    // ...
}
catch (unknown_class) {
    cerr << "unknown class on input";
    // ...
}
```

A `catch` clause is entered if (and only if) an exception of its specified type is thrown by code in or invoked from the try block.

We could, of course, define class `Shape` the usual way by deriving it from `io_obj` as required by user():

```
class Shape : public io_obj {
    // ...
    virtual void draw() = 0;      // pure virtual function
    // ...
};
```

However, it would be more interesting (and also more realistic) to use some previously defined `Shape` class hierarchy unchanged by incorporating it into a hierarchy that adds the information needed by our I/O system:

```
class iocircle : public Circle, public io_obj {
public:
    io_obj* clone() // override io_obj::clone()
      { return new iocircle(*this); }

    iocircle(istream&);    // initialize from input stream

    static iocircle* new_circle(istream& s)
    {
      return new iocircle(s);
    }
    // ...
};
```

The `iocircle(istream&)` constructor initializes an object with data from its `istream` argument. The `new_circle` function is the one put into the `io_map` to make the class known to the object I/O system. For example:

```
io_map["iocircle"]=&iocircle::new_circle;
```

Other shapes are constructed in the same way:

```
class iotriangle : public Triangle, public io_obj {
    // ...
};
```

If the provision of the object I/O scaffolding becomes tedious, a template might be used:

```
template<class T>
class io : public T, public io_obj {
public:
   io_obj* clone() { return new io(*this); }

   io(istream&);   // initialize from input stream

   static io* new_io(istream& s)
   {
     return new io(s);
   }
};
```

Given this, we could define `iocircle` like this:

```
typedef io<Circle> iocircle;
```

We would still have to define `io<Circle>::io(istream&)` explicitly, though, because it needs to know about the details of `Circle`.

This simple object I/O system may not do everything anyone ever wanted, but it almost fits on a single page, is general and extensible, is potentially efficient, and the key mechanisms have many uses. Undoubtedly, you would have designed and implemented an object I/O system somewhat differently. Please take a few minutes to consider how this general design strategy compares to your favorite scheme, and also think about what it would take to implement this scheme in pre-ISO C++ or some other language.

THE LIBRARY

I have long regretted that I was not initially able to provide C++ with a good enough standard library. In particular, I would have liked to provide a string class and a set of container classes (such as lists, vectors, and maps). However, I did not know how to design containers that were elegant enough, general enough, and efficient enough to serve the varied needs of the C++ community. Also, until I found the time to design the template mechanism, I had no good way of specifying type-safe containers.

Naturally, most programmers want essentially everything useful included in the standard library. That way, they assume, all that they need will be supplied elegantly, efficiently, and free of charge. Unfortunately, that is just a dream. Facilities will be designed by people with different views of how to do things, limited time, and limited foresight. Also, implementors will find some way of getting paid for their efforts. As the library grows, so does the chances of mistakes, controversy, inefficiencies, and cost.

> **TIP**
>
> The scope of a standard library must be restricted.

Consequently, the scope of the standard library had to be restricted to something a relatively small group of volunteers could handle, something that most people would agree to be important, something most people could easily learn to use, something that would be efficient enough for essentially all people to use, and something C++ implementors could ship without exorbitant cost. In addition, the standard library must be a help, rather then a hindrance, to the C++ library industry.

The facilities provided by the standard library can be classified like this:

1. Basic runtime language support (for allocation, RTTI, etc.).

2. The standard C library (with very minor modifications to minimize violations of the type system).

3. Strings and I/O streams (with support for international character sets and localization).

4. A framework of containers (such as, vector, list, set, and map) and algorithms using containers (such as general traversals, sorts, and merges).

5. Support for numeric computation (complex numbers plus vectors with arithmetic operations, BLAS-like and generalized slices, and semantics designed to ease optimization).

This is quite a considerable set of facilities. The description of the standard library takes up about two thirds of the space in the standards document. Outside the standard C library, the standard C++ library consists mainly of templates. There are dozens of template classes and hundreds of template functions.

The main criteria for including a class in the library were that it would somehow be used by almost every C++ programmer (both novices and experts), that it could be provided in a general form that did not add significant overheads compared to a simpler version of the same facility, and that simple uses should be easy to learn. Essentially, the C++ standard library provides the most common fundamental data structures together with the fundamental algorithms used on them.

The standard library is described in Stepanov[7] and Vilot[8] so let me just give a short—but complete—example of its use:

```
#include <string>            // get the string facilities
#include <fstream>           // get the I/I facilities
#include <vector>            // get the vector
#include <algorithms>        // get the operations on
                             // containers

int main()
{
  string from, to;           // standard string of char
  cin >> from >> to;         // get source and target file
names

  istream_iterator<string> ii
    = ifstream(from.c_str()); // input iterator
  istream_iterator<string> eos; // input sentinel

  ostream_iterator<string> oo
    = ofstream(to.c_str());   // output iterator

  vector<string> buf(ii,eos);         // standard vector
class
                             // initialized from input

  sort(buf.begin(),buf.end());        // sort the buffer
  unique_copy(buf.begin(),buf.end(),oo);// copy buffer to
                             // output discarding
                             // replicated values

  return ii && oo;                    // return error state
}
```

As with any other library, parts will look strange at first glance. However, experience shows that most people get used to it fast.

I/O is done using streams. To avoid overflow problems, the standard library `string` class is used.

The standard container `vector` is used for buffering; its constructor reads input; the standard functions `sort()` and `unique_copy()` sort and output the strings.

Iterators are used to make the input and output streams look like containers that you can read from and write to, respectively. The standard library's notion of a container is built on the notion of "something you can get a series of values from or write a series of values to." To read something you need the place to begin reading from and the place to end; to write simply a place to start writing to. The word used for "place" in this context is `iterator`.

The standard library's notion of containers, iterators, and algorithms is based on work by Alex Stepanov and others.[7]

THE STANDARDS PROCESS

Initially, I feared that the standardization effort would lead to confusion and instability. People would clamor for all kinds of changes and improvements, and a large committee was unlikely to have a firm and consistent view of what aspects of programming and design ought to be directly supported by C++ and how. However, I judged the risks worth the potential benefits. By now, I am sure that I underestimated both the risks and the benefits. I am also confident that we have surmounted most of the technical challenges and will cope with the remaining technical and political problems; they are not as daunting as the many already handled by the committee. I expect that we will have a formally approved standard in a year plus or minus a few months. Essentially all of that time will be spent finding precise wording for resolutions we already agree on and ferreting out further obscure details to nail down.

The ISO (international) and ANSI (USA national) standards groups for C++ meet three times a year. The first technical meeting was in 1990, and I have attended every meeting so far. Meetings are hard work; dawn to midnight. I find most committee members great people to work with, but I need a week's vacation to recover from a meeting—which of course I never get.

In addition to coming up with technically sound solutions, the committees are chartered to seek consensus. In this context, consensus means a large majority plus an honest attempt to settle remaining differences. There will be "remaining differences" because there are many things that reasonable people can disagree about.

Anyone willing and able to pay the ANSI membership fee and attend two meetings can vote (unless they work for a company who already has a representative). In addition, members of the committee bring in opinions from a wide variety of sources. Importantly, the national delegations from several countries conduct their own additional meetings and bring what they find to the joint ANSI/ISO meetings.

All in all, this is an open and democratic process. The number of people representing organizations with millions of lines of C++ precludes radical changes. For example, a significant increase or decrease in C compatibility would have been politically infeasible. Explaining anything significant to a large diverse group—such as 80 people at a C++ standards meeting—takes time, and once a problem is understood, building a consensus around a particular solution takes even longer. It seems that for a major change, the time from the initial presentation of an idea until its acceptance was usually a minimum of three meetings; that is, a year.

Fortunately, the aim of the standards process isn't to create the perfect programming language. It was hard at times, but the committee consistently decided to respect real-world constraints—including compatibility with C and older variants of C++. The result was a language with most of its warts intact. However, its runtime efficiency, space efficiency, and flexibility were also preserved, and the integration between features were significantly improved. In addition to showing necessary restraint and respect for existing code, the committee showed commendable courage in addressing the needs for extensions and library facilities.

Curiously enough, the most significant aspect of the committee's work may not be the standard itself. The committee provided a forum where issues could be discussed, proposals could be presented, and where implementors could benefit from the experience of people outside their usual circle. Without this, I suspect C++ would have fractured into competing dialects by now.

CHALLENGES

Anyone who thinks the major software development problems are solved by simply using a better programming language is dangerously naive. We need all the help we can get and a programming language is only part of the picture. A better programming language, such as C++, does help, though. However, like any other tool it must be used in a sensible and competent manner without disregarding other important components of the larger software development process.

I hope that the standard will lead to an increased emphasis on design and programming styles that takes advantage of C++. The weaknesses in the compatibility of current compilers encourage people to use only a subset of the language and provides an excuse for people who for various reasons prefer to use styles from other languages that are sub-optimal for C++. I hope to see such native C++ styles supported by significant new libraries.

I expect the standard to lead to significant improvements in the quality of all kinds of tools and environments. A stable language provides a good target for such work and frees energy that so far has been absorbed tracking an evolving language and incompatible implementations.

C++ and its standard library are better than many considered possible and better than many are willing to believe. Now we "just" have to use it and support it better. This is going to be challenging, interesting, productive, profitable, and fun!

Acknowledgments

The first draft of this paper was written at 37,000 feet en route home from the Monterey standards meeting. Had the designer of my laptop provided a longer battery life, this paper would have been longer, though presumably also more thoughtful.

The standard is the work of literally hundreds of volunteers. Many have devoted hundreds of hours of their precious time to the effort. I'm especially grateful to the hard-working practical programmers who have done this in their scant spare time and often at their own expense. I'm also grateful to the thousands of people who—through many channels—have made constructive comments on C++ and its emerging standard.

References

1. Ellis, M.A. and B. Stroustrup. THE ANNOTATED C++ REFERENCE MANUAL. Addison-Wesley, Reading, MA. 1990.
2. Kernighan, B.W., and D.M. Ritchie. THE C PROGRAMMING LANGUAGE, second ed. Prentice-Hall, Englewood Cliffs, NJ, 1988.
3. Koenig, A., and B. Stroustrup. As close as possible to C—But no closer, C++ REPORT, 1(7), 1989.
4. Koenig, A., Ed. THE WORKING PAPERS FOR THE ANSI-X3J16 /ISO-SC22-WG21 C++ Standards Committee.
5. Stroustrup, B. THE C++ PROGRAMMING LANGUAGE, second ed. Addison-Wesley, Reading, MA, 1991.
6. Stroustrup, B. THE DESIGN AND EVOLUTION OF C++. Addison-Wesley, Reading, MA, 1994.
7. Stepanov, A., and M. Lee. THE STANDARD TEMPLATE LIBRARY, ISO Programming language C++ project, Doc No: X3J16/94-0095, WG21/N0482, May 1994.
8. Vilot, M.J. An introduction to the STL Library, C++ REPORT, 6(8), 1994.

INTRODUCTION TO ITERATOR ADAPTORS

ANDREW W. KOENIG

M Y LAST FEW ARTICLES HAVE TALKED ABOUT ITERATORS AND RELATED CON-
cepts in the Standard Template Library (STL). This one continues that
discussion with the idea of *iterator adaptors*—templates that take iterators
as parameters and convert them to other iterators. This notion can be tricky
to understand, so we will lead up to it a step at a time in the context of a few
key examples.

MOTIVATION

The following function should be familiar:

```
template<class T, class X>
T find(T begin, T end, const X& x)
{
    while (begin != end && *begin != x)
      ++begin;
    return begin;
}
```

This function performs s a linear search on a (more or less) arbitrary data
structure, which is characterized only by the type of the template parameters `begin` and `end`. We use `begin` and `end` as *input iterators*. That is, we
require that they support only those operations necessary to read the contents of the data structure we are searching.

Ordinary pointers can act as input iterators. Thus, for example, if we have
declared:

```
int x[100];
```

and we want to find the first place 42 appears in x, we can say

```
int* p = find(x, x+100, 42);
```

after which p will either point to the first element of x that is equal to 42 or will be equal to x+100 if no element of x is 42.

Suppose, now, that instead of finding the first instance of some particular value, we wanted to find the last instance. How would we do that?

We want to write a function that will find the last element equal to x in a sequential data structure characterized by a pair of input iterators called begin and end. Clearly that is easy to implement if we find the element we seek. What if it isn't there? Then we must return some value that refers to none of the elements of the data structure; the only such value we have available is that of end. Evidently, both forward and reverse searching must return the same value on failure; this breaks what would otherwise be complete symmetry.

Once we've decided what to do, we can do it. The straightforward way is to keep searching until we reach the end:

```
template<class T, class X>
T find_last(T begin, T end, const X& x)
{
    T result = end;
    while (begin != end) {
        if (*begin == x)
            result = begin;
        ++begin;
    }
    return result;
}
```

Indeed, if all we can assume about T is that it is an input iterator, we have little choice about how to implement find_last. But it is clear that this strategy has a serious disadvantage: it always looks at all the elements of the data structure it is searching, even if the value being sought is at the very end of that structure.

If instead of input iterators we have bidirectional iterators, that opens up new possibilities. Now we need not rely only on ++; we can use -- as well. That means we can scan the data structure starting from the end and moving toward the beginning:

```
template<class T, class X>
T rfind(T begin, T end, const X& x)
```

```
{
  if (begin != end) {
    T p = end;
    do {
      if (*--p == x)
        return p;
    } while (p != begin);
    return end;
  }
}
```

Why is this function so much more complicated than the original `find`? The fundamental reason is that the value returned when x is not found is less "natural" than when searching forward.

In the original `find`, we could use `begin != end` as our loop termination, destroying the value of `begin`, secure in the knowledge that we would eventually be able to return the value of `begin` regardless of whether x was found or not. In `rfind` we do not have that luxury. Instead, we must save the value of `end` so that we can return it later if x is not found. Moreover, we must make a special test for an empty array, because in that case there is no guarantee that we will successfully be able to compute the value of `--begin`.

DIRECTIONAL ASYMMETRY

This illustrates an important point in algorithm construction: it is not always possible to preserve symmetry exactly when reversing the direction of an algorithm. In this case, the asymmetry stems from a characteristic of iterators that, in turn, comes from the C language definition: although iterators generally guarantee that there is an "off-the end" value available, there is no comparable guarantee for any "off-the beginning" value.

> **TIP**
>
> It is not always possible to preserve symmetry.

To illustrate this more directly, consider a simple loop that sets the elements of a 10-element array a to zero:

```
int a[10];
for (int i = 0; i < 10; i++)
  a[i] = 0;
```

At the end of this loop, i will be 10, which, of course, causes no particular problem. If we want to zero the elements of a in reverse order, there is still no problem:

```
for (int i = 9; i >= 0; i--)
    a[i] = 0;
```

At the end of this loop, a will be -1, which is certainly a plausible value for it to have.

If, however, we change this loop to use pointers instead of subscripts, we begin to see the source of the asymmetry:

```
for (int* p = &a[0]; p < &a[10]; p++)
    *p = 0;
```

At the end of this loop, p will be equal to &a[10], which is the address of an element of a that does not exist. This program works only because the C and C++ languages guarantee the ability to form the address of the element that is one past the end of any array. In other words, &a[10] is legal but &a[11] is not—and neither is &a[-1].

That means that if we want to rewrite the backwards loop to use pointers, we must be careful never to form the address of a[-1]. In particular, we cannot do this:

```
// This does not work
for (int* p = &a[9]; p >= &a[0]; p--)
    *p = 0;
```

because for the loop to terminate, we must reach a state where p < &a[0], and there is no assurance that such a thing can ever happen. That evidently means that we must contrive to use p > &a[0] as our comparison instead and assign to *p immediately after we have decremented it:

```
// This works
int* p = &a[10];
while (p > &a[0])
    *--p = 0;
```

This way we guarantee that p never takes on a prohibited value.

CONSISTENCY AND ASYMMETRY

We have learned so far that we can search data structures both forward and backward, but with a catch: the value returned in case of failure must always be the "off-the-end" value. This can be a nuisance, especially if we use find or rfind to search portions of sequential structures.

For example, it is common to look for a particular value in a data structure and then append that value if it is not found. It is convenient that `find` returns a pointer to the place to put that value if it was not already in the structure. The `rfind` function is not similarly considerate: if the value sought is not found, it returns a pointer that, although an "off-the-end" pointer in a strict sense, must really be treated as an "off-the-beginning" pointer because we are searching backward. This puts us at exactly the wrong end of the data structure for appending a new value—unless we want to append at the beginning. Is there anything we can do about this?

At first glance, one would think not. An *n*-element data structure makes available only *n*+1 iterator values: those referring to the n elements and the off-the-end value. But what if we offset everything by one? What if, instead of using the iterator values directly, we pretended that each iterator pointed to the spot in the data structure immediately *after* the element we were seeking?

That would mean we would use the off-the-end value to point at the last element of the structure, a pointer to the last element to refer to the next-to-last element, and so on. That would then free up the pointer to the first element to use as an off-the-beginning value.

This is easier to demonstrate than to describe. The following function, called `rnfind` (for "reverse neighbor find") searches a sequential data structure from end to beginning and returns an iterator that points to the element *after* (one element closer to the end than) the one sought. If the value is not found, it returns an iterator that refers to the first element (that is, one past the nonexistent off-the-beginning element):

```
template<class T, class X>
T rnfind(T start, T end, const X& x)
{
    while (end != start && end[-1] != x)
      --end;
    return end;
}
```

Of course, this function cheats a tiny bit by using `end[-1]`: doing so means that T must be a random-access iterator and not just a bidirectional iterator. We can remove the cheating by rewriting `end[-1]` in terms of `--`, but doing so would obscure the important point: `rnfind` actually looks much more like `find` than any of the previous reverse find functions.

It is the "neighbor" technique that allows it to look that way. Indeed, it appears that, in general, we can reverse the direction of sequential algorithms if we swap starting and ending values, swap `++` and `--`, and *adopt the*

TIP

Iterators point to
the element after
the one we "really"
want.

*convention that iterators point to the element after the
one we "really" want.*

AUTOMATIC REVERSAL

The argument so far has involved a lot of hand waving.
It is time to try to make it more precise. Suppose type
T is a bidirectional iterator. Then we can imagine cre-
ating a new type called, say, TR (for T *reversed*) that behaves just like T but
goes in the opposite direction.

Our neighbor convention says that converting a T to a TR must result in
something that appears to point to the element before (or is it after?—we'll
see) the one that the T pointed to. Also, the senses of ++ and -- must be
reversed and the usual copy, assignment, comparison, and dereferencing
must work too.

Can we do all that as a template? Well, almost. Dereferencing causes the
one significant problem. For example, suppose we said:

```
template<class T> class Rev<T>
{
    // ...
    ??? operator*();
};
```

We would not know what type to make operator* return. That implies
that we need an extra template parameter for the type of the objects the iterator yields, along with the type of the iterator. After that observation, we can
actually declare the template:

```
template<class It, class T> class Rev {
    friend bool operator==
      (const Rev<It, T>, const Rev<It, T>);
    friend bool operator!=
      (const Rev<It, T>, const Rev<It, T>);
public:
    Rev();
    Rev(It i);
    operator It();
    Rev<It, T>& operator++();
    Rev<It, T>& operator--();
    Rev<It, T> operator++(int);
    Rev<It, T> operator--(int);
    T& operator*();
};
```

Nothing here is particularly difficult. We declare exactly the operations we need for a bidirectional iterator: construction, dereferencing, (in)equality, and prefix and postfix increment and decrement. We do not explicitly declare destruction, copying, and assignment because we expect that will be handled correctly by the corresponding operations on our iterator type.

Implementation is straightforward also. The only thing to remember is that dereferencing must actually look at the element immediately before the one at which our private data member points. The implementation below includes that data member, as well as definitions for everything:

> **TIP**
>
> Dereferencing must actually look at the element immediately before the one at which our private data member points.

```
template<class It, class T> class Rev {

    friend bool operator==
      (const Rev<It, T>, const Rev<It, T>);
    friend bool operator!=
      (const Rev<It, T>, const Rev<It, T>);

public:
    Rev();
    Rev(It i): it(i) { }
    operator It() { return it; }

    Rev<It, T>& operator++()
      { --it; return *this; }
    Rev<It, T>& operator--()
      { ++it; return *this; }

    Rev<It, T> operator++(int) {
      Rev<It, T> r = *this;
      --it;
      return r;
    }

    Rev<It, T> operator--(int) {
      Rev<It, T> r = *this;
      ++it;
      return r;
    }

    T& operator*() {
      It i = it;
      --i;
      return *i;
    }
```

```
private:
  It it;
};

template<class It, class T> bool operator==
    (const Rev<It, T> x, const Rev<It, T> y)
{
  return x.it == y.it;
}

template<class It, class T> bool operator!=
    (const Rev<It, T> x, const Rev<It, T> y)
{
  return x.it != y.it;
}
```

The neighbor rule appears as part of operator*:

```
T& operator*() {
  It i = it;
  --i;
  return *i;
}
```

How do we know that `--i` is correct here and not `++i`? Note first that variable `i`, of type `It`, is the original iterator type. Its value might refer to any element in the (original) structure or might be an off-the-end value. If we said `++i`, there would be no way to get at the first element of the structure because there is no value to which we can apply `++` and make it refer to that first element. As written, on the other hand, `--i` translates the off-the-end value into a pointer to the last element of the original structure, so it must be right.

We can use it this way:

```
typedef Rev<int*, int> R;

int* p = find(x, x+100, 42);
R r = find(R(x+100), R(x), 42);
```

Here we have introduced R as a convenience; we could also have written:

```
Rev<int*, int> r = find(
   Rev<int*, int>(x+100),
   Rev<int*, int>(x), 42);
```

After this, p points to the first place 42 occurs in x and r "points" to the last place.

DISCUSSION

What we have achieved is the ability to use a single algorithm to search a data structure forward and backward, subject only to the availability of a bidirectional iterator type that describes that data structure. In effect, we have written a template that does interface matching: we have one interface, we need a different one, and so we make what we have into what we want.

The particular task we accomplished is a little more complicated than we would have thought at first. This is because of the asymmetrical nature of C arrays: we are guaranteed an off-the-end value but not an off-the-beginning one. It is tempting to argue that C++ should allow off-the-beginning values as well, but that would not solve the problem because this whole technique is intended to work with arbitrary data structures and not just arrays. Insisting on off-the-beginning values would therefore require implementors of all kinds of data structures to complicate them just to take the off-the-beginning convention into account. Instead, we solve the problem just once in the reverse iterator adaptor and then don't worry about it any more.

> **TIP**
>
> This whole technique is intended to work with arbitrary data structures.

STL has a template called `reverse_bidirectional_iterator` that is a slightly more general version of `Rev`. In addition, if you have a random access iterator, you can use `reverse_iterator`. It requires full random access iterator semantics from its argument, in return for which it presents random access iterator semantics to its user.

This technique is obviously more generally applicable. One example is a bounds checking adaptor. Given an iterator type, it might yield another iterator type with the ability to confine its values to be within a pair of bounds given when creating an object of that type. Used carefully, iterator adaptors can greatly reduce the number of variations of an algorithm one must write, or increase what one can accomplish with fixed effort.

Availability

The Standard Template Library is primarily the work of Alex Stepanov and Meng Lee at Hewlett-Packard Laboratories. The C++ standards committee adopted it for inclusion in the standard at their July 1994 meeting. You can obtain more information about STL, including C++ source code, free of charge by anonymous FTP from `butler.hpl.hp.com` in directory `stl`.

FUNCTION OBJECTS, TEMPLATES, AND INHERITANCE

ANDREW W. KOENIG

I N SOME PROGRAMMING LANGUAGES, FUNCTIONS ARE FIRST-CLASS VALUES. IN such languages, it is possible to pass functions as arguments, return them as values, use them as components in expressions, and so on.

C++ is not quite one of those languages, though the reason is less than immediately obvious. After all, it is common for C++ programs to pass functions as arguments and store their addresses in data structures. Suppose, for example, that we want to apply a given function to all the elements of an array. If we know that the function takes an `int` argument and yields `void`, we can write something like this:

```
void apply(void f(int), int* p, int n)
{
    for (int i = 0; i < n; i++)
        f(p[i]);
}
```

Doesn't this show that C++ treats functions as first class?

The first subtlety in this example is that, despite appearances, f is not a function at all in this example. Rather, it is a function pointer. As in C, it is not possible to have a variable of function type, so any attempt to declare such a variable is immediately converted into a declaration of a pointer to a function. Also as in C, an attempt to call a function pointer is equivalent to a call of the function to which that pointer points. So the example above is equivalent to

```
void apply(void (*fp)(int), int* p, int n)
{
```

```
    for (int i = 0; i < n; i++)
        (*fp)(p[i]);
}
```

So what? What is the big difference between functions and function pointers? The difference is similar to the difference between any pointers and the objects they point to: it is not possible to create such objects merely by manipulating pointers. The total store of C++ functions is fixed before program execution begins. There is no way to create new ones once the program has started to run.* To see how this is a problem, consider how one might write a C++ function to compose two functions. To keep things simple for the moment, we will assume that each of our functions takes an integer argument and returns an integer result. Suppose, then, that we have a pair of functions f and g:

```
extern int f(int);
extern int g(int);
```

and we want to be able to say something like

```
int (*h)() = compose(f, g);
```

with the property that for any integer n, h(n) (which you will recall is equivalent to (*h)(n)) will be equal to f(g(n)).

C++ offers no direct way to do that. One might imagine doing something like this:

```
// this does not work
int (*compose(int f(int), int g(int)))(int x)
{
    int result(int n) { return f(g(n)); }
    return result;
}
```

TIP
C++ does not support nested functions.

but this fails for two reasons. The first is that C++ does not support nested functions, which means that the definition of result is illegal. Moreover, there is no easy way of working around that restriction because result needs access to f and g from the surrounding

---

*Of course, individual implementations may choose to modify this restriction, perhaps by offering some form of dynamically linked library. This does not apply to the language in general, though, and does not affect the discussion that follows.

scope. Thus, we cannot simply make `result` global:

```
// this also does not work
int result(int n) { return f(g(n)); }

int (*compose(int f(int), int g(int)))(int x)
{
   return result;
}
```

because now `f` and `g` are undefined in `result`.

The second problem is more subtle. Suppose C++ did allow nested functions—after all, there are some C++ implementations that do so as an extension. Wouldn't that do the trick?

The answer, unfortunately, is "not really." To see why, let us rewrite our compose function a tiny bit:

```
// this does not work either
int (*compose(int f(int), int g(int)))(int x)
{
    int (*fp)(int) = f;
    int (*gp)(int) = g;
    int result(int n) { return fp(gp(n)); }
    return result;
}
```

The change here has been to copy the addresses of `f` and `g` into two local variables `fp` and `gp`. Now, suppose we call `compose` and it returns a pointer to `result`. Since `fp` and `gp` are local variables of `compose`, they will go away as soon as `compose` returns. If we now call `result`, it will try to use those local variables even though they have already been deleted. The result will probably be a crash.

This should be fairly easy to see from inspecting the last version of `compose` above. However, exactly the same problem exists in the first version. The only difference is that now, instead of being ordinary local variables, `f` and `g` are formal parameters. This makes no difference: they still go away when `compose` returns, which means that when `result` tries to access them, disaster ensues.

Apparently, then, writing our `compose` function requires some kind of automatic memory management beyond the usual function stack-based implementations. Indeed, languages that treat func-

> **TIP**
>
> Languages that treat functions as first-class values also usually support garbage collection.

tions as first-class values also usually support garbage collection. While it would be nice in many ways for C++ to have garbage collection, there are enough difficulties involved that C++ does not have garbage collection as a standard part of the language. Is there any way to circumvent this restriction and treat functions as values in a more general way?

FUNCTION OBJECTS

The difficulty with our `compose` function is that its result needs to be able to store additional information—namely, the identities of the functions being composed. Whenever we are faced with such a problem, we should think about using a class object to express the solution. If `compose` cannot return a function, perhaps it can return a class object that acts like a function.

> **TIP**
>
> A function object is an object that includes the `operator()`.

Such objects are called function objects. Typically a function object is an object of some class type that includes the `operator()` member function. Having that member function makes it possible to use the class object as if it were a function. So, for example, if we write

```
class F {
public:
    int operator() (int);
    // …
};
```

then objects of `class F` will behave somewhat like functions that take integer arguments and return integer results, so that in

```
int main()
{
    F f;
    int n = f(42);
}
```

the call of `f(42)` is equivalent to `f.operator()(42)`. That is, it takes the object `f` and calls its `operator()` member with argument `42`.

We can use this technique as the basis for a class that can be used to compose functions:

```
class Intcomp {
```

```
public:
   Intcomp(int (*f0)(int), int (*g0)(int)):
     fp(f0), gp(g0) { }
   int operator() (int n) {
     return (*fp)((*gp)(n));
   }
private:
   int (*fp)(int);
   int (*gp)(int);
};
```

Now, if we have our functions f and g as before, we can use an Intcomp to compose them:

```
extern int f(int);
extern int g(int);

int main()
{
   Intcomp fg(f, g);
   fg(42);        // equivalent to f(g(42))
}
```

This technique solves the problem, at least in principle, because every Intcomp object has a place to store the identities of the functions being composed. However, it is still not quite a practical solution because it can compose only functions and not function objects. This means, for example, that we cannot use an Intcomp to compose an Intcomp with anything. In other words, although we can use our Intcomp class to compose two functions, we cannot use it to compose more than two. What can we do about this?

FUNCTION OBJECT TEMPLATES

We would like to be able to create a class whose objects can be used to compose not only functions but also function objects. The usual way in C++ of defining such a class is to use a template. Such a template will have the types of the two things being composed as template parameters. Looking ahead, we will also give it two more parameters, which will be the types of the value we give the composed function object when we call it and of the value it returns. That way, we will not be stuck dealing only with functions that return int:

```
template<class F, class G, class X, class Y>
   class Comp {
public:
   Comp(F f0, G g0): f(f0), g(g0) { }
```

```
    Y operator()(X x) { return f(g(x)); }
  private:
    F f;
    G g;
};
```

We can now use our `comp` class to compose the integer functions `f` and `g` from before:

```
int main()
{
   Comp<int (*)(int), int (*)(int), int, int>
       fg(f, g);
   fg(42);        // calls f(g(42))
}
```

This works, after a fashion, but the need to specify the function type `int(*)(int)` twice is far from elegant. Indeed, if we wanted to compose, say, `fg` and `f`, the type of the object we would need is truly awesome because the full type of `fg` must appear as its first template parameter:

```
Comp<
    Comp<int (*)(int), int (*)(int), int, int>,
    int,
    int>
       fgf(fg, f);
```

Is there any way to simplify this enough to make it useful?

HIDING INTERMEDIATE TYPES

Let's think for a moment about where we are trying to go. At this point we have a way of composing two functions or function objects, but the type of the function object that represents the composition is too complicated. Ideally we would like to be able to write something like this:

```
Composition fg(f, g);     // too optimistic
```

but that is too much to hope for. The reason is that later on when we try to evaluate `fg(42)`, how does the compiler know what type that expression should have? Whatever the result type is, it must be implicit in the type of `fg`, and similarly for the argument type that `fg` expects. The best we can hope for, therefore, is something like

```
Composition<int, int> fg(f, g);
```

where the first `int` is the type of the argument the function object expects, and the second one is the type of the result it will return. Given that definition, it is not hard to write down at least part of the class definition:

```
template<class X, class Y> class Composition {

public:
    // ...
    Y operator() (X);
    // ...
};
```

but how do we implement it? For that matter, what does the constructor look like?

The constructor is an interesting problem, since a `Composition` must be capable of accepting any combination of functions and function objects—particularly `Compositions`. That suggests that the constructor must itself be a template,* so as to cater to all these possibilities:

```
template<class X, class Y> class Composition {
public:
    template<class F, class G>
      Composition(F, G);
    Y operator() (X);
    // ...
};
```

but this just begs the question. Types `F` and `G` are not part of the type of class `Composition` because they are not template parameters there. Yet, presumably, class `Composition` is going to work by storing an object of class `Comp<F, G, X, Y>`. How can it do that without making `F` or `G` a template parameter to class `Comp` itself?

ONE TYPE COVERS MANY

Fortunately, C++ has a mechanism for that—namely, inheritance. Suppose we rewrite our class `Comp` so that `Comp<F, G, X, Y>` is derived from some other class that does not depend on `F` or `G`. We might call that class `Comp_base<X, Y>`. Then in our class `Composition` we will be able to store only a pointer to `Comp_base<X, Y>`.

---

*This is a facility that the standards committee approved only in 1994, which means that many compilers will not yet support it.

It is probably easiest to unravel this tangle from the inside out and begin with `Comp_base`. Conceptually, a `Comp_base` object will be something that will represent an arbitrary function object that takes an `X` argument and gives a `Y` result. We will therefore give it a virtual `operator()`, since the `operator()` in every class derived from `Comp_base<X, Y>` will take an argument of the same type (namely, `X`) and return a result of the same type (namely, `Y`). Because we do not want to define `operator()` specifically for a plain `Comp_base`, we will make it a pure virtual. Moreover, since inheritance is involved, it will need a virtual destructor.

Looking ahead again, we see that we will want to be able to copy `Composition` objects. Copying a `Composition` object will involve copying an object of some `Comp` type without necessarily knowing the exact type. That means that we will need a virtual function in `Comp_base` to make a copy of the derived class object.

With all that, we have the following base class:

```
template<class X, class Y> class Comp_base {
public:
   virtual Y operator()(X) = 0;
   virtual Comp_base* clone() = 0;
   virtual ~Comp_base() { }
};
```

Now we will rewrite class `Comp` to use `Comp_base` as a base class and add an appropriate `clone` function to `Comp` that will override the pure virtual in `Comp_base`:

```
template<class F, class G, class X, class Y>
   class Comp: public Comp_base<X, Y> {
public:
   Comp(F f0, G g0): f(f0), g(g0) { }
   Y operator()(X x) { return f(g(x)); }
   Comp_base<X, Y>* clone() {
     return new Comp(*this);
   }
private:
   F f;
   G g;
};
```

Now we can make our `Composition` class contain a pointer to a `Comp_base`:

```
template<class X, class Y> class Composition {
```

```
public:
   template<class F, class G>
     Composition(F, G);

   Y operator() (X);
private:
   Comp_base<X, Y>* p;
   // ...
};
```

Whenever a class gains a member of pointer type, we should think about what to do with the pointer when copying an object of that class. In this case, we want to copy the underlying object—after all, that is why we put a clone function into class `Comp_base` in the first place. That means we must write an explicit copy constructor and destructor in class `Composition`:

```
template<class X, class Y> class Composition {
public:
   template<class F, class G>
     Composition(F, G);
   Composition(const Composition&);
   Composition& operator=
     (const Composition&);
   ~Composition();
   Y operator() (X);
private:
   Comp_base<X, Y>* p;
};
```

IMPLEMENTATION

At this point, it should be fairly straightforward to implement class `Composition`. When constructing a `Composition<X, Y>` with a pair of objects of types `F` and `G`, we will create a `Comp<F, G>` object and store its address in the pointer `p`:

```
template<class X, class Y>
   template<class F, class G>
     Composition<X, Y>::Composition
       (F f, G g):
       p(new Comp<F, G, X, Y> (f, g)) { }
```

This works only because class `Comp<F, G, X, Y>` is derived from class `Comp_base<X, Y>`.

The destructor just deletes the object to which `p` points:

```
template<class X, class Y>
Composition<X, Y>::_Composition()
{
    delete p;
}
```

The copy constructor and assignment operator take advantage of the virtual `clone` function in class `Comp_base`:

```
template<class X, class Y>
Composition::Composition(const
Composition& c):
    p(c.p->clone()) { }
template<class X, class Y>
Composition& operator=
    (const Composition& c)
{
    if (this != &c) {
      delete p;
      p = c.clone();
    }
    return *this;
}
```

Finally, `operator()` uses the virtual `operator()` in class `Comp_base`:

```
template<class X, class Y>
    Y Composition::operator() (X x)
{
    return (*p)(x); // p->operator()(x)
}
```

At this point we have our wish: we can say

```
extern int f(int);
extern int g(int);
extern int h(int);

int main()
{
    Composition<int, int> fg(f, g);
    Composition<int, int> fgh(fg, h);
}
```

and have `fg` and `fgh` be the same type even though they do very different things internally.

DISCUSSION

One way of looking at this example is that it is quite a bit of work to get around a seemingly simple language restriction. Another viewpoint is that the example shows that the language extension is not quite as simple as it appears at first. Moreover, if the work of defining these function objects is done once, it can be used again later.

My experience is that C++ programmers do not ask for function composition as such all that often. However, there are related things that do come up more frequently, and which are therefore part of the standard library. For example, there is a standard library function called `transform` that applies a function or function object to every element in a sequence, possibly yielding a new sequence. If `a` is an array with 100 elements, then

```
transform(a, a+100, a, f);
```

will apply `f` to each element of `a` in turn and store the result back into the same element of `a`.

Suppose we want to use `transform` to add an integer `n` to every element of our array. Then we could define a function object that adds an integer:

```
class Add_an_integer {
public:
    Add_an_integer(int n0): n(n0) { }
    operator() (int x) { return x+n; }
private:
    int n;
};
```

and call

```
transform(a, a+100, a, Add_an_integer(n));
```

but it is a nuisance to have to define a separate function object class for this purpose.*

The library therefore offers a collection of function object templates that can make it unnecessary to define special-purpose function object classes.

---

*To test your understanding, explain why we had to use a function object here instead of a function.

SMALLTALK

MANAGING CONCURRENCY CONFLICTS IN MULTI-USER SMALLTALK

JAY ALMARODE

T HERE ARE A NUMBER OF ADVANTAGES WHEN MULTIPLE USERS ACCESS SHARED objects in a single object space: Users share behavior as well as object state, developers do not have to write mapping code between Smalltalk and a persistent store, and delivering and updating applications is simply a matter of making the changes public. However, when multiple users can view and modify shared objects, there is a potential for conflict.

Concurrency conflicts occur when one user reads an object that another user has modified, or when two users modify the same object. For example, if one user reads an account balance that has been modified and committed by another user, it is imperative that the transaction experience a conflict. This is because any decision made and subsequent code executed is based upon a value that is no longer valid. When the transaction attempts to commit, the attempt is unsuccessful due to the concurrency conflict.

> **TIP**
>
> This is the classic "racing" problem in computer science.

When building applications in single-user Smalltalk systems, developers do not have to consider the possibility of concurrency conflicts on their Smalltalk objects because they can treat all of object memory as their own private domain. Instead, they must map the application's concurrency requirements onto the concurrency control mechanisms provided by some persistent store. In multi-user Smalltalk, the underlying execution engine and transaction manager provide the concurrency control mechanisms. This column will describe the mechanisms for concurrency control in multi-user Smalltalk and describe some techniques for resolving concurrency conflicts.

TIP

There are two approaches to con-currency control.

There are two approaches to concurrency control. One approach is to acquire locks on objects. This approach, called "pessimistic," allows a user to prohibit other users from reading or writing a particular object. Acquiring a lock on an object guarantees that at commit time, certain kinds of conflict will not occur on that object. Locking has its drawbacks, though. When an object is locked, its availability is reduced for other users. Acquiring a lock typically requires the arbitration of a centralized lock manager, which may involve additional network communication in a client/server architecture. And using the pessimistic approach requires that application developers understand which objects will be read or written. For single objects, this might not be too difficult to do. But for networks of objects, it might not be obvious which object will eventually be written when an operation is invoked on the root node in the network.

A second approach to concurrency control, called "optimistic," does not use locking, but instead determines concurrency conflicts when a transaction attempts to commit. With this approach, an application reads and writes objects without explicitly worrying about other users. At commit time, the system determines if any of the objects read or written by this transaction were also read or written by other committed transactions. If so, then a conflict occurs and the attempt to commit fails. This might sound drastic, but in many cases, applications are only reading the majority of objects anyway, so the chance of conflict may not be too high. If an application knows that it will be writing objects also accessed by other applications, it can always acquire locks on the object. The two approaches are not mutually exclusive. If a conflict should occur at the time of commit, the user can find out which objects experienced the conflict and perhaps take steps to resolve the conflict. In SmalltalkDB, the data definition and manipulation language for GemStone, a user can find out which objects experienced conflict by sending the message System transactionConflicts. This message returns a dictionary whose keys are symbols indicating the kind of conflict, and whose values are arrays of objects that experienced the conflict. Using this information, an application can take steps to save information that might be lost when the transaction is aborted (for example, by writing information into a newly created object or by writing data to a file).

In discussing concurrency conflicts on objects, I've discussed conflicts in terms of reading and writing an object at the physical level. Most persistent

TABLE 1. DESCRIBES THE VARIOUS KINDS OF CONFLICTS THAT CAN OCCUR

#'Read-Write'	My transaction read an object that another transaction wrote
#'Write-Read'	My transaction wrote an object that another transaction read
#'Write-Write'	My transaction wrote an object that another transaction wrote
#'Read-ExclusiveLock'	My transaction read an object on which another transaction acquired an exclusive lock
#'Write-ReadLock'	My transaction wrote an object on which another transaction acquired an exclusive lock
#'Write-WriteLock'	My transaction wrote an object on which another transaction acquired a write lock
#'Rc-Write-Write'	My transaction wrote an RC object that another transaction wrote, and the conflict could not be logically resolved.

object-based systems detect conflicts by recognizing when concurrent transactions have read or written the same objects, irrespective of the logical operations that caused those reads or writes. There has been much work in concurrency control for abstract data types that is applicable to object-based systems.[1–3] The main thrust of this work is that even though there may be conflict on the physical level, the logical specification of an object and its operations may allow the physical conflicts to be resolved. For example, two concurrent transactions may add some objects to an instance of Bag. The second transaction that attempts to commit will experience conflict since the first transaction wrote the same bag (this is a write–write conflict). However, there is no logical reason why two concurrent transactions cannot add objects to the same bag. If the underlying system can resolve these physical conflicts so that the end result is that the bag contains both transaction's additions, then the second transaction should be allowed to commit successfully. Some systems solve this problem by using locking protocols, but this reduces concurrency by making the bag unavailable for concurrent modifications.

In using objects in a multi-user setting, a developer must not only think about the functional semantics of an object (what an operation does to an object), but also its concurrency semantics (what concurrent operations are allowed on the object). In SmalltalkDB, the kernel class library has been

TABLE 2. VARIOUS RC CLASSES AND THEIR SEMANTICS

RcQueue	multiple adders to the queue will not conflict
	a single remover from the queue will not conflict with adders
	multiple removers from the queue will conflict
RcBag	multiple adders to the bag will not conflict
	a single remover will not conflict with adders
	multiple removers of disjoint objects will not conflict
	multiple removers of the same object will conflict if they attempt to remove more than the number of occurrences in the bag
RcHashDictionary	multiple updaters of entries with disjoint keys will not conflict
	multiple updaters of an entry with the same key will conflict
	multiple removers of entries with disjoint keys will not conflict
	multiple removers of an entry with the same key will conflict
	readers of an entry will not conflict with updaters of the same entry
RcCounter	multiple incrementers or decrementers will not conflict
	readers of the counter value will not conflict with modifiers of the value

TIP

All developers must consider concurrency semantics.

extended to include classes particularly tailored to multi-user access. These 'reduced-conflict' classes (called RC classes, for short) have functional semantics the same as their single-user counterparts, but have been specifically implemented to provide more concurrency. The cost of this additional concurrency is greater memory usage per object, and potentially slightly longer time to commit. Table 2 lists the reduced-conflict classes and their concurrency semantics.

In SmalltalkDB, programmers have a number of ways they can manage concurrency conflicts. They can lock objects to ensure a successful commit; they can abort their transaction when a conflict occurs and retry operations; they can utilize RC classes when appropriate in their applications. The following code examples illustrate these three approaches for adding an object to a shared bag. The example in Listing 1 illustrates the optimistic approach. After adding the object to the shared bag, we attempt to commit the transaction. If another transaction has modified the bag, we may get a concurrency conflict, and the attempt to commit will fail. In this case, we abort the transaction, causing the view of the bag to be updated. We can then add the object

LISTING 1. EXAMPLE USING OPTIMISTIC CONCURRENCY CONTROL

```
"The Bag and The Object are global variables for the purpose of
 this example"

 | addToBag |
 addToBag := true.
 [ addToBag ] whileTrue: [
  " add the object to the bag "
  TheBag add: TheObject.
  " attempt to commit the transaction "
  System commitTransaction
       " if commit was successful, exit the loop "
     ifTrue: [ addToBag := false ]
       " if unsuccessful, abort the transaction and try
         again "
     ifFalse: [ System abortTransaction ]].
```

LISTING 2. EXAMPLE USING LOCKS

```
 | tryAgain |
 tryAgain := false.
 [
  " Attempt to acquire a write lock on the bag "
  System
     writeLock: TheBag
       " if lock was denied, keep trying "
       ifDenied: [ tryAgain := true ]
       " if lock is dirty, abort the transaction to
           update your view "
     ifChanged: [ System abortTransaction ].

  tryAgain

 ] untilFalse.

 " at this point, we've acquired the lock on the bag "
 TheBag add: TheObject.
 System commitAndReleaseLocks
```

to the bag and attempt to commit again.

The example in Listing 2 shows one way to acquire a lock on an object. It attempts to acquire a write lock since we know we will be modifying the bag by adding an object to it. It is possible that the lock may be denied because another transaction has already acquired a lock on the bag or because we do

Listing 3. Example Using RC Bag

```
" TheBag is now an instance of class RcBag "
TheBag add: TheObject.

"by the concurrency semantics of RcBag, this transaction
can successfully commit "
System commitTransaction
```

not have write authorization for the bag (object authorizations will be the subject of a future column). For this example, we assume we have authorization to modify the bag; otherwise we would add code that checks our authorizations and takes some other course of action. If the lock is denied, we set a boolean flag so that we continue trying to acquire the lock (presumably until another transaction releases its lock). It is possible that the lock may be acquired but a modification to the bag has been committed by another transaction since this transaction began. This is called a "dirty" lock. In this case, we abort the transaction to update our view of the bag, then proceed with our addition to the bag since we continue to hold the lock after the abort operation.

The final example in Listing 3 illustrates the ease of use of RC classes in SmalltalkDB. Since an adder to the RcBag will not conflict with other adders, removers, or readers of the bag, the transaction will not conflict. The implementation of RcBag uses various strategies to avoid physical conflict on the bag. When a physical conflict does occur, the underlying system attempts to resolve those conflicts if they are determined not to be logical conflicts.

Hopefully this column has given you some insight into managing concurrency in multi-user Smalltalk applications. When multiple users share objects, the application programmer must be aware of the potential for conflict. There are a number of techniques for avoiding concurrency conflicts and when they do occur, the application can take steps to resolve those conflicts.

References

1. Weihl, W. Local atomicity properties: Modular concurrency control for abstract data types, ACM Transactions on Programming Languages and Systems 11(2), 1989.

2   Herlihy, M. Apologizing versus asking permission: Optimistic concurrency control for abstract data types, ACM TRANSACTIONS ON DATABASE SYSTEMS 15(1), 1990.

3. Schwarz, P., and A. Spector, Synchronizing shared abstract types, ACM TRANSACTIONS ON COMPUTER SYSTEMS 2(3), 1984.

Coverage Analysis in Smalltalk

Mark L. Murphy

How Much Is Enough?

Quality assurance, unfortunately, is largely a guessing game. You know when programming is complete on a project, because all the requirements have been met. However, the standard against which quality assurance is held is, "Are there any bugs left?" which is impossible to know. You could test until the end of time and still miss bugs. Every project, therefore, makes a decision as to how much testing is enough.

Project managers are charged with ensuring that the testing is done, and done properly. It is not always easy to tell, however. Suppose you ask to see the unit test plan for a 24-class subsystem, and the developer hands you a 7-page document outlining a dozen tests. It is quite likely, just by looking at it, that the test suite is insufficient to really test out all the subsystem's functionality—it is simply too short. Suppose, however, that the test plan were 70 pages, or 700. How do you know if the tests really do thoroughly exercise the subsystem? A 700-page test plan may seem to be good based on size alone, yet might miss entire classes, if the suite is really bad. You just do not know for sure.

What we need is an objective measurement and set of criteria for determining test completeness. *Coverage analysis* is one such metric. This article will describe what coverage analysis means and how one can use it in practice. It includes an overview of some classes for measuring method coverage in Visual Smalltalk 3.0.1 (VST).

Enter Coverage Analysis

Coverage analysis involves "teaching" the subsystem to track what portions of it a test suite executes. For example, each method might note that a test

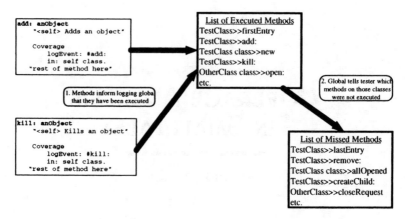

FIGURE 1. *Method coverage in action.*

executed it before evaluating the body of the method itself (see Figure 1). One can run a test suite, collect coverage tracking information, and determine specifically what the test executed and what it did not.

Now you have real-world information to determine how thorough a test suite is. The spots that were missed represent areas that the suite cannot audit. If they were not tested by hand in some other way, they have not been tested at all, and may contain bugs. You can even express coverage data in metric form (e.g., "we covered 87% of the subsystem's methods") for use in overall project benchmarking.

COVERING WHAT? AND HOW?

A generic coverage analysis tool will not know specifics about an application. Hence, it cannot say: "You missed testing the X-Base file filter."

All the analyzer can do is report on abstract coverage metrics. For example, method coverage asks the question, "Has every method been executed at least once?" If you've never tested a method, you cannot know if it works!

Researchers and practitioners have identified several types of useful coverage metrics, each asking a different question. These include:

- **Statement**: Has each line of code been executed at least once?
- **Branch:** Has every logical branch (e.g., `ifTrue:` and `ifFalse:`) been tried in both the true and false directions?
- **Loop:** Has every loop (e.g., `do:` on a `collection`) been tried with 0, 1, and several passes through the loop? Zero passes means that the loop body (e.g., the block passed to `do:`) is never evaluated.
- **Path:** Has every logical path through a method been tried? Figure 2 shows a sample Smalltalk method and the four paths that an application could take. Branch coverage would be satisfied by testing only two of the paths: A and D.

ANALYZING THE RESULTS

From a quality-assurance perspective, coverage analysis will provide a list of missed pieces of code, along with an overall percentage of code coverage. Developers must decide on an acceptable coverage level for a project. If a unit test for a subsystem fails to meet that metric, developers can add more tests based on the list of missed coverage spots.

> **TIP**
>
> Developers must decide on an acceptable coverage level for a project.

Note, however, that some coverage "misses" may actually be expected. For example, perhaps there is some code that specifically handles the exception raised when a database server is not responding. Testing that code in a live situation means bringing down the server, which database administrators typically dislike. Hence, the test suite intentionally might skip a test for that exception handler, but the coverage analysis will still report that the suite missed it. Hence, a sub-100% coverage value may still be acceptable.

What you really want is 100% practical coverage, where testers justify each missed method. Note that those methods still must be tested somehow, even if it is by hand. Since you cannot continually re-test that method (regression testing), make sure it is right the first time!

METHOD COVERAGE IN VST

If you want to employ method coverage in your Smalltalk application, you have three main choices:

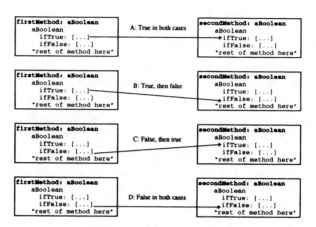

FIGURE 2. *Paths to be covered.*

1. Hand-code messages to a coverage-logging routine, as was shown in Figure 1—but this is time consuming.

2. Use the profiler that comes with the Smalltalk development environment.

3. Use or construct custom classes specifically for doing method coverage analysis in an automated fashion.

Using a Profiler

Many Smalltalk implementations come with profiling tools used for measuring the performance of pieces of Smalltalk code. One could, in principle, use them for method coverage analysis as well, since they watch over what a test executes. The TimeProfiler that comes with VisualWorks would not work in this case, because it uses a statistical sampling technique that might miss methods.

The profiler that comes with VST, however, does catch each and every message an application sends. Why, then, build another set of classes for method coverage? There are two reasons:

1. The VST profiler watches all methods in the image. Even the simplest test generates dozens to thousands of messages, most of which are for Smalltalk kernel classes. It would be difficult to determine the use of application classes with all this "noise."

2. The profiler does not report the methods the test missed, only those that it executed (and how long they took). Developers would have to

TABLE 1. METHOD DICTIONARY BEFORE INSTRUMENTATION

Selector	Method
log:forClass:	**log: aSymbol forClass: a Class** "Execute real code here"

TABLE 2. METHOD DICTIONARY AFTER INSTRUMENTATION

Selector	Method
real_log:forClass:	**log: aSymbol forClass: a Class** "Execute real code here"
log:forClass:	**log: p1 forClass: p2** "Execute instrumentation code here" ^self real_log: p1 forClass: p2

manually cross-reference against the class to figure out which ones the test missed.

Technique: Method Wrapping

What we want to do is create a mechanism of "instrumenting" methods: adding code that does not change their original behavior but adds in new functionality. For coverage analysis, the instrumentation will simply inform some Smalltalk global that this method has been invoked. That global will have to track the called methods and provide coverage results on demand when the test is done, as shown in Figure 1.

> **TIP**
>
> Create a mechanism of "instrumenting" methods.

The term for this instrumentation technique is "method wrapping." There are two ways one can wrap a method. One is simply to add new Smalltalk code to the source of the existing method and recompile it. This will work in many situations, but not all. Primitive methods cannot be wrapped this way, because Smalltalk code and a primitive call cannot coexist. It also requires one to parse Smalltalk methods, which is a nuisance.

Another approach, moving the existing method, is used both by the TimeProfiler that comes with VisualWorks Advanced Tools and the classes in this article. The `CompiledMethod` to be wrapped is moved in the class' method dictionary from its original selector to a new, unused selector. Then, a new `CompiledMethod` is created and installed under the original selector. This new method executes the instrumentation code, then sends a message, using the temporary selector, to invoke the original behavior. Since the original `CompiledMethod` remains unchanged, any type of method can be wrapped. Tables 1 and 2 show a fragment of a class' method dictionary, both before and after instrumentation.

In either case, to "unwrap" the method one simply restores the original compiled method under its original selector. While a method is wrapped, it will perform the added code (e.g., log method execution to a global) in addition to its old behavior. Once you unwrap it, everything returns to normal.

The VST implementation of coverage analysis via method wrapping for this article involves three classes:

- `SRInstrumentedMethod`—can wrap and unwrap a specified method.
- `SRCoveredMethod`—a subclass of `SRInstrumentedMethod` that wraps methods with coverage-logging statements.
- `SRCoverageMonitor`—logs coverage events created by the `SRCoveredMethod` instances.

These classes are available on the Internet at http.//www.evro.com /STReport/Oct 95.htm.

Using the Monitor

The only class that developers need to use directly is `SRCoverage-Monitor`. The following steps describe how to start and stop coverage and get results:

1. Create a new instance of a `SRCoverageMonitor` via the `new` class method.
2. Tell the monitor which classes and methods to watch. There are three methods that one can use:
   - `cover: aClass`—covers all methods for that class (or metaclass)
   - `cover: aClass including: aCollection`—covers the indicated methods for that class
   - `cover: aClass excluding: aCollection`—covers all methods for the class except the specified ones
3. Start monitoring these methods, by sending `enableCoverage` to the monitor.
4. Perform the tests to be monitored.

5. Stop monitoring by sending `disableCoverage` to the monitor.

6. Inspect the results, using these methods:

- `coveredMethods`—returns a list of all methods that were executed during the tests, along with how many times they were sent

- `notCoveredMethods`—returns a list of those methods on the covered classes that were not executed

- `browseNotCoveredMethods`—brings up a `MethodBrowser` on those methods that were missed during the test

The following code fragment illustrates the use of these methods:

```
| mon today |
mon := SRCoverageMonitor new.
mon cover: Date.
mon enableCoverage.

"This is the test that coverage for which is being mea
        sured"
today := Date current.
Transcript show: 'The date is: ', today printString; cr.

mon disableCoverage.
mon browseNotCalledMethods.
```

A few caveats about using these classes:

- Because method wrapping does change classes at a low level, it is best to save your image before using it, in case of disaster. If the test crashes and fails to run to completion, one can restore the original versions of the instrumented methods via `SRInstrumentedMethod class>>restoreAllOldMethods`. Each wrapped method is tracked in a class variable, which this method uses to unwrap them all.

- Enabling coverage on methods that the coverage analysis classes use will cause an infinite loop. Only enable coverage on application-specific classes or method extensions.

- The `enableCoverage` and `disableCoverage` methods may take a while to run if a lot of methods are being monitored.

- Methods whose selectors are made up solely of punctuation (e.g., `<=`) cannot be wrapped. The algorithm for coming up with a temporary selector (the original with a "`real_`" prefix) will not work. `SRInstrumentedMethod` could be modified to use an alternate scheme that would overcome this limitation.

OTHER SMALLTALKS, OTHER COVERAGE METRICS

Coverage analysis is not limited to VST. Both VisualWorks and IBM Smalltalk/VisualAge can employ method coverage using the same technique. Note that configuration management tools, such as ENVY, will require slightly different code, as they typically have different methods for compiling methods into classes. Also, we do not want the instrumented version of the method to go into the revision history, lest it grow out of control.

You could also implement other coverage metrics, but with some difficulty. Ideally, one could do loop and branch coverage by creating modified versions of Boolean and the block classes (e.g., VST's `ZeroArgumentBlock`). However, most Smalltalks inline a lot of that code, so real messages are not sent; hence, the modified versions would not get triggered. One could modify the Smalltalk compiler classes to overcome this problem.

SUMMARY

Coverage analysis is an important component in the quality-assurance program for software development. It is the only real way to feel confident that the test suite is doing its job. These classes for VST will give you a head start toward incorporating method coverage on your project.

Acknowledgments

It should be noted that the research for this article was conducted as part of work done for American Management Systems. Also, the author thanks Doug Kittelsen for his able editorial assistance.

PROCESSES

ALEC SHARP AND DAVE FARMER

THIS ARTICLE TALKS ABOUT SMALLTALK PROCESSES, THE THREADSAFENESS OF shared resources, and communication between processes. Because the implementation of processes varies quite a bit between Smalltalk vendors, we want to note up front that in this article we are describing VisualWorks 2.0 from ParcPlace Systems.

CREATING PROCESSES

Smalltalk allows you to create separate processes so that your application can do several things in parallel. For example, our application creates a process for handling input from sockets, another process for handling output to sockets, and separate processes to handle I/O to each robot tape library that is connected to our UNIX server. These processes all run in a single Smalltalk image.

The Smalltalk image is a single process being run by the operating system, but internal to Smalltalk is another process scheduler that allocates time among the various Smalltalk processes. So the operating system scheduler allocates time to Smalltalk, and the Smalltalk scheduler allocates time to the various Smalltalk processes.

> **TIP**
>
> The Smalltalk scheduler allocates time to the various Smalltalk processes.

Smalltalk processes can be forked at different priorities, with higher priority processes being given preferential treatment if they have anything to do. To fork a process, you send a `fork` or `forkAt:` message to a `BlockClosure`. For example,

```
[SocketInput new start] forkAt:
    Processor userSchedulingPriority.
```

When assigning priorities, it's a good idea to use names to avoid problems when values change in new software releases. For example, in VisualWorks 1.0, user background priority was 3, but in VisualWorks 2.0 the number of priorities has been significantly increased and user background priority is now 30. The priority names can be found in the "priority names" instance protocol of `ProcessScheduler`.

You can also create a process that does not immediately run, using the

> **TIP**
>
> You can create a process that does not run immediately.

newProcess or newProcessWithArguments: message to a `BlockClosure`. A process created this way does not run until you send it a **resume** message. (Interestingly, the `fork` message is actually implemented as a `newProcess` message followed by a resume.) We won't go into this aspect of processes except to say that you might use this capability if you wanted to gain more control over process scheduling.

PROCESS SCHEDULING

VisualWorks does not have a preemptive scheduler, which means that a process will continue execution until either it explicitly gives up control, using `Processor yield`, or it does an operation that yields the processor, such as reading a file or waiting. So, for example, in the following code, process1 will never give up control and so process2 never runs. In fact, if we had used fork to create the new process, it would have inherited the priority of the creating process, and would have never given up control to the parent, so the parent would not be able to terminate it. Unfortunately, you won't be able to terminate it with ctrl-C; try it and see!

```
| process1 process2 |
process1 := [[Transcript show: '1 '] repeat]
    forkAt: Processor userBackgroundPriority.
process2 := [[Transcript show: '2 '] repeat]
    forkAt: Processor userBackgroundPriority.
(Delay forSeconds: 7) wait.
process1 terminate.
process2 terminate.

Results: 1 1 1 1 1 1 1 1 1 1 1 1 1 1 1 1 1 1 1 1 ....
```

In these examples we don't want the processes to run forever, so we terminate them after seven seconds. We have shown all the code above, but in future examples we will only show the `process1` and `process2` code to save space. We will also use a tighter formatting than we would use in production code. Another thing to note is our use of the `Delay` class. Every time we want to wait, we create an instance of `Delay` then immediately ask the instance to wait. In a production system, it might be more appropriate to create the instance in a separate operation from the wait, especially if the wait occurs inside a loop. For example,

```
delay := Delay forMilliseconds: 100.
[...
delay wait] repeat.
```

In the next example, we yield the processor and now `process2` gets a chance to run. Similarly, we could have done an operation that caused a wait, such as `(Delay forMilliseconds: 10) wait`, and this would have the same result:

```
process1 := [[Transcript show: '1 '. Processor yield]
                repeat]
            forkAt: Processor userBackgroundPriority.
process2 := [[Transcript show: '2 '.
              Processor yield] repeat]
                forkAt: Processor userBackgroundPriority.

Results: 1 2 1 2 1 2 1 2 1 2 1 2 1 2 ......
```

Let's now give `process2` a higher priority (`userSchedulingPriority`) than `process1`. Even though `process2` does a `Processor yield`, `process1` is never scheduled after `process2` gets into the picture because `process2` always has work to do. This is unlike timesharing processes in a UNIX system, where each process in effect has two priorities: a base priority and a current priority. The UNIX process scheduler computes the current priority from the base priority, how much time the process has been sleeping, how much CPU time it has used, and other factors. This way, all processes have a chance to run, even if they have a low base priority. Smalltalk processes are more like UNIX real-time processes, where the highest priority process always gets the CPU if it has something to do.

```
process1 := [[Transcript show: '1 '] repeat]
                forkAt: Processor userBackgroundPriority.
(Delay forMilliseconds: 100) wait.
process2 := [[Transcript show: '2 '. Processor yield]
                repeat]
```

```
        forkAt: Processor userSchedulingPriority.

Results:  1 1 1 1 2 2 2 2 2 2 2 2 2 2 2 2 2 2 2 2 2 2 .....
```

Let's take a brief look at how VisualWorks itself uses some of the different priorities; we'll specify the priority by the message that you send to Processor. The incremental garbage collector runs at `systemBackgroundPriority`, so it only gets activated if there is nothing else going on. Once running, if it decides that memory needs compacting, if forks a process to do so at `userInterruptPriority`, which is a higher priority than the typical user application running at `userSchedulingPriority`. The Profiler also runs at `userInterruptPriority`, since it needs to periodically interrupt the application it is profiling.

Keyboard and mouse input are done at a higher priority still, `lowIOPriority`, as is the process that handles low space conditions. An example of a `highIOPriority` process is a C routine calling back into Smalltalk. The highest priority, `timingPriority`, is used by system processes that handle delays and process termination.

TERMINATING PROCESSES

Once a process has been forked, how does it terminate? There are two ways this can happen. It can simply finish what it was doing, or it can be terminated. This example shows a process finishing up its job then terminating. We print out the value of the process twice, once while it's still doing work, and again after it's finished and the garbage collector has done its thing.

```
proc := [(Delay forSeconds: 1) wait.] fork.
Transcript cr; show: proc printString.
(Delay forSeconds: 2) wait.
ObjectMemory garbageCollect.
Transcript cr; show: proc printString.

Results:   a Process in [] optimized
           a Process in nil
```

To terminate a process, we send it a `terminate` message. Generally this message will be sent by another process, but there's no reason why a process can't send itself a `terminate`. Of course the process will need a handle to itself if it wants to send a `terminate` message to itself. Generally you should be able to structure the code that is executed in a forked block to simply finish, but it's certainly possible that the termination condition may be buried deep in your code, and rather than filtering up the condition it's easier to terminate the process when the condition is found (alternatively, you could raise an exception). A process could also terminate itself by sending the terminate message to the active process (i.e., itself):

```
Processor activeProcess terminate
```

The example that follows shows a process being terminated by another process. The main difference between this example and the previous one is that in line one, the process waits for 10 seconds, then in line three we terminate the process. The Transcript shows that the process is nil long before the 10 seconds are up.

```
proc := [(Delay forSeconds: 10) wait.] fork.
Transcript cr; show: proc printString.
proc terminate.
(Delay forSeconds: 1) wait.
ObjectMemory garbageCollect.
Transcript cr; show: proc printString.

Results:    a Process in [] optimized
            a Process in nil
```

SHARED RESOURCES

Sometimes we have resources that the various processes need shared access to. For example, in our application, we log information from the various processes and we need to make sure that we don't get interleaved data. We also keep a ThingsToCleanUp object in a pool dictionary, in which we store all the opened files and external devices, and the forked processes. We want to make sure that we provide threadsafe access to these shared resources. If we don't make access to shared resources threadsafe, we could end up in the situation illustrated by the following example.

```
array := #(1 2 3 4 5 6 7) copy.
process1 := [array do: [:element | Transcript show: element
                                    printString, ' '.
       (Delay forMilliseconds: 500) wait ] ] fork.
(Delay forMilliseconds: 1000) wait.
process2 := [array at: 6 put: nil.
     Transcript show: '<Setting 6=nil> '] fork.

Results: 1 2 <setting 6=nil> 3 4 5 nil 7
```

We want to protect the array so that only one process can access it at a time. We do this with a mutual exclusion semaphore, which we create by sending the forMutualExclusion message to Semaphore. We ask the semaphore to run the code by sending it the critical: message with the block of code to run, and the semaphore is smart enough to only run one block of code at a time.

```
array := #(1 2 3 4 5 6 7 ) copy.
sem := Semaphore forMutualExclusion.
process1 := [sem critical:
    [array do: [:element | Transcript show: element
                        printString, ' '.
    (Delay forMilliseconds: 500) wait]]] fork.
(Delay forMilliseconds: 1000) wait.
process2 := [sem critical:
    [array at: 6 put: nil.
    Transcript show: '<setting 6=nil> ']] fork.

Results: 1 2 3 4 5 6 7 <setting 6=nil>
```

As a brief aside, Semaphores work by having processes wait until a signal is sent to the semaphore. The mutual exclusion semaphore sends itself a signal when it's created, so that the first block of code to be run by the semaphore already has a signal waiting. That is, it doesn't have to wait. Once the code has been executed, the semaphore sends itself another signal, priming itself in advance for the next code block. It does so by:

```
^mutuallyExcludedBlock valueNowOrOnUnwindDo: [self signal]
```

How do the priorities of the different processes affect mutual exclusion? Fortunately, mutual exclusion works as you'd want it to work, regardless of priority. If we change the previous example so that process1 is forked with forkAt: Processor userBackgroundPriority and process2 is forked with forkAt: Processor userSchedulingPriority, we get the same results. The critical block is still run to completion before the higher priority process can get access to the shared resource.

The next question is can another process get access to a shared resource if it's not cooperating by sending the critical: message? As the following example shows, the answer is yes:

```
array := #(1 2 3 4 5 6 7 ) copy.
sem := Semaphore forMutualExclusion.
process1 := [sem critical: [array do: [:element |
    Transcript show: element printString, ' '.
```

```
    (Delay forMilliseconds: 500) wait]]] fork.
(Delay forMilliseconds: 1000) wait.
process2 := [array at: 6 put: nil.
    Transcript show: '<setting 6=nil> '] fork.

Results: 1 2 <setting 6=nil> 3 4 5 nil 7
```

So, to protect shared resources, the processes must cooperate. Both processes have to agree to use the same semaphore to protect the shared resource. Let's go ahead and implement access to a shared resource, a Dictionary, as we might do in a real application. We will create and initialize the object, then provide read, write, and delete access to the resource. Our first decision is whether to subclass off Dictionary or create a new class that has a Dictionary as an instance variable. Since we want to restrict access to just a few messages, it's easier to create a new class than worry about all the possible ways someone might try to access a subclass of Dictionary. So, we'll create a new class with two instance variables, collection and accessProtect:

```
new
    ^super new initialize

initialize
    collection := Dictionary new.
    accessProtect := Semaphore forMutualExclusion.

at: aKey put: anItem
 ^accessProtect critical: [collection at: aKey put: anItem]

at: aKey
 ^accessProtect critical: [collection at: aKey ifAbsent:
    [nil]

remove: aKey
 ^accessProtect critical: [collection removeKey: aKey
    ifAbsent: [nil]]
```

Having got this far, we now need to say that the Transcript is not thread-safe. It so happens that all our examples work in VisualWorks 2.0, but writing to the Transcript from multiple processes is not guaranteed to work correctly. In fact we have an innocuous looking Transcript example that in VisualWorks 1.0 hangs until you press ctrl-C. So, while we use the Transcript in our examples, we don't recommend writing to it from multiple processes in production code. Much of the time, code that is not threadsafe will work because the Smalltalk scheduler is non-preemptive and so many code segments will run to completion. However, if you ever add code that causes the process to give up control, you may find that your code no longer works correctly.

INTERRUPTING ANOTHER PROCESS

Now, suppose you want to ask a particular process about its state. Perhaps you want to know if it's waiting for a particular input, or whether it's finished some part of its processing. In our product, where we have separate processes handling different robot tape libraries, we sometimes want to know the status of the library; for example, if it's on-line or off-line. There are several ways to handle this desire for information.

One solution might be to restructure your application so you don't need access to this information, but we'll ignore this one because it's not very interesting to this article! Another solution would be to have the process post the needed information in a shared resource, protected by a mutual exclusion semaphore. This has the potential disadvantage that the process may be updating the shared resource with a lot of information, but perhaps no one is reading it very often.

Another approach would be to send an object to the process using a shared queue and have the object figure out the information then send it back on another shared queue. We'll talk more about shared queues later, but a disadvantage of the shared queue approach is that the process needing the information will usually have to wait until the process can get to the shared queue, pull the object off it and process it. It's not an approach to use if you are in a hurry.

The approach we are going to look at is one where you can actually interrupt a process and ask it to do something for you. The mechanism is to send an `interruptWith: [aBlock]` message to the process, passing as a parameter the block of code you want executed. The process saves its context, executes the passed-in block, restores its context, then resumes its business. Here's an example. `Process1` is simply waiting for time to pass before doing anything. We interrupt it and ask it to print something.

```
process1 := [(Delay forSeconds: 4) wait.
    Transcript cr; show: 'process1 done waiting'] fork.
process2 := [(Delay forMilliseconds: 100) wait.
```

```
process1 interruptWith:
    [Transcript cr; show: 'process2 interrupt']] fork.

Results:    process2 interrupt
    process1 done waiting
```

That's all well and good, but what happens if the process is doing something that it really doesn't want interrupted? Fortunately, there's a way to prevent interrupts, which is to protect the special block of code with a `valueUninterruptably` message. The `valueUninterruptably` method sends the active process an `uninterruptablyDo: [aBlock]` message.

`uninterruptablyDo:` takes the parameter block and asks a semaphore named `interruptProtect` to run the block in critical mode. `interruptWith:` also asks `interruptProtect` to run its block in critical mode. Since `valueUninterruptably` and `interruptWith:` both ask the same semaphore to run their blocks critically, only one of the code blocks executes at a time.

Here's the previous example with `process1` protecting its work against interruption:

```
process1 := [[(Delay forSeconds: 4) wait.
    Transcript cr; show: 'process1 done waiting']
        valueUninterruptably] fork.
process2 := [(Delay forMilliseconds: 100) wait.
    process1 interruptWith:
        [Transcript cr; show: 'process2 interrupt']] fork.

Results:    process1 done waiting
    process2 interrupt
```

Are the `interruptWith:` and `valueUninterruptably` messages ones that you should use? Our view is to use them if you have to, but use them sparingly. ParcPlace recommends against their use. The method comments for `valueUninterruptably` and `uninterruptablyDo:` both say "Use this facility VERY sparingly." One problem with running a process uninterruptably is that you can't even use ctrl-C to interrupt it should things go wrong. Another is that if a process running uninterruptedly does something time consuming, such as reading a file, no one else can get the processor during that time. The only classes that send `valueUninterruptably` are Profiler and SharedQueue. ControlManager and Process are the only classes that send `interruptWith:`.

SHARED QUEUES

Our main objective in talking about `interruptWith:` and `valueUninterruptably` is to illustrate some interesting capabilities, then let this lead to a discussion of `SharedQueues`. So here we are. `SharedQueues` are the general mechanism for communicating between processes. They contain an `OrderedCollection` so that all objects that go onto a shared queue are taken off in chronological order. To set up communication between processes, you create an instance of `SharedQueue` and tell both processes about it. One process will put objects on the shared queue using `nextPut:` and the other process will use `next` to get objects from the queue. When a process sends the `next` message, it blocks until there is something on the queue. If the process doesn't want to block it can send `isEmpty` or `peek`.

Because shared queues are so important for communicating between processes, they need to be as safe as possible. For this reason, all access to shared queues is protected by a mutual exclusion semaphore using the `critical:` message, and this block of code is protected by a `value Uninterruptably` message. For example, here's how ParcPlace implements the `size` message to a shared queue.

```
size
    ^[accessProtect critical: [contents size]]
            valueUninterruptably
```

Again, the `critical:` message makes sure that only one operation happens at a time, so for example, it makes sure that one process is not getting an object from the queue while another process is adding an object. The `valueUninterruptably` makes sure that the shared queue operations can't be interrupted by a process sending an `interruptWith:` message.

Here's an example of shared queues in use. `Process2` prints the number and puts it on the shared queue, and `process1` reads the queue and prints the number:

```
sharedQueue := SharedQueue new.
process1 := [[number := sharedQueue next.
    Transcript show: ` R', number printString] repeat] fork.
process2 := [1 to: 5 do: [:index |
    Transcript show: ` W', index printString.
    sharedQueue nextPut: index.
    (Delay forMilliseconds: 500) wait]] fork.
Results: W1 R1 W2 R2 W3 R3 W4 R4 W5 R5
```

Try this again after removing the `Delay` in `process2`. Because `process2` now always has something to do, it does not give up control and so `process1` waits for the processor until `process2` is completely finished. The `Transcript` output now looks like:

```
Results: W1 W2 W3 W4 W5 R1 R2 R3 R4 R5
```

OUR PRODUCT

In our product we make heavy use of processes and therefore of shared queues (See Figure 1). We have one process that does nothing more than block on a socket waiting for input. It puts the input on a shared queue and another process takes it off. This second process sends each object a `queueYourself` message, telling the object to put itself on the appropriate shared queue for the robot tape library that the request is going to. Each library controller blocks on its own shared queue, waiting for a request to process. Finally, after the request has done what it needs to do, a response is created and put on an output shared queue. The output process gets response objects from this queue and sends them out over a socket to the appropriate UNIX process. Because Smalltalk gives a process control while it has things to do, we put a `Processor yield` after each shared queue `nextPut:`. This gives each process the opportunity to run, even when other processes have more they could be doing.

There is actually a lot more going on than this, and to solve our specific problems we created a subclass of `SharedQueue`, which we call a `PrioritySharedQueue`. Rather than keeping objects in chronological order in the shared queue, it orders them by priority then time. It also has methods to search for specific types of object and to delete objects. However, that's a story for another day. This just about wraps the article up, but before we leave, we'd like to mention briefly a new class that appeared in VisualWorks 2.0 that makes use of processes.

PROMISES

VisualWorks 2.0 introduces a new class, the `Promise` class. An instance of Promise promises to do something for you while you go off and do other things. It does this by forking a new process to carry out the work. You create the promise by sending the `promise` or `promiseAt:` message to a

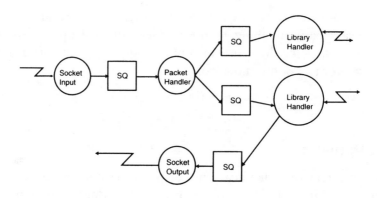

`BlockClosure`. Once the promise has been created, you can query it for its value (if the promise has been kept), or to find out if it has a value (it may still be doing its work). In fact, promises are a little more complex than this because if the promise fails or terminates, an exception is raised, so to be robust, you should wrap the promise in a `handle:do:` message. But since we are only mentioning promises in passing, we'll just show a simple example of a promise in action.

```
count := 0.
Transcript cr.
promise := [DialogView confirm: 'Is it true?'] promise.
[promise hasValue]
    whileFalse:
        [Transcript show: count printString, ' ' .
        count := count + 1.
        (Delay forSeconds: 1) wait].

Transcript show: promise value printString.
```

TRANSACTIONS IN SMALLTALK

JAY ALMARODE

THE KEY CHARACTERISTIC OF MULTI-USER SMALLTALK IS THAT A SINGLE OBJECT identity domain is accessible by multiple, concurrent users. Users share the same objects, not proxies to a remote system or duplicate copies mapped from a persistent store. This means that users share object behavior, as well as state. Rather than duplicating the same behavior in each application (and having to update each application when the behavior changes), the application sends messages to objects that reside in a single, globally shared image.

Since multiple users may be reading and modifying shared objects, the underlying Smalltalk system must make sure that a single user's view of objects is consistent. When a user reads or modifies an object, the user's operations must not be invalidated by other user's changes. For example, suppose an application maintains financial accounts with objects that encapsulate the account balance. A user that wants to transfer funds from account A to account B would cause the value in the account object for A to be decremented by some amount, and the value in account B to be incremented by the same amount. Since multiple users may be allowed to view the account balance in account A, it is important that concurrent users are not allowed to transfer funds based upon a view of the account that has since been decremented (unless we are allowed to make money out of thin air).

The way that a multi-user system maintains a consistent view of objects is with the notion of a transaction. A transaction is a bounded sequence of

> **TIP**
>
> When a user reads or modifies an object, the user's operations must not be invalidated by other user's changes.

operations such that either all of the operations are executed to completion, or none of them are executed. This is called atomicity. In the example above, when transferring money between accounts, both the debit of account A and the credit of account B must occur, or neither must occur. Otherwise, the account balances may become logically inconsistent. In a transaction-based system, when a user invokes the "commit" operation, the underlying system guarantees that either all modifications that occurred since the transaction began are made persistent, or none of them are. If a user wishes to discard all modifications, then he or she invokes the "abort" operation. In a limited sense, single-user Smalltalk systems support the notion of a transaction with the operation to save the image (by writing all of object memory to a file). When the image is saved, all modifications that occurred since the last save operation are made permanent, analogous to a commit operation. Correspondingly, if the user quits the image without saving, it is equivalent to the abort operation. If you've ever made low level changes to the user interface or kernel classes, you know the practicality of being able to quit the image without saving. It is a convenient way to back out of changes that have made the system inoperable.

The notion of a transaction has another important ramification concerning object visibility. When a user begins a transaction, the user is presented a view of the world of objects that is based upon the last committed state. This is sometimes called a "transaction's point of view." As a user modifies objects, these changes are not visible to other users until these changes are committed. In addition, any new objects that a user creates are not visible to other users until the transaction is committed. There is another model of object visibility where a user is allowed to see uncommitted modifications performed by other concurrent transactions. In this model, when a transaction views an uncommitted modification to an object, the transaction becomes dependent upon the committal of the other transaction. If the other transaction should abort its changes, then the current transaction must be aborted as well. With this model of object visibility in a transaction, the application may not get "repeatable reads" of an object. Accessing the state of an object depends upon the time that it is accessed within the transaction, and may not yield the same result every time the object is accessed. This is problematic in object-based systems, since complex (and side-effect causing) behavior may be executed based upon the state of an object. This model also leads to the potential problem of "cascading aborts," where the aborting of one transaction causes a domino effect by requiring dependent transactions to abort.

In multi-user Smalltalk, the underlying system is responsible for managing transactions and maintaining logical object consistency. Since objects reside in a single object memory, this task is greatly simplified. The internal object manager has knowledge of which objects have been read or written, and directly coordinates the updating of object memory that is sharable by all users. In SmalltalkDB, the data definition and manipulation language for GemStone[1], the underlying system uses shadowing techniques to provide a transaction's point of view. When a transaction begins, the user is presented a view of objects based upon the last committed state of object memory. This view appears to the user as a private copy of all of object memory. Any modifications that the user makes are not seen by other users. When the user modifies an object, the modification is actually performed on a shadow copy of the object. When the transaction is successfully committed, the shadow copy is merged into shared object memory by the underlying object manager. At this time, other users gain visibility of the transaction's modifications and any new objects that were created during the transaction. In addition, the user's view of objects is refreshed to include any modifications committed by other transactions in the interim. When a transaction is aborted, any modifications that were made to objects are lost, and the user's view of objects is refreshed. However, the user does not lose any new objects that were created before the abort occurred. As long as the application retains a reference to the newly created objects, it can continue to access them, and possibly commit them at a later time.

> **TIP**
>
> The underlying system is responsible for managing transactions.

The task of maintaining logical object consistency is slightly more complex for other architectures where a relational database (or other persistent store) or remote object messaging is used to share objects in single-user Smalltalk systems. In applications where a relational database is used to store an object's state, the application must transfer modifications that are performed on an object into updates to a relational table. Since the Smalltalk image exists independently from the database, an application developer must decide upon some means to keep object memory in synch with that state of the database. This problem is commonly called the "two-space problem."

When using a relational database or other persistent store to share objects, the Smalltalk application must make sure that when modifications are flushed to the database (for example, by causing the execution of SQL update commands), the modifications are atomic. This usually means utilizing whatever transaction mechanism is provided by the database. In the earlier example where the Smalltalk application has objects that represent account A and account B, there are corresponding rows in a relational table that holds the account balances for both of these objects. An application developer must make sure of at least two things when the modifications to the two objects are flushed to the database: 1) the state of the corresponding rows have not changed from the time they were initially read when constructing the account objects (or at least have not changed in such a way as to invalidate the fund transfer), and 2) the two SQL update operations are performed atomically. The first problem is solved by acquiring locks on the rows of the table or by re-reading the rows prior to the update to validate that they have remained unchanged. The second problem is solved by placing both update operations in a database transaction.

In applications where objects in one Smalltalk image can send messages to remote objects in another Smalltalk image, these same issues must be addressed. The developer must design the application so that when changes are committed in one Smalltalk image (i.e., the image is saved), any modifications that occurred to remote objects in other images are also committed. For example, if the object for account A resides in one Smalltalk image, and the object for account B resides in another, both images must commit their changes, or the objects may become logically inconsistent. If both account objects reside in the same image, but their modifications are caused due to a message sent from a remote image, their changes cannot be committed unless the remote sender notifies them that it expects them to commit. This is because the remote sender may have determined that the changes should not occur after all. This problem is solved using two-phase commit protocols. In this scheme, a Smalltalk image must ask all remote images in which it caused modifications if they can commit their changes. If a remote image answers yes, then it must guarantee that if asked to do so, it can commit its changes, even in the face of hardware failure. This is typically done by writing some logging information to disk before answering affirmative to the request. If all remote images answer yes, then the coordinating Smalltalk image can send a second command to the remote images, telling them to commit their changes. Note that this scheme does not allow a Smalltalk image to execute messages from more than one remote transaction at a time and maintain logical object consistency. This is because one remote transaction may request that the local Smalltalk image commit its changes, while another remote transaction might request it to abort. Since a save operation will write all of object memory, an image cannot selectively commit modifications to some objects and not others.

To build industrial strength multi-user applications in Smalltalk, the system must support the notion of transactions. Sometimes a transaction may not be allowed to commit to ensure that objects remain logically consistent. The inability to commit a transaction is necessary when other transactions have performed operations that invalidate the operations in the current transaction.

Reference

1. Bretl, B., et al. The GemStone Data Management System, OBJECT-ORIENTED CONCEPTS, DATABASES, AND APPLICATIONS, W. Kim and F. Lochovsky, Eds., ACM Press, 1989.

Building a Gopher from Sockets and Widgets

Patrick Mueller

No, THIS ISN'T AN ARTICLE ON CYBERBIOLOGY. I'LL BE DESCRIBING HOW TO BUILD an Internet Gopher client within IBM Smalltalk, using the Widgets user interface programming model and the sockets communications protocol used on the Internet. Plan on learning a couple of things after reading the article:

- what an Internet Gopher looks like
- how the Gopher protocol works
- an introduction to socket programming in IBM Smalltalk
- an introduction to user-interface programming in IBM Smalltalk.

What is Gopher?

First let's talk about Gopher. If you don't already know what Gopher is, the best way to learn is to play with a Gopher client. Ask your local Internet guru for a test drive. In case you don't have one locally available, here's a description.

You start up a gopher client by running the gopher program and specifying a gopher server to start at. The gopher client will contact the server and ask for a list of items. Those items will be displayed by the gopher client, with some kind of user interface for you to select items (see Figure 1 for an example of my Gopher client displaying a menu of items). Each item in the list is typed: common types are:

- another gopher menu
- a text file
- a graphics file

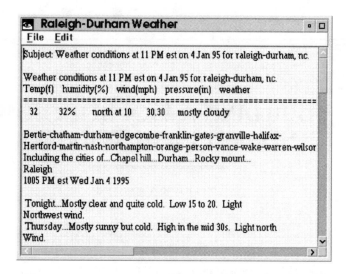

FIGURE 1. *Sample Gopher menu.*

When you select one of the items, the gopher client will send a command to get the appropriate type of item from the server and return it to the client. In the case of another gopher menu, another menu will be displayed. In the case of a text file, a text editor will be displayed with that text (see Figure 2 for an example of my Gopher client displaying a text file). You get the picture. It's a very simple program to use. And there's lots of information available. Within IBM, for example, we have more than 60 well-known gopher servers, servicing more than 8000 different menu items (sorry folks, this is primarily IBM-only information).

THE GOPHER PROTOCOL

The protocol a gopher client and server use to exchange information is one of the simplest used over the Internet. To get a gopher item from a server, the client needs to know three pieces of information: the name of the server (TCP/IP hostname), the TCP/IP port for the server, and a selector string. Most gopher servers use port 70. The main menu for a gopher server uses an empty selector string. So, to get the main menu from a gopher server, you really only need one piece of information: the name of the gopher server.

The client creates a new TCP/IP socket and connects it to the server at the port requested. It then writes the selector string, followed by carriage return

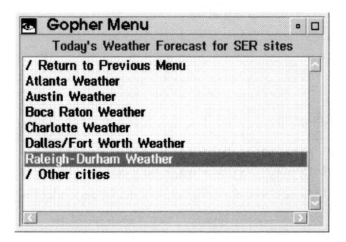

FIGURE 2. *Example Gopher text window.*

and linefeed to the socket. At this point, it starts reading from the socket, terminating when the socket is closed by the server. The data returned by the server is interpreted depending on the type of the item. After receiving the data, the client closes the socket.

The most common type of gopher item is a menu; that is the type of item returned for the main gopher server, when passed an empty selector string. The data returned for a menu consists of a set of lines, separated by carriage return and linefeed characters, up to the line that contains nothing but a period ("."). For each line, the first character is a type indicator. The rest of the string is tab delimited. The field after the type indicator is a string to display in the user interface for the item. The next field is the selector. The next is the server name, and the last is the port. The selector, server name and port are all used to get that item. The type indicator (first character in the line) indicates what type of item this is (e.g., menu, text, graphics, etc).

For the text type, the data returned from the server is just the text to display back to the user. For the graphics type, the contents of a GIF or TIFF file might be returned.

CLASSES IMPLEMENTED

First a little class hierarchy creation. We're going to implement a class called GopherItem, with a subclass for each of the gopher data types. GopherItem is defined with instance variables:

```
display     description of the item to display to the user
selector    selector to send to the server
host        name of the server
port        port number for the server
data        data returned by the server
```

Besides defining accessors for these variables GopherItem contains:

- the logic to get the data for an item from a server
- the logic to parse a line of menu information returned from the server
- the logic to determine what type of data a particular line is

We'll create the following subclasses of GopherItem:

- GopherItemMenu to display menus.
- GopherItemSearch to prompt for a search string, and display a resulting menu (used to search phone books, for instance).
- GopherItemText to display textual information.
- GopherItemUnknown to handle Gopher data our client does not understand.

We'll create a class named Gopher to manage the user interface.

USING TCP/IP SOCKETS IN IBM SMALLTALK

Now we'll actually implement the main processing of the gopher client: connecting to a server to get the some data.

If you aren't already familiar with sockets, here's a brief overview. Sockets are a lot like file handles. You open them, read from them, write to them, and close them. Except, instead of having a disk drive to read from or write to, there's another program over the network who is reading what you are writing, or writing what you are reading. And instead of specifying a file name, you specify a host name and a port number to connect to.

The logic to get the data for an item from the Gopher server is implemented in the instance method GopherItem>>getData. GopherItem supplies instance methods to return the host, port and selector of the Gopher server we want data from. Example 1 contains the Smalltalk code for this method.

Data is first initialized by `getData` to an empty string, and defaults its port and selector if not set. It then obtains an instance of `AbtTCPInetHost`, `AbtTCPPort`, and `AbtSocket` from the host and port information. `AbtTCPInetHost` is used to convert host names into TCP/IP addresses. `AbtPort` is used to associate a TCP/IP port with a TCP/IP address. `AbtSocket` is used to manage the actual socket, based on the `AbtPort` it was created with.

Up to this code, we have defined what we want to connect the socket to, but haven't actually connected it. Sending connect to the socket will cause the socket to connect to the server.

Once connected, we send the selector, followed by carriage return and linefeed, then start reading from the server. As long as the socket is connected, we receive the data from the socket and append it to the end of a local variable. When the server finally closes the socket, `isConnected` will return false. At this point, we close our end and set the data to the entire string returned from the server.

That's the only TCP/IP related code in the entire gopher client. Each gopher item subclass is responsible for interpreting the data received by this code.

USING WIDGETS IN IBM SMALLTALK

Widgets are the programming interface used for user interface programming in IBM Smalltalk. The terminology comes from Motif, upon which the user interface classes are based on. If you're already familiar with Motif Widgets, I have real good news for you—you're already familiar with IBM Smalltalk's Widgets. If not, don't worry—it's a simple and elegant model.

Widgets are used to model all the visual building blocks needed to create a user interface:

- the shell, to contain the frame, system menu, title bar, and minimize/maximize buttons
- main windows to contain the menu bar
- forms and bulletin boards to contain other widgets
- core widgets like buttons, list boxes, text fields, etc.

Each type of widget is a subclass of `CwWidget`. There are two primary ways to change the behavior of a widget: through resources and through callbacks.

Resources control the basic state of a widget, such as color and font information. Most widgets have a unique set of resources associated with them,

```
getData
"Set data instance variable to the data returned for
the gopher menu item."

    | abtHost abtPort abtSock dataChunk allData |

    self data: ''.

    self port isNil ifTrue: [self port: 70].
    self selector isNil ifTrue: [self selector: ''].

    abtHost := AbtTCPInetHost getHostByName: self host.
        abtHost isCommunicationsError ifTrue: [^nil].

    abtPort := AbtTCPPort usingHost: abtHost portNumber:
self port.
        abtPort isCommunicationsError ifTrue: [^nil].

    abtSock := AbtSocket newStreamUsingPort: abtPort.
        abtSock isCommunicationsError ifTrue: [^nil].

    abtSock bufferLength: 8192.

    (abtSock connect) isCommunicationsError ifTrue:
[^nil].

    (abtSock sendData: (self selector, Cr asString, Lf
asString))
        isCommunicationsError ifTrue: [^nil].

    allData := ''.
    [abtSock isConnected] whileTrue: [
        dataChunk := abtSock receive.
        dataChunk isCommunicationsError ifTrue: [^nil].
        allData := allData, dataChunk contents asString
        ].

    abtSock disconnect.
    self data: allData.
```

EXAMPLE 1. *GopherItem>>getData method.*

and resources are inherited down the `CwWidget` class hierarchy. Resources are set and queried via instance methods named after the resource. For instance, to query the width of a widget, send it the message `width`.

Callbacks are a way to get feedback from the user when they interact with the system. Like resources, each widget class implements its own set of callbacks, which are inherited down the `CwWidget` class hierarchy. As an example, to be notified when the user presses a button, the following code may be used.

```
buttonWidget
    addCallback: XmNactivateCallback
```

```
receiver: self
selector: #pressed:clientData:callData:
clientData: nil.
```

Each callback has a name, in this case `XmNactivateCallback`. This particular callback is invoked when a button is pressed. When the button is pressed, the message `pressed:clientData:callData:` will be sent to the object that executed this code (since the receiver was specified as self). The callback message is passed the widget, the client data specified when the callback was added (in this case, nil), and an object containing information specific to this type of callback.

Ok, so those are the basics, let's dive right into our gopher client. Our user interface is going to be a new window, with a read-only text field at the top giving a description of the current gopher menu item we're viewing and a list box containing the items available on this gopher menu. Gopher text items will be displayed in a separate window (a Workspace), which is not described here.

The widgets we'll need are:

- a shell, to contain the frame, system menu, title bar, etc.
- a form, to contain the text field and list box
- a text field
- a list box

A form is a widget that knows how to resize the widgets contained within it. We're using it to allow the user to resize the window and have the widgets contained in the form automatically resize themselves.

As mentioned before, we'll be implementing a class called `Gopher` to handle the user interface. Gopher is defined with the following instance variables:

`data`	to hold the data associated with the menuitems (i.e., the selector, server, and port of the menu items)
`listWidget`	to hold our list box widget
`textWidget`	to hold our text field widget
`shellWidget`	to hold our shell widget
`menuStack`	to keep track of where we came from, so we can backtrack through the gopher.

The instance method `createWindow` is used to create and setup all the widgets. Example 2 contains the code for this method.

```
listWidget items: (OrderedCollection with: a with: b
                   with:c)

createWindow
    "Create the gopher menu window"

    | shell main form text list |

    shell := CwTopLevelShell
        createApplicationShell: 'gopherMenu'
        argBlock: [:w| w
            title: 'Gopher Menu';
            width: (CgScreen default width) // 2
        ].

    form := shell
        createForm: 'form'
        argBlock: nil.
    form manageChild.

    text := form
        createLabel: 'label'
        argBlock: [ :w | w
            labelString: ' '
        ].
    text manageChild.

    list := form
        createScrolledList: 'list'
        argBlock: [ :w | w
        selectionPolicy: XmSINGLESELECT;
            visibleItemCount: 20
        ].
```

EXAMPLE 2. *Gopher>>createWindow method.*

The first thing we do is create a shell window. This is done with the message `CwTopLevelShellclass>>createApplicationShell:argBlock:`. The first parameter is the name of the widget. All widgets have a name, which is usually not externally visible to the user. The second parameter is a block used to set resources when the widget is created. In this case, we're going to set the title of the shell window, which will be placed in the frame's window bar, and the width of the frame, making it half the size of the screen.

```
list manageChild.

text setValuesBlock: [:w | w
    topAttachment: XmATTACHFORM; topOffset: 2;
    leftAttachment: XmATTACHFORM; leftOffset: 2;
    rightAttachment: XmATTACHFORM; rightOffset: 2
    ].

list parent setValuesBlock: [:w | w
    topAttachment: XmATTACHWIDGET; topWidget: text;
    bottomAttachment: XmATTACHFORM; bottomOffset: 2;
    leftAttachment: XmATTACHFORM;leftOffset: 2;
    rightAttachment: XmATTACHFORM; rightOffset: 2
    ].

list
    addCallback: XmNdefaultActionCallback
    receiver: self
        selector: #selectItem:clientData:callData:
    clientData: nil.

shell realizeWidget.

self listWidget: list.
self textWidget: text.
self shellWidget: shell.

self menuStack: OrderedCollection new.
```

EXAMPLE 2. (CONT.)   *Gopher>>createWindow method.*

You might be wondering why we use the `argBlock` parameter (and the `setValuesBlock:` later in the code) to set our resources.

The message to create the shell widget could also have been written as:

```
shell := CwTopLevelShell
    createApplicationShell: 'gopherMenu'
    argBlock: nil.
shell
    title: 'Gopher Menu';
    width: (CgScreen default width) // 2
```

In IBM Smalltalk, widget resources are "hot"—that is, when changed, the user interface is immediately updated. In order to allow the system to optimize changes to a widget, the `argBlock` parameter and `setValuesBlock:` message are the recommended ways to set resource values for a widget.

Next, we create the form. Most widgets are created using widget creation convenience methods named `createXXXX:argBlock:`, where XXXX is the type of widget to create. These messages are sent to the widget that will contain the widget to be created. In this case, we'll create a form with the name form, and don't need to set any resources.

After the widget is created, we send it the message `manageChild`. This is a Motif-ism, which you don't need to be too worried about, but will need to call it after creating your widgets. Managing and mapping widgets allows some interesting behaviors, such as causing widgets to instantly appear and disappear as needed.

Contained within the form will be a label widget, created with `createLabel:argBlock:`. We'll set the initial text of the label to a blank string.

Also contained within the form is a list box, created with `createScrolled List:argBlock:`. The `selectionPolicy` resource sets the type of selection allowed—single select, multiple select, etc. The `visibleItemCount` resource sets the initial size of the list box, e.g., the list box will be sized to contain 20 items.

As mentioned previously, we're using a form so that the widgets inside the form can be automatically resized. In order to make this happen, we have to attach the widgets to the form.

For each of top, bottom, left and right, there are three basic types of attachment:

- attach the widget to the edge of the form
- attach the widget to a position in the form (position based on 100—setting to position 50 attaches the widget to the middle of the form)
- attach the widget to another widget.

In our case, we attach the label widget to the top, left, and right sides of the form. We don't need to attach the bottom, since a label field has a default height (the height of the font the text is being displayed in). The list box is attached to the bottom, left and right sides of the form, and it's top is attached to the label widget. Note also an offset is specified for aesthetic reasons (to keep the user interface from looking as if it's all crammed together).

Now when the window is resized, the label and text windows will have their widths changed automatically, since they are attached to the sides.

When the height changes, the label won't change size but the list box will, since it's attached to the label widget at the top and the form on the bottom.

As a further example of attachments, if we change the label widget to attach the bottom as in:

```
bottomAttachment: XmATTACHPOSITION;
    bottomPosition: 25;
```

the label widget would take the top 25% of window and the list box would have take the bottom 75%.

Note that for the list box, we send `setValuesBlock:` to the parent of list, not list itself. This is because a `CwScrolledList` widget is a list box with a set of scrollbars around it. It's the widget (which we don't see) that contains the list box and scrollbars that we need to attach to the form.

To be able to execute some code when an item in the list is selected, we need to use a callback. In the previous code, the `XmNdefaultAction-Callback` is used on the list widget. This callback is invoked when an item is double-clicked in the listbox. We specify sending the message `selectItem:clientData:callData:` to self. The actual callback is implemented as follows:

```
selectItem: widget clientData: clientData callData: callData
    "Callback sent when an item is selected.  Open a
    viewer for the appropriate GopherItem subclass for the
item."

    | pos menuItem |
    pos := callData itemPosition.
    menuItem := (self data) at: pos.
    menuItem view: self.
```

`callData` is an object containing information specific to this callback; in this case, sending it `itemPosition` answers the one based offset of the item within the menu that was selected. The data instance variable of `Gopher` contains an ordered collection of `GopherItem` instances returned from the server. We just get the appropriate menu item and tell it to view itself.

Finally, we tell the shell to realize itself, which causes it to be displayed, and set our instance variables.

The contents of the list box are maintained with the items resource. The data associated with this resource is an `OrderedCollection` of `Strings`. For instance, to set the contents of a list box to the items a, b, and c, you would use the code in Example 2.

CONCLUSION

The source for the gopher client is available via anonymous ftp to st.cs.uiuc.edu, and will work on OS/2 and Windows, with IBM Smalltalk or VisualAge with the Communications Component.

Author Index

Subject Index

A

ABC (abstract base class), 334, 336, 339
abort operation, 412
abstract
   architectures, 321
   classes, 51, 211, 256, 294, 334, 336, 340
   coverage metrics, 392
   data types, 3, 13, 18, 237, 385
   domains, 282
   factors, 292
   functions, 339–340
   polymorphic interface, 340
   use-case class, 144, 172–174, 176, 178
   use-case extends, 175
Abstract Factory design pattern, 298, 310
abstraction links, 101
abstraction
   layers, 336
   techniques, 237
abstractionist, 232
abstractions, 23, 27–28, 30, 95, 98, 103, 260, 320
Accepter design patterns, 292–293, 296–300, 304–305, 310–311, 318–319, 321
accepter object, 317
access
   shared, 403
   threadsafe, 403
accessor operations, 63
acquaintance, 159
acquire method, 304
active process, 403
actors, 88, 129–130, 134, 136, 141–143, 145–146, 154–155, 157–158, 164, 166, 168, 172, 178–179

behaviors, 143
class, 143
Ada, 126
ADAPTIVE project, 322
Adaptive Service eXecutive (ASX), 289
   components, 292
   framework, 290, 292, 298, 300, 322
addresses, 362
   TCP/IP, 421
administration, 28
Advanced C++, 250, 255
aesthetics, 238, 319
aggregate class, 343–345
aggregated types, 19
aggregates, 153
aggregation, 13, 19, 21, 105, 107, 164, 173
   object, 114
air-traffic control system, 228
Alexander, C., 238, 240, 244, 247, 263, 268–269, 281
algorithms, 285, 289, 292, 313, 318, 321, 367, 397
alternative courses, 172
American Management Systems, 398
American software industry, 168
analysis, 82, 152, 167, 181, 190
   coverage, 391–392, 396, 398
   model, 46, 207, 282, 287
   object model, 86, 140
   pattern, 284, 286
   phase, 122, 341–342
analyst, the, 113
analysts, 179
analyzer, 392
ANSI standards group, 356

ANSI/ISO C++ standards committee, 347,356
anthropology, 239
application
    behavior, 292
    C++, 339
    distributed, 321
    engineer, 232
    environment, 28
    generators, 286
    multi-user, 415
    requirements, 65
architects, 25, 230, 232–233, 238, 261, 263
    novice, 263
architecture
    abstract, 321
    blueprints, 293
    building, 246
    client/server, 384
    components, 293
    document, 233
    documentation, 274
    layered, 336
    legacy, 267
    patterns, 286
    team, 230, 233
architectures, 30, 89, 91, 130, 221, 244, 267, 298
argument polymorphism, 341
arguments, 369, 372
arithmetic operations, 256
ARM, 347
arrays, 367, 369, 379, 404
artisans, 221
assembly, 19, 221
assertions, 216
assignment, 365
    operator, 378
associated objects, 63
associations, 3, 5, 7–8, 11–13, 15, 18–21, 59, 107, 122–123, 157
    mapping, 7
    multiplicty, 3, 5–6, 8, 11
    multiplicty constraints, 9
    traversal, 3, 14
associative array, 351
asymmetric, 19
asymmetry conditions, 21, 361–362
asynchronous communication, 122, 125
AT&T, 239, 243, 245
ATM, 293
atomic, 414
atomic unit of change, 205
attributes, 3, 13, 18, 20–21, 98, 102, 105, 113, 161, 163, 283

audit, 392
authoritative source, 273
automated regression test, 211, 217
automatic teller machine (ATM), 125
Automobile, 6
autonomous systems, 129

B
"Backing Store" remapping, 165
bag, 385, 388
base class, 251, 253, 257, 305, 333–334, 336–337, 341
base class operations, 251
baselines, 199–205
basic course, 172
Beck, K., 238, 243
behavior, 24–25, 73, 161–162, 180, 182, 191, 257, 260, 270–271, 282–283, 292, 335, 343–344, 383, 396, 411–412
behavioral
    analysis, 163
    pattern, 281
    requirements, 85
behaviors of actors, 143
Berczuk, S., 256, 258, 263
Berczuk's synopses, 256
Biblical metaphor, 211
bidirectional
    iterators, 360, 363–365, 367
    mapping, 3, 6, 11, 13, 19
Biggerstaff, T., 270
Bilow, P., 168
binary propositions, 97
blackbox, 87
blackbox functional requirements, 175
BLAS, 354
blocking, 299–300
blueprints, 240
Boehm, B., 282
Booch, G., 67, 175, 199, 238
Booch
    diagrams, 185, 192
    mechanisms, 178
    method, 23, 182, 184–185, 187, 189, 225, 230, 233
bool, 348
Boolean, 398
    flag, 388
    operation, 65
boundary lines, 199
bounds checking adaptor, 367
branching, 144, 206
bridge, 249
bridge pattern, 258–260, 262

SIGS BOOKShelf

Applying OMT
Kurt W. Derr

Applying OMT is a how-to guide on implementation processes and practical approaches for the popular Object Modeling Technique (OMT) created by James Rumbaugh et al. The book begins by providing a thorough overview of such fundamental concepts as modeling and prototyping and then moves into specific implementation strategies using C++ and Smalltalk. By using a typical business application as a case study, the author illustrates the complete modeling process from start to finish.

1995/557 pages/softcover/ISBN 1-884842-10-0/Order# 6S01-2100/$44/£ 34

Object Technology Strategies and Tactics
Gilbert Singer

Designed for both managers and software developers interested in understanding OO concepts, this book will help you make intelligent analysis, design, and management decisions. Language independent, this nuts-and-bolts guide is designed to help minimize the risks and maximize the benefits of OT.

May 1996/Approx. 250 pages/softcover/ISBN 1-884842-38-0/ Order# 6S01-2380/$39

The Java Source
The Worldwide Guide to Java Companies, Products, Services and Books
Marisa Urgo

For the first time ever: comprehensive information on Java products, vendors, consultants, resources, and more.

1997/approx. 500 pages/softcover/ISBN 1-88-4842-57-7/Order# 6S01-2577/£ 28

The Object Primer
Scott W. Ambler

The Object Primer is the ultimate introductory text on object-oriented technology. By reviewing this easy-to-read book, you'll gain a solid understanding of object-oriented concepts and object-oriented analysis techniques.

The Object Primer provides all a developer needs to know to start using object-oriented technology immediately.

November 1995/250 pages/softcover/ISBN 1-884842-17-8/ Order# 6S01-2178/$35/£ 28

What Every Software Manager Must Know to Succeed with Object Technology
John Williams

This book shows managers what object technology is and how to manage it effectively. It provides readers with a no-nonsense approach to object technology management, including effective guidelines on how to track the development of projects.

1995/294 pages/softcover/ISBN 1-884842-14-3/Order# 6S01-2143/$35/£ 29

Managing Your Move to Object Technology
Barry McGibbon

Written for software managers, **Managing Your Move to Object Technology** clearly defines and illustrates the management implications associated with the transition to object technology. Although other books may cover the technological benefits of OT, this is one of the few to address the business management issues associated with new technology and the corporate environment. It covers what OT will do to the corporate culture, not simply what it will do for it.

1995/288 pages/softcover/ISBN 1-884842-15-1/Order# 6S01-2151/$35/£ 29

Successful Enterprise Modeling Techniques
Getting Results with the Object-Oriented Enterprise Model
Thornton Gale and James Eldred

Enterprise modeling is the primary tool used in business reengineering. Historically, the number-one problem with enterprise modeling has been the lack of formalism. **Getting Results with the Object-Oriented Enterprise Model** tackles this dilemma head-on and prescribes a formal methodology based on object technology.

1996/650 pages/softcover/ISBN 1-884842-16-X/Order# 6S01-216X/$45/£ 30

The Blueprint for Business Objects
Peter Fingar

The Blueprint for Business Objects provides a clear and concise guide to making informed decisions about emerging object technology and to mastering the skills you need to make effective use of the technology in business.

Based on the workplace experiences of several major corporations, **The Blueprint for Business Objects** presents a framework designed for business and information systems professionals. It provides the reader with a road map, starting at the level of initial concepts and moving up to the mastery level. It also includes information on how to select and find additional learning resources.

1996/300 pages/softcover/ISBN 1-884842-20-8/Order# 6S01-2208/$39/£ 26

Reliable Object-Oriented Software Applying Analysis and Design
Ed Seidewitz and Mike Stark

Reliable Object-Oriented Software presents the underlying principles of object orientation and its practical application. More than just another text on methodology, **Reliable Object-Oriented Software** focuses on the fundamental concepts of software development and architectural design, and lays the foundation necessary to develop robust, maintainable and evolvable software.

November 1995/425 pages/softcover/ISBN 1-884842-18-6/Order# 6S01-2186/$45/£ 30

Inside the Object Model
David M. Papurt

Inside the Object Model serves two key functions: it teaches object-oriented analysis and design from first principles and clearly explains C++ mechanisms that implement object-oriented concepts.

With over 100 figures, hundreds of working code examples, and comparisons of coding techniques, this is the book you will need to gain a complete understanding of both C++ and the object model. Professional software analysts, designers, programmers, and advanced computer science students will benefit from reading this book.

1995/540 pages/softcover/ISBN 1-884842-05-4/Order# 6S01-2054/$39/£ 26

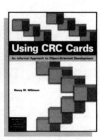

Using CRC Cards
An Informal Approach to Object-Oriented Development
Nancy M. Wilkinson

Using CRC Cards is a comprehensive introduction to CRC (Class, Responsibility, Collaborator) cards. It includes a description of the cards and how they can be used in interactive sessions to develop an object-oriented model of an application.

In this book, the author draws on her years of project experience to describe how CRC cards can contribute at every stage of the software life cycle. It includes practical examples of how to use CRC cards in projects using either formal or informal development techniques.

1995/243 pages/softcover/ISBN 1-884842-07-0/Order# 6S01-2070/$29/£ 19

Object Lessons
Tom Love

In this usable guide to developing and managing OO software projects, well-respected consultant and OOP pioneer Tom Love reveals the absolute do's and don'ts in adopting and managing object-oriented technology. **Object Lessons** is filled with applicable advice and practical suggestions for large-scale commercial software projects.

If you are an applications programmer, project leader or technical manager making decisions concerning design and management of large-scale commercial object-oriented software, this book is for you.

1994/275 pages/softcover/ISBN 1-9627477-3-4/Order# 6S01-7734/$29/£ 19